DOWN TO THE WIRE

DOWN
TO THE
WIRE

· · ·

UPI's FIGHT
FOR SURVIVAL

Gregory Gordon
and
Ronald E. Cohen

McGRAW-HILL PUBLISHING COMPANY
New York   St. Louis   San Francisco   Hamburg   Mexico

1 2 3 4 5 6 7 8 9 DOC DOC 8 9 2 1 0 9

ISBN 0-07-023804-9

Library of Congress Cataloging-in-Publication Data

Gordon, Gregory.
    Down to the wire : UPI's fight for survival / Gregory Gordon and
Ronald Cohen.
        p.   cm.
    Includes index.
    ISBN 0-07-023804-9
    1. United Press International—History.   2. News agencies—United
States—History.   3. Journalists—United States—Biography.
I. Cohen, Ronald, 1937–   II. Title.
PN4841.U66G67   1989
070.4'35—dc20   89-2629
                                                                    CIP

Book design by Mark Bergeron

To my loving parents; and to my enduring wife, Nancy Derr,
who has lived with this book nearly as long as she has lived with me.
—Greg Gordon

To the fine, strong women in my life—Jill, Rachel and Jennifer,
Mildred and Diane, Florence and Marcia—for their love, inspiration,
and boundless patience; and in loving memory to my dad, Maurie,
the real writer. —Ron Cohen

And to the generations of "Unipressers" whose spirit, astonishing
dedication, and unbending fealty to the highest standards of their
profession have made United Press International unique in the world.

ACKNOWLEDGMENTS

This book never could have been written without the cooperation of more than 200 people, including executives, accountants, lawyers, and employees who talked freely and openly because they felt the story of UPI needed to be told. We deeply appreciate their trust, assistance, and time.

We wish to thank scores of UPI employees for keeping us abreast of the company's operations in recent years, and for their support, valuable contributions, and abiding interest in our project.

We are deeply grateful to our editors at McGraw-Hill: first, Thomas Miller, who recognized the significance of the UPI story and helped us with the manuscript; then Dan Weaver, who poured his energy into the final product and was always there when we needed him.

We would like to thank those who made special contributions: Chicago lawyer David Andich, who gave generously of his own time; ex-Unipressers, Dr. Norman Sims, head of the Journalism Department at the University of Massachusetts, and Dr. Leonard Granato, journalism professor at Queensland Institute of Technology in Australia, who spent many hours offering important feedback and advice; good friend Michael Landes, who provided his New Jersey mountain hideaway for our search for the muse; and Phil Serafino, who later joined UPI, for his important legwork; and our wives, Nancy Derr and Jill Cohen, never shy about telling us, as the project progressed, what was good and what was lousy.

CONTENTS

TO THE READER

In a real sense, this book was born on March 4, 1985, when we (Ronald Cohen as managing editor and Greg Gordon as chief investigative reporter) decided United Press International must cover its financial crisis and the open warfare raging in its executive suite straightforwardly, factually, and aggressively. We felt that if UPI were not going to survive, the company's last story should be its own obituary. We realized the task could pose personal risks. Indeed, the decision, which led to hundreds of stories moving on UPI's national news wires, ultimately may have contributed to the company's separate actions in firing both of us in later years.

Regularly for fifteen months, in the period up to and including UPI's bankruptcy, Gordon reported and wrote, and Cohen edited and signed off on, stories for transmission to newspapers and broadcast stations worldwide. At times UPI's dirty linen was displayed for the world to see. Yet, we never had second thoughts about the decision to cover our company. UPI always had guarded jealously its rich and storied tradition of reporting the news without fear or favor. For three quarters of a century the name UPI had stood for innovative, balanced, and fair journalism. There could be no thought now of abrogating that mission. The stories were controversial. Some clients were astonished that company executives continued to permit such intensive public scrutiny of private matters.

While the coverage exerted a calming effect by keeping information flowing about a turbulent situation, frequently UPI executives were dismayed and discomfited. To its credit, the management never sought to censor the stories.

We decided to write *Down to the Wire* in part because it was impossible to tell the whole story in truncated news articles. We felt the American public, the world's news media, and UPI employees were entitled to know the full and shocking details of the inner turmoil that beset the institution. We also felt that, while UPI is a private company, in many ways it is a public trust whose owners and executives should be accountable for their actions and decisions.

In the fall of 1986, several months after we began work on the book outside the office, Cohen was fired during one of UPI's many management shake-ups. While no full explanation ever was offered, it seemed clear that the new owner was not pleased that UPI had covered its own story.

As the book neared completion in May 1989, UPI executives demanded that Gordon, still an employee, turn over the unfinished manuscript for their review. When he refused on grounds that it would abridge his First Amendment rights, he, too, was fired, a dismissal that drew widespread national attention. While we were disappointed with the company's actions in both cases, we vowed from the outset not to allow our employment status with UPI to affect the overall content or tone of this book in any way.

The book is a no-holds-barred recounting of events, including episodes that many current and former UPI people might rather forget. Even so, we consider ourselves loyal "Unipressers." After spending a total of forty-three years with the wire service, we feel deep affection toward the institution and the thousands of journalists who since its founding in 1907 have dedicated themselves to the highest principles of their profession.

1

. . .

Down and Almost Out in Beverly Hills

Luis Nogales was a man who usually concealed his emotions, but as he stood alone listening to the fateful words over the phone in Beverly Hills a dark scowl contorted his face. Trembling with anger, Nogales dropped the receiver on the bed, keeping alive the connection to Nashville. His heartbeat quickened. He walked from the bedroom and turned down the fifty-foot hallway to the mansion's paneled den. Normally, his stride would have carried him there quickly, but now his gait slowed. Nogales, the young president of United Press International, was pondering the unthinkable. In the doorway to the den he paused a moment, composed himself, then turned to deliver devastating news to a gathering of lawyers, bankers, and company executives.

In this moment of despair, Luis Nogales could never have guessed that he and his company were embarking on a bizarre and remarkable adventure, one that would alter the fabric of American journalism.

. . .

UPI. Three letters instantly recognizable to millions. UPI. A trusted, comforting institution that always had been on the scene to report on the biggest stories of the day and send them clacking on teletype machines to newsrooms around the world.

In reality, on this first Sunday of March 1985, the world's second largest news service was out of cash and on the brink of financial collapse. UPI had lost money unceasingly for two decades, prompting the E.W. Scripps Company to unload it in 1982 to self-styled Tennessee entrepreneurs Doug Ruhe and Bill Geissler. By early 1985 it was clear that Ruhe and Geissler had not been the answer for UPI. Their stewardship had been a disaster. The storied, seventy-five-year-old wire service was flirting with bankruptcy and, further, was paralyzed by an internal power struggle between the owners and Nogales's management team.

UPI's flickering hopes rested with Nogales, its gutsy, Stanford-educated president, who had been born on a roadside forty-one years earlier to Mexican-American migrant fruit pickers. Nogales was convinced that unless the owners yielded control, UPI was dead. Among their other failings, Ruhe and Geissler lacked the one commodity UPI could not do without: money.

The two men had not only failed miserably in their turnaround efforts and rung up enormous debts, but also had stubbornly resisted Nogales's blunt suggestions that they relinquish control. Instead, they had demanded that he find a minority investor, a task he felt would be all but impossible. Surely no serious investor would hand money over to two men bereft of credibility in the financial world. As the weeks dragged on and UPI's debts and problems mounted, Nogales had grown more frustrated with his bosses. He wasn't alone.

The Los Angeles-based Foothill Capital Corporation, the primary cash lender, had grown increasingly worried about protecting its investment. Foothill long ago had lost faith in Ruhe and Geissler. The lender had been more than generous to UPI and its owners, several times rescuing the company from desperate situations by raising its $4 million lending limit to cover payroll. By late February, patience gone, Foothill's executives summoned the owners to Los Angeles and threatened to turn off the cash spigot unless they stepped aside.

Suddenly the squeeze was on, and Ruhe and Geissler seemingly were without options. True, it was their company, but if they insisted on retaining control, UPI's future was in jeopardy. They negotiated, reluctantly, for several days. Finally, on February 26, they agreed to let Nogales run the company and sell it—if he could find a buyer. Then they flew back to Nashville. Everything would be wrapped up at a meeting at the Beverly Hills home of Foothill president John Nickoll on the first

Sunday in March 1985. Foothill had warned that the deal must be sealed or paychecks might begin bouncing the next day.

Despite his agreement with the owners, Nogales was worried. He had watched Doug Ruhe operate for two years and didn't entirely trust him. He had seen Ruhe flip-flop in negotiations before. While Ruhe and Geissler had not seemed bitter before they flew home to Nashville, Nogales knew they considered his effort to seize control treasonous. As Nogales and his top advisers gathered in John Nickoll's mansion on this balmy, late-winter night, they hoped that Ruhe's handshake would be his bond. They had told themselves that even though the owners were erratic, they wouldn't dare gamble with UPI's future. Or would they?

• • •

UPI's 1,500 staffers in more than 200 bureaus around the globe were ignorant of the drama being played out in Beverly Hills. Had they known, it probably wouldn't have mattered. For more than two decades UPI employees had stoically shrugged off rumors of imminent demise.

UPI was the Avis of the news business, second best numerically, financially, and in stature to its fierce rival, the Associated Press. For decades its employees had been underpaid, uncomplaining foot soldiers of the news industry, working anonymously in cramped bureaus with old and creaky equipment, churning out the latest news stories, sports, stock-market quotes, and human-interest features. By sheer hard work and ingenuity they often beat their giant rival on major stories. These were sweet victories that only tremendous underdogs could truly savor. To Unipressers, their company always had been more than a business. It was an institution, a crusade.

This was the news agency, after all, that had been first to tell the world about the assassination of President Kennedy, about the attempts on the lives of Presidents Ford and Reagan, about the presidential election victory of a self-effacing Georgia peanut farmer named Jimmy Carter. UPI had been there to provide the competition to keep AP staffers from getting complacent and lazy.

And UPI had been there when the AP was wrong. The existence of competing wire services, their machines side by side in newsrooms, had saved countless editors from misinforming the public. On September 18, 1961, UPI correctly informed the world that U.N. Secretary General Dag Hammarskjöld had died in a plane crash in a Rhodesian jungle. The AP had reported his plane had landed safely. When an AP story sent network TV crews scurrying to Charleston, West Virginia, in 1984 to cover the deaths of seventy people in a supermarket explosion, UPI calmly and accurately reported that no one had died at all. Of course there had been occasions when the reverse happened. Editors long had cherished the security blanket provided by having both wires. Even when there was no factual conflict, the presence of UPI helped them choose the better story or allowed them to combine the best elements of each.

UPI's ability to challenge and often surpass the AP's coverage, despite its rival's almost limitless resources, had earned it the respect of the industry. Editors marveled at how Unipressers sustained their competitive spirit despite the company's endless financial woes, and staffers wore that respect as a badge of honor.

• • •

As Luis Nogales stood at the doorway to John Nickoll's luxurious den that Sunday night, he was stunned by the message that owner Doug Ruhe had just delivered over the phone. Nogales, a newcomer to UPI, was fully mindful of UPI's rich legacy and tradition. He had arrived at the meeting praying that Ruhe and Bill Geissler would, for the good of the wire service, lay aside their ambitions and bow out gracefully. But he and the other guests had barely settled into their seats when the phone rang.

Nickoll's wife, Ann, had picked it up in the bedroom and called, "It's for you, Mr. Nogales."

Ruhe, calling from Nashville, was typically blunt. Nogales had bridled at his boss's words and protested angrily, but in vain. Finally he had placed the receiver on the bed. As he reappeared at the door of the den, heads swiveled expectantly and the room fell quiet.

"Well," Nogales said, "I've been fired."

No one spoke. Everyone knew the consequences of Doug Ruhe's reckless decision. Foothill would yank its financial backing, employee paychecks would bounce like India rubber, and UPI would plunge into bankruptcy. Staffers around the globe would be stranded, jobless. Fearful of being left without news coverage, clients would scurry to the AP. A prime source of the world's news and information would be silenced.

For several seconds those in the room sat stunned, incredulous.

UPI, an institution that each day touched the lives of hundreds of millions of people, appeared doomed.

2
· · ·

With Scotch Tape and Baling Wire

This unseemly tug of war for control of a failing company could hardly have been what Edward Wyllis Scripps had envisioned when he founded the United Press in 1907. The wire service was Scripps's proudest legacy, a powerful institution that was a gift to his profession. He would have been shocked to see its disintegration.

Yet the news agency always had been a paradox: its worldwide impact and reputation had far outstripped its meager resources. Finding itself both reliant on other major media companies for business and competing with them for clients and news, the wire service had fought unsuccessfully for decades to turn the corner to prosperity.

Indeed, as Luis Nogales struggled to save UPI in 1985, he not only was battling the company's owners but also far greater forces. Snapping up every available property, media giants were monopolizing ownership, cutting into UPI's potential subscriber base, and bringing a disturbing homogeny to America's free press and airwaves.

Watching big business consume the media, Nogales and others felt it even more vital that independent voices like UPI's not be stilled. Perhaps the wire service's struggle was a sort of symbolic battleground in the effort to maintain diversity in the journalism world. Its fight ultimately would have to be waged without the backing of many of the barons of the American newspaper industry, whose indifference would cast UPI into the hands of owners either incompetent, greedy, ignorant of or even willing to abandon its role as a defender of the public's right to know. UPI's fight for survival was a tale of employee commitment, a classic story of love of company and profession.

It was only fitting that E.W. Scripps was himself the personification of the company's tenacious, enterprising spirit. In 1872, at eighteen and with $80 in his pocket, he left the family farm in Rushville, Illinois, to seek fame and fortune in Detroit. He clerked in a drugstore for several years, and with his two brothers and a sister started a two-penny newspaper, the *Detroit Evening News*. It was so successful that Scripps began a similar paper in Cleveland, *The Penny Press*, which would become the *Cleveland Press*, flagship of his empire.

Scripps proved such a good, skinflint manager that he was able to add other Ohio dailies to his fledgling newspaper chain.

From the beginning his view of journalism was considered radical. He opposed the concentration of corporate power, championed labor unions, and inveighed against political corruption. Although he was all business when it came to his newspapers, the bewhiskered E.W. played hard. He smoked the best cigars and drank the finest whiskey almost to the day he died; he delighted in a rowdy game of poker and, in the words of the official Scripps handbook, "enjoyed wholesome pleasures of the flesh." Many joked that his nickname, "Doc," stood for "Damned old crank."

When Scripps's papers in Cincinnati, Cleveland, Columbus, and Toledo were frozen out of national and international news coverage by the severely restrictive membership policies of the well-established Associated Press, Scripps fought back by placing his own correspondents in key cities. His loose network so enhanced his newspapers' coverage that Scripps contemplated creating his own news service. By refusing to sell to more than one newspaper in each market, he concluded, the AP was all but inviting competition. On June 21, 1907, Scripps gave it to them. He launched the United Press.

Scripps wanted to be able to sell news to anybody, anywhere, at any time. He decreed his new wire service had to concentrate on reporting about people, had to be colorfully written, had to be scrupulously independent and free of domination by any large group of newspapers. Scripps' United Press would rise to engage the AP in the most intense and bitter rivalry in the news business.

Although Scripps owned a ranch in California and a yacht, the "Ohio," his austere new United Press quickly earned what would become a legendary reputation for journalistic penury. The UP began with correspondents in a handful of cities transmitting each day about 12,000 words of Morse code over leased telegraph lines to 369 afternoon newspapers. Those at the paper transcribing the dots and dashes of the code often used an empty tobacco can to amplify the clatter.

To run his wire service, Scripps tapped Roy Howard, an ambitious, inventive twenty-four-year-old banty rooster of a man who exhorted his small team of staffers to use cunning and guile to outdo the AP. In his 1957 book, *Deadline Every Minute*, Joe Alex Morris described how the newborn UP scrounged to cover the Mexican revolution in late 1910. UP engaged a reporter named Cook, who worked for an AP paper in El Paso. After providing excellent coverage the first day, Cook sent a telegram saying he must resign because AP management insisted no staffer work for the United Press.

"Have arranged for competent reporter Brown to cover for you," Cook wired. The next day, in the same flashy style, "Brown" kept UP clients apprised of the fighting. But that night he, too, resigned, wiring, "Have arranged for good man Gordon to protect you." After UP received the same kind of sharp writing and reporting for a third day, "Gordon," too, submitted his resignation, acknowledging, to nobody's surprise, that Cook had been the author all along. By then UP staffer Bill Shepherd had arrived from New York.

Shepherd, who later became one of the most famous European correspondents during World War I, also scored one of the biggest reporting triumphs of UP's early years. One spring day in 1911, he saw flames shooting out of New York's Triangle Shirtwaist Factory. He watched in horror as terrified sweatshop workers leaped from the upper stories.

"Thud—dead! Thud—dead! Thud—dead!" began Shepherd's frighteningly graphic account. "Sixty-two 'thud—deads.'

"I call them that because the sound and the thought of death came to me, each time, at the same instant. . . ."

"I learned a new sound—a more horrible sound than description can picture. It was the thud of a speeding, living body on a stone sidewalk."

Asked years later his secret, Shepherd replied, "I just write for the milkman in Omaha." Unipressers soon adopted that as their credo.

• • •

Fighting to make its mark, UP had to be innovative. It was the first to give reporters bylines and to leaven its news report with feature stories. Encouraged by E.W. Scripps, it pioneered coverage of the union as well as the management side of the fledgling U.S. labor movement.

Feisty little UP performed so well that many AP members soon added a second wire service. When UP began using Teletype machines to speed communications, its newspaper clients in North America swelled to 700.

In the early days of twentieth-century America, way before television and even before radio news, agencies like AP and UP were virtually the only source of immediate, mass information. Papers everywhere relied on them heavily. In bureau after bureau, country after country, the men and women of the United Press turned out news stories around the clock, their financially fragile network held together with Scotch tape and baling wire. Their surroundings were spartan, their pay barely covered life's necessities. There never were enough of them to do the job properly. Their equipment was makeshift and unreliable. Yet for decades they hammered away, seemingly beyond their talents, to bring news from around the world to millions of newspaper readers. Their victories often were measured in minutes and preserved like battlefield decorations in the treasured front-page acknowledgment "By United Press."

The reporting and writing of UP's correspondents covering World War I did much to embellish its growing reputation. But ironically, Roy Howard, the dapper, diminutive man who was the brains and guts behind the news service's meteoric rise, nearly destroyed the UP as the war came to a close. On November 7, 1918, en route back home after visiting UP war correspondents, Howard had stopped in the office of Admiral Henry Wilson in the French coastal town of Brest. Wilson handed Howard a slip of paper, an official dispatch from the U.S. Embassy in Paris.

"Armistice signed at 11 a.m.," it said.

Howard rushed to the cable office to flash the news to UP's New York office. Moments later the UP bulletin pronouncing the war's end hit newspaper offices around the world. "Extra" editions with screaming headlines soon were being snatched out of the hands of newsboys. On the strength of Howard's monumental scoop, tens of thousands of Americans poured into the streets to celebrate. New Yorkers danced on Fifth Avenue, deliriously embracing total strangers.

At their lower Manhattan headquarters, AP's top executives refused to be stampeded into matching UP's story despite scores of telegrams from subscribers threatening to resign membership immediately, charging the AP, the nation's largest news agency, was pro-German. Outside the AP offices at 51 Chambers Street, angry demonstrators brandished fists at the windows. Then AP's editors broke into grins. Undersecretary of State Frank Polk had personally told AP news chief Jackson Elliott at 2:15 p.m. by phone from Washington that the Germans had yet to sign an agreement. AP rammed out a bulletin.

UP executives, growing increasingly edgy at the lack of confirmation, nervously stood behind Howard's story. Now it was their turn to take the heat. Frantic editors barraged UP's New York office with demands that the discrepancy be resolved.

In France, two hours after the UP flash, Howard had been handed an official denial dismissing the previous announcement as premature. Using his only means of communication, Howard had cabled a correction. It never reached the New York bureau because military censors channeled it instead to Secretary of the Navy Josephus Daniels, who was away from Washington and whose office held it until his return the next day. UP had blown the story of the decade and the whole nation knew it.

Livid, Howard traced the phony announcement: the American Embassy had been victim of a hoax by a caller using a private, official channel and purporting to be from the French Foreign Office. The armistice was officially announced three days later, but UP would spend decades trying to erase its black eye. One paper, the New York *Globe*, editorialized that UP's erroneous flash was "probably the greatest fake in newspaper history."

• • •

Stung by that humiliation, Roy Howard vowed anew to safeguard UP's accuracy. Overcoming the armistice episode, the young wire service continued to flourish, adding morning newspapers and scores of reporters. Aggressively hunting down stories around the globe, UP by 1923 had a $3 million budget, served 1,000 newspapers in thirty-six countries, and boasted it covered the news "Around the World, Around the Clock."

In 1922, Scripps moved to ensure his heirs would carry on his sacred tradition of hard-hitting, independent journalism. He established "The Edward W. Scripps Trust," assigning to it 89 percent ownership control of the UP and his other holdings. He made Roy Howard chairman of the board and renamed his chain the Scripps–Howard newspapers. Through good years and lean, in the decades after Scripps died in 1926, his wire service would fiercely protect his legacy.

In May 1927, UP restored some of the luster lost in the armistice debacle by flawlessly covering Charles "Lucky" Lindbergh's historic solo transatlantic flight to Paris. The AP, which had vigorously castigated its rival over the bogus armistice, had to eat crow when it first prematurely announced that Lindbergh had landed safely, then was twenty-one minutes behind UP when he actually did arrive.

UP reporters resorted to any means to get news to the wire, at times employing carrier pigeons as a backstop delivery system. In 1935, when tribesmen clashed with spears and shields in the remote Ethiopian war, the UP turned to native runners to rush copy to telegraph operators.

It was also in that year that UP seized on a new market. Until the 1930s newspapers were the only real source of news. Television news was two decades away and radio networks had largely provided only entertainment. While AP doggedly refused to sell to radio stations, UP brilliantly divined that the broadcast market was the lucrative wave of the future. In 1935 it began tailoring a present-tense newswire for broadcasters, who until then had relied almost solely on swiping stories from newspapers. Several years later the newspaper-oriented AP reluctantly joined the broadcast market, but it would not catch up until the mid-1970s.

• • •

The clackety-clack of a dozen Teletype machines in the Kansas City United Press bureau on a summer day in 1938 fairly drowned out the screeching siren of the ambulance heading up the hill to nearby General Hospital. Sirens always sent one eager UP reporter bounding from his chair. Hands, face, and clothing smeared with the carbon of his toils, young Walter Cronkite, instinctively curious, rushed to the window, spotted the ambulance, and telephoned the hospital in hopes of landing a scoop.

Here, in the nation's heartland, the UP Kansas City bureau was a vital link connecting the coasts, the relay point where copy was written and edited for San Francisco, Mexico City, New York, Boston, and other cities that were just names on a map to many of the staffers. Unipressers bustled about the bureau shuffling copy to a battery of Teletype operators for transmission to newspapers. The material ranged from the vital to the mundane to the trivial, from the latest stock-market quotes off the Western Union ticker to the rumblings in Nazi Germany; from baseball scores, Omaha stockyard prices, and traffic fatalities to stories about how Franklin Roosevelt's New Deal was revolutionizing post-Depression America.

The bureau, on the top floor of an old factory that also housed the *Kansas City Journal-Post*, resembled nothing so much as a factory sweat-shop. With extra generators on the south wall keeping the wires humming, and the newspaper's lead type-melting furnace in the next room, the tiny thermometer easily registered 100-plus temperatures on summer days. Sweltering staffers typed stories on eight-copy carbon books. They had only to blacken their hands and faces a few times before learning to wear old clothing to the office. One young reporter, Maggie Richards, stashed gloves and a hat in a desk drawer in case she was sent out to cover a story.

But covering a story firsthand was rare. UP was so badly understaffed that virtually all its news was gathered by telephone or through special stringers willing to feed news tips for a buck or two a month.

Cronkite, one of a group of eager young Unipressers who later would go on to great renown in the newly born field of network television news, was earning the princely sum of $25 a week. He soon learned how ingenuity could overcome the UP's legendary budget constrictions. His expenses, a few phone calls back to the office from the scene of a story, were not reimbursed. Instead, his bureau manager taught Cronkite how to jiggle two pins through a phone cable to make the connection without having to deposit coins.

Like their counterparts in most UP bureaus, Cronkite and other Kansas City staffers were a tight-knit group that worked and played together, whether they all converged on the office, unsummoned, to help relay news about the bombing of Pearl Harbor; or whether they gathered at parties to marvel as Cronkite and his wife, Betsy, danced at racehorse speed to the "Beer Barrel Polka." Years after he left the UP for the greener pastures of broadcast journalism, Cronkite often nostalgically recalled his stint in Kansas City as his most demanding and enjoyable job.

• • •

In the mid-1930s most cities had at least two competitive newspapers, and in the big metropolitan areas readers could choose from half a dozen or more. In papers buying more than one wire service, a "beat" of even a minute or two could spell the difference between landing on page one or in the trash barrel. The story that arrived first generally made the afternoon papers, which were fighting for street sales with "extra" editions and screaming headlines. The battle for wire service supremacy among UP, AP, and INS, the William Randolph Hearst-owned International News Service, was fierce and furious. It reached a fever pitch with the outbreak of World War II.

On the lovely tropical evening of December 6, 1941, UP Honolulu bureau chief Frank Tremaine and his wife, Kay, were guests of the Coast Guard commandant at a dinner dance at Fort DeRussy on Waikiki Beach. Next morning Tremaine awakened to the sound of antiaircraft fire. Still groggy from partying, he crawled over his sleeping wife and hurried to the living-room window of his hillside home so he could glimpse Pearl Harbor.

Tremaine spotted a few puffs of smoke. Eight o'clock on Sunday morning is an odd time for a drill, he thought, and headed back to bed. Moments later the gunfire grew louder, and he bolted back to the window. A pillar of black smoke, which he later learned came from the stricken aircraft carrier USS *Arizona*, billowed high above the harbor. Tremaine grabbed his phone and quickly tracked down Army Captain Harry Albright, an old friend, who confirmed the harbor was under siege. Phoning Commercial Cable Company, Tremaine flashed the news to New York and Manila: "Pearl Harbor Under Attack."

Then he asked a telephone operator to try to make a connection to the UP San Francisco bureau. When he confirmed the obvious, that the attacking planes were Japanese, he fired off another cable to New York, where UP editors were frantically transmitting the stunning news to the world.

Tremaine threw on clothes and left for Pearl Harbor, instructing his wife to dictate more details if the call to the UP San Francisco bureau ever came through. Moments later, Kay Tremaine found herself on the phone with UP's Jim Sullivan in San Francisco. She read her husband's notes and described what she could see from her window. Ignoring a misdirected antiaircraft shell that whistled past the house and exploded nearby, she painted a vivid eyewitness account of Japanese bombers destroying the USS *Ward*.

For three hours, until Navy censors imposed a news blackout, UP filed sporadic details of the horrible beginning of the Pacific war. While regular communication to Honolulu was cut off for the next four days, UP alone among the news agencies was able to use its private receiver to relay news from the outside world to the petrified, isolated inhabitants of Hawaii.

At his home in Arlington, Virginia, UP White House reporter Merriman Smith, expecting relatives for Sunday dinner, was shaving at 2:25 p.m. when his wife opened the bathroom door.

"You know what the radio just said?"

"No, what?" Smith asked.

"It said the Japanese bombed Hawaii."

Smith wiped the lather off his face, threw on some clothes, dashed to his car, and started out in the heavy traffic. He spotted a motorcycle cop, told him of the Japanese attack, and asked for an escort to the White House.

"Why, those little bastards!" the officer spat out. "What entrance do you want?"

During the next several hours, the most hectic of Smith's young career, he dictated to his editors eight bulletins and four flashes, reserved for the most momentous news. America was plunging into war.

In Lafayette Square, across Pennsylvania Avenue from the White House, thousands of fearful Washingtonians massed in support of President Roosevelt. As Smitty filed his bulletins he could hear them singing "God Bless America" in the cold, bleak wintry night.

• • •

World War II proved another boon to the United Press. Papers locked in bitter readership wars sought the most complete news reports possible and willingly paid for the dispatches of UP's quickly beefed-up foreign staff. UP's client base in the United States alone leaped to 1,715 newspapers and radio stations.

After the armistice fiasco of 1918, with Roy Howard's old admonitions of "accuracy first" ringing in their ears, Unipressers covered World War II with spirit, ingenuity—and extreme care. UP scored exclusives such as the first Western interview with Adolf Hitler, authored by Richard Helms, who a quarter century later would became director of the Central Intelligence Agency.

The young war correspondents, earning about $50 a week and outnumbered 3–1 by their higher paid AP rivals, worked under the continual prodding of their editors in New York who were acutely aware of the insatiable market for fast, accurate war news. World War II would be on the front pages of American newspapers every day for four years; readers simply couldn't get enough.

J. Edward Murray, UP's chief correspondent on the Western Front, was stationed at the Scribe Hotel in Paris to cover SHAEF—Supreme Headquarters, Allied Expeditionary Forces. Writing about SHAEF was grueling work, requiring enterprise and hustle. Murray sent his dispatches over half a dozen different routes to beat the inevitable cable communications snafus.

Unipressers also became adept at skirting regulations to get their stories on America's front pages. Once Murray was suspended for a week by General Dwight D. Eisenhower for cagily breaking censorship on a story about the Battle of the Bulge. Murray, in a cable to UP foreign editor Harrison Salisbury in New York, had concealed a sentence confirming a major exclusive already run by *Time* magazine. When Salisbury spotted the confirmation, he rewrote the *Time* story and sent a UP dispatch screaming out under Murray's byline. An irate Ike stood up at a press briefing and shouted, "Ed Murray, you're grounded!"

Murray, about to yield the assignment to colleague Boyd Lewis anyway, smiled smugly. The suspension was a small price to pay for scooping AP and INS.

• • •

Many young Unipressers cut their journalistic eyeteeth in Europe, carving out reputations that ultimately would lead them to better jobs and big reputations at other news organizations.

Walter Cronkite, based in London, had supplemented his regular editing duties in the bureau by becoming expert in all facets of air warfare. For months his byline appeared on UP's daily story slugged "airwar."

On the night of June 5, 1944, he cashed in on his expertise. He was awakened at his London apartment by an Air Force press officer and learned he had been chosen by lot to accompany the 303rd Bomber Group in a B-17 in the next morning's D–Day invasion of Normandy. Taking off before dawn, Cronkite was witness to the most massive military mission ever mounted. Returning to London, he crafted a riveting story that captured the drama and scope of the invasion. Although his was a pool report distributed simultaneously to all the correspondents left behind in London, the story was a tremendous coup for UP. Now everyone knew Cronkite's name.

Three months later, when he learned that Eisenhower was preparing a daring airborne drop of troops into Holland behind the Siegfried Line of German troops, Cronkite finagled permission to use military communications to transmit to his London office up to 100 words during the first six hours after the invasion. Cronkite, who never had flown in a glider, joined paratroopers headed for Holland. The furtive mission worked perfectly—the engineless planes nose-dived silently behind enemy lines and crash-landed south of Arnhem.

Clambering out of the wreckage, Cronkite reached for the first available helmet and started to crawl across a potato field. Soon a dozen soldiers were following him. When they reached a ditch, one of the men asked the UP correspondent, "Are you sure we're going in the right direction, sir?"

Bewildered, Cronkite doffed his headgear to discover that in the landing scramble he had picked up a major's helmet.

As the war drew to a close UP scored major scoops with stories about the crossing of the Rhine River by Allied forces and the joining of American and Russian troops in Germany. The brilliant successes paid off in a rapidly expanding client base. UP was raking in money like never before.

UP's European news manager, Boyd Lewis, had replaced Murray in 1944 at SHAEF headquarters and was holed up in the Scribe Hotel. Lewis yearned to write about the inevitable German surrender, a story he felt would be the highlight of his nearly two decades with United Press.

On May 6, 1945, Brigadier General Frank A. Allen, Jr., hurried Lewis, James Kilgallen of INS, and Edward Kennedy of AP aboard a C-47 transport and announced, "We're off to witness the end of the war [in Europe]. We are going on a mission to cover the signing of the peace." En route to Reims, Allen, chief of public information at SHAEF, laid down stringent ground rules to prevent premature release of the armistice information. Lewis, mindful that UP had been burned badly by blowing the armistice signing in 1918, agreed along with the others to the news blackout restrictions aimed at permitting the Germans to surrender before they would be slaughtered by rapidly advancing Russian troops.

Lewis laid careful plans to ensure his story would be the first transmitted back to New York, even promising his jeep driver a bottle of gin if he would break the speed limits back to the filing center at the Scribe. After watching Ike accept the German surrender, Lewis and his rivals returned to Paris. Lewis, met at the airport by his trusty, lead-footed driver, beat both Kilgallen and Kennedy back to the hotel. He watched in satisfaction as his historic story was placed at the head of the queue for transmission to UP headquarters, to be held until the next day's 3 p.m. simultaneous announcement by Stalin, Truman, and Churchill.

Still gloating over his enterprise, Lewis was stunned to receive a "rocket" message from New York: AP already had reported Germany's surrender! Enraged, Lewis protested to SHAEF's chief communications officer, demanding that his copy immediately be released. No dice.

Enterprisingly, Kennedy had bypassed the system by posing as a colonel and arranging to be connected through a French military phone line to his London bureau. Before his line collapsed he managed to dictate 300 words, giving AP a full day's beat on Germany's surrender. The filing privileges of Kennedy and the AP immediately were revoked, and 54 other SHAEF correspondents angrily sent Eisenhower a letter assailing Kennedy for "the most disgraceful, deliberate, unethical double-cross in the history of journalism."

Once again a war in Europe had ended with bitter rivals AP and UP ensnarled in charges of unprofessional conduct.

• • •

During the war UP logos had become commonplace on the front pages of major American dailies such as the Chicago *Sun*, a tabloid launched by department-store tycoon Marshall Field to compete with the mighty Chicago *Tribune*. Still, Field was furious that he was barred from joining the exclusive AP club, and he sued to force the Associated Press to serve his UP-only paper. In 1945 the Supreme Court ruled that AP's exclusionary provision violated antitrust laws, and it must sell its service to all who wanted it.

While AP lost the case, the real loser turned out to be the United Press. Without captive clients, the smaller, weaker, poorer wire service had to spend money to expand its state coverage to compete with the AP. For the court ruling had left intact AP's exclusive right to transmit over its wires the news generated by its member papers, giving the cooperative free access to vast amounts of copy. Although it would cost UP dearly to add large numbers of reporters to its state bureaus, it had little choice. Newspapers often decided which wire service to buy based on their state coverage.

The Supreme Court had dealt the UP a staggering blow it never would overcome.

Another serious setback occurred even as the United Press was reaping the benefits from its sparkling war and postwar coverage, including a scoop from Clinton "Pat" Conger on the suicide of Nazi leader Hermann Goering during the Nuremberg trials. Despite the successes, the American newspaper market was suddenly beginning to shrink. While nearly a score of papers had flourished on the streets of New York in the war years, by the 1950s the number had dwindled by half. Over the next three decades, as television proved it could deliver hot-breaking news stories faster and stole away advertising dollars, newspapers continued to fold or merge in competitive markets.

UP's ink remained black, but only with the help of the Scripps-owned United Features Syndicate, which held the rights to such gold mines as the comic strip "Peanuts."

• • •

As the market changed, newspaper subscribers—even Scripps's own papers—had little notion of the money and manpower problems UP faced. After the war the UP was so short-staffed that it often had to leave its bureaus temporarily unattended and sometimes missed stories. While resources were in short supply, resourcefulness rarely was.

When Babe Ruth lingered near death at French Hospital in Manhattan in 1948, UP assigned to the story a couple of rookie sports writers. Milton Richman and Jack Griffin, both of whom later became sports editors for the news service and respected names in the profession, knew they couldn't be at the hospital twenty-four hours a day, so they devised a scheme novel to the penurious wire service. They spent some money. They bribed everybody in the hospital. Whoever called UP first would collect $100. On August 16, at 8:01 p.m., Ruth's heart finally stopped and the phones started ringing. UP's flash cleared at 8:04, and AP trailed by two minutes, an enormous beat for UP's broadcast subscribers.

• • •

Russell Jones, a short, soft-spoken correspondent whose wife was Hungarian, was the only American reporter who refused to leave Budapest during the 1956 revolution that triggered a Soviet invasion. Tirelessly,

Jones fed short, tightly written takes to the London bureau, which forwarded them to New York. There, cables editors Jack Fallon, a quick-witted Irishman with an extraordinary writing touch, William J. Fox, and Walter Logan pounded out under Jones's byline straightforward, hard-hitting accounts of the mesmerizing David-and-Goliath conflict. Their anonymous efforts sent Jones on his way to UP's first Pulitzer Prize, an award he helped secure by finally fleeing to London and writing a series of articles on what he had witnessed.

Jones and his rewrite team were not UP's only heroes during the bloody fighting. When communication to the West from Budapest was temporarily cut off, Anthony Cavendish, a young British reporter assigned to the Warsaw bureau, fired a message to European News Editor Roger Tatarian offering to fly there on a Polish Red Cross plane.

"For God's sakes go, man," Tatarian responded.

UP's London desk heard nothing from Cavendish for more than twenty-four hours. Then, suddenly, the telex machine in the bureau awakened, clacking a message from the foreign ministry in Budapest. Cavendish had walked into the Hungarian government's deserted headquarters and started typing away!

"Tatarian," he wired. "Arrived Budapest yesterday. No transport to city. I finally hitched a ride into town on a truck. As we were going into the city, Russian tanks with the bodies of dead Red army soldiers across them were pulling out of Budapest."

UP London correspondent Daniel Gilmore, looking over Tatarian's shoulder, quickly rapped out a bulletin informing the world: "Red army troops pulled out of Budapest today, carrying their dead with them."

• • •

On January 2, 1952, Scripps sold to United Press its Acme Newspictures photo agency, which it had set up twenty-seven years earlier. Now, for the first time, a wire service was able to offer photographs to go with its news stories.

UP also improved on its invention of the Teletype machine by pioneering use of the Teletypesetter, a revolutionary device that permitted its stories to automatically be set in type at newspaper composing rooms, a great money-saver that lured many small newspapers from the AP.

Still, a stream of innovations and an occasional Pulitzer Prize were not enough to permit UP to overtake its main rival, the AP. The Supreme

Court decision had led a number of UP subscribers to switch to the bigger wire service. And evidence mounted that UP and INS could not individually challenge a nonprofit cooperative that could cover any deficits simply by raising its members' assessments.

In the late 1920s the Scripps Howard chairman, Roy Wilson Howard, a gnome-like man with an enormous "Charlie Brown" round head and no evident neck, had traveled to San Simeon Castle on California's Pacific coast to visit the legendary, imperial William Randolph Hearst, baron of the sensationalist tabloids. It was the first known discussion about the possibility of merging the Scripps and Hearst services, and it was as brief as it was unproductive.

"Bill, you know how to run newspapers, but we know how to run a wire service," Howard said. "Why not join INS and UP?"

"Well, Roy," Hearst replied, "you know a mother is always fondest of her sickest child. So I guess I will just keep the INS."

A quarter century later, in 1954, merger talks resurfaced and ranged for the next several years from cool to tepid. When things finally began to get serious, Hugh Baillie, the flamboyant, burr-headed president of UP, coined a code name for the proposed merger, "Company X," in hopes of keeping the negotiations secret.

Baillie and others had surmised that should word leak repercussions from both the AP and the Justice Department's antitrust lawyers might kill the offspring before it could draw a breath.

By the spring of 1958 all major hurdles had been cleared. Frank H. Bartholomew, who succeeded Baillie as UP president, recalled the fateful weekend in his autobiography, *Bart*.

At 4:40 p.m. on Friday, May 16, 1958, in suite 404 of New York's Drake Hotel, he and Hearst president Richard E. Berlin signed the merger agreement. Then, Bartholomew, a California winemaker when he wasn't running a wire service, cracked out four bottles of his best Buena Sonoma champagne to toast the historic occasion.

To allow time for transferring equipment from INS, the men set the announcement for three days later, Monday, May 26. But late Friday afternoon the Justice Department ordered Bartholomew to delay any merger until it investigated a complaint by the American Newspaper Guild that union members' jobs were in jeopardy. Bartholomew and Berlin flouted the warning and sent this announcement over the wires at noon Saturday:

"This is the first dispatch of the news service which will embrace the largest number of newspaper and radio clients ever served simultaneously by an independently operated news and picture agency."

It would be known as United Press International, an organization that already had spawned Cronkite and David Brinkley; Merriman Smith, Howard K. Smith, and H. Allen Smith; and Eric Sevareid, Harrison Salisbury, Marquis Childs, Westbrook Pegler, James Kilgallen, Hugh Baillie, Roy Howard, Oscar Fraley, Raymond Clapper, William Shirer, Charles Collingwood, and Helen Thomas.

The UP finally had its "I."

Alone, UP and INS had been unable to compete with the mighty AP, which had been institutionalized, perhaps in perpetuity, by the Supreme Court ruling. The two private wire services hoped that, with upwards of 6,000 employees and 5,000 newspaper and broadcast clients, they could succeed together where individually they had failed.

The taste of Bartholomew's champagne soon would turn bitter.

Within three years this newly formed giant of the news industry would begin a long, inexorable slide that would erode the company and leave it an object of both ridicule and sympathy.

3
· · ·

Scripps Ponders the Unthinkable

At the sound of gunfire Merriman Smith lunged for the mobile radio telephone in the press limousine.

As the black auto lurched forward, Smith crouched in the front seat, knuckles white on the phone, and barked the news to his colleague in UPI's Dallas bureau.

Shots had been fired at the limousine carrying the President.

Seated behind Smitty, Associated Press reporter Jack Bell squirmed helplessly as he watched his long-time rival beat him to the only phone in the press car that had been part of a triumphal presidential motorcade through downtown Dallas. Not so quick to react, Bell was powerless to inform AP clients what was happening that fateful autumn afternoon, Nov. 22, 1963.

As the press car dashed after John F. Kennedy's limousine toward Parkland Hospital in a race with death, Merriman Smith and Jack Bell were playing out a dramatic subplot: the intense, no-holds-barred competition between UPI and AP.

"Smith, here," he growled into the phone.

"This is Fallon, Smitty," UPI's Southwest Division boss, Jack Fallon, responded.

"Bulletin—three shots were fired at President Kennedy's motorcade

21

in downtown Dallas,'' said Smith. Barely pausing to react, Fallon, the ex-cables editor who had helped UPI win its first Pulitzer Prize four years earlier, slapped the words into the hands of a teletype operator.

The reverberations of rifle fire in Dallas's Dealey Plaza had barely stilled when the bulletin arrived in newsrooms around the world.

Calmly, professionally, rapidly Smith dictated, telling himself to ignore the sirens, the flashing lights, the horror of the moment.

When he had finished dictating, Smith told Fallon, ''Read that back, will you, Jack?''

Even in the confusion, Fallon sensed Smith was stalling to keep the phone line open. Slowly, very slowly, Fallon began reading back Smith's words. Jack Bell had been angry enough that Smith had beaten him to the phone, but he was furious at this stunt. His frustration boiling over, Bell aimed a wild, roundhouse right at his competitor. Smith ducked, and the punch grazed the driver. Still grasping the phone in a death grip as Bell tried to wrestle it away, Smith kept talking slowly, evenly to Fallon. He was on his way to scoring a stunning competitive beat on the story of the decade.

Arriving at the hospital, Smith spotted Kennedy's limp body in the back seat of the presidential car, head cradled in his wife's arms. Shaken at seeing dark bloodstains on the side of Kennedy's gray suit, he turned to Secret Service Agent Clint Hill and asked, ''How badly was he hit, Clint?''

''He's dead,'' Hill replied curtly. Smith dashed into the hospital, grabbed a phone, and called Fallon again.

Nine minutes after the shooting, UPI flashed the news around the world:

''Kennedy seriously wounded, perhaps fatally, by assassin's bullet.'' Hill was quoted by name as saying the wounds were fatal.

The bells on UPI Teletype machines still echoed as Walter Cronkite interrupted the CBS soap opera *As the World Turns*. Voice quivering, Cronkite read his old colleague's words: John Fitzgerald Kennedy had been shot and might be dead.

Smith, dean of White House reporters, was Jack Bell's friend. But as in all UPI-AP relationships they were fierce rivals as well, and their friendship had vanished in the fight for the telephone. Poor Jack Bell, himself a journalist of high repute, had been trounced on the biggest story he ever would cover. His career and his relationship with Smitty never would be quite the same, and he would carry his anger and bitterness to his grave.

UPI had scored an incredible triumph over the giant AP, which later complained so bitterly to the White House that on subsequent trips the wire service reporters would ride in separate cars—each equipped with a phone.

In its desperate struggle to catch up on the story, the AP ran an "unconfirmed report" that Vice President Lyndon Johnson also had been shot, and another that a Secret Service agent had been fatally wounded in a separate incident. The AP's erroneous stories fed panicky rumors of an assassination conspiracy.

The AP was no match that day for UPI's Dallas crew, quarterbacked by Fallon, a hard-nosed newsman whose writing style was so crisp and clean it often could be detected by colleagues even when a story carried someone else's byline. Sitting over a typewriter in UPI's old bureau on McKinney Avenue and banging out stories from his staff's notes, Fallon would not leave the office for the next five days, stopping only occasionally to catch a catnap on an office couch.

Aboard Air Force One back to Washington hours after the shooting, Smith fought to make sense of the chaos. Could all this really have been telescoped into three hours? It seemed years. Before the presidential jet had left Love Field in Dallas bearing the body of America's slain leader, Smith had again been a witness to history. Jack Kennedy's widow, Jackie, stockings and pink wool suit drenched with her husband's blood, had watched Lyndon Baines Johnson take the oath as America's thirty-sixth President.

Smith now was in his familiar seat in the press section of Air Force One, pounding out on his portable the biggest news story of his life. Although he had dictated hundreds of words on the run to Jack Fallon, this was his first opportunity to collect his thoughts, to compose a complete and coherent story.

When the plane carrying both the dead President and the new one touched down at Andrews Air Force Base outside Washington, Smith spotted colleague Helen Thomas, who herself would rise to become perhaps UPI's most famous byliner.

Before rushing with the presidential party back to the White House, he thrust his story to Thomas. Grabbing an airfield phone, fighting back tears, she dictated to the UPI Washington bureau Smith's simple but poignant description of the tragic hours in Dallas, a story that landed on front pages nationwide.

Smith's wire service had lived up to its slogan, "A UPI man is on the scene." Claiming his place in a pantheon of famous Unipressers, he had handed UPI another Pulitzer Prize.

• • •

Despite the heroics of correspondents like Merriman Smith, UPI's profits, which had peaked in the years after World War II, continued to shrink dangerously.

Scripps Howard had quickly dampened hopes that the 1958 merger creating UPI would spawn a blockbuster news agency. In consummating the merger, Scripps had stripped the lucrative United Features Syndicate, including the popular "Peanuts" comic strip, from the new corporate umbrella. UPI lost a big revenue source. By 1962 the ink turned red. Although operating losses totaled only a few hundred thousand dollars at first, it was the start of a decline that would continue for a quarter of a century.

Forces always seemed to conspire against UPI. The emergence of television news in the late 1950s, spawning such heroes as ex-Unipressers Cronkite, Eric Sevareid, and David Brinkley, robbed the afternoon newspaper of its most precious commodity: speed in delivering the day's news. To survive, many of UPI's biggest newspaper clients merged or slashed their operations, often keeping just one wire service. Generally that was the AP, beneficiary of the perception that it was more comprehensive and reliable.

As the industry tides began to turn, UPI had trouble sustaining even its profitable ventures. One example was a newsreel service it had set up in the 1950s with 20th Century Fox Movietone to fly news film across the Atlantic each day. The service helped John Cameron Swayze launch TV's first newscast, *Camel Caravan*, in 1952 and provided Fox with film for its movie newsreels. UP had reaped $300,000 in annual profits until development of the transatlantic coaxial cable enabled the TV networks to handle the film themselves. Fox, its newsreel service now a dinosaur, pulled out and stuck UPI with a loser.

As losses mounted in the mid-1960s, UPI executives concluded their Achilles' heel was the vital but costly European operation, which provided sexy datelines such as Paris, London, and Rome.

Rod Beaton, fast-rising vice president for Europe, Africa, and the Middle East, had been dispatched to London by UPI president Mims Thomason to cut the European losses, which were putting the entire company in the red. Beaton severely curtailed the costly services that translated news stories into French, German, and other languages, even from "American English" to "English English" for British subscribers. Modeling his plan after a deal cut with the Italian news agency ANSA by his predecessor, Beaton negotiated news exchanges with the Scandinavian countries, the German news agency DPA, and Agence France-Presse. Although the agreements saved UPI money and reduced its London staff from 800 to 300, the wire service soon became increasingly dependent on often questionable foreign journalists. Further, UPI's diminished presence deprived newspapers in those countries of an important alternate source of news.

• • •

In the newsroom, ambitious UPI editors hoping to find the key to long-term financial stability groped for innovations and competitive victories that would distinguish the service. Most editors always had considered UPI livelier and brighter than AP; now UPI had cultivated a stable of extraordinary writers like H.D. "Doc" Quigg, Jack Fox, David Smothers, Louis Cassels, and Oscar Fraley, who in his spare time wrote the script for the hit TV series *The Untouchables*.

Roger Tatarian, now managing editor, showcased UPI's writing talents. In 1961 he sent Smothers from Chicago to Sheldon, Iowa, where the FBI had arrested the cashier of the First National Bank. Three UPI reporters from the Des Moines bureau joined Smothers, introducing the concept of "team reporting" that would become a UPI trademark. They crawled over the tiny farm community like locusts.

Eschewing the traditional matter-of-fact lead paragraph—that Sunday-school teacher Burnice Geiger had embezzled $2,126,850.10 over forty years from her father's bank—Smothers began his story:

"Three signs tell the story of Sheldon, Iowa. One of them is on the outskirts of town. It says, 'Bank with confidence at the First National Bank.' Another is on the cash register of every store in town. It says, 'Sorry, we can't cash checks from the First National Bank.' The third is on the door of the bank itself. It says, 'Closed by order of the federal bank examiner.' "

Two decades later such treatment would be standard, but in the 1960s the approach was so radical that UPI offered "alternate leads" for more timid papers.

The same year Tatarian was given a copy of a front-page editorial by Thomas Storke, publisher of the Santa Barbara *News-Press*, criticizing a new right-wing organization espousing racial and religious hatred. Tatarian, who had never heard of the John Birch Society, queried UPI bureaus. He struck gold. Information poured in from across the country revealing how deeply the society was entrenched. Tatarian assigned New York staffer Barbara Bundschu to write a five-part exposé, UPI's longest to date. Although Storke ultimately won a Pulitzer Prize, it was UPI's stories that shone the national spotlight on the secretive Birch Society.

The series stirred a furor. UPI received cancellations from newspaper subscribers in Texas and Ohio who thought it a terrible attack on a patriotic American organization.

Tatarian went to UPI president Mims Thomason with good news and bad.

"Play has been terrific, but we got three cancellations."

"Was our story okay?" Thomason asked.

"Our story was okay," Tatarian told him.

"Fuck 'em!" Thomason growled, demonstrating the kind of independence that would have made E.W. Scripps proud.

Since UPI could not compete with the AP army of reporters on every story, it made sure it pounced on the big ones, such as the civil rights movement in the early 1960s.

In early June of 1966, reporter James "Ken" Cazalas was assigned to James Meredith's 220-mile voting-rights pilgrimage from Memphis, Tennessee, to Jackson, Mississippi. Meredith had created a fire storm in 1962 when he integrated that Jim Crow bastion, the University of Mississippi.

Jack Griffin, the former sportswriter who had risen to Southern Division chief, knew the march was fraught with danger.

"Watch Meredith every minute!" he warned.

Late on the afternoon of June 6, Cazalas was right where Griffin had told him to be, while AP reporter Ron Alford was back in his Memphis bureau filing a story. When a shotgun blast rang out, Cazalas raced to a phone and dictated a bulletin: Meredith had been shot and wounded.

AP, caught without a staff reporter present, filed a bulletin at 6:33

p.m., based on information from a stringer, that James Meredith was dead.

Al Kuettner, whose name was bylined on virtually all the major UPI civil rights stories that decade, phoned the hospital from Atlanta and tracked down a doctor who confirmed that Meredith had dozens of superficial scalp, leg, and back wounds—but was still very much alive.

Meanwhile, messages flowed in to UPI's Atlanta bureau from around the globe: ''AP says Meredith dead!'' ''CBS says Meredith dead!'' Feeling deadline pressure from UPI-only subscribers to match the AP, Mims Thomason phoned Griffin from New York.

''Jack,'' he said, ''are you absolutely sure we're right?''

''Yes, sir, I am.''

''You know what's riding on this?''

''Yes, sir, I do.''

''Okay,'' Thomason said, and hung up. If UPI were wrong on such a big story, it could lead to a flurry of subscriber cancellations.

At 7:08 p.m., thirty-eight minutes after declaring Meredith dead, AP pulled back its bulletin—far too late for the networks' evening newscasts. AP's official explanation said that reporter Alford, desperate to catch up on the story, had misunderstood. The AP's Memphis stringer had said ''shot in the head.'' Alford heard—and reported—''shot dead.''

Kent Cooper, the AP general manager, later called the episode the worst black eye his agency had suffered in twenty years.

But when you're number two, things just seem to conspire against you. AP and UPI photographers at the scene, shooting from opposite sides of the road, each got pictures of the fallen Meredith. AP discovered, upon developing its film, that the would-be assassin was visible in the background. Despite botching one of the major stories of the civil rights era, AP won a Pulitzer Prize for photography—an irony that left Griffin and other Unipressers bitter for decades.

• • •

In 1971, at the height of the Vietnam War protests, UPI stumbled on a story that would astound the world. Four young members of the militant Weatherman faction of the radical Students for a Democratic Society had died when homemade explosives blew up their Greenwich Village headquarters. The news that the radicals were children of middle-class America caused an uproar that lasted for days.

Tatarian learned that a London staffer, Lucinda Franks, knew one of the bombing victims, a young woman from Kankakee, Illinois, named Diana Oughton. Realizing immediately the sensational potential, Tatarian brought Franks back from London and teamed her with Tom Powers, a bright, twenty-nine-year-old New York City desk staffer, on an assignment to write Diana Oughton's story. Leave no stone unturned, Tatarian directed, no lead unchecked, no road untraveled.

Powers and Franks tramped across the Midwest piecing together the tale of the daughter of a wealthy family, the recipient of the best education money could buy, dead in the rubble of a New York City bomb factory.

Returning to New York for money and a breather, they excitedly told their editor, "We think you're going to be proud of us."

"Good God, this is terrific!" Tatarian exclaimed as he listened to their unfolding story.

After five weeks on the road, Franks and Powers holed up in a twelfth-floor conference room at UPI's New York bureau. Working nonstop for ten days, they turned out a five-part, 12,000-word series, "Diana: Making of a Terrorist." It won the 1971 Pulitzer for national reporting.

For many young stars like Powers and Franks, UPI was but a springboard to success. Although the opportunities to shine were extraordinary at the wire service, the pay was low. And even the most experienced staffers had to spend much of their time performing scut work. Unlike reporters on newspapers, Unipressers had no guarantees their stories would break into print. Their fate was in the hands of powerful, unknown newspaper wire editors who often heartlessly whacked the bylines off wire copy.

After making their splash with the Diana Oughton series, Powers and Franks took leaves, never to return to UPI. Powers expanded the series into a book and later became a nationally known free-lance writer. Franks signed on as a correspondent for *The New York Times*.

• • •

Despite its editorial innovations, however, UPI was becoming an albatross for the wealthy Scripps Howard group. By 1972 the wire service's annual operating losses had inched perilously close to $2 million and there seemed no immediate hope of reversal.

It wasn't as if Scripps executives didn't have plenty of other problems to worry about, including mounting losses from several of the afternoon newspapers that were the core of founder E.W. Scripps's empire. While most of the Scripps newspapers still were healthy and profitable, its papers in Cleveland and Columbus were losing ground to morning competition and ultimately would fold. The foundering Cincinnati *Post* and the Pittsburgh *Press* would be saved only by merging production and business operations with rival morning papers.

To Scripps, UPI's problems not only posed a financial drain but seemed to confound solution. The AP was able to command far higher rates from the great majority of newspapers, capitalizing on its special relationship with "members." When UPI tried to approximate AP's rates, many papers threatened to cancel. And the more clients that canceled the more important it became for UPI to raise the rates. AP executives watched with ill-concealed glee as their rival sank deeper into the red.

As UPI's fortunes worsened, Scripps accorded its biggest and most prestigious property the kind of tentative affection a parent might give an adopted orphan. The boldness and innovation that had been a UPI trademark rapidly were disappearing, replaced by a creeping malaise. Rather than exploiting the dawn of the worldwide information revolution by searching for profitable new products and services, Scripps executives timidly watched from the sidelines, resigned to merely trying to contain UPI's losses.

For Scripps it rarely was "How can we make money with UPI?" Rather, it was "How little can we lose?"

Because Scripps's newspaper and broadcast profits vaulted it into a 48 percent bracket, as long as UPI's losses were reasonable they could be justified as a useful tax write-off. After experiencing a decade of ever-increasing deficits, disheartened Scripps executives had begun to realize that their wire service was on shaky ground, facing a shrinking newspaper market, sharply escalating costs, and a perhaps invincible rival.

The tight financial situation was reflected in the inhospitable appearance of most UPI bureaus. In contrast to comfortable working conditions enjoyed by many other news organizations, most UPI offices still resembled the early years: they were dark and dismal, and furnishings and typewriters often were ancient and decrepit.

UPI employees, who watched other big media companies change and prosper, began to fear Scripps's commitment was waning. Whenever paychecks arrived a few hours late, rumors flared that their wire service might fold.

• • •

Mims Thomason, frail, fighting a drinking problem and weary of battling a decade of UPI financial woes, stepped down as president in late April of 1972.

Scripps, typically staying within the family in naming a successor, tapped Rod Beaton, who had lobbied for the job since being recalled from Europe in 1969 to become general manager. The appointment of Beaton, a rawboned man at six feet five, foreclosed the futures of some of the company's most talented vice presidents, and several soon departed.

Two weeks after assuming the presidency, Beaton asked the UPI board of directors for $5 million for an improved facsimile photo transmission system to serve newspapers about to enter the age of color.

Charles Scripps, dean of the Scripps family, flinched—but he and the board approved it.

In another big investment, Scripps authorized $10 million that enabled UPI to retire scores of Teletype operators and replace them with computers able to transmit stories twenty times faster. UPI had pioneered the use of computer terminals that would be standard fare in most newspapers a decade later, but many later believed that Scripps and UPI squandered a golden financial opportunity in the next few years by failing to aggressively develop new computer-driven products or sell technical consulting services.

UPI also failed to fully capitalize on a news-gathering revolution, triggered by the Watergate scandal, that would make investigative reporting a staple of America's best papers. On June 17, 1972, when members of a White House "plumber's unit" broke into Democratic National Headquarters, *Washington Post* reporters Bob Woodward and Carl Bernstein pounced on the story with extraordinary verve. UPI's coverage of the ensuing Watergate scandal was respectable, but, like other news organizations, it could not equal the *Post*'s. More important, the Woodward-Bernstein style of dogged sleuthwork signaled a new era in investigative journalism—one that would provide exclusive, heavily documented stories that would help major newspapers compete with TV news. The more traditional AP was leery of in-depth reporting, and UPI, often innovative in the past, was slow to seize the opportunity.

Even when UPI executives tried to initiate new products they got precious little support from Scripps. For years the wire service had struggled to keep alive its television service, known as UPITN. In 1973, UPI joined with Paramount Pictures and a British commercial television network to create a daily, hour-long syndicated TV news show that would be broadcast electronically to subscriber stations rather than shipped by overnight mail. Within months, even though business was growing, Paramount dropped out because of financial losses suffered on the movie *The Great Gatsby*. Stuck with all the liabilities, UPI and its remaining partner, ITN, abandoned the project after a year, frightened off by $1 million in start-up losses and by a competitor financed by Colorado brewing magnate Joe Coors. UPITN executives Burt Reinhardt and Reese Schoenfeld later capitalized on the still untapped TV news market by using a similar concept to develop Ted Turner's Cable News Network.

Although Scripps continued to invest in UPI, as the losses grew its commitment somehow seemed less than enthusiastic. While Scripps rarely rejected outright Beaton's requests for money, the chilly atmosphere at UPI board meetings made him loath to push expensive new ideas. Many other media leaders, seizing on brilliant advances in technology, were plunging headlong into the communications revolution. By standing still, UPI was losing ground.

Beaton, a man with a legendary temper, felt the pressure to reverse UPI's slide. He commonly returned from board meetings and vented his frustration by firing off the communiqué that since the 1920s had struck fear: DOWNHOLD. The term, a truncated version of "hold down expenses," was a throwback to the days when cable costs were measured in words and thrifty Unipressers saved money by inventing their own telegraph vocabulary, dubbed Cable-ese.

To Unipressers, a Downhold was a constant reminder of the company's troubles—dig even deeper, cut even more. No more transfers, no more hires, no more overtime, no more "temps" for vacation or sick leave. As economy moves piled up, even the "Downhold" edicts from on high lost their impact.

• • •

Unipressers who had seen their company survive more than a decade of losses developed an almost blind faith in its importance: in a real crisis, they reassured each other, the news industry would not let UPI die—someone would come charging to the rescue.

Despite its drawbacks, UPI had plenty of allure to keep talented staffers from defecting. It was a perfect training ground—the pace was furious, the work varied, and even beginners could cover stories of national and international import. Advancement often was rapid, and possible overseas assignments beckoned the footloose.

UPI's forces were like troops in a battle zone aware their mates were also under siege. While many staffers knew their colleagues only as a voice on the phone or by initials on wire messages, they nurtured enduring, if long-distance, friendships. Urgent calls for help rarely went unanswered. Unipressers knew that the next time they might be the ones needing help.

And, in sharp contrast to AP's stuffy, button-down image, Unipressers enjoyed a far more casual working environment. There were no dress codes and there were precious few behavioral strictures—iconoclastic staffers often turned the air blue with shouts and curses.

Managers shrugged, ascribing outbursts to enthusiasm and grit. In the late 1950s, cub reporter Richard Growald, a young man with a hair-trigger temper, hurled a telephone through the window of UPI's Hartford bureau, located, appropriately enough, on the corner of Asylum Street. UPI tolerated the talented Growald's often erratic behavior, and he later rose to become a star reporter during the Vietnam War and then White House correspondent.

Most employees loved the unstructured atmosphere at UPI, but even the most loyal had their breaking points. In 1974, two years into Beaton's reign, long-simmering resentment over low pay and long hours bubbled to the surface. The union, heretofore a weak sister, demanded wage parity with the AP. Scripps refused.

At 8 a.m. on St. Patrick's Day, as afternoon newspapers in the East were choosing their front-page stories, hundreds of Unipressers hit the picket lines, some wearing buttons emblazoned "Hire 'em cheap, use 'em up, throw 'em out."

The strike lasted twenty-three days. Nonunion employees worked themselves into exhaustion producing a truncated news and picture report. UPI's millions of words a day slowed to a trickle.

Worried about their limited bargaining power, the strikers resorted to dirty tricks. In the closing seconds of the NCAA basketball tournament in Greensboro, North Carolina, Charlie Aldinger, UPI's Memphis manager, was about to call the Atlanta bureau when suddenly his courtside phone rang.

"This is the desk," growled a voice at the other end. "Are you ready to start dictating?"

For twenty minutes Aldinger rattled off his story, then headed into the jubilant North Carolina State locker room for quotes and color. When he returned the press-box phone rang again.

"This is Atlanta. The game has been over half an hour. Where the hell is your story?"

"I just got finished dictating it to you," Aldinger protested.

"Like hell you did! Start over!"

Aldinger realized he had been hoodwinked into dictating to a striker. The long delay in getting the story on the wire assured AP a mammoth competitive advantage on one of the biggest sporting events of the year, and invigorated picketing Unipressers.

But many publishers, staunchly anti-union, brushed off the fact that UPI's news report was far from adequate and supported the company's position. Realizing they had no leverage, the union caved in after twenty-three days and returned to work for a token wage increase.

Management had won, but the strike left a bitter aftertaste. It enraged employees, exposed UPI as a company with severe labor strife, and sent more subscribers fleeing to the AP.

• • •

While UPI's cub reporters were brimming with enthusiasm, they occasionally made embarrassing mistakes that hurt the company. Less than two hours after the Teamsters Union called a nationwide strike at 12:01 a.m. on April 1, 1976, UPI's Chicago bureau sent out a bulletin quoting sources as saying it had been settled. A correction moved minutes later, explaining that it was only a small local that had settled and that 400,000 Teamsters still were on strike. It was too late for those West Coast papers that had rushed the earlier scoop onto the front pages.

But on the biggest story of 1976, struggling UPI once again amazed the news industry. As returns rolled in on the presidential election, the sophisticated computers and high-priced political analysts of the major TV networks could not project a winner. UPI, relying on state political experts to analyze the returns and historic voting patterns to determine when a candidate had carried their states, sent a flash at 2:57 a.m. EST on November 3: Jimmy Carter had upset President Gerald Ford. Moments later, Walter Cronkite appeared on CBS to announce UPI's flash and plaintively asked CBS reporters why they had been beaten. It took fifteen minutes for CBS to match UPI, then the other networks straggled in. AP limped home behind them all.

The last shall be first, the biblical saying goes, and on that Election Day in 1976 Unipressers scored a beat that filled their scrapbooks and fed their egos.

• • •

Still, the profit-loss figures grew gloomier. The news industry was changing. Broadcast journalists had cornered the market on speed, and wire-service victories measured in minutes would not be enough to sustain UPI. *The New York Times* and *Washington Post* capitalized on their successes covering the Watergate scandal and began to syndicate, further eroding UPI's subscriber base.

Bernard Townsend, a financial vice president for Scripps, had been urging since the early 1970s that UPI diversify to capitalize on the burgeoning worldwide market for financial and business information. Townsend, who foresaw the bonanza Reuters ultimately would reap in that area, shook his head in frustration when both Rod Beaton and Charles Scripps repeatedly ignored his entreaties. He was convinced their tunnel vision about the industry prevented them from grasping that UPI, a money-loser for so long, might yet be made wildly profitable.

For Beaton, trying to control the burgeoning deficit was like squeezing marmalade. By the mid 1970s, UPI's financial woes seemed irreversible. In 1976 and 1977 operating losses crept to about $3.5 million a year. In 1978 the pretax deficit surged to $5.3 million.

Beaton, never very imaginative, grew even more conservative. In presenting the latest bleak financial picture to the UPI board, he hastened to add, "We'll have a Downhold."

Even Scripps officials began to view Beaton's Band-Aid measures with skepticism. Chairman Edward Estlow, a nature-loving Robert McNamara look-alike, would respond to Beaton's cost-cutting suggestions by citing UPI's most loyal subscribers—Scripps's own newspapers.

"Rod, I know from talking to our own editors that you're already too thin. You're into the bone already. A Downhold's not the answer. Sales are the answer."

Beaton, trying to keep the payroll spare, never increased UPI's skeletal sales force, which was preoccupied with trying to dissuade subscribers from dropping the service. When aides suggested hiring more salesmen who would concentrate on luring new clients, he snapped, "What the hell do we need more salesmen for? The twenty-nine we have aren't selling anyway!"

UPI's editors had begun wondering why Scripps and Beaton were not more aggressively searching for solutions. In 1976, Beaton told a lunch meeting of top company officials that UPI had been offered an opportunity to join a project that would convert the ancient Central Commercial High School into an office building. UPI would then move into the building, next to its midtown Manhattan headquarters, and capitalize on the exploding real estate market. Beaton's lieutenants listened to their boss with growing enthusiasm, only to have their hopes quickly dashed.

Of course, he told them, he had turned down the offer—"We're not in the real estate business."

"Maybe we ought to be," someone at the table muttered unhappily.

Not too long after, real estate tycoons Harry and Leona Helmsley tore down the high school, built a luxury hotel, and made a fortune.

• • •

By the late 1970s, UPI's dismal bottom line was creasing the brows of even the stone-faced barons at Scripps headquarters in Cincinnati.

As long as UPI's losses were modest, Scripps had shrugged them off as tax breaks. But UPI's $5.3 million actual loss in 1978 still translated to a net loss of $2,538,000. More worrisome, the figures kept rising.

Scripps executives had devised clever schemes to minimize UPI's drain on the parent company. But even smart lawyers, imaginative accountants, and UPI's editorial staff could not solve the biggest problem looming: Scripps's officers were legally responsible for the family trust that owned more than 80 percent of the company stock.

In an effort to insulate his media empire, E.W. Scripps had created the trust primarily for his six grandchildren—Bob, Charles, Sam, and Ted Scripps, and Peggy Buzzelli and Nackey Loeb. When the last one died the trust would revert to their heirs, more than two dozen Scrippses and Howards, who would have the option of cashing in the assets.

E.W. could not have foreseen that the terms of the trust would, ironically, be a disincentive for his grandchildren to continue underwriting UPI. For if Scripps were ultimately forced to fold the wire service, it might have to shoulder up to $50 million in pensions, severance, and other shutdown costs. And the Scripps executives and directors—even E.W.'s grandchildren—worried that in such a case they might personally be vulnerable should the heirs decide to sue them for squandering assets by continuing to underwrite UPI's losses.

Atop its other woes, disaster struck UPI on a sweltering July evening in 1977 when lightning plunged the Northeast into darkness. Without its computer in New York, UPI had no way to transmit the bulk of its news report. As fate would have it, AP soon was able to jerry-rig a regional transmission system, but UPI was all but out of business and its single-service newspapers and broadcast clients were virtually without a news report for twenty-four hours. The embarrassment that AP was able to operate almost normally, while UPI could not, left Beaton and his managers vowing never to let it happen again. Bowing to UPI's lobbying, Scripps bought a new, $10 million computer and leased the wire service space in a new building in Dallas, a city less prone to power failures. But the parent company's resolve was wavering.

• • •

Reeling from the burgeoning losses, Beaton, never a gregarious man, grew even more distant from rank-and-file Unipressers, rarely ever sticking his head into the newsroom. He worried how long Scripps would continue to underwrite UPI—and about his own future. Beaton lost his notoriously short temper even more frequently, exploding when managers brought him more bad news.

"I can't believe it, I can't believe it!" he would shout, pounding his desk in frustration.

Beaton's top aides so dreaded his outbursts that some decided to accentuate the positive. At Monday morning staff meetings, general manager Bob Page and Jim Buckner, UPI's marketing head, played down client defections and emphasized new sales. Glossed over was the reality that added revenues from new sales would not kick in for months or even years, until existing AP contracts expired.

Part of controller Fred Greene's job was bringing Beaton the sad financial tidings, including the fact that 1979 losses were projected to approach an unprecedented $7 million. Contrasted with the encouraging sales reports Beaton was getting from Page and Buckner, the ominous projection further confused and enraged the president. One day when Greene walked into Beaton's office to announce that UPI had lost another million, the boss erupted. He hurled his pen and it caromed off his desk, struck a picture on the wall, and landed on the couch.

"I don't believe it! I don't believe it!" Beaton roared. "You don't know what you're talking about!"

"Rod, take a look at the advances we've drawn from Scripps. Look at the cash . . . We're taking a million-dollar bath a month!" Greene insisted.

Scripps executives never moved to shake up UPI's management or replace Beaton. But he had reason to wonder how long Scripps would continue subsidizing the wire service. The demand for news and information was exploding, and Scripps executives knew competing with the rich and entrenched AP would be ever more costly.

Despite UPI's deepening losses, Scripps still had failed to adequately respond to drastic changes in the marketplace. Television gobbled advertising dollars and papers continued to fold or merge, further reducing the number of cities with daily competition. No longer worrying about being scooped, it became easy for papers in monopoly markets to comfortably drop one of the major wire services—almost always UPI. Newspapers used their savings to pad operating profits, to hire more reporters, or to purchase the mushrooming supplemental wire services being peddled at bargain rates by papers like *The Washington Post, Los Angeles Times, New York Times*, and *Chicago Tribune*, and by chains like Knight-Ridder, Cox, Newhouse, Hearst, and even Scripps Howard itself. These supplementals also had become UPI's competition, but the wire service conducted business as usual, continuing to focus on its direct warfare with the AP.

UPI was so obsessed with beating its giant rival that the underdog wire service seemed to lose sight of the fact that the game was unfair, perhaps unwinnable. As a nonprofit cooperative not overly concerned with the bottom line, the AP could haughtily treat its smaller rival like a bothersome gnat, meeting any serious challenges by pouring in money and manpower. Further, the clubby AP lavished coveted memberships on its many boards and committees to editors and publishers.

UPI never could come close to challenging what its rival charged big metro papers. For basically the same service in the mid-1970s, AP reaped $2.33 for every dollar UPI made from the twenty-three largest U.S. papers. *The Wall Street Journal* in 1974 paid AP $36,000 a week, UPI $19,300; the LA *Times* paid AP $20,500 a week, UPI $13,000. Such discrepancies, which only continued to widen, enabled AP to plunge with economic abandon into broadcast rate wars.

While beating AP was a UPI fixation, AP knew time was its relentless ally. So long as UPI was supposed to make money and the AP didn't have to, the playing field never would be level.

AP's top brass had made it clear they would do nothing that might help UPI. They had been approached by UPI executives on several occasions about sharing a common communications network to combat the soaring costs of telephone lines, and each time categorically rejected the idea.

Seeing all these signs in the late seventies, Ed Estlow and chief financial officer Larry Leser quietly began lobbying the Scripps family. Before it was too late, they argued, the heirs must consider disposing of E.W. Scripps's proudest legacy.

• • •

The seeds had been planted when Scripps financial vice president Bernard Townsend held three meetings with CBS to discuss a merger he felt would save money by streamlining two worldwide communications networks, and create the world's most powerful news organization. The talks broke down, however, over the issue of who would be in control.

In 1979, Estlow and Leser persuaded the Scripps that it was time to go public with the full dimensions of UPI's financial problems and seek industry help.

Beaton was generally a team player in dealing with the parent company—some even viewed him a toady. To this idea, though, he strenuously objected. If Scripps revealed UPI's true plight, panicky subscribers might cancel.

"Why," he mused, "would I want to drop off my dirty clothes at a laundry I felt might go bankrupt?"

Beaton thought Estlow had lost his mind.

But mindful of the imprecations from the Scripps lawyers to solve the UPI "problem," Estlow decided to ask his publishing brethren to purchase partnership shares to help prop up UPI. At a convention in September 1979 at Scottsdale, Arizona, Estlow tested his bombshell on a group of subscribers serving as members of the UPI Newspaper Advisory Board. UPI was in deep financial trouble, he said, and the terms of the family trust made it mandatory for Scripps to put its financial house in order.

The advisory board members were generally supportive and understanding. They knew Scripps had subsidized UPI to the tune of $80 million over the past two decades and urged Estlow and Leser to press on with a limited partnership plan. Finally, UPI would learn how deep was the industry commitment to the tradition of wire service competition.

Beaton and editor H.L. Stevenson, a dynamic, quick-tempered Mississippian who had succeeded Roger Tatarian in 1972, were seated at opposite ends of the conference-room table in Scottsdale when Estlow announced his intentions. They wrestled with their emotions. After seventy years of steadfast support from Scripps, here was the first real chink. If UPI's parent no longer could support it, who would?

Flying back to New York, Estlow himself was torn. Practically, this was a step Scripps had to take. Emotionally, because UPI was the old man's legacy, conceding defeat would be torture for his grandchildren. But Estlow swallowed hard and made his public pitch, emphasizing the need for the industry to support the idea of competing wire services.

The grand plan for putting UPI on a sound financial footing, hatched by lawyers at the prestigious Cleveland firm of Baker and Hostetler, called for phasing down Scripps's role over a five-year period. Up to forty-five media interests would be offered a 2 percent limited partner's share for $180,000. As general partner, Scripps would absorb all losses the first year and 75 percent the second, gradually phasing down so that by the fifth year it would hold only 10 percent of UPI.

Even had it been met with wild enthusiasm, the plan would have generated but $8.1 million, scarcely covering UPI's 1979 operating loss and hardly a major cash infusion to underwrite new technology or products. But Scripps reasoned that, if it could entice such giants as Gannett, Times-Mirror, Knight-Ridder, *The New York Times*, and the networks to invest and subscribe handsomely, revenues would soar and UPI could be profitable at last, even if it far more resembled the AP cooperative than the fiercely independent little wire service E.W. Scripps had founded. In taking a chance by being open about UPI's financial woes, Ed Estlow and his Scripps team were confident newspapers would rally behind the partnership idea. But they had badly overestimated the reservoir of industry support.

When Beaton, general manager Bob Page, and controller Fred Greene hit the road to try to help sell the limited partnership, they met a chilly reception. The reasons ranged from loyalty to AP to fears that a perpetual money-loser like UPI could not be made profitable, to reluctance to buy into a cartel where they would not have voting rights. After three months only eighteen prospects had expressed interest, among them the Quincy, Massachusetts, *Patriot-Ledger*; the Boston *Globe*; the Copley family in San Diego; the *Providence Journal*; the Bonneville broadcast group, and Len Small of the Moline, Illinois-based Small Newspapers. Some big newspaper groups informed Scripps they feared stockholders would protest.

Beaton, Estlow, and Charles Scripps were crushed. For years Scripps had been the mule, packing the weight for the industry. Now, when it begged for help, the answer was a flat no. The limited partnership idea was dead. No autopsy was necessary.

Privately, some UPI executives and Scripps officials complained that Estlow and Leser had done a lousy job selling the idea, and that a more innovative, determined, and less hasty approach might have saved the proposal.

On January 31, 1980, Beaton sent a memo to staffers announcing the campaign had fallen "substantially short of our goal." He pledged to "go back to the drawing board."

Employees, who had assumed Scripps would have little difficulty rounding up financial help for UPI's renaissance, were dumbstruck. For years they had deluded themselves that the news business treasured their efforts as indispensable.

Now they had to worry about Scripps's commitment, too. Whatever its faults, for almost three quarters of a century UPI's owner always had been there with the paychecks, underwriting their dreams of wire service domination and professional glory. Their bulwark crumbling, Unipressers pondered the unthinkable: Scripps might dump their wire service on some untested, ill-equipped new owner, or, even worse, simply let it die.

4
· · ·
Dreams of Glory

One day in late 1981 a newspaper article set Doug Ruhe's imagination dancing. It was just a small blurb, but it didn't take much to ignite Ruhe, who, with his partner, Bill Geissler, was always searching for new ideas and opportunities from a pie-shaped office in the steel-and-glass Union Commerce Bank Tower in downtown Nashville.

Ruhe and Geissler had come a long way from their 1960s days as civil rights hell-raisers, using sheer brains and hustle to gain ownership of a Chicago television station. Now they were big-time dreamers.

The two had worked together at the Baha'i National Center in Wilmette, Illinois. In 1977 they borrowed money from Ruhe's mother-in-law to launch a public relations and marketing firm from the attic of Ruhe's modest home in nearby Evanston. So cramped was their office that the lean, lanky duo could stand straight only in the middle of the room. With partner Joon Chung, a Korean-born graphics designer, they soon moved into a one-room office in a nondescript shopping center, Bell and Howell being the centerpiece of their small handful of clients.

Ruhe and Geissler had dreams of acquiring several television stations and stitching together an alternate Independent Quality Network. They were undaunted at having no money and no experience, and even ap-

41

proached Ted Turner with their idea long before his Cable News Network hit the airwaves.

One day Ruhe learned that a license was available for a UHF station in the Chicago area and decided it could be the linchpin for their network. Ruhe, earning all of $15,000 a year, boasted, "If I get the right deal, I can put the capital together."

Guided by a Washington communications lawyer who agreed to wait for his $10,000 fee, the two business novices soon found themselves in competition for a license in Joliet, Illinois, with a cable subsidiary of Time-Life, Inc., and Dallas Cowboys owner Clint Murchison.

Facing far richer rivals, Ruhe and Geissler used the legal avenues of the Federal Communications Commission to receive preferential treatment. They were a local group, and half their partners were minorities: Ruhe's wife, Beverly, was black; Chung was Korean and his wife, Irene, an American Indian.

Cannily, Ruhe wheedled and finagled until he had cut programming and franchising agreements with his competitors that won his group the license and also helped finance the project. To be sure, Ruhe bargained away a substantial part of the deal. But he and Geissler, energy and chutzpah their sole capital, had leveraged entree to one of the nation's most lucrative media markets and landed what they felt would be a $30 million commodity. They had done it even though they were so short of cash that they had to ask employees to forgo paychecks until Channel 66 got on the air. Once the station was operating with subscription movie programming in 1981, Ruhe and Geissler would share a nice piece of its $2 million annual revenues, enough for less ambitious men to live off.

Ruhe and Geissler were not about to quit now. They set up a new office in Nashville. Sticking pins on a color-coded map of America to plot their own television network, they recruited Baha'i friends as partners and flooded the FCC with minority applications for low-power stations.

They were on a roll. With Channel 66, they had triumphed once against tough competition and were not frightened to try again. So it was no surprise Ruhe's eyes lighted up that morning when he spotted *The Wall Street Journal* article. Instantly, he smelled pay dirt: the E.W. Scripps Co. wanted to sell UPI.

He rushed to the office and waved the *Journal* article at Geissler and Chung. UPI's terrible financial woes worried Chung, but, like Ruhe, Geissler brimmed with excitement. UPI might be suffering huge losses, but the world was on the brink of an information explosion that would transform the marketplace, and the wire service needed only their vision and enthusiasm to become a gold mine. What a perfect mesh! UPI's worldwide news resources could be the foundation for their independent television network. What an opportunity! There were only two news wholesalers offering a worldwide communications highway and one of them, the AP, would never be for sale.

The mere thought of acquiring a sprawling, problem-plagued company like UPI would have intimidated many with far more business experience. Nor did anything in Ruhe and Geissler's backgrounds suggest that they were qualified to run such a major corporation, even to bid on it. A media giant like Scripps probably would sneer at small fry, anyway. Yet these brash entrepreneurs had airily convinced each other that they could be Davids with slingshots, giant-slayers who could succeed where the richer and more powerful had failed.

Ruhe read in the *Journal* article that the First Boston Corporation was providing a sales prospectus to potential buyers. He phoned First Boston.

"We're not dealing with little companies," sniffed a spokesman for the investment banking firm.

Ruhe feigned shock.

"Wow, man! You know, UPI is losing a lot of money. Maybe you should just give me the information. Maybe you aren't going to have any buyers."

"We've got plenty of buyers. We've got big companies interested."

Ruhe hung up, disappointed. First Boston, stalking a big commission, perhaps had overrated the prospects of enticing a substantial, well-financed buyer.

And, to be sure, it had vastly underrated Doug Ruhe and Bill Geissler.

• • •

By the time the partners learned UPI was on the block, Scripps had been trying to ditch it—quietly and futilely—for three years. Panic was beginning to set in as Scripps executives realized getting rid of UPI would be far more difficult than they had imagined.

They had concluded in the late 1970s that there was no reason to believe almost two decades of mounting losses could be reversed and decided there was no reason to throw good money after bad.

UPI executives had been lobbying for a major investment in satellite technology because soaring ATT charges had cost the wire service $60 million just to transmit the news to subscribers in the past seven years. Technical wizard Jimmy Darr contended that if UPI had switched to satellites in 1975, it would have reaped a $4.1 million profit instead of suffering a $43.2 million loss over the seven years. That would easily have paid for the $37 million cost of converting to satellites. But the mere thought of investing $37 million more on a money-loser like UPI had sent Scripps diving for cover. Estlow and Leser cringed at the prospect of jeopardizing other bright Scripps expansion opportunities by tying up cash in a shaky proposition like UPI. They believed that even if they approved the satellite project, UPI would soon be back pleading for millions more to keep limping along.

"If we gave you the satellite program, we know you could cut your losses," Leser bluntly told controller Fred Greene. "But there isn't enough business in the broadcast and newspaper industry to share with the AP. Ten years from now you'll be right back in the same boat. And this time there won't be any satellite program to cut your losses."

The message could not be misread. Scripps, heretofore always UPI's guardian angel, had been captured by the guardians of the bottom line, who were divining the wire service's future with stunning accuracy.

• • •

As Rod Beaton had feared, the industry's rejection of Estlow's 1979 public solicitation for limited partners had made it increasingly difficult for UPI to attract business. The industry was now aware that the wire service had serious financial problems, and that nobody seemed to care enough to help. There was a growing perception that UPI might never climb out of its hole. Facing 1980 operating losses of $12 million and a net loss of $6,394,000, Estlow spent a bundle for First Boston to undertake a detailed analysis of UPI.

Its bleak report underscored what Scripps executives had come to fear: Unless UPI could attract a dramatic influx of customers with innovative new products, the wire service was doomed.

"From a standpoint of purely hard-nosed economics, your number one choice is to shut it down immediately," a First Boston analyst told Scripps. "Just looking coldly at the numbers, that's the way they come out."

Believing they had not exhausted their options, Estlow and Leser substantially revamped their unsuccessful limited partnership scheme. Now they proposed a general partnership in which media heavyweights would share control and liability for UPI. The plan made sense. Changing the very form of UPI, either by broadening the ownership or merging with a media giant, seemed the best and perhaps the only hope for survival. At a lunch at the Pinnacle Club atop the Mobil building in Manhattan, they outlined their plan to many of the nation's largest media groups—among them Gannett, *The Wall Street Journal*, Knight-Ridder, Hearst, *The Chicago Tribune*, and the New York *Daily News*.

Estlow and Leser apparently had not learned enough from their failure the year before to sell the idea of a limited partnership. Had they laid the groundwork for the meeting by winning advance commitments from one or two newspaper giants, the results might have been different. Perhaps the enthusiasm would have been contagious. Instead, Estlow gambled that the plan would all but sell itself. Once again the response left the Scripps president angry and disappointed, but not surprised. Although friendly and sympathetic to UPI's plight, the media leaders sat on their hands when Estlow asked for volunteers.

For many years fellow publishers had refused to pay UPI anything near the rates they willingly gave AP. Now they had turned their backs once more. While UPI wallowed, the titans of the newspaper business were busily expanding their own empires, marketing supplemental wire services that stood to flourish should UPI fail.

Even in his rage Estlow conceded a basic truth: in a year when covering national politics and the Olympics was sending UPI's losses soaring to $12 million, suitors were hard to come by. His wire service, after all, was less graceful swan than ugly duckling.

• • •

Word of the latest ill-fated attempt to secure UPI's future rippled through the industry and riddled the company with anxiety and uncertainty. The 1980 contract negotiations were a microcosm of the tension gripping UPI. Scripps, having no success finding a buyer, was seeking major concessions from the union. For their part Unipressers, still angry that they had been forced to accept a wage freeze two years earlier, were fully aware they had little leverage—a strike might prompt Scripps to shut down their company.

Union leaders shrewdly waited for months for the perfect moment to exercise their clout, setting a strike deadline for the second day of the Republican National Convention in Detroit, just as the GOP was to nominate Ronald Reagan as its presidential candidate.

In bureaus across the country, Unipressers nervously watched the clock hands inch toward the 4 p.m. witching hour, a time when every available staffer was needed and a walkout would be an embarrassing setback for UPI. Then, at 3:58 p.m., a phone rang in UPI's convention workroom in Detroit's Cobo Hall. It was guild negotiator Cheryl Arvidson in New York, announcing that Scripps had agreed to a three-year settlement with modest wage hikes. The strike nobody wanted had been averted.

Cheers swept the newsroom. The pact, which carried the promise to pay severance if the company folded, seemed a long-term commitment from Scripps. Worries about the future again submerged, UPI's political junkies fanned out to cover the big story.

As UPI's drama unfolded, Reagan's political advisers played for far higher stakes nearby in the top-floor suites of the Detroit Plaza. In a bold gamble that might have ensured a GOP win before the Democrats even chose their nominee, Reagan strategists tried to persuade former President Gerald Ford to agree to be Reagan's running mate. As dramatic negotiations stretched toward midnight, the Associated Press ran a bulletin saying Ford had agreed to run with Reagan. This was huge news indeed. Never had a former President agreed to come back as second banana.

Under immense competitive deadline pressures, UPI reported more cautiously that Ford had not accepted Reagan's offer but that negotiations were continuing. The "deal" soon collapsed. Before the AP could issue a correction, its erroneous story already had been bannered in a number of morning newspapers. The Chicago *Sun-Times*'s front page proclaimed, "It's Reagan-Ford!"

UPI, up for sale and struggling to survive, with its staffers having just withstood a strike scare that might have been a death knell, had demonstrated again the necessity of wire service competition.

Were clients listening? Did they even care?

The competitive message was underscored on March 30, 1981, in a chaotic scene outside the Washington Hilton Hotel after a speech by President Reagan. Secret Service agents were whisking Reagan out a side door to his waiting limousine when a young man mingling in the crowd suddenly drew a revolver.

UPI's Dean Reynolds, trailing the President by a few steps, watched in horror as the young man later identified as John W. Hinckley, Jr., dropped to a crouch and fired several shots, hitting Reagan and critically wounding White House press secretary James Brady and Secret Service agent Timothy McCarthy. Reynolds, a short, athletic bundle of energy who a few years earlier had given UPI a major victory while covering the attempted assassination of Alabama Governor George Wallace, sprang to action.

He dashed back into the hotel, bolted up a down escalator, grabbed a phone at the reception desk, and dialed UPI Washington editor David Wiessler. Instantly the news was screaming around the world. UPI again had hit the wire first with an assassination attempt, just as Merriman Smith had eighteen years earlier from Dallas.

UPI's Washington staff was galvanized, tracking every development as Hinckley was carted off to jail and Reagan and Brady were rushed into surgery at George Washington University Hospital.

Within an hour the AP and all three networks were reporting Brady had died. UPI was starkly alone in reporting that Brady was fighting for his life.

At ABC, anchorman Frank Reynolds read to a live television audience the UPI bulletin, written by his son Dean, that said Brady was alive. Emotionally, he pounded his fist and beseeched, "Is he dead or is he alive? We're talking about a man's life! Can't we get these facts right?"

UPI had it right. Brady survived. Despite their flawless coverage, Unipressers later learned disappointedly that they had only been runners-up for the 1981 Pulitzer Prize for national reporting.

● ● ●

Much of the newspaper industry seemed oblivious to UPI's performances on some of the biggest stories of the century—at least indifferent to the need for both wire services. Sensing the industry's lack of commitment and worried about Scripps's, Rod Beaton reluctantly flipped a dangerous wild card.

Reuters, the rival British-based news agency, always had coveted UPI in hopes of gaining a foothold in America. Since its decision a decade earlier to concentrate on selling financial information services to banks and brokers, once-foundering Reuters had become a huge success, flush with cash.

Beaton had been wary of approaching Reuters, fearing the risks of exposing UPI's most sensitive financial information to its prosperous rival. But with all other avenues blocked in early 1981, Beaton picked up the phone and asked his old friend, Reuters chief executive Glen Renfrew, to meet him for lunch.

On St. Patrick's Day Beaton left the UPI offices and jostled his way through throngs of revelers toward the New York Athletic Club. Over corned beef and cabbage, he made his overture.

"Lookit, Glen, UPI is shopping around and making itself available. Does Reuters have an interest?"

Renfrew said he would get back to Beaton and picked up the lunch tab. Frugality still was a UPI hallmark.

Renfrew quickly checked with his board of directors, and, suddenly, UPI found itself immersed in serious negotiations with Reuters.

As daffodils poked their blossoms through the dirty Central Park snow, Beaton set his strategy. Hoping to avoid an outright takeover that might lead to layoffs of hundreds of Unipressers, he talked up the idea of forming one super news agency. But as Reuters's numbers crunchers combed UPI's books, they were startled by the gloomy portrait they uncovered. Beaton's mood darkened as Reuters executives fanned out across the nation to UPI bureaus and clients, spending six months stockpiling a massive intelligence file about their American rival. He began to fear the Brits were interested only in plucking UPI's plums—its newspictures, radio, Latin American services, and a few top editorial employees—and dumping the rest. Glumly, Beaton concluded Reuters was bent on murder, not merger.

Actually, Reuters was agonizing over its decision. Renfrew told Beaton that his company had problems of its own—trying to go public with its stock and undertaking major internal expansion.

Reuters executive John Stevens, seeing the potential in a merger with UPI if the price was right, suggested at one negotiating session that the Brits should be given $20 million to take the wire service off Scripps's hands.

Estlow and Leser laughed in his face.

• • •

Beaton didn't know it, but Ed Estlow was getting another intriguing feeler about UPI from a personal friend, Maurice Mitchell, chairman of National Public Radio. Mitchell bluntly suggested Scripps donate UPI to his non-profit network.

"You can probably put a value on it for tax breaks far greater than anything you can get selling it," Mitchell said.

Estlow was excited. NPR was highly reputable, and the plan seemed perfect, freeing Scripps of liability if UPI failed and permitting it to take up to $100 million in tax deductions as a charitable contribution.

When Mitchell raised the idea with NPR president Frank Mankiewicz, a former Kennedy confidant who loved making the news, Mankiewicz joyfully envisioned the headlines: "NPR Takes Over UPI."

In his office in Cincinnati, Leser declared, "I want this deal so bad I can taste it."

• • •

Leaks to the press about Scripps's negotiations with Reuters and NPR further frayed Unipressers' nerves. Some openly resented their wealthy owners balking at undertaking the financial commitment they felt certain would make UPI a success. They had tolerated second-class status for years. Now Scripps was jeopardizing their careers.

There could hardly have been a starker contrast than the one between the Scripps hierarchy and the emotional, earthy people who called themselves Unipressers. Among the most volatile was Kenneth Braddick, vice president for UPI's long-profitable New England division. Braddick could be smooth and charming when sober, rowdy and abrasive when not. As a reporter Braddick had refused to join the Guild, and he contrived to win the undying enmity of many colleagues by crossing a picket line during the 1974 strike. Some New York co-workers drove twenty miles to suburban Mamaroneck to pelt his house with raw eggs.

Most Unipressers would not have chosen Braddick, a slight, blunt, short-fused Australian, to carry their banner of bitterness and frustration, but they were not surprised that he was the one to explode. Few, though, could have foreseen the intensity of the eruption in the fall of 1981—or guessed its unwitting victim.

The scene was New York's Grand Hyatt Hotel, the occasion, UPI's most important yearly gathering of newspaper editors—the EDICON meeting. Braddick, who had launched the cocktail hour early, found himself in an elevator with Charles Scripps. As the tipsy Braddick gaped at the bearded sixty-one-year-old family dean, the same anger and anguish that had festered in hundreds of Unipressers erupted, and he berated the soft-spoken patriarch for trying to sell UPI.

"You motherfucker!" Braddick spat. "Do you understand what you're doing?" Charles's wife, Beano, watched in shock and disbelief as Braddick ranted.

After an eternity the elevator stopped at the floor where the fancy UPI reception was being held. Still there was no holding Braddick back. Pursuing Scripps into a corridor, he continued his attack.

Jabbing a cigar and flicking ashes on Scripps's jacket, Braddick lectured him for several minutes on why such a great institution must be preserved. UPI was a company with unique morale and spirit. How could Scripps even consider selling it?

Shocked by Braddick's rude outburst, Scripps tried to squirm away. But it was too late. The embarrassing scene had riveted the attention of UPI's important clients. Softly, Scripps tried to explain to Braddick that the family trust almost compelled the sale of UPI. Scripps just could not continue subsidizing these huge losses forever, he said. Problems existed that were far beyond Braddick's ken.

Braddick's faux pas quickly dominated the cocktail party chatter. UPI's top brass tried to smooth things over with hurried apologies to Scripps executives.

The next morning Ed Estlow angrily phoned Beaton.

"Jesus, what the hell is the matter with this guy Braddick?"

"I suppose he had too much to drink, and that happens to the best of us," said Beaton, struggling to patch things up. Deep down, he was livid. Pulling Braddick aside, he tore into him for his indiscretion and heatedly informed him his job was in jeopardy. Braddick asked whether Charles Scripps would accept a personal apology.

"I think that's the right thing to do," Beaton replied.

At the big UPI luncheon that noon, heads turned as Braddick approached the eldest Scripps. Estlow, a burly ex-football and track star at the University of Denver, protectively moved in, towering ominously over the diminutive Aussie. Scripps quickly and graciously accepted Braddick's apology, explaining that putting UPI up for sale had been a wrenching decision for the family, but that they had no choice.

If Charles Scripps could forgive and forget, his wife, Beano, could not. "I will remember this as long as I live," she told friends. (Years later, Charles Scripps denied any recollection of the incident with Braddick.)

Beaton contemplated firing Braddick, but decided to let him off with a stern warning letter.

● ● ●

Watching Scripps lavish energy and attention on NPR, Reuters's ambivalence turned to irritation. Finally, the Brits decided enough was enough.

Beaton couldn't mask his joy one cold November day in 1981 when he summoned controller Fred Greene, who had labored for months to provide financial information to Reuters and had become convinced a sale to the Brits was UPI's best hope.

"I know you're not going to be happy," Beaton said, smiling, "but Reuters just pulled out of the deal."

Greene, who had been certain the deal would be cut, felt his heart sink at the devastating news. One by one, potential saviors had dropped by the wayside. What options were left? What would happen to his company? If Reuters couldn't love UPI, who would?

The joint announcement that negotiations had broken off came on November 30, 1981. Reuters, filthy rich and knowledgeable about the wire service business, had concluded publicly that UPI was a loser.

Estlow and Leser tried to shrug off the bad news, concentrating on tying up the deal with NPR, which planned to raise $25 million through foundation grants. Armed with a strong vote of approval from the Scripps board, Estlow told Mitchell, "I think this deal will work."

Despite Estlow's enthusiasm, many UPI executives were worried because NPR had traditionally experienced its own financial problems. They didn't have to worry long. Negotiations quickly fell apart when NPR's financial consultants concluded UPI was too big a pill to swallow. On February 23, 1982, Mankiewicz announced the deal was dead.

Another possible escape hatch had been slammed on the fingers of Estlow and Leser. In three short months, two attractive opportunities to extricate Scripps from the UPI mess had slipped away. Had Estlow and Leser, in their zeal for a deal with NPR, passed over the best choice of a new owner for UPI? Reuters had money, prestige, and experience running a wire service. Scripps clearly had not pursued the Brits as aggressively as it could have. Now that opportunity was lost.

Estlow and Leser knew they had to get rid of UPI, and wanted to avoid the massive costs that would accompany a shutdown. There also were equally compelling face-saving considerations. They didn't want to fold E.W. Scripps's legacy, and they wanted to be sure that any buyer would be prestigious and well financed, to reduce the chances of a major embarrassment.

By early 1982, with time and their options fleeting, Estlow and Leser were forced to broaden their net. Some new names surfaced in the press, including Gannett, the nation's largest newspaper group, and Richard Mellon Scaife, an archconservative who owned the Sacramento *Union* and some small dailies. Former Treasury Secretary William Simon made an inquiry. Scripps also contacted Australian publishing tycoon Rupert Murdoch, who had become deeply involved in newspapers in England. Murdoch listened, but would not bite.

In the spring of 1979 flamboyant First Amendment lawyer John Jay Hooker had approached Scripps along with Gannett executive Karl Eller, whom he had helped to acquire *The Tennessean* in Nashville. Hooker was a folksy charmer with a predilection for vested blue suits, red- and blue-striped ties, white felt homburgs, and outrageous homespun homilies, who had lost three statewide political campaigns in Tennessee. He was a wheeler-dealer of the first magnitude who loved center stage.

"Ah want to be President of the United States," he had told Estlow with typical grandiloquence, "and if ah can't be President of the United States, ah want to be president of UPI!"

Estlow had been cordial but noncommittal, sizing up Hooker as a glad-handing blowhard who lacked the cash to do the deal alone.

Now, three years later, Hooker's interest had not waned. He made another try at Scripps, this time with Fred Smith, chairman of Federal Express, who might bail UPI out of its communications problems with his "Zap Mail" satellite delivery network. Once again Estlow and Leser did not take the flamboyant Hooker seriously and, after a meeting at the Cincinnati airport, correctly divined that Smith was not a bona fide contender.

Estlow and Leser cast about, pursuing reasonable inquiries. Sometimes they even initiated the courtships, such as with Jack Taub and Jack Ault of National Information Utilities Corporation of Falls Church, Virginia.

Taub had demonstrated his vision by developing and selling to computer customers a data base service called "The Source," which carried UPI's news reports. The two suggested that if Scripps gave them a share of UPI, in a joint venture arrangement, their communications wizardry and management skills could cut transmission costs, provide new products, and turn the company around.

While Estlow and Leser had first broached the idea, they quickly developed serious misgivings about Taub, a brash, unpredictable man who never graduated high school and whose business résumé included some sparkling successes and a glaring bankruptcy. The Scripps executives remembered their incredulity when, during a UPI outing at a rodeo in Texas, Taub had bounded out of the stands and volunteered to try to wrestle a bra and panties onto an uncooperative calf, which tossed him around the dusty arena like a beanbag.

Estlow and Leser told Ault that they would listen to his proposal, but only if he would leave his partner home.

Imploring Taub to stay behind was like waving a muleta before a bull. He refused to believe that Estlow and Leser wanted nothing to do with him. Arriving at the airport in early spring to catch a flight to Cincinnati, Ault spotted his partner and knew he could kiss any deal for UPI good-bye.

That day during lunch at the staid Queen City Club near the Scripps tower, Ault watched his worst nightmare come true.

Years earlier, Taub had owned a Los Angeles bar, The Promised Land, that advertised "the largest topless dancer in the world"—350-pound "Sadie the Whale." Taub also kept a caged lion cub at the bar and frequently delighted patrons by wrestling his pet. Without hesitation, Taub began to describe the bar to Estlow and Leser, and Ault cringed. He knew the story all too well, was powerless to prevent Taub from telling it, and couldn't bear to watch.

Taub energetically described how he had to stop the little wrestling matches once "Charlie" had matured to 300 pounds, too big to control. One night, he said, he got a call from police at 3 a.m. informing him that the beast had escaped, and they had cornered it against a nearby building.

Taub rushed to the scene to find that high beams and flashing red lights from a dozen squad cars were blinding the terrified lion. Approaching gingerly, he tried to calm his pet. Suddenly, Charlie crouched. Taub knew he was in deep trouble. He began to retreat, but the beast sprang and pounced on him, sinking its teeth into his shoulder. As Taub rolled on the ground, struggling to keep the lion's jaws from his throat, police officers watched passively, unsure whether Taub was merely once again playfully wrestling with his pet.

Now, in the dining room of the Queen City Club, Taub transformed himself from storyteller to actor. While startled Cincinnati businessmen rubber-necked in amazement, he dropped to the floor and re-enacted his predicament, complete with lion roars.

Finally, he told his audience, one of the officers had asked, "Are you okay?" Taub said he knew somebody would write a story the next day, either about poor Jack or poor Charlie. "No," he gasped, as if the Los Angeles police were right there in the club dining room. "Shoot him! Shoot him!"

Although Estlow and Leser smiled politely, they clearly were embarrassed by Taub's one-man theatrics. Fellow club members would not soon let them forget this astonishing breach of lunchtime etiquette. Although the performance had been brief, to the Scripps executives it had seemed an eternity before the lion finally was dead and Taub had scrambled back to their table.

Mortified, Ault knew their bid for UPI was as dead as the lion.

When he returned to Washington he phoned Leser for a status report.

"Not so good," Leser said simply. No further explanation was needed.

Ault broke the news to Taub, who, disbelieving, insisted, "They *don't* feel that way about me!"

• • •

Like land speculators, entrepreneurs love bad news about their quarry. The harder it became for Scripps to sell UPI, the easier it might be for unknowns with skimpy resources to pull off a dream deal.

Not long after being spurned by First Boston, Ruhe's and Geissler's enthusiasm was rekindled by an article in *The New York Times* about the collapse of UPI's negotiations with Reuters. Intensifying their efforts to get the UPI prospectus from First Boston, they phoned Porter Bibb, an investment banker at New York's Bankers Trust Co., who had been the first husband of Geissler's wife, Diti.

Bibb advised him to deal directly with Scripps, and that Bankers Trust would be glad to represent the partners for a fee of $100,000 if the deal closed.

While pondering Bibb's proposal, Ruhe read another article in *The Wall Street Journal*, this one saying that there was such a paucity of potential suitors for UPI that Scripps had considered donating it to cash-poor NPR. Ruhe's juices started to flow, and he thrust the article at Geissler and Chung.

"It's insane," Ruhe cried. "How can they even contemplate that? That's a mark of desperation. NPR's about to go down the tubes. If we can't get it now, when there's nobody at the table, something's wrong with us."

He immediately phoned New York and had Bibb paged on his beeper. "We're ready to go," Ruhe said.

Within twenty-four hours Ruhe finally had in hand the First Boston prospectus and sage advice from Bibb:

"The key is not whether you will buy UPI, but whether Scripps will buy you guys as the new owners."

A fast reader, Ruhe whipped through the prospectus and gave a copy to Tom Haughney, a short, intense accountant he had met when both were summoned to the private University School in Nashville because their seven-year-old sons kept getting into mischief in Mrs. Martin's second-grade class. Haughney, working for a metals processing firm in Chapter 11 bankruptcy proceedings, had considered Ruhe's periodic requests for advice a welcome diversion.

As the two looked over the prospectus, they became convinced UPI was ripe for the plucking. Ruhe quickly overwhelmed Geissler with his infectious enthusiasm, but Chung, an artist, not an entrepreneur, soon left the firm.

Haughney, who had attended the prestigious Wharton School of Business at the University of Pennsylvania, hatched a financing scheme based on convincing Scripps to lend the buyers $5 million in operating cash.

Ruhe also sought advice from Bob Thompson, an acquaintance involved in television start-ups.

"You know," Thompson said, "that thing's owned by a trust. There's just a chance you could be the buyer of last resort."

"What's that?"

"Well, they're fiduciaries of a trust, and if they're being pressured by the heirs they've got a responsibility to get rid of this thing that's losing money. And if they've got a bona fide offer—but it's got to be a bona fide offer—then you're the buyer of last resort, and they don't really have any choice but to take it."

Did he think Scripps would accept Ruhe's offer?

"It would depend on what kind of losses they would sustain if they had to shut it down or take it into bankruptcy."

"Wow, this is going to be a tricky one," Ruhe said.

"You'd have to make a real offer, a bona fide offer," Thompson said. "And you'd have to make it in writing."

"I'd be nuts to offer anything," Ruhe said. "They should pay me to take the company."

"Yeah, they should," Thompson said with a chuckle. "That's a good idea. That's happened before."

Ruhe was elated. His long-shot dream was looking better. Before he left the office for the weekend, he banged out a mailgram—cheaper than a telegram—to Charles Scripps. It contained a formal offer to buy UPI and included Haughney's suggestion that Scripps loan Ruhe and Geissler $5 million in return for a percentage of future profits.

Doug Ruhe may have been a novice, but his advisers had been right on target. The following Monday morning, Ruhe answered his office phone. It was Larry Leser.

"Charles Scripps received your telegram and we're taking your offer very seriously," Leser said. Now desperate to be rid of its millstone, Scripps had been reduced to negotiating with the likes of Doug Ruhe and Bill Geissler over the fate of one of the world's biggest news agencies.

"We'd like you to come to Cincinnati," Leser said.

Ruhe, fighting to keep calm, agreed and hung up the phone. Then he burst out laughing. These guys must really be in a panic! This might be easy! Leaping from his chair, he rushed to break the news to Geissler.

• • •

In late February, Ruhe arrived at the Central Trust Tower in Cincinnati, hard by the Ohio River, for his first meeting with Ed Estlow and Larry Leser. Ruhe felt as if he had entered a time warp. Scripps's headquarters reminded him of some musty financial institution, with severe furniture and trappings and the unmistakable aroma of old money. Sounding authoritative when he talked about new communications technology, he asked whether Estlow and Leser had considered switching UPI to cheaper satellite transmission. He was confident and direct. Ruhe knew his hosts were anxious to be rid of UPI.

Ruhe also asked probing questions about UPI's finances and said he needed much more information than had been contained in the First Boston prospectus. He was promised a look at the books.

Certain that he was being taken seriously, Doug Ruhe started to feel warm inside. "Maybe Bob Thompson was right," he thought. "Maybe I *am* the buyer of last resort!"

Indicating they would be very selective, Estlow and Leser pressed Ruhe to state his general plan for operating UPI. They stressed that E.W. Scripps had directed his heirs and the family trust to ensure UPI's survival.

During the warm and cordial lunch at the nearby Queen City Club, Charles Scripps stopped to shake hands, then joined his own guests at another table. Ruhe headed back to Nashville convinced he had scored important points.

To impress Leser and Estlow further, Ruhe and Geissler plunged into researching UPI. At a second meeting in Cincinnati, the partners peppered the Scripps executives with trenchant questions. Their performance only heightened their enthusiasm. On the way home they agreed jubilantly that they just might pull it off if they played their cards carefully.

In mid-March, shortly after the second meeting, Ruhe phoned his lawyer, Cordell Overgaard, in Chicago for advice.

"There were some areas where we thought we knew more about UPI than they did!" Ruhe boasted.

Although Overgaard, a former chairman of "Family Weekly" magazine, considered Ruhe and Geissler highly intelligent, he had dismissed their pursuit of UPI as unrealistic. Now he realized things were getting serious and decided to help them map strategy. Overgaard was familiar with UPI. Another client, the Small publishing family of Kankakee, Illinois, had been interested in buying a limited partnership share in 1979.

In late March Fred Greene was visiting UPI's London office when he got a message to phone Leser.

"Fred, I want you to get back," Leser said. "You've got to meet with two groups of people. They're interested in buying the company."

Concerned, Greene hopped a plane to New York. As UPI's chief financial officer, he understood better than anyone how bad things really were and that no big-name prospects were banging at UPI's door. Lost in thought during the flight, he couldn't shake nagging questions about what might be in store. He worried that a hurried, careless choice could doom the wire service.

At Scripps Howard's New York offices on the forty-third floor of the Pan Am Building, Greene met with Ruhe, Geissler, and Overgaard in the morning. In the afternoon he met with Tom Quinn, head of the successful Los Angeles City News Service, a former campaign manager for California Governor Jerry Brown; and with another former Brown aide, Doug Faigin, owner of a Colorado radio station.

Quinn and Faigin were baffled by the chaos masquerading as UPI's financial records. Yet, even though they felt it might take as much as $30 million to turn UPI around, they still were interested.

Estlow and Leser also had talked for months with at least one other prospect, Thomas Wise, formerly of *The Wall Street Journal*, who had a successful business venture tracking newspaper advertising lineage. Wise and Herbert Muschel, founder of the PR Newswire that distributed corporate press releases, had submitted a conditional, preliminary offer of $15 million for UPI.

• • •

When Ruhe and Overgaard flew to Cincinnati April 2 for another meeting, they were elated that Scripps seemed unfazed at the prospect of giving away a company with more than $100 million in revenues. Now they felt that to win the inside track, they had to assemble a credible team.

Overgaard urged Ruhe and Geissler to try to attract partners with stature in the news business. He said that even if they convinced Scripps to sell them UPI, their chances for success hinged on establishing credibility with major newspaper subscribers. Overgaard himself began to lean toward joining the partnership, and he told Estlow and Leser he knew some media people who might also be interested.

Overgaard phoned his client, Rob Small, in Kankakee. The Small family published seven dailies and had reaped $9.5 million from the sale of their 25 percent interest in the Sunday magazine insert "Family Weekly." The Smalls were known nationally, mainly because Rob's late father, Len Small, had been popular in the industry and was president-elect of the American Newspaper Publishers Association when he died in a car accident. For years the family had loyally supported UPI.

"Do you want to own a wire service?" Overgaard asked Rob Small.

The younger Small always had cherished his six-month stint two decades earlier as an intern in UPI's London and Paris bureaus, where he worked with some of the wire service's most storied correspondents. Small well knew that UPI was a shoestring operation. But when Overgaard told him no money or financial risk would be involved, he became intrigued. Small, his younger sister, Jennifer, and their sixty-eight-year-old mother, Jean Alice, agreed to meet with Ruhe, Geissler, and Overgaard.

Learning of the Smalls' interest in UPI, Ruhe and Geissler felt that if they could only attract them into the partnership, their own stock with Scripps would rise dramatically. Overgaard had been right, they agreed. Unknowns like themselves needed people like the Smalls to front for them.

At their first meeting with the Small family, Ruhe and Geissler offered to make Jean Alice chairman. She was flattered but noncommittal.

Rob Small, however, sized up Ruhe and Geissler as street-smart, imaginative, hardworking and energetic, and began leaning toward accepting their offer to join the partnership.

Overgaard also phoned some other media clients, including Florida businessman Robert "Woody" Sudbrink, a station owner who turned over radio properties like other people changed socks. Sudbrink licked his chops. Should UPI hit it big, he thought, he might make a tidy, no-risk profit.

• • •

Of E.W. Scripps's six grandchildren, none felt more genuine affection for UPI than the youngest. Ted Scripps had worked for UP in Reno in 1952, straight out of the University of Nevada, and had spent two years in UPI's Washington bureau in the mid-1960s. Sometimes he would drop unannounced into the Washington office to help on election nights.

His allegiance was fostered by the staff's loyalty and esprit de corps, his belief in competing wire services, and his feeling that UPI could be salvaged by upgrading its product and sales effort.

He had spearheaded efforts to save money by getting AP to merge news and picture transmission systems with UPI. He also proposed that Scripps try a last-ditch, five-year, $30 million salvage operation. But members of the Scripps board still smarted from the industry's refusal to support its proposal for an industry-wide partnership and resented the idea of having to heavily invest anew to prop up UPI.

In April 1982, Ted Scripps saw that if he failed to do something fast, it would be too late. His only hope of staving off a sale was to offer to assume the responsibility of running UPI himself. He approached his brother Charles and Estlow and beseeched them to make him the wire service's chief executive officer.

Charles Scripps and Estlow were touched by his dramatic plea, but it was too late. They said they were committed to a sale and that the family trust could not afford an eleventh-hour effort to resuscitate the wire service.

The Scripps family, they told Ted sadly, had done everything it possibly could for UPI. Now it was time to let go. There would be no looking back.

Eleanor Howard, wife of Roy Howard's son Jack, told her husband she would be willing to invest from her own fortune to keep UPI in the family. She would later recall that he advised her it would be against the family's wishes.

• • •

On April 30, Ruhe sent an artfully constructed three-page letter to Estlow formally offering to "buy" UPI. The letter, drafted with the help of Overgaard and Porter Bibb, invoked the name and memory of E.W. Scripps and was an unabashedly sentimental pitch pledging to "perpetuate a great journalistic institution."

It was also a slick business proposition, requesting a $5 million, interest-free, five-year loan and other concessions. Ruhe said his group was contemplating naming Jean Alice Small chairman and widely respected industry consultant Mort Frank as president. Conveniently omitted was any mention that neither had agreed to serve.

"If the foregoing is acceptable to you," Ruhe wrote, "we would diligently proceed to work with you to prepare the definitive purchase agreement with the expectation that it would be signed in not more than two weeks."

While Ruhe had taken Overgaard's advice in approaching the Smalls, he could not possibly have guessed how important it was to Scripps that UPI be sold to an American publisher. Rob and Jean Alice Small loaned the brash young entrepreneurs a patina of respectability they never otherwise could have enjoyed. Estlow, later asked to explain his interest in Ruhe and Geissler, said it was his recollection that Rob Small first approached Scripps on behalf of the consortium.

During a May meeting in Nashville, Overgaard continued to follow his instincts. Pressing the Small connection, he phoned Frank, a close friend and former partner of the Smalls who for seventeen years had published "Family Weekly." Might he be interested in serving as UPI's president?

Frank declined, partly because of the travel that would be required to mend fences with clients, largely because he was skeptical that Ruhe and Geissler could make a success of UPI.

• • •

UPI president Rod Beaton had lunch with Ruhe and Geissler at the Pinnacle Club on Forty-second Street near UPI's offices in May, still not aware how seriously the Scripps executives were treating their offer. Although he found Ruhe garrulous, bright, and full of intelligent questions, Beaton simply could not fathom that Scripps might sell UPI to somebody with no newspaper background. Little did he know of the Smalls' involvement or that the men he was dining with already were searching for his successor.

For Ruhe's and Geissler's effort was rapidly gaining momentum. Soon their would-be consortium gathered at the City Club atop Nashville's thirty-story Life and Casualty Building. Ruhe and Geissler were flanked by accountants Haughney and Bill Ahlhauser, their Baha'i friend, as they unveiled to the Smalls and to Woody Sudbrink their grand plan for acquiring and reviving UPI.

But as they passed around draft documents designating Jean Alice Small as UPI's new chairman and tried to agree on a corporate strategy, the meeting degenerated into petty bickering over who would play what role. Ruhe and Geissler felt they had given their proposed partners a nice share of the deal in return for the stature they would lend. The two majority shareholders made it absolutely clear that they intended to make the decisions about how UPI would be run. Whenever the Smalls and Sudbrink made suggestions indicating they did not intend to be mere figureheads, Geissler, afflicted with a nervous stammer that sometimes made it agonizingly difficult for him to verbalize, uncharacteristically erupted in anger. Although the others were stunned by the outburst, Ruhe made no effort to calm his friend. Finally, irate over the developments, Geissler stomped out of the room.

To Overgaard and Sudbrink, the melodramatic departure was a portent of long-term trouble. Overgaard, usually a gentle, soft-spoken professional, pulled Ruhe aside and said with uncharacteristic fervor, "Look, Doug, I don't need this kind of stuff. If you don't want anybody else involved, that's fine with me."

Sudbrink also was troubled by his perceptions of how Ruhe and

Geissler planned to run so big and complex a company. As the two had described how they would set up various UPI operating accounts through Focus Communications, their Nashville television company, Sudbrink thought the arrangement sounded too much like a slush fund.

He told himself that Ruhe and Geissler were babes in the business world who inevitably would squander UPI's money. He decided to bow out, and was not surprised to learn soon after that Jean Alice Small also had withdrawn.

• • •

In late April, Leser flew to Los Angeles International Airport to meet Tom Quinn, who had produced a major financial backer for his effort to buy UPI: Peter Ueberroth, head of the Los Angeles committee hosting the 1984 Summer Olympics. Ueberroth, who had earned millions in the travel business, said he had others interested in investing. In the conference suite of United Airlines' Red Carpet Room, Quinn and Ueberroth told Leser they wanted to submit an offer. Quinn came away from the meeting convinced they had a couple of months to prepare it. But Estlow and Leser were driving hard now to close a deal, and it seemed nothing would stop them.

Soon after, at the Scripps offices in New York, they drafted a preliminary contract to sell UPI to Tom Wise and Herb Muschel. Beaton had worked closely with Wise, and, at a meeting at the Pinnacle Club, the three men talked enthusiastically about prospects for a fresh start for UPI.

Although Wise and Muschel felt they had the inside track, a hitch developed, apparently over concerns about millions of dollars in severance and pension liabilities if UPI were to shut down. Wise and Muschel bided their time, awaiting further word, unaware the Scripps executives were continuing to negotiate with Ruhe and Geissler.

As Memorial Day approached, Ruhe and Geissler's confidence grew. While Jean Alice Small, Mort Frank, and Woody Sudbrink had said no, it appeared as if Rob Small would join the bid.

Ruhe and Geissler reshaped the deal, increasing Overgaard's share from 5 to 15 percent to match Small's.[1] They allotted another 5 percent

---

[1] Overgaard divided his share. He gave one block to his law partners to cover the time he would be spending on UPI business, the other to his cable television venture in which Woody Sudbrink was a partner.

each to financial men Ahlhauser and Haughney, and split the remaining 60 percent.

But Ruhe and Geissler, although tantalized by the prospect they might get a $5 million loan from Scripps, still were skeptical about UPI's financial condition. They worried about the exodus of newspaper clients and about confusion surrounding the company's monthly losses.

"We really need more money than $5 million," Ruhe told Estlow and Leser during a meeting in Cincinnati. "We need more like $20 million, because the company's in a lot worse shape than the numbers indicated."

When Estlow and Leser challenged his statement, Geissler asserted that UPI had lost 180 newspaper clients during the last eighteen months.

Estlow minced no words. "We'll shut it down rather than pay you $20 million. We're not going to give anyone $20 million. That's what Reuters wanted, and we told them no."

Ruhe hardly was disheartened. Scripps had agreed to lend UPI $5 million for working cash and put another $2.362 million into UPI's pension funds.

One night in mid-May the phone rang at Haughney's Nashville home.

"Tom, they've drawn the line," Ruhe exulted, bursting into laughter. "They'll give us seven and a half million dollars to take it off their hands—and not a penny more!"

It had been five years since Scripps had decided to unload UPI, and many suitors had stopped by to kick the tires.

Now, instead of demanding cash for its battered jalopy, Scripps was about to *pay* Doug Ruhe and Bill Geissler to haul it off the lot.

5

. . .

Entrepreneurs to the Rescue

Doug Ruhe and Bill Geissler, excited as kids on Christmas morning, trooped into a meeting room of the Harley Hotel on East Forty-second Street. Several others trailed, struggling to match their strides.

Long rows of chairs filled the room, but some people still had to stand. For on this balmy June 4, 1982, employees at UPI's world headquarters in Manhattan were meeting their new owners, and journalists are a curious lot. Managers and staffers from the New York bureau and top executives hastily flown in from around the country converged on the posh hotel.

Barely could they contain their eagerness to meet and make journalistic snap judgments about the strangers who twenty-four hours earlier had purchased their venerable wire service. When word leaked of the secret sale, the media world was stunned. Who were these guys? Where had Scripps dug them up?

Seated on a platform were Ruhe, thirty-eight, and Geissler, thirty-six, tall, mustachioed partners in a Nashville, Tennessee, television company who were UPI's new majority owners; Bill Ahlhauser, their baby-faced financial manager. Rob Small, thirty-nine, a straight-arrow midwesterner who was introduced as the company's new chairman; and Cordell Overgaard, forty-eight, a short, dapper senior partner in a prominent Chicago law firm. Joining them was UPI president Rod Beaton, looking bewildered.

Except for Small, whose family published medium-sized newspapers and had been a loyal supporter of UPI, Unipressers knew zilch about their would-be saviors.

Ruhe and Geissler monopolized the presentation, often delivering effusive, rambling pledges that they would take whatever steps, conventional or unconventional, necessary to breathe life into the moribund company. Ruhe likened himself to a riverboat gambler, willing to accept high risks if that was what it took to bring UPI back. Promises flowed like dark beer at Octoberfest. Unipressers, desperate hopes for their company's survival clashing head-on with traditional journalistic cynicism, listened intently.

When the new owners invited questions, never-shy editor in chief H.L. Stevenson was first to speak up. His tone was challenging.

"You have compared yourself to a riverboat gambler," he told Ruhe. "We don't know anything about you. How would you describe yourself?"

"Lots of people get called lots of things," Ruhe replied, "but the word we would apply to ourselves would be entrepreneurs."

Entrepreneurs. Over and over, Ruhe and Geissler used that word to describe themselves and their business philosophy.

Unipressers shared two basic emotions. The first was a feeling that "anything has got to be better than what we've been going through." The second was a healthy skepticism. They worried that Scripps, the corporate sugar daddy, had entrusted its sickly child to rank amateurs. With the ghost of its founder looming, had Scripps turned over United Press International to people without the necessary brains, experience, connections, and cash to have a chance to succeed?

It was left to Larry DeSantis, bald, roundish, crusty New York picture editor, to verbalize the doubts.

"I'm not a businessman. I'm just a newsman, just a photographer," he growled in Brooklynese. "Tell me. What da fuck is an entrepreneur?"

Nervous laughter greeted his words, but DeSantis merely was first to question whether the new emperors really wore clothes.

Others, more delicately than their blunt-speaking colleague, also began to ask whether Ruhe and Geissler were prepared to pour in the kind of cash Unipressers had dreamed about during endless downholds.

"We plan to turn this thing around on its own revenues," Ruhe said.

Dismay greeted his words. It was clear the new owners did not bring with them a pot of gold.

Ruhe and Geissler had arrived at the meeting proud and excited, hoping the staff of one of the world's great news organizations would welcome them as conquering heroes. Instead, they were met with a marked absence of enthusiasm from skeptical journalists weary of operating on the cheap, of having to settle for less than the best, and worried about the future of their company and themselves.

Continuing to field questions, the owners began to feel as uncomfortable as their inquisitors. As Ruhe looked out over his new domain, he told himself this reclamation project certainly wasn't going to be easy.

After the meeting Unipressers strolled in small clusters back to the bureau next door, buzzing over the surreal scene. A little bewildered, a lot worried, they had one burning question: Why had Scripps entrusted UPI to novices whose idea of how to do business sounded to journalists like something from another planet? How could anybody turn UPI around on its own revenues?

Who were Doug Ruhe and Bill Geissler, and why had Scripps passed UPI's torch to them?

• • •

It was summer, 1965, in the southwest Texas border town of Laredo—dusty, sweltering, the air so thick that the squat downtown buildings shimmered as if in a blurred snapshot.

The early morning sun blazed relentlessly as thousands of Mexican day workers trudged across the International Bridge from their shacks in Nueva Laredo, little green daily work permits tucked in their pockets and purses.

There was an official U.S. welcome center, but Laredo's workers hardly felt a rush of neighborliness. The bridge walkers, willing to work for twenty-five, thirty-five, forty cents an hour because it was double what they could earn in Mexico, drove down wages for the Americans whose city they invaded each morning.

Doug Ruhe, only twenty-one but already a veteran of civil rights protests in his native South and his adopted state of Kansas, watched the Mexicans stream daily across the Rio Grande. Joining the war on poverty in Laredo with other VISTA volunteers, Ruhe vowed to help overcome the abject poverty he saw on both sides of the river.

Ruhe had joined Richard Geissler, Bill's older brother, and several dozen other VISTA volunteers in Laredo, living in a roofless, concrete block house in a dusty section inhabited by low-paid working-class families. In addition to their regular VISTA assignments, Ruhe and Richard Geissler helped organize residents of poor sections into the neighborhood councils that were the backbone of the "domestic peace corps" of Presidents John Kennedy and Lyndon Johnson.

One day Bill Geissler, an impressionable nineteen-year-old about to enter his sophomore year at Syracuse, arrived for a visit. Feeling his first stirrings of social conscience, Bill saw in Doug Ruhe a kindred spirit. Both were confrontational, headstrong young men, passionate fighters against society's iniquities.

Ruhe and the Geisslers were puzzled that the war on poverty in the border town seemed barely a skirmish, but they soon discovered a possible reason. Mayor Joseph Claude "Pepe" Martin chaired the local Office of Economic Opportunity and there were allegations he was diverting into Laredo's political machinery federal money aimed at helping the poor.

"That's not the way it's supposed to be," they told neighborhood residents. "It's backwards. The mayor has his money, you should have yours. You should elect your own council officers. That's what it says in the OEO charter."

Having studied OEO regulations that declared decisions should be made with "maximum feasible participation of the poor," they quietly laid the groundwork for a tiny revolution in Laredo's barrio, coaching the residents for a confrontation with Martin.

When the mayor personally presided over a meeting of the local neighborhood council, he found himself facing a packed audience. Abruptly, one tough hombre with a face scarred from a losing battle with a socket wrench rose and said, evenly, "Mr. Mayor, I would like to move that we elect a new slate of officers."

"What is your name?" Martin asked, coldly.

"Juan Guevara."

"Somebody take that man's name down!" Martin shouted. "Take his name down!" But others quickly rose, joining the challenge to Martin's leadership. Ruhe and his friends exulted in the electricity sweeping the room.

"Take down their names! Take down their names!" screamed Martin's henchmen until several frightened people ducked under their chairs. But Ruhe and the Geisslers had proselytized well. Many more rose to complain—far too many names to take down. The Chicanos, goaded by the VISTA activists, had wrested control of their council from the most powerful man in Laredo.

To Doug Ruhe and Bill Geissler, a couple of middle-class kids, this was heady stuff. In the name of the poor and the downtrodden, they had won a small victory over the establishment. This was certainly better than sitting in a classroom listening to a professor spout theoretical abstractions.

• • •

Even in these formative years, Ruhe and Geissler were complicated young men, a strange blend of idealism, arrogance, anger, bluster. Unconventional and unorthodox, they were cut from different cloth than most of corporate America, not to mention the nation's media barons.

Willingly challenging authority, they did what they thought was right, regardless of the consequences—a kind of "we know best" philosophy they later would carry into UPI.

After their success in the barrio, Ruhe, the Geisslers, and Neil Birnbaum, a roughneck, hotheaded Chicagoan, next tried to unionize badly paid cafeteria workers and farmhands, despite warnings from fellow volunteers that such activities could anger Washington and endanger the budding programs for the poor. Soon workers were picketing the Deliganis Cafeteria. Ruhe and the Geisslers further aroused the community by organizing night rallies that bulged the seams of the town square. His business badly hurt, cafeteria owner Milton Deliganis finally capitulated, agreeing to quadruple wages to $1.25 a hour and provide uniforms for the workers.

Deliganis took a grudging liking to Bill Geissler, insisting on buying him a new shirt and paying to have his shoulder-length hair trimmed. That constituted big TV news in Laredo.

Soon after, as fellow volunteers had predicted, Ruhe and his gang were bounced from VISTA. But Doug Ruhe and Bill Geissler had begun to believe themselves conquering knights, riding in on white chargers to save the day.

• • •

From his childhood in Atlanta, Doug Ruhe was profoundly influenced by the Baha'i faith and its championing of the underdog. His father, Dr. David Ruhe, embraced the religion of his strong-willed wife, Margarite, rising to become a member of the elite nine-person Universal House of Justice, the Baha'is' world governing council.

In 1954, when Ruhe was ten, the family moved to Leawood, a Kansas City suburb. Introduced to blacks at Baha'i meetings in his home, Ruhe soon began questioning the restrictive covenants that prevented Jews and blacks from buying homes in his subdivision. Once he angered friends from his all-white high school, Shawnee Mission East, when he chastised them for throwing garbage and shouting "Nigger!" at black maids waiting for a bus.

Ruhe was torn—his parents were color blind, but many of his class-mates' families were openly racist. He found an answer at fourteen, when he and his family went to hear Dr. Martin Luther King, Jr., at a Kansas City synagogue.

Doug Ruhe sat transfixed by King's eloquent plea for racial justice and equality. Afterward, he and his older brother, Chris, stood in line to meet the civil rights leader. As they shook hands Doug was mes-merized by King's shirt cuffs, which had been stitched and patched many times.

In 1960, Martin Luther King's greatness still was undiscovered. But Doug Ruhe could see it, and was troubled by the fact that, in affluent America, a prophet preaching justice, dignity, and equality couldn't afford a new shirt.

• • •

Ruhe's passion for racial equality never flagged. He taught black kids in church summer schools, joined civil rights marches with King, hired blacks in his businesses, and married a black, Beverly George.

At sixteen Ruhe became the only white to join weeks-long picket-ing that forced a number of Kansas City merchants to hire blacks. Ruhe's joy was tempered by the middle-aged white women who spit in his face and shouted, "How much are these niggers paying you, Commie?"

The next summer Ruhe graduated to the big leagues, hitching to Alabama to join tens of thousands marching to King's drumbeat demands for racial justice; from Dothan, where he ducked under a cop's billy club, to Birmingham, where the confrontation of King versus Police Chief Bull Connor splashed Dixie's aging iron-and-steel capital across every front page in America.

In the summer of 1964, Ruhe was the only white instructor in a program preparing black children in Greenville, South Carolina, for the public school integration that fall under Lyndon Johnson's Civil Rights Act. Then he marched with King to Selma, Alabama, bloody landmark in the struggle for racial equality in America, sleeping along the way on the floors of shacks and shanties. Ruhe also joined demonstrations in Washington and Chicago and marched in Memphis with striking garbage workers. Before quitting his teens he had become a hardened veteran in the war against segregation.

Along the way Ruhe managed to get arrested twice. In 1963, during a brief return to Kansas City, he and a group of civil rights activists were hauled off in a paddy wagon after trying to integrate a local amusement park, Fairyland. Police Chief Clarence Kelley, who later would become FBI director, arrived at the station sleepy-eyed and with hair mussed, an overcoat thrown over his pajamas, and tried to persuade the group to leave quietly. Ruhe and his colleagues refused, spending the night in jail and drawing widespread publicity.

At the University of Kansas, Ruhe and football hero Gale Sayers, later a Hall of Famer with the Chicago Bears, were among those arrested for seizing the chancellor's office in a struggle to integrate the university's sororities and fraternities.

Ruhe's academic performance was undistinguished. He spent two years at Earlham College before transferring to Kansas. A man who liked to be center stage, Ruhe found formal classwork boring. Four times he flunked a required algebra course. Yet his combativeness and fast tongue won him a place on the debating team.

Always an iconoclast, Ruhe made no attempt to hide his opposition to the Vietnam War. When he was drafted in 1968 he claimed conscientious objector status as a Baha'i. Rather than fight, he served a year as a medic in a field hospital in Vietnam's Central Highlands. When he learned a little Vietnamese, some branded him "Gook-lover" and questioned his patriotism. Ruhe's beliefs were unshakable.

Shortly after his discharge in 1970, he resumed his efforts to help the down-and-out in Springfield, Massachusetts, where he soon met up again with a man who deeply shared his ideals—Bill Geissler.

• • •

Geissler's affable but often defiant personality perhaps could be traced to his turbulent childhood. His early years in Caracas, Venezuela, were unsettled because both his mother and then his stepmother abandoned his father, a plumbing contractor. Bill and his older brother, Richard, were cared for by Elsa Wick, a German immigrant who lived with her husband in the Geissler home. When Papa Geissler died in 1957, Elsa whisked eleven-year-old Bill and his brother off to the United States to prevent their father's business partners from gaining custody and controlling the small estate. Bill and Richard went to live in the blue-collar town of Eastchester, New York, with their childless aunt and uncle, who found it hard to cope with their roustabout nephews.

Bill Geissler hung around the streets, getting into small-scale trouble with a band of rowdies who dubbed themselves the "Tree Stump Gang"—their rendezvous was a stump on a strategic downtown corner that permitted quick getaways when the cops interrupted their pranks.

Geissler was a "greaser," hair slicked back in a duck's-ass, comb jutting from the back pocket of his pegged pants. He also was a voracious reader, frequently consuming a book a night. After his sophomore year at Eastchester High, disturbed that his friends had started shoplifting, breaking into homes, and stealing hubcaps, he abandoned the gang life and informed his uncle he wanted to go to military school. Geissler was enrolled at Massanutten Military Academy in Virginia's Shenandoah Valley, light-years from the Tree Stump Gang. There he blossomed, making the honor roll. He found it exciting to learn he could learn.

But Geissler couldn't completely shake his roots. He was far from a model soldier. When he decided he wanted to go on to West Point, his guidance counselor declined to recommend him. So Geissler enrolled instead at Syracuse in 1963. There he discovered that blacks were not the despised "niggers" berated by the folks in Eastchester. In his second semester he moved from his all-white dorm to share an apartment with his first black friend, Brian Bassingthwaite, a gentle, homesick Southwest African, and soon found himself joining local CORE demonstrations against discriminatory hiring practices. When he visited his brother in Laredo in 1965, just before he was to begin his sophomore year, he landed smack in the middle of a hotbed of radical activism. Meeting Doug Ruhe and getting caught up in the emotional campaign, Geissler quickly forgot college.

Ruhe, handsome and self-assured, profoundly influenced young Geissler. A teetotaling Baha'i, Ruhe sipped pop and talked politics and religion in the cantinas across the border as Neil Birnbaum and Geissler engaged in prodigious beer- and tequila-drinking contests.

Geissler, not religious himself, absorbed a lot of Ruhe's philosophy along with the booze. If you have to have a religion, Geissler thought, this Baha'i stuff seems harmless. Later, visiting Ruhe's parents in Wilmette, Illinois, near the Baha'i temple, Geissler got into a heated religious discussion with Ruhe's father, who gave him the Koran, the Baha'i bible, along with tracts explaining the faith. Reading and rereading the Koran, Geissler a couple of years later embraced the faith.

• • •

While in Laredo, Geissler had met Rogers Worthington, a reporter for the Kansas City *Star*. Many nights in the cantinas they talked of hunting for the exiled Cuban Communist leader, Che Guevara. In August 1967 the dream became more than just bar talk. Worthington's editors agreed that if the two undertook the quixotic search, the paper would purchase and print stories about their adventures.

Before departing, Geissler and Worthington made crucial decisions. Geissler ignored a draft notice. Worthington skipped his honeymoon with his new bride, Jolene Bluejacket, granddaughter of a legendary Sioux general who had battled the U.S. Cavalry.

Dawdling at their first stop in Mexico City, they picked up the October 9 morning newspaper to discover the Bolivian Army had captured and executed Guevara. Nevertheless the young men, fluent in Spanish, continued on to Panama, Colombia, and Venezuela, interviewing rebel leaders in their mountain hideouts and filing stories back to Kansas City. Geissler helped his experienced colleague with the writing, and they pooled their skimpy funds for cheap bus rides from country to country.

Finally they descended on Elsa and Richard Wick in Caracas. A few days later a blunt cable arrived from Jolene Bluejacket Worthington: be back to Kansas City by Christmas or be gone.

Worthington returned to his bride, but Geissler wangled a job on the English-language Caracas *Daily Journal* covering Venezuela's presidential election and the burgeoning radical and Communist movements. Still, his decision to ignore the draft hung over his head. It had not been a move made lightly. A Chinese history course at Syracuse had stiffened his opposition to U.S. involvement in Southeast Asia.

"Why would I go and interfere with the process of human liberation?" he asked himself. "Just because it's policy? To hell with that."

When Geissler learned after eighteen months in Caracas that his return was being sought, he decided it was time to face the music. "I'm not going to run away and hide," he told the Wicks, and three days later he was back in New York.

Indicted on charges of draft dodging on May 29, 1969, he surrendered and pleaded guilty at federal court in Manhattan. Judge Edmund Palmieri directed him to write an essay on why he had ignored his draft notice.

Geissler arrived in court August 13 for sentencing during a recess in a Black Panther trial whose disruptive defendants had been bound, gagged, and dragged from the courtroom. He watched the fuming judge with dread. Could there possibly be a worse time to be sentenced?

When Geissler's case was called, Palmieri announced, "I'm going to sentence you like a common criminal."

Holy mackeral, Geissler thought, this guy's going to throw the book at me! He decided he had nothing to lose.

"Well, your honor, can I ask a question? What's more important to you, order or justice?"

Palmieri's stern visage softened. "Actually, they're indivisible," he said. "There can be no justice without order."

For a moment the Black Panther disruptions were forgotten as the judge peered down at this thoughtful young man, remembering that Geissler's compelling essay had used religious, political, and philosophical arguments to explain why he could not serve in Vietnam.

"I read your document, young man, and I have given this a lot of thought," Palmieri said. "I wish I could let you go. But other men have been called, and they're serving and dying in Vietnam. I cannot let you go. I'm going to sentence you to one year." Palmieri ordered Geissler to report to the federal prison in Danbury, Connecticut in two days.

Geissler was lucky. Three others who had refused to plead guilty got five years.

Leaving the courthouse, Geissler spotted famed baby doctor Benjamin Spock in a rumpled suit waiting for a streetlight. Spock's conviction for conspiring to counsel young men like Geissler to avoid the draft and face jail instead had been overturned by an appeals court a month earlier.

"Dr. Spock!" cried Geissler. "How's it going?"

"Fine."

Geissler, realizing that he was about to go to jail while Spock would be free, could not contain himself. On the busy downtown Manhattan street corner, he bitterly assailed Spock for not accepting the kind of prison sentence being given the young men he had been counseling.

"That stinks," Geissler said. "I'm on my way to jail. You ought to come with me to jail, man."

Bewildered, Spock began to cross the street. As he disappeared into the crowd, Geissler shouted after him, "You ought to be going to jail with me, man!"

Geissler was still in the Danbury jail when Ruhe returned from Vietnam and settled in Springfield. Nearly every weekend Ruhe commuted three hours to the prison, bringing books to his lonely, frustrated friend. But the visits and Geissler's job in the prison library could neither sate the young prisoner's literary appetite nor shake his deepening depression. Geissler emerged from prison in July of 1970 sober and introspective, unable to come to grips with having left a chunk of his life and a piece of his soul behind bars. Scars lingered long after his release, even though he and other Vietnam War resisters were pardoned by President Gerald Ford in May 1976.

Geissler rejoined Ruhe in nearby Springfield, where, without undergraduate diplomas, they won admission to the University of Massachusetts graduate School of Education. Perhaps not coincidentally, the school was headed by brilliant, controversial Dwight Allen, a national Baha'i leader, who during his seven-year stewardship recruited more Baha'i faculty members and admitted more students of that faith than any university department in the land.

Allen contended lack of an undergraduate diploma need not be an impediment to earning an advanced degree, and he replaced letter grades with pass/fail. Class attendance was spotty, and one semester eighty-five students got credit for two "education methods" courses not even offered.

Detractors said Allen ran a diploma mill. Indeed, although his college was but one of sixty graduate departments on campus, during his last three years it awarded 45 percent of the university's doctoral degrees. Rejecting the usual safeguards against academic inbreeding, Allen appointed twenty-six of his own doctorate recipients to the faculty. He resigned when the FBI found that some of the $15 million in federal grant money he had raised had been improperly diverted.

Ruhe and Geissler left the University of Massachusetts with master's degrees, even though most of their energy had been spent not in the classroom but with their own novel education experiment. Shortly before

Geissler left prison, Ruhe and Bill Smith, an old civil rights friend, had launched a storefront school called SASSI (Street Academy System of Springfield, Inc.) to help dropouts, delinquents, druggies, and pregnant teens written off as incorrigible. Raising $150,000 through solicitations from local business and educational grants, they soon had a minority-dominated enrollment of 200 and a faculty of a dozen earning subsistence wages. Ruhe taught English, social studies, and writing; Geissler, writing and journalism. They seemed successful. Some of their best students went on to prep school, then college.

Using SASSI students, Ruhe and Geissler also began a weekly paper, *SALT—Springfield Area Life and Times*. Before Vietnam, Ruhe had worked briefly as a reporter in Allentown, Pennsylvania. Geissler now was free-lancing for the Springfield dailies and sold several stories about SASSI. Without mentioning his own connection, Geissler liberally quoted Smith and Ruhe, and even inserted himself in the articles, a journalistic no-no.

Once he wrote, "It was during a hectic morning of fund-raising for SASSI Prep that this reporter spoke with Smith and his co-director, Douglas Ruhe, both graduate students at the UMass School of Education."

Despite Ruhe and Geissler's growing belief that they could overcome meager experience and humble resources to beat the odds, their little newspaper folded in 1973 for lack of advertising. If that was a portent, the two cocksure young mavericks paid little heed. A decade later, before reaching forty, they would scratch and claw their way to become owners of UPI, whose staffers and the rest of the journalism world would be astounded that Scripps could find no better candidates to take over the troubled wire service.

• • •

Rod Beaton's heart had pounded when, in late May 1982, he met with Ruhe, Geissler, Cordy Overgaard, and Bill Ahlhauser at the Pan Am Building and it suddenly dawned on him that they had the inside track. If UPI fell into the clutches of total unknowns, he feared, the news industry would erupt in protest.

"Lookit," he told Ruhe and Geissler, "you may think you're going to take over a news service and everything will go smoothly. But nobody knows anything about you, and you're going to become news. A lot of editors and publishers are going to want to know who they're doing business with.''

"We'll handle them," Ruhe said glibly. "No problem."

Beaton didn't know it, but Scripps had set a meeting for June 2 to close the deal.

Ruhe and Geissler summoned Rob Small to New York on Memorial Day weekend to work out last details and finally tell him of Woody Sudbrink's withdrawal. Small, the conservative Midwesterner, was alarmed. But he again remembered with affection his days at UPI, knew his financial risk would be modest, and realized Ruhe and Geissler needed him if they were to succeed. He agreed to come along, unaware that the next six months would be among the most trying of his life.

Secrets never stayed that way long at UPI. On the Tuesday night after Memorial Day, veteran Tennessee manager Duren Cheek got a tip from newspictures vice president Bill Lyon that Nashville entrepreneurs Ruhe and Geissler probably would be the new owners.

"There's no way," Cheek told Lyon, incredulously. He had never even heard of Ruhe and Geissler. "I've been around Nashville forever. I know every sonovabitch in town who's anybody.''

Cheek made some fast checks. Eddie Jones, executive director of the Nashville Chamber of Commerce, hadn't heard of Ruhe and Geissler, either. Neither had *Tennessean* publisher John Seigenthaler, who interrupted a dinner party at his home to make a few phone calls and reported back two hours later that he, too, had run into a brick wall.

• • •

Wednesday morning, Ruhe and Overgaard flew separately to Cincinnati to sign the momentous deal at Scripps's Central Trust Tower. There was little pomp and less ceremony. Except for the presence of Charles Scripps and a UPI photographer clicking away, the two sides could have been cementing a real estate deal instead of transferring title to the news agency Scripps had nurtured for three quarters of a century.

Estlow, Leser, and stocky Scripps lawyer Sherman Dye, his cigar as long as a salami, officiously shuttled between rooms for three hours, collecting signatures on transfer papers.

Shortly before closing, Scripps executives expressed disappointment on learning that Woody Sudbrink and Jean Alice Small had decided not to join the partnership. But they rationalized that as long as Rob Small was going to be UPI's new chairman, everything would be okay.

At the last minute, to the shock and delight of the new owners, Scripps officials decided to sweeten the pot to give UPI a fighting chance to succeed. The promised $5 million loan became an outright gift. Scripps would pay off most of UPI's short-term debts, and for five years UPI would keep as clients the Scripps broadcast properties and dozen-plus newspapers. Scripps also continued its agreement to pay UPI to market the lucrative "Peanuts" cartoon strips and other features overseas.

Perhaps Scripps made these gestures because it was worried that if UPI failed, shutdown costs might revert to the seller. Or perhaps it was a last try to honor the family legacy before UPI was cut loose.

The board vote approving the sale was all but perfunctory. Only Ted Scripps manifested the emotion of the parting. Trying to forestall the inevitable, he made one last attempt to lobby his brother Charles. It was far too late. Yet, even though his little crusade was doomed, Ted simply could not find it in his heart to join the otherwise unanimous vote. Instead, he abstained.

All the Scripps people, even those who supported the sale, felt saddened. Some believed Scripps Howard was abandoning its most vital public obligation, the one thing that made it an important international media company. Loss of its wire service would substantially diminish its stature worldwide.

Estlow and Leser, concerned lest word leak that Scripps had paid cash in its zeal to be rid of UPI, extracted from the new owners a pledge of secrecy.

Bernard Townsend, recently retired Scripps director, had not been consulted about recent sale negotiations and was absent from the closing ceremony, convinced he had been frozen out because Scripps officials knew he would vigorously oppose unloading UPI to Ruhe and Geissler. Although he kept his silence, Townsend considered Scripps's abandonment of UPI his greatest professional failure. So sensitive, embarrassed, and defensive were the Scripps brass that, seven years after the sale, company officer Jack Howard still had never spoken of it to his best friend, Townsend, whom he saw almost every day.

Before their partners had signed the last documents in Cincinnati, Geissler and Small showed up at UPI's New York office and Beaton and other top executives of the wire service were informed privately about the ownership change.

Sitting in his thirteenth-floor office with Geissler and Small, Beaton fought to conceal his dismay. But he felt sick to his stomach. Scripps had given away his wire service to two men he considered dangerously unqualified. Distressed, concerned about his heart condition, and worried that he almost certainly would be shunted aside, Beaton had had enough. Then and there he told himself it was time to retire.

As the UPI executives tried to make small talk, Geissler picked up a phone to hear Ruhe say, jubilantly, "It's done! We've got it!"

Douglas Ruhe and William Geissler, operators of a small Nashville company barely capable of covering its payroll, had pulled a business coup beyond comprehension. Stepping from anonymity to center stage, they had become the new owners of UPI.

And it hadn't cost them a dime.

• • •

Scripps and the new owners had agreed to keep the sale secret for two days, until important clients such as Thilo Pohlert, president of the powerful German news agency Deutsche Press Agentur, could be notified privately.

But abruptly, stunningly, the veil of secrecy cracked.

Terry Bochatey, a Cincinnati-based UPI photographer, had been summoned to record the modest signing ceremony. No one bothered to tell Bochatey not to send the photos on UPI's picture wire. He dutifully took the elevator to the UPI bureau, processed the film, typed a caption, and transmitted the news of the sale to hundreds of UPI newspaper subscribers.

The switchboard in New York soon began lighting up, but UPI had no news story, not even a press release, prepared. The new owners had not provided personal bios, and the news world was clamoring for information on these strangers who suddenly owned United Press International.

William Adler, UPI's director of information, was aghast at the lack of preparation and sensed a public relations catastrophe brewing. Adler, editor H.L. Stevenson, and UPI's marketing officials scrambled to assemble enough information to satisfy subscribers and reporters rushing to cover the breaking story. Geissler used an old typewriter to knock out bare-bones bios of himself and Ruhe.

Camera crews and reporters soon swarmed all over UPI's offices in the Daily News Building. Geissler and Small, both shy men, declined to hold a news conference, so UPI officials simply confirmed the sale; its terms were secret, unknown even to them. The only public comments from the owners came in a brief statement from Ruhe and in a short interview Small granted the UPI Audio Network.

Ruhe and Overgaard hopped a plane to New York and gathered at dinner to rejoice with their partners. Sobered by the botched announcement and the enormity of their task, their celebration was strangely subdued.

They had accomplished the difficult. The impossible was dead ahead.

• • •

Meanwhile, word of the sale reached the others who had expressed interest in UPI. New York businessmen Thomas Wise and Herb Muschel, who had continued negotiations with Scripps, were stunned.

"Who's Focus?" Wise blurted upon learning he had lost out to Ruhe, Geissler, and their fledgling TV enterprise. He would not discover until much later that Scripps had given away UPI, passing over his preliminary bid of $15 million in favor of the prestige of Rob Small.

And when word reached Honolulu, where he was vacationing, Tom Quinn's jaw dropped. He couldn't believe Scripps would renege on Leser's assurance that there was plenty of time for him and Peter Ueberroth to submit a bid. Quinn immediately called Leser, angry the announcement had been made without even the courtesy of a warning phone call. Leser apologized, explaining the deal had jelled too quickly to notify other interested parties. Estlow and Leser never gave a public explanation. They declined to describe details of their discussions with the losing bidders.

The rapidly unfolding developments made Beaton's head swim. Exhausted and distraught, he rode home alone to Cos Cob, Connecticut, in a rented limo, bitterly drowning his sorrows with a few stiff belts. During the forty-five-minute drive to elegant, moneyed Fairfield County, Beaton fought his emotions and tried to rationally analyze the situation.

"Oh, shit," he muttered. "It's finally happened. It's done. We've got to get the debris cleaned up and turn a clean company over to these guys—and get on with our lives."

• • •

UPI employees were hungry for information, and their first meeting with the new owners at the Hotel Harley two days later at least had served to calm some fears. Ruhe and Geissler had provided assurances that they planned to continue UPI as a full-service news agency and had said that no jobs were in danger.

Despite their own growing anxieties, Ruhe and Geissler glowed after the Harley parley as they strolled through the New York bureau, showing off their new toy to their families.

Stopping periodically, they chatted with employees bitter that their ideas had been ignored for years. The new owners glibly left the impression that the bad old days were gone forever.

"Write me a memo on that, will you?" was heard again and again.

Veteran Patricia McCormack urged them to begin a special-features wire and charge clients extra.

"That's a good idea," Ruhe snapped expansively. "We'll do it."

But Rod Beaton was not the only veteran Unipresser with doubts about the new owners. Jimmy Darr, who had helped launch UPI into the computer era, treated as just so much hot air Ruhe's boasts of having the technical expertise to solve UPI's communications problems. Darr, who was semiretired after forty-five years with UPI, marched into Beaton's office after the Harley meeting and exercised the ninety-day notice clause on his consulting contract.

"I don't want to work with these people," Darr told his longtime colleague and friend. "I don't like them."

• • •

Major newspapers were skeptical too. They did not idly accept the unadorned announcement about the men who now owned the world's second-largest news service.

In Nashville the story was even bigger because of the "hometown boys make good" angle. Both newspapers, the *Tennessean* and the competing afternoon *Banner*, assigned reporters to scour public records and chase every possible tip about the mysterious young owners of UPI.

One particularly curious Nashville resident was John Jay Hooker. The day after the sale announcement Hooker drove downtown to the Commerce Union Bank Building, where Focus had its office.

Hooker, yet another Nashvillian who had never heard of Ruhe and Geissler, wanted to look them in the eye and find out how they had pulled off the coup that had eluded him. Looking about their small eighth-floor offices, Hooker was bewildered. How could guys who did business in such spartan surroundings ever have managed to snare UPI?

Ruhe and Geissler were not there, so Hooker scrawled a note.

"Dear Gentlemen:

"Congratulations. You did something I couldn't do. If you get a chance, give me a buzz. John Jay Hooker."

• • •

Activity at UPI headquarters in New York was fast and furious. In the hours following the Harley meeting, Beaton was on the phone reassuring worried clients. But when he learned the secret terms of the sale, he had to struggle anew to control his strange feelings of emptiness and renewed anger. Not only had Scripps paid off UPI's debts, but it had bankrolled the new owners with $5 million. Beaton told himself that had he guessed what the bargain price would be, he might have assembled his own group to "buy" UPI. And why, if Scripps was intent on giving the company away, hadn't it turned it over to those who deserved and loved it most —the employees?

After still another fourteen-hour day, Beaton wearily dragged himself home late Friday night. At 1:30 a.m. the phone roused him from a deep sleep. It was Duren Cheek, calling from Nashville. Cheek read Beaton a lengthy story from the early edition of Saturday's *Tennesseean* containing stunning revelations about Ruhe and Geissler.

Under the headline, "2 UPI Owners Had Brushes with Law," the copyrighted story quoted from their FCC television license applications.

It said Geissler had been convicted and served a year in federal prison for resisting the draft, while Ruhe had been arrested twice for participating in civil rights demonstrations in Kansas in the 1960s. It also said the two were members of the little-known Baha'i religious group.

As he sat on his bed scribbling notes in shorthand, Beaton's heart sank. These were significant details, things that Ruhe and Geissler had not volunteered. Undoubtedly, the AP would pick up *The Tennessean* story and it would be national news by the next morning, immediately putting the new regime on the defensive.

Beaton thanked Cheek, hung up, and began trying to reach *Tennessean* publisher John Seigenthaler, an old friend, to ask him to remove the story from subsequent editions until he could check the facts. But Seigenthaler was out of town, unreachable. Without his approval the story could not be yanked.

Face ashen and fingers trembling, Beaton dialed Estlow's Denver condominium.

''Good lord, Ed! What do you know about these guys?'' Beaton demanded. ''What do you know about their background?''

He read aloud *The Tennessean*'s revelations. Estlow who had publicly praised the new UPI owners as ''a group of experienced media people,'' sounded surprised, taken aback. If he already had known those things about Ruhe and Geissler, he did not let on.

Beaton pressed on. Was Estlow satisfied that the Scripps lawyers had thoroughly investigated the two new owners?

Estlow's reassurances rang hollow.

Perhaps Estlow, Larry Leser, and the Scripps family had been sold by Rob Small's involvement. If so, they had ignored the obvious—Ruhe and Geissler, not Small, were the ones who would be running UPI.

Ruhe and Geissler were gritty men long on social conscience. But the harsh reality of the business world and the challenges of running a major corporation were a far cry from organizing migrant workers in a cafeteria in dusty Laredo, or setting up a street school for down-and-out teens.

Scripps had gambled big. UPI would be the loser.

6

...

Who Are These Guys, Anyhow?

Doug Ruhe, Bill Geissler, Cordy Overgaard, and Rob Small felt a twinge of nervous anticipation as they entered the office of *New York Times* executive editor Abe Rosenthal, the most powerful man on the world's most powerful newspaper. It had only been a couple of weeks since they had taken over UPI, and the owners knew they had to make a good impression on a client whose business and approbation they sorely needed.

They trooped to the executive editor's office in the *Times*'s vast third-floor newsroom, introduced themselves to Rosenthal and his assistant, managing editor Jim Greenfield, and slid into chairs at the very conference table where top *Times* editors mulled over the next day's front-page stories.

Doug Ruhe, who never had been more than a small-town cub reporter, was about to square off against one of journalism's true giants, a man whose reputation for striking terror among those he considered beneath him was legend in the *Times* newsroom. But Ruhe liked a scrap. He hadn't gotten where he was by being a milquetoast.

Rosenthal, blunt and caustic, skipped the usual pleasantries. He wanted the specifics, all the undisclosed details, of the UPI sale. A *Times* story on June 9 had quoted Porter Bibb, a vice president of Bankers Trust

Company who had helped arrange the deal, as saying money had changed hands at the time of the sale. Indeed it had—but in the opposite direction than people assumed. The story also quoted wildly inaccurate industry analysts who said UPI had been sold for between $17.5 million and $20 million.

Rosenthal, like his fellow editors around the world, wanted to find out whether the "purchase" had been financed by Ruhe and Geissler's Baha'i friends or even with money from the Middle East, where their religion had its roots.

The owners tried to deflect his sharp questions by expansively describing their plans for rebuilding UPI. Rosenthal, not long on patience, stared them down and declared ominously, "We really don't need UPI. We can get along fine without it."

Rosenthal continued to demand details of the sale.

Ruhe, mindful of the secrecy pledge Scripps had extracted, responded firmly, "I don't know why we need to tell you that. That's confidential. We're a private business. We don't need to disclose that."

Then Small's and Overgaard's worst fears were realized. Abe Rosenthal, accustomed to getting his way, suddenly became agitated. The friendly, get-acquainted meeting was about to descend toward disaster.

"UPI is not just a company, it is a public trust, a journalistic institution!" Rosenthal said, his voice rising. "You are, in effect, holding a trust. You have an obligation to disclose the terms of the deal."

Overgaard and Small cringed, then sat in disbelief as Doug Ruhe's voice rose too.

"*The New York Times* makes acquisitions from time to time," Ruhe retorted, deciding the best defense was a strong offense. "We see these little notices in the paper—'The terms were not disclosed.' "

Rosenthal protested. "We don't know anything about you. You could be the CIA."

Ruhe was incredulous. The CIA? "Are you suggesting the deal is crooked? This is Scripps Howard, these are people you know, for crissakes! You're in the same business!"

Here Geissler jumped in, explaining that the details could not be divulged because Scripps had insisted on secrecy. Perhaps Geissler should have remained quiet. Rosenthal immediately demanded particulars about his "draft-dodging."

"I was *not* a draft dodger!" Geissler shot back. "I came back from

Venezuela and turned myself in. I opposed that war. I thought it was morally wrong.''

Why, he asked, hadn't Rosenthal used his paper's influential editorial pages to strongly condemn America's involvement in Vietnam? If Rosenthal had bristled before, now he was livid.

Overgaard and Small, with front-row seats to this battle, were horrified at the disintegration of a visit aimed at cementing relations with UPI's most prestigious customer. They tried in vain to restore civility to what had become a shouting match.

"We can talk about this some other time," Overgaard pleaded, but his peacemaking efforts were swallowed by the din.

"Tell them about UPI," Rosenthal snapped at Greenfield, who enthusiastically came to the aid of his boss.

"It's not even number two, it's number four," declared Greenfield, his hyperbole solidifying his reputation as one of UPI's most obdurate critics. "At best it's a tip service. It's inaccurate, poorly written, poorly edited.''

The new owners were stunned, but had no rejoinder. They had not thought to bring along someone authoritative enough to defend UPI's editorial product. Editor H.L. Stevenson could have done it, but he already was being shunted aside.

When Rosenthal saw he was getting nowhere with his demands for details of the sale, he threatened to assign a reporter to write about the supposedly private meeting in his office.

"Now I know what you mean by 'off the record,' " Ruhe sneered. "I've got your number.''

"You *don't* have my number!" Rosenthal shouted. "Don't talk about having my number, because you don't have my number!''

Rosenthal continued to bait Ruhe and Geissler while Small and Overgaard squirmed awkwardly, powerless to reverse the meeting's disastrous course.

"Well, you guys must really have made a bad deal if they won't let you tell us what it is," Rosenthal taunted. How could he have guessed the new owners, and not Scripps, had received cash from the transaction?

Finally, things calmed somewhat and the four took their leave. But the icy atmosphere lingered. As they walked through the newsroom they felt mystified glances from those in earshot of Rosenthal's office.

Ruhe and Geissler headed back to the UPI office while Overgaard and Small repaired to a Midtown bar. They knew the disagreement had to be patched quickly. Yet they agreed that Ruhe and Geissler had as much right as Rosenthal to protect a business confidentiality.

Over drinks Small and Overgaard shook their heads and chuckled wryly—they had to laugh or they'd cry. Capped by this fresh trouble at the *Times*, the first couple of weeks had been replete with errors, bad luck, and industry hostility that threatened to ground the venture before it could become airborne.

The trouble had started the day of the sale. Tennessean Editor and Publisher Seigenthaler, besieged by phone calls from media friends around the country, had quickly assigned reporters to investigate the local strangers. Within three days his paper had broken the story that Ruhe and Geissler had been arrested for civil disobedience during the turbulent 1960s, and that Geissler had spent ten months in federal prison. Although those scrapes hardly constituted common criminality, the story caused a huge stir. The media pressed for more information about their backgrounds.

The owners then had tried to seize the offensive. In a UPI story Ruhe said he was not ashamed at having been arrested during civil rights demonstrations in the early 1960s, and Geissler explained that the Vietnam War had been a watershed for him and other young people.

"I did what I thought was honorable," Geissler said. "I believe in obedience to law and government, and in the principles for which the country is founded. If called upon to serve today, I would do so."

Asserting their Baha'i faith was apolitical, Ruhe and Geissler also declared they had "no intention of imposing our religious beliefs on UPI and its news-gathering operation."

Then *The Tennessean* had followed with another front-page story challenging the accuracy of Geissler's claim to have been a reporter in Springfield, Massachusetts. An editor in Springfield was quoted as saying Geissler had been an infrequent free-lance contributor, not a staffer. The controversy was snowballing and, to the deep dismay of Unipressers, Ruhe and Geissler were becoming the talk of the media world.

Barely had *The Tennessean* hit the streets with its second story than Irby Simpkins, publisher of the competing *Nashville Banner*, said in a front-page editorial that he was canceling UPI because of ethical questions raised by the "deceiving information" Ruhe and Geissler had put out about their backgrounds. He, too, demanded details of the sale.

Every time one of the Tennessee papers came out with a new story, UPI's Nashville staff punched the text into the computer system, and bureaus across the country soon were worriedly buzzing about the latest revelations.

In another UPI interview the new owners again tried to lay the controversies to rest. They denied the purchase money had come from outside sources, again wryly concealing Scripps's charity.

The media pressed on. Several papers sent reporters scurrying to see if they could dig up dirt. Editors especially were concerned about the Baha'i connections because Sun Myung Moon's Unification Church had just bankrolled the new *Washington Times* in the nation's capital. To many Americans the Baha'is—like the Moonies—were little more than a cult. Overgaard, whose house in Wilmette, Illinois, was coincidentally three blocks from the enormous national Baha'i shrine, looked up one Saturday and saw a photographer hanging out the window of a hovering helicopter. He felt sure it was part of the media frenzy to uncover everything about UPI's new owners.

Flustered, Ruhe and Geissler finally had found a way to quell some of the controversy—by consenting to a lengthy face-to-face interview with the highly respected Seigenthaler himself. The resulting 5,000-word copyrighted story that carried Seigenthaler's rare byline delved deeply into Ruhe's and Geissler's backgrounds and religious beliefs. It helped dispel misconceptions about the century-old Baha'i faith, built on the precepts of the spiritual unity of mankind.

Still editors and publishers grumbled. For decades industry leaders had been confident that Scripps Howard would guard UPI's integrity; now they openly feared for its future.

As Small and Overgaard sipped their drinks in the Midtown bar and rehashed the turmoil, they sympathized with Ruhe and Geissler over what they considered unfair religious slurs. After all, the Baha'is were a humanistic sect preaching world peace and equal rights—concepts held dear by most journalists—and did not deserve to be lumped together with the Moonies.

But Small and Overgaard also agreed that their partners should not have glossed over the damaging personal information reporters inevitably would uncover. They wrestled with ways to smooth the bumps rutting UPI's uphill road.

Time was precious. UPI was losing $500,000 a month. Every move had to be perfectly planned and quickly executed to cut the losses or the $5 million from Scripps would not last a year. UPI had to quickly find a cheaper communications system and take the unpopular step of increasing rates to subscribers chary about the new owners.

Disheartened, Overgaard and Small finished their drinks. The venture, which needed to hit the ground running, was limping and disorganized.

• • •

If Small and Overgaard were upset over the contretemps with Rosenthal, it was a mere harbinger of the troubles ahead. Rather than proving themselves young geniuses of the corporate world, Ruhe and Geissler would quickly demonstrate just how shallow their business experience was.

Short of cash and facing problems that had defied solution for decades, they needed a mistake-free transition, and they needed help from their partners and outside experts. Instead, in their anxious rush to succeed on their own, Ruhe and Geissler would, curiously, ultimately ignore or reject sound advice from others.

In July, just a few weeks after the sale, Rob Small mentioned UPI's problems to a friend, New York investment banker Cy Brown. Brown suggested that Richard Farkas, a turnaround expert who had helped save one of Britain's most debt-riddled companies, might help. Small soon persuaded Ruhe to meet with Farkas.

The session at the Third Avenue offices of Farkas's International Management Consultants Group lasted most of the afternoon. Listening to Ruhe detail the acquisition of UPI and talk glowingly about its future while he stared at the trend of growing losses, Farkas concluded Ruhe did not fully grasp his peril. Farkas lived by this theory: to have any chance of reviving a losing company you must concentrate on controlling the minuses; the pluses will take care of themselves. Farkas, who had gotten rich solving other people's business problems, thought Ruhe's penchant for glossing over negatives was naively unrealistic.

Ruhe seemed receptive to Farkas, hiring him to perform a short review of UPI's financial condition. But Farkas feared the damage already had been done, that Scripps had suckered these guys. More experienced negotiators could have taken advantage of Scripps's panic to cut UPI loose. They might well have extracted guarantees against losses the first year, guarantees of revenues from continuing business, and perhaps even indemnifications against pension-fund liabilities.

Ruhe and company had not even conducted a full audit of UPI before taking possession. Since he had wanted UPI so badly and was paying nothing for it, Farkas felt, Ruhe had been too hesitant to push for the kind of concessions he surely could have won.

After his visitors left Farkas told associates that UPI's owners were hardly the slick entrepreneurs they liked to think. Rather, they had been patsies for Scripps.

• • •

Barely anything can match the frenzied pace of the news business. Each day reporters pump the phones, pore over the latest government reports, read the newspapers, and monitor television and radio news broadcasts, always racing the clock and each other.

At short-staffed, deadline-every-minute UPI, things never seemed to slow. The summer and fall of 1982 proved no exception. UPI reporters scrambled to try to beat the AP during the dramatic, nine-week trial of Ronald Reagan's would-be assassin John W. Hinckley, Jr.; chased the first revelations that Reagan's defense buildup had included $500 toilet seats and $9,600 Allen wrenches; and pursued the latest developments in Lebanon.

The flurry of activity in UPI's executive suite that summer and fall, however, almost rivaled the tempo of its newsrooms. Searching for ways to polish the company's image, Ruhe and Geissler hired the consulting firm of Yankelovich, Skelley, and White to study UPI's market, and began talking about opening new bureaus. A search was under way for a new company president. The owners discussed how they would deal in upcoming contract negotiations with employees unhappy over their salaries. And Ruhe personally assumed the critical task of finding a way to switch over to cheaper satellite delivery of UPI's news reports.

While there was much action, there was little direction. Watching Ruhe and Geissler make key decisions in helter-skelter fashion while shuttling between Nashville and New York, Overgaard, Small, and president Rod Beaton, who was about to retire, were convinced UPI needed a strong, hands-on manager. Ruhe's attention span seemed too short for the important details in the day-to-day management of a large company.

The newly formed UPI Executive Committee, which met weekly in New York, might have helped, but Ruhe and Geissler never really gave it a chance. Rambling, agendaless meetings quickly bogged down in trivial pursuits, such as Ruhe's grand plan for cash-poor UPI to buy the buildings housing its bureaus. Small, Overgaard, and chief financial officer Tom Haughney dreaded the sessions: Ruhe was squandering precious time UPI did not have.

Beaton particularly was angry that Ken Braddick, the slim Australian who finally had resigned eight months after his drunken outburst at Charles Scripps, suddenly had been reborn. Braddick owed his resurrection to Geissler, who had met him at the staff meeting at the Harley and, upon learning he had quit, apparently figured a defector would be the best source of information about UPI. The two had spent the next day together. Soon Braddick was a consultant with the title of vice president in charge of development. As their friendship and mutual admiration deepened, other UPI executives theorized that the owner was charmed by Braddick's feistiness—perhaps his impertinence reminded Geissler of himself during the rebellious days of the sixties. Ruhe, not so impressed with Braddick, suffered his presence as a sop to his partner.

Beaton was also irritated at Ruhe's braggadocio in touting himself a communications expert who could save UPI millions by pulling off a satellite deal. Beaton recalled old colleague Jimmy Darr's departure warning: "Ruhe doesn't know as much as he thinks about communications." And Beaton was disappointed that chairman Rob Small, on whose experience and stature he had placed such high hopes, was being reduced to figurehead status. Ruhe, who had assumed the title of managing director, clearly was calling the shots. Finally, in mid-July, well before his scheduled departure, Beaton went to Ruhe.

"Doug, lookit, I don't think it's really necessary for me to stay. I think I should get on my way."

Ruhe made no effort to dissuade Beaton. The private search for a new president had, in fact, already begun.

In mid-August, on the last day of his thirty-four-year UPI career, Beaton lunched with close associates at The Palm, then raised a glass at a farewell party in the thirteenth-floor executive offices. He exhorted everyone to ignore the negative signs and the owners' inexperience; the battle to save UPI was too noble to abandon.

As the bittersweet festivities came to a close, Beaton bade farewell and headed out the door.

Suddenly he burst back into the hallway, grabbed information officer Bill Adler by his jacket lapels, and, emotions boiling over, growled, "Don't let these bastards screw it up!"

• • •

After the acrimonious meeting in Abe Rosenthal's office, the owners should not have been surprised at the bombshell *The New York Times* editor dropped in midsummer. The nation's leading newspaper said it would not renew when its contract expired in June 1983.

The cancellation threatened to be devastating—UPI could hardly hope for a financial renaissance without a visible presence in "the newspaper of record." Adler, worried that the news might start a landslide of client defections, told inquiring newspaper reporters such advance cancellations were merely a tactic for negotiating lower rates.

Small and Overgaard, also fearful of fallout from the *Times*'s stunning announcement, felt UPI must quickly hire a big-name president. Small's close friend Mort Frank, former publisher of "Family Weekly," had declined the job but had agreed to serve as a virtual one-man search committee. After approaching about two dozen industry leaders with little success, Frank mentioned the job to his friend Bill Small, 55, recently sacked as president of NBC News. Small was interested.

The prospect of enticing a news celebrity like Bill Small excited Overgaard and Rob Small—no relation to Bill—and they began pitching him to their partners.

But Ruhe and Geissler had ideas of their own. Three years earlier, during the Channel 66 negotiations in Dallas, Ruhe had met Luis Nogales, a vice president for Gene Autry's Los Angeles-based Golden West Broadcasters. The two had swapped yarns about their days as civil rights activists, and Ruhe since had occasionally phoned Nogales to invite him to join their Focus Communications venture.

Nogales had always politely declined. But when he read that Ruhe and Geissler had bought UPI, he was impressed. After all, just two years earlier, Ruhe had been grateful when Nogales picked up lunch and dinner tabs in Dallas. Nogales recalled an incident that week when they had shared a late-night cab to the airport, where Nogales's hotel was located. Ruhe had said he planned to catnap in the terminal until his early morning flight departed.

"Why don't you get a room?" Nogales asked.

Ruhe hesitated a long moment, then admitted, "I'm short on cash."

"C'mon," Nogales said, "I'll take care of it."

Now in the early fall of 1982, Ruhe phoned Nogales again:

"Would you be interested in coming to join us at UPI? Why don't you come out, look the place over, and then, you know, you decide what you want to do.''

This time Nogales was interested enough to make inquiries. When he mentioned UPI to Peter Jones, a fellow board member of Levi Strauss Company, he was surprised to learn that Jones's father had been a career Unipresser who had helped set up its highly successful Latin America operations. As Nogales investigated further, he was struck by the incredible loyalty and warmth UPI engendered from clients, staff, and ex-employees. This certainly was no ordinary company. In late summer he flew to New York.

Arriving at UPI's headquarters in the Daily News Building, Nogales found Ruhe's office a most casual place. Ruhe would fly in from Nashville, stash his luggage in a corner, hold a meeting or two, then rush off. When he was absent he generously let other UPI officials use the office.

Ruhe arranged for Nogales to meet with Overgaard and Rob Small. Nogales was surprised when their questions focused not on him but on whether he knew anything about Bill Small.

Nogales said he never had met Small, choosing not to repeat some tales he had heard—that while the acerbic Small was highly regarded as a journalist, many NBC employees had feared and loathed him. Nogales assumed from the conversation that Bill Small might wind up UPI's new editor in chief. Neither Rob Small nor Overgaard volunteered that they were pushing Small for president.

Nogales, who had come to New York expecting to be offered a high-level company job, spent most of the day waiting, first for Ruhe, then for Rob Small and Overgaard. Perplexed and irritated over the seeming disarray, and with no specific job offer from Ruhe, Nogales flew back to California, dismissing the cross-country jaunt as time ill spent.

He did not know he was caught in a tug-of-war between Ruhe and Geissler on one hand and Overgaard and Rob Small on the other. The struggle over the choice of a new UPI president was the latest manifestation of a deepening rift between the two factions. Nor could Nogales guess he would become a central character in UPI's fight for survival.

• • •

Chris Huffman, Jean Alice Small's secretary, froze one late August day when she answered the phone in Kankakee, Illinois, and heard a voice say, ''Dan Rather calling from New York.''

The CBS anchorman wanted to offer Rob Small a rave recommendation for his former boss, Bill Small, to be UPI's new president. During Bill Small's seventeen years at the network he often had been Rather's staunch defender.

Then came a gushing call from former CBS news executive Fred Friendly: "I may be in the springtime of my senility, but Bill Small's a terrific guy, a terrific newsman."

Rob Small was deeply taken with the former network chief. In three-plus years at NBC, Bill Small had recruited a number of top correspondents and producers, including CBS stars Roger Mudd and brothers Marvin and Bernard Kalb. Small, he thought, was the kind of respected, world-class schmoozer who could comfort those concerned about the new owners and the direction UPI would take.

So vigorously did Rob Small and Cordy Overgaard campaign for Bill Small that Ruhe finally, reluctantly, gave in, only to incur a vehement protest from Geissler, who thought it was a horrible idea. Ruhe finally prevailed. This was no time to risk so antagonizing Rob Small that he might bail out on UPI. Besides, the strong support for Bill Small from all the media big shots left Ruhe and Geissler little choice. Rob Small and Cordy Overgaard had won their first, and last, big victory.

UPI's announcement on September 14 bore encomiums from Mudd and Rather. Swallowing hard, Ruhe called Small "one of the news industry's true leaders."

Small's hiring gave UPI a patina of respectability, but he did not come cheap. His three-year contract far surpassed Beaton's salary, starting at $220,000 a year—a princely sum for a struggling company.

Another part of Ruhe and Geissler's planned facelift for UPI included replacing editor H.L. Stevenson. They had developed a deep respect for John Seigenthaler, whose paper had been most vigorous in investigating their backgrounds. Just a few weeks after *The Tennessean's* lengthy story, over dinner at a pricey Italian restaurant in Nashville, Ruhe and Geissler offered Seigenthaler a quarter-million-dollar salary to run UPI's news report. Seigenthaler declined, saying he already had the best job in journalism. He cautioned them not to precipitously dump Stevenson, highly popular with subscribers.

When Geissler pressed him to reconsider, Seigenthaler replied, "I just can't." He was far too gracious a southern gentleman to mention his doubts that Ruhe and Geissler had either the experience or talent to resuscitate the failing wire service.

• • •

Bill Small came aboard just in time for the annual October EDICON meeting where UPI hosted key newspaper editors and publishers and their spouses. Heading into the meeting in Denver, the owners tried to capitalize on Small's appointment with a slick public relations barrage. The New York PR agency of Lois Pitts Gershon disgorged upbeat trade publication ads and press releases, then trotted out a classy new logo in black block letters: "UPI: One Up On the World."

At the meeting Geissler painted a rosy forecast, saying UPI had signed $2.3 million in new business and cut cancellations by 2.7 percent. "We feel we've rounded a corner," he declared.

It was obvious, however, that the newspaper community had not warmed to the teetotaling Baha'is; Ruhe and Geissler still were outsiders in the old-boy network. When Small left EDICON early for a broadcast convention in Las Vegas, the clients' enthusiasm waned.

Rob Small and Overgaard felt somewhat comforted that Bill Small would be a wonderful goodwill ambassador, traveling about to reassure clients that UPI was turning the corner and spinning yarns about journalism's good old days. But their hope that Small also would be the take-charge manager UPI desperately needed soon would vanish.

• • •

As the months dragged on Overgaard and Rob Small grew increasingly concerned that their partners were not attacking UPI's most costly problem, the critical, complicated satellite switch.

Before leaving UPI, Jimmy Darr had warned Ruhe, "Don't screw up the satellite program. You'll never get out of trouble."

Darr's warning proved prescient.

Ruhe was proud of his communications expertise and brooked no interference in his pet project. For months he had negotiated with the Harris Corporation over a plan to install thousands of the firm's ten-foot, $9,000 satellite dishes at client sites across the country, with subscribers splitting the cost. Scripps had used such a scheme for an earlier pilot project to equip more than 400 broadcasters with Harris dishes, but had been unwilling to underwrite the massive costs of switching all clients to satellites. Whenever Overgaard and Rob Small nervously inquired about his progress in resuming the conversion, Ruhe gave his stock answer: "I'm working on it."

As the owners' self-imposed Labor Day deadline for switching to satellites came and went, it seemed to his partners that Ruhe was like a haggler at a Persian bazaar, always holding out for a "better deal." Also discouraged that Ruhe's attention kept wandering to far less crucial things, Rob Small told Overgaard, "Cordy, we're disorganized."

Surely Ruhe knew the Scripps money was disappearing at the rate of a half-million dollars a month, and further delays in the satellite program would be devastating. They decided to confront their partner.

"We've got just too many things going on," Overgaard told Ruhe. "We've got to assign priorities. There are just too many balls in the air."

Ruhe lightly brushed aside the imprecations. "We can handle it," he said.

One day Overgaard got a call from a legal client who had invested in Equatorial, Inc., a satellite communications company.

"The people at Equatorial can't get in to talk to UPI," the client said.

Overgaard and Small were astonished. Despite his airy assurances, Ruhe not only seemed to be making little progress but had also ignored a potential supplier. Overgaard asked Ruhe to meet with Equatorial. Ruhe was soon surprised to learn that Equatorial's smaller receiving dishes would cost only about a fourth as much as the 1,000 dishes he already had ordered from Harris for $9 million. Still, he faced a quandary. Harris's satellite "uplink" fee was less than half of Equatorial's $80,000 monthly rate.

Ruhe kept juggling, always searching for just a little better deal. Finally, with even Geissler prodding him, he elected to begin a pilot project with Equatorial, using big Harris dishes only at large-city receiving hubs. Ruhe was proud of setting the stage for a conversion that even Scripps had not achieved.

But with UPI still paying for ATT's expensive telephone lines, his months of delay in even beginning the embryonic move toward satellite transmission would prove a disaster.

• • •

Even chief financial officer Tom Haughney, who had helped mastermind the purchase, was growing queasy. Haughney had already been through a Chapter 11 bankruptcy with a previous employer and did not like what he was seeing at UPI.

Haughney worried that Bill Ahlhauser, a shiny-faced Harvard Business School graduate, was improbably young and inexperienced to be treasurer. He was convinced that Ahlhauser did not even seem to know what the functions of a treasurer were. Besides, Ahlhauser was gaining a reputation among UPI executives for rather curious behavior. In the hallways he would peer through wire-rimmed glasses and, almost mimicking Ruhe's effusiveness, confidently brush aside the latest crisis.

"I don't know why you people have trouble here," he would tell concerned executives. "I think UPI is the easiest company in the world to turn around."

Haughney, his subordinate, shrugged off such oddities until he discovered one day in the fall of 1982 that Ahlhauser had ordered controller Fred Greene to withhold from Small and Overgaard copies of UPI's monthly financial statements.

Haughney marched into Ahlhauser's office.

"Why?" he asked.

"Because Doug said so," Ahlhauser said.

Haughney was aware of his corporate responsibilities to keep all stockholders, including Small and Overgaard, fully informed about financial matters.

"Why did Doug say so?" Haughney demanded sarcastically.

"Because they might become confused."

Aghast, Haughney protested.

"Look, they've got to have them," he insisted.

Ahlhauser, a Baha'i who seemed to revere Ruhe, refused to back off.[1] Haughney decided to ignore the directive, and chose not to tell Rob Small and Overgaard of Ruhe's attempt to circumvent them.

Haughney grew even more disturbed when Ahlhauser told him that Focus Communications—Ruhe and Geissler's Nashville company—needed money and wanted to transfer cash from UPI.

Until now Ruhe and Geissler had been idiosyncratic, headstrong young men loath to listen to people with more experience. This was different. Now it appeared the owners might secretly try to divert UPI's precious cash. This gambit troubled Haughney deeply, and he spoke up.

"That would require authorization from the Executive Committee," he told Ahlhauser.

---

[1] Ahlhauser declined several requests for an interview.

Ahlhauser hinted Ruhe probably would be reluctant to take such a transaction to the committee. Haughney was wary of being drawn into anything that might be considered improper and suggested an alternative. Remembering Ruhe and Geissler were being paid $400-a-day management fees, he proposed to Ahlhauser that the owners receive the money on a quarterly basis—and in advance.

Ahlhauser agreed. In early 1983, without telling Overgaard and Small, Ruhe and Geissler began drawing the first of their advance consulting fees that would add up to tens of thousands of dollars.

• • •

Most of the company's serious problems, including its precarious cash position, had been kept from the rest of the media. In fact, to outsiders things seemed to be getting better. Once aboard, Bill Small had quickly visited *The New York Times* to begin patching the strained relations, and an expensive public relations blitz had been unleashed. Marketing efforts also seemed to be gaining momentum and the owners were quick to hype any successes, although most of the business came from renewed or extended contracts.

One company press release announced a fivefold increase in ''new'' sales to $11.1 million for the third quarter, and said UPI had reversed the exodus that had cost it 287 subscribers in 1981.

On November 30, sales vice president Tom Beatty announced UPI's rate increase would be held to 6.3 percent, the lowest in two decades.

''What we're saying here is, 'Yes, UPI needs more money,' '' Beatty said. '' 'But we're going to go out and get most of it in the form of new business.' ''

While it was undeniable that UPI had made some headway in its marketing efforts, the glowing reports were vastly overstated.

Rob Small and Overgaard knew the truth about UPI's finances and urged their partners to consider bringing aboard investors with cash— perhaps American publishing tycoon Ralph Ingersoll and Finnish publisher Aatos Erkko.

But Ruhe and Geissler were through taking their advice. Just months after they had used Small and Overgaard to help win UPI from Scripps, they now exhibited no concern over their partners' growing disenchantment.

• • •

Although the owners had hired Dick Farkas and his turnaround crew for an intense, three-month review of the company's books, they did not even consult Farkas before plunging into negotiations over a new union contract.

Geissler, in his first labor negotiations as a manager, and Ken Braddick would handle the crucial bargaining. Geissler still empathized with workers because of his days in Laredo, and was determined to avoid the kind of acrimony with the union that had marred UPI's recent past. Aware that Unipressers had been badly compensated for years, Geissler felt a moral commitment to pay them at least as well as Associated Press staffers, even if it ultimately cost millions of dollars. But he also decided to go far beyond that, to voluntarily agree that UPI would have an agency shop, a treasured concession the guild had been seeking for years. For the first time all employees under guild jurisdiction would be required to pay dues, giving the union far greater financial clout. Alan Berger, a St. Louis labor attorney hired to represent UPI, was unaware of the company's financial crises but was nonetheless flabbergasted to learn the depth of Geissler's compassion for the workers.

Informed of Geissler's plan to grant an agency shop, Berger told him, "That is a very handsome item, and it could have a very handsome sale price on it. What do you expect to get for it?"

"Well, we're getting their cooperation."

Berger was amazed. Could Geissler really be so naive?

Berger, a Don Rickles look-alike with a wit to match, marched into the office of management negotiator Bobby Ray Miller and asked, with feigned sarcasm, "Did you know your bosses are pro-union?"

Had Berger known how bad things were financially, he might have fought harder to convince the owners to extract every dime's worth of union concessions. Instead, his marching orders were to seek a three-year contract holding the line on costs the first year but granting wage increases in the second and third years that would bring Unipressers close to parity with the AP. He was to finance the increases with innovative, cost-saving contract modifications.

Unlike past union negotiations where the UPI lawyer led its bargaining team, Berger was a benchwarmer. UPI was represented at the table mainly by Braddick and labor relations chief Miller, a bearded, rotund survivor of years of internecine company battles who, like Braddick, had won a senior management job after cozying up to Geissler. So entrenched had Braddick become that his inexperienced young wife, Elaine Clisham, had been hired by Geissler as chief UPI sales coordinator, a move that stunned and enraged sales staffers far better qualified.

It was on a Sunday, at an opening negotiating session at the Grand Hyatt Hotel in New York, that the guild raised the agency shop issue. So vehement was its demand that, during a recess, union negotiator Judy Dugan urged caution lest the issue set too hostile a tone and "blow the whole negotiations."

"The hell with that," said veteran officer Drew Von Bergen. "Let's just see what happens."

When the recess ended UPI's representatives casually broke the news. "Okay, you've got your agency shop."

The union was thunderstruck. Almost off-handedly UPI's negotiators, on Geissler's orders, had handed the union a coup that had eluded it for decades.

Struggling to hide his glee, Guild president William Morrissey said, "Well, okay, let's break for the day." He wanted to announce the victory before the company could change its mind.

Bill Geissler had no second thoughts, despite the warnings of virtually every UPI executive—even Ruhe. Geissler felt a bond with UPI's young, liberal, well-educated work force, and wanted to prolong the honeymoon. He was convinced that if he could negotiate a contract with no first-year cost increases, anticipated satellite savings and the big sales push would more than cover the cost of the hefty pay raises in the final two years. It certainly was worth the risk, he felt.

During the unusually speedy, twenty-three-day negotiations, Overgaard and both Smalls had been left largely in the dark. When they inquired Geissler would reply enigmatically, "It's fine. We're going to work everything out."

Rob Small, with extensive experience in labor relations on his family newspapers, knew the contract talks were critical because labor costs were by far UPI's biggest operating expense. Annoyed and increasingly alienated by being shut out, he feared the negotiations were being bungled.

In mid-December, UPI celebrated its seventy-fifth anniversary with a fancy, expensive, cocktail party at National Geographic Society headquarters in Washington hosted by Rob and Bill Small. The company unveiled its exhibit of classic UPI news pictures, including a number of Pulitzer Prize winners, which would tour other major cities.

While Vice President George Bush and other guests surveyed the exhibit, sipped cocktails and munched giant shrimp, UPI staffer Paula Schwed casually asked the Smalls their opinion of the new union contract just announced on the wires. UPI's chairman and its president were dumbfounded. They had been frozen out of a monumental management decision.

In New York, Geissler and Braddick took the agreement to controller Fred Greene and asked him to tote up the damages.

"Don't you know how much you signed for?" Greene asked.

When they replied no, Greene's jaw dropped.

Discovering that the management negotiators' handwritten notes were incomprehensible, Greene had to pluck details of the agreement from a union bulletin. He was astonished to find the company had committed to more than $10 million in new expenditures over three years and to raise salaries by more than 25 percent in the final two years.

Geissler immediately was assailed from nearly every quarter. Even publishers called to complain. "Are you guys crazy?" asked one. "We're trying to hold everybody down, and you're giving people big raises!"

While publicly supporting Geissler, Ruhe never would forgive his partner for blowing the negotiations.

Overgaard, too, was horrified. Both he and Rob Small were keenly aware that UPI was headed in 1984 into a so-called quadrennial year where presidential campaigns and the Olympics would send costs soaring. UPI's losses of $12.1 million in 1980, the last quadrennial under Scripps, were its worst ever.

Now, they fretted, the fat pay-raise provisions of the new contract would frighten away any possible outside investors and doom UPI's hopes for profitability. And they were offended that they had not even been consulted. They were partners in name only.

The union contract raised the rare possibility that UPI employees would earn a few bucks more than their AP counterparts by the time it expired in 1985. During separate negotiations with the AP, Guild president Morrissey jabbed the needle.

"You know you can't let that [higher UPI wages] happen," he told Tom Pendergast, AP's vice president for personnel.

Pendergast's retort was chillingly clairvoyant: "You don't really think you'll ever see that money, do you?"

• • •

When Rob Small and Overgaard returned to New York after the Christmas holidays, they ran smack into still more depressing news. Dick Farkas's IMC consulting team had delivered its report: debts were mounting so rapidly that the harshest medicine was needed. UPI must be treated as if it were already in bankruptcy.

Farkas knew the new union contract was a killer. A hard-nosed veteran of numerous corporate turnaround efforts, Farkas was neither delicate nor courteous. He urged Ruhe and Geissler to reopen negotiations immediately and to demand substantial concessions. UPI should raise its rates, lay off 400 employees, and shrink to a forty-state national supplemental news agency.

"Bite the bullet right now—hard," he told them. "What you've just agreed to give the union is going to make the company go bankrupt."

"You don't understand, man," Geissler replied.

"I *do* understand."

"I'm an ex-union man," Geissler said. "I believe you've got to be competitive."

"If we don't face up now, later is academic," Farkas said.

Ruhe and Geissler argued that such drastic staff cuts would be suicidal, that subscribers would not accept a UPI that did not cover all fifty states.

Farkas suggested that Geissler and Ruhe go back to Nashville and let IMC be the villains.

"You're new here," Farkas said. "Nobody knows you guys. You leave now, we shed the blood, you guys come back. Everybody who is left says, 'Whew, we survived.' The company is in the black."

But Ruhe feared Farkas might be trying to seize UPI for himself.

Farkas was also shocked at Ruhe's laggard performance in converting UPI to satellite delivery. Indeed, Ruhe had concocted a shortcut solution to the pressing problem and it had been a disaster. After signing the agreement with Equatorial, Ruhe had decided UPI could save money by installing the dishes itself. He established a subsidiary in Miami, Focus Service Systems, under friend and fellow Baha'i Lee Moynahan.

Her tiny crew included Don Whitfield and his son, David, also Baha'is, and a couple of former employees of Harris Corporation, the satellite dish manufacturer. But they operated from a truck out of geographically isolated Miami. Installation delays were killing UPI, which continued to bear ATT's long-distance phone-line charges that sometimes exceeded the rates clients were paying. And the delays also meant some newly signed clients were missing start-up dates. "Ludicrous," sniffed Farkas.

Farkas's report underscored the belief of Small and Overgaard that UPI's only hope was to convince Ruhe to hire a general manager and give him day-to-day operating control.

Overgaard was deeply upset by IMC's bleak assessment. The minority partners, whose credentials had helped Ruhe and Geissler close the deal, never had been given any real authority. They felt used and they didn't much like it. Ruhe and Geissler, they felt, were lost in dreamy idealism that distorted their business judgment. If their partners were going to run UPI into the ground, Small and Overgaard wanted no part of it.

Yet, when Overgaard suggested they pull out, Small still felt stirrings of old loyalty to UPI.

"Before we resign," he said, "let's just put it to Doug that we think we need a manager here, to see if he'll go along with that."

Even though their past prodding had failed, Overgaard reluctantly obliged. Perhaps an ultimatum would shock Ruhe and Geissler back to reality.

Ruhe agreed to a meeting, but again he was a step ahead of his partners. Shortly after the sale, at a media banquet in Nashville, he and Geissler had been introduced to John Jay Hooker, the man who had left a congratulatory note in their office.

Shaking Hooker's hand, Ruhe told him warmly, "We got your note. Let's have lunch."

One December day Hooker picked up Ruhe and Geissler at the Focus office building and aimed his gray Lincoln Continental south toward Arthur's, an elegant restaurant in Nashville's Green Hills section.

The three hit it off from the start. Reclining in unaccustomed luxury in the back seat, Ruhe and Geissler described how they had put together their partnership to buy UPI, while Hooker spun tales about his political and show-business friends and his past business adventures.

Lingering over lunch, they were oblivious to time. Hooker did not hide his interest in UPI, and suggested his new friends think about how he might join their venture. Ruhe and Geissler were enthusiastic. They told Hooker they had brought in Rob Small because they needed his prestige, but now they had grown disenchanted.

Sensing an opening, Hooker pressed his pitch.

"Look, you'll make more money and have more fun with me in the deal than without me."

Ruhe and Geissler found Hooker appealing and amusing. They laughed and kidded him about his "uniform"—blue suit, blue- and red-striped tie, blue vest with gold watch fob, white homburg, and white handkerchief neatly folded in his vest pocket.

"What is a man dressed like you going to do with a couple of fellows like us?" Ruhe asked.

"To each his own," Hooker replied. "I'm not trying to be Doug Ruhe, and you're not trying to be John Jay."

By the time Rob Small and Overgaard prepared to confront them, the UPI owners had secretly cut an arrangement to make Hooker their partner. The showdown with Overgaard and Small was set for Wednesday, January 26, 1983.

On Tuesday evening Ruhe and Geissler invited Small to dinner. At the bar in the lobby of the Grand Hyatt Hotel in Manhattan, Ruhe introduced him to John Jay Hooker. Then he caught Small completely off guard, casually disclosing that the flamboyant Tennessee lawyer not only was joining them for dinner but also was coming aboard as a partner.

Before Small could catch his breath, Ruhe told him reassuringly, "Now I know you've felt alienated, but I think we can fix things up."

Small, a quintessential gentleman, suffered his shock and resentment in silence. He was well beyond being offended by Ruhe's strange ways and was soon fascinated by Hooker's garb, gregarious charm, and studied folksiness. He thought he already had seen every variety of character parade through UPI in six months, but this Hooker was a work of art.

During dinner at a Midtown Spanish restaurant, Small was taken aback when Hooker said bluntly, in a low voice, "Let me ask you this, Rob. Are these fellows coachable?"

"If you don't watch out," Small cautioned, "they'll end up coaching you. They're very opinionated fellows, and they're not going to accept anyone's leadership. They're going to do it the way they want to do it. I don't know if there's a place for me in light of the overall situation."

• • •

Next morning Overgaard flew in from Chicago. Scarcely had he and Small settled into their chairs at Ruhe's suite at the Grand Hyatt Hotel when Ruhe dropped a new bombshell. Hooker was coming in as an equal partner, receiving a third of Ruhe and Geissler's shares. The three would vote their stock as a block. Small and Overgaard immediately understood the ramifications. Hooker would have more clout than they.

Small finally found his voice.

"Cordy and I have two major points we want to discuss. First of all, we need capital. We need somewhere between $6 million and $15 million.

"Second, Doug, you're a very creative guy, but we're frustrated. We feel we are disorganized. We need an administrator-type person to run this company, because we're in trouble."

Ruhe shook his head, but Small pressed on.

"You need to do the deals and have the ideas. But we need somebody else to run this company."

Ruhe would hear nothing of the sort. He made it clear that he and Geissler had no intention of loosening their grip on UPI.

"I think it can be turned around," Ruhe said. "We're confident."

Overgaard, who had done legal work for Ruhe and Geissler for five years, knew full well just how bull-headed Ruhe could be.

"Rob and I both recognize that you two had responsibility for bringing about the acquisition of UPI, and that this is your deal," he said. "We're not seeking power or confrontation, but we have increasingly felt our positions have become ambiguous and less relevant.

"We are increasingly frustrated with what we perceive to be inadequate management. Anyway, it must be annoying to you to have two partners tugging and pulling at you. Under the circumstances, Rob and I have decided to withdraw."

Ruhe listened, impassive. Then, almost as if on cue, the phone rang. Geissler answered and informed Ruhe they were late for their next meeting.

Ruhe nodded, then suddenly turned to Overgaard and Small and said, "What do you intend to do with your stock?"

Again they were taken aback. They had resolved to resign if Ruhe proved unshakable, but had not even dreamed he might suggest they return their stock. They were angry, too. Who did Ruhe think he was? Without them in the deal, Scripps might have tossed Ruhe and Geissler out on their ears.

Fighting to conceal his emotions, Small reminded himself that the important thing was to try to ensure UPI's future.

"I didn't get into UPI to make money, and I'm sure something can be worked out," he said, reaching for his coat. "We'll think about it."

The great showdown had lasted less than half an hour. Small and Overgaard walked the block back to UPI, cleared out their desks, bade good-byes, and—confused, upset, disappointed and a little relieved—flew back to Illinois.

Doug Ruhe stubbornly had spurned their counsel, convinced he alone should determine UPI's course. Yet he and Geissler had failed virtually every major test in their first six months, and UPI was in greater peril than ever.

These two small-time businessmen had gambled by squeezing out their respected partners, men who had shown every willingness to accommodate. In their place now was the mercurial, controversial John Jay Hooker, who, after trying for four years, at last had his hands on UPI.

7

...

UPI's First-Class "Chay-ah-man"

U PI's Washington staff caught sight of John Jay Hooker one day early in February when the new chairman breezed into their messy, cramped, low-ceilinged office on the third floor of the National Press Building.

He marched up to Washington vice president Grant Dillman, thrust out his hand, and drawled, "Hi, ah'm John Jay Hooker. Pleased to meet you."

With Dillman trailing in his wake, and without seeming to rush the job, Hooker managed in less than an hour to greet individually several dozen staffers. Approaching a group of veteran writers in the dingy corner of the office jokingly dubbed by its denizens "Poets' Alley," he grabbed the hand of Clay Richards.

"Hi, I'm UPI's national political reporter," Richards offered.

Hooker's eyes brightened and a broad grin creased his face.

"Ah love politics like a hog loves slop!" exulted Hooker, a liberal Democrat who had been denied both the governorship and a U.S. Senate nomination by the voters of Tennessee.

Hooker's arrival was met with a mix of skepticism, deprecation, and hope. Like all journalists, Unipressers professed hard-bitten cynicism. But even though Hooker seemed like a glib Dixie drummer, they found it difficult to dislike this smooth-talking, wavy-haired charmer.

His brash gregariousness was a stark contrast to Rob Small and Cordy Overgaard, reserved men who never mingled with the editorial staff. John Jay Hooker was born to mingle, a man as much at ease with the lowliest reporter as he was hobnobbing with stars and celebrities.

He had befriended heavyweight boxing champion Muhammad Ali while chairman of the STP Corporation in the early seventies. One day Kentucky Governor John Y. Brown phoned and asked Hooker for a $25,000 contribution for the Muhammad Ali boxing school in Louisville, Ali's home town. Hooker obliged, and later, when Ali's plane was grounded in Natchez, Mississippi, Hooker picked him up in the STP corporate jet and whisked him to Louisville.

Ali had been stripped of his heavyweight championship and received a five-year prison sentence in 1967 for refusing induction into the military during Vietnam, but the Supreme Court later had ruled he was entitled to conscientious objector status.

"You are mah hero," Hooker told Ali.

Ali was puzzled. "You're a white boy," he replied. "You belong to these country clubs. You're in favor of that [Vietnam] war. Why are you saying that?"

Hooker persisted. "You are mah hero because you were willin' to give up the championship of the world, and you paid your dues. The thing ah admire most in life is courage."

On October 1, 1975, before the entire world, Hooker was rewarded. At the close of the ballyhooed "Thrilla in Manila," one of history's most memorable prizefights, Ali dragged his aching body off the canvas to reclaim the heavyweight crown in a fourteen-round TKO of Smokin' Joe Frazier. As Ali gasped for breath an announcer jammed a mike in his face.

"Before I say anything," he croaked, "I want to say hello to my friend John Jay Hooker."

Watching in a closed-circuit movie theater in Fort Lauderdale, Florida, Hooker's jaw dropped to his blue vest. Hundreds of thousands of bewildered fight fans around the world wondered if Frazier's powerful left hooks had scrambled Ali's brain.

Next day, Hooker phoned Ali in Manila. The champ crowed.

"John Jay Hooker! John Jay Hooker! SE-VUN HUN-DRED MIL-YUN PEOPLE! John Jay Hooker!" The jubilant Ali knew he had given his friend his own thrill from Manila.

Besides Ali, Hooker numbered among his close celebrity friends actors Warren Beatty and Lorne Greene, singers Andy Williams and Abbe Lane, odds-maker Jimmy "the Greek" Snyder, and former Miss America Phyllis George. The friendships paid dividends. Beatty even cast Hooker as a U.S. senator in *Reds*, a three-and-a-half-hour movie epic. Hooker, unable to persuade Tennessee voters to send him to Washington, gloried in his bit part.

Hooker loved to stand out in crowds. Continuing a custom he started at Vanderbilt Law School, he made sure he wore the same outfit every day.

"If a fella met me today, ah want him to start out tomorrow remembering ah'm the same fella," Hooker, who won acclaim as one of America's best-dressed men, loved to say.

• • •

Hooker had had a checkered career. In fifty-two years he had made and lost several fortunes dabbling in law, hospitals, electronics, motor-oil additives, politics, and fried chicken. When things went badly he reached into a bottomless bag of ideas. Friends he had helped make rich often were willing to chance a new venture.

After opening a law practice in Nashville in 1957 with his brother Henry, Hooker had become a prominent First Amendment lawyer for *The Tennessean*, where he grew friendly with the paper's star investigative reporter, John Seigenthaler. When Seigenthaler later became an aide to Attorney General Bobby Kennedy, Hooker was tapped to help negotiate the release of American prisoners held by Fidel Castro after the Bay of Pigs invasion and to help prepare the government's case against Teamsters boss Jimmy Hoffa.

Between two losing campaigns for governor and one for senator, Hooker concentrated on entrepreneurial business ventures. In 1966 he and his brother launched Minnie Pearl fast-food fried chicken franchises. After the Hookers reported initially booming sales, the Securities and Exchange Commission filed a formal complaint that Minnie Pearl dramatically overstated its revenue figures and income in a public stock offering. Although Hooker amended the public filing, his venture crashed. Hooker partially blamed the bad publicity and charged the SEC investigation was politically motivated by Republican Senator Bill Brock and U.S. Attorney General John Mitchell.

Another venture, Whale, Inc., a publicly traded electronics firm, fell into untimely bankruptcy the same day in 1970 on which Hooker announced a second run for governor. But Hooker was resilient. In 1973 he succeeded former race car driver Andy Granatelli as chairman of STP Corporation, and his marketing wizardry sent sales of the oil additive soaring.

After losing his last political race, an effort to unseat Brock, Hooker searched for new opportunities. In 1979 he helped arrange Gannett's $50 million purchase of *The Tennessean* and, in gratitude, Gannett executive Karl Eller offered to help him buy the city's smaller paper, *The Banner*. Hooker, who had waged bitter wars with *The Banner* during his political campaigns, didn't hesitate.

"Ah'd rather own *The Banner* than be president of General Motors," he declared.

With Eller opening doors, Hooker and two partners bought *The Banner* for $25 million, a deal so leveraged that it ultimately netted him $6 million without a nickel's investment. About then Scripps had begun trying to sell UPI. That, thought Hooker, is what I really want.

Ruhe and Geissler hoped Hooker's experience in the news business and his skills as a promoter and a dealmaker would be the answer to UPI's desperate need for investment capital. Before accepting their offer that he buy in for $1.00, Hooker sought the advice of Gannett Chairman Al Neuharth.

"Look," Neuharth told his friend, "for one dollar you're getting a look at what could be a great opportunity. The risk-reward ratio is very handsome. If it doesn't work, what have you lost?"

• • •

UPI's upbeat announcement of Hooker's arrival on February 1 contained the news that he had "purchased" an interest in Media News Corporation, UPI's parent company, and would replace Rob Small as chairman. It cleverly skipped mention of the purchase price. At the same time the departures of Small and Overgaard were papered over as coincidental and unrelated.

A story in *The Tennessean* quoted Hooker as saying he had been trying to persuade Ruhe and Geissler to let him join the venture and felt "greatly blessed" to be their partner.

"They have already made substantial headway at UPI, and the plans they have are going to transform the company back to profitability."

Then, with typical hyperbole, he added, "I want everybody to know that I'd rather be chairman of the board of UPI than governor of Tennessee.''

Despite the flourish attending Hooker's arrival, many Unipressers and industry leaders were distressed by Small's abrupt exit. Ken Braddick told Geissler, ''Rob Small has a very good reputation in the industry, and a lot of people will read his departure as an indication something is wrong.''

In reply, Geissler shrugged off the rift as a fundamental disagreement over the direction of the company. Hiding any bitterness, Small graciously said in an interview in *Editor and Publisher*, the industry magazine, that he and Overgaard had left UPI to spend more time on their businesses and with their families.

•   •   •

Hooker quickly demonstrated he was no shrinking violet. Even Doug Ruhe sometimes found himself on the defensive.

At a restaurant during their first meeting after Hooker came aboard, Ruhe got a taste of what life with the flamboyant Tennessean would be like. Returning from the men's room, Ruhe was greeted by Hooker's booming voice.

''Doug, ah'm chay-ah-man, ah'm the chay-ah-man! Bill and ah just voted!''

Ruhe cringed, stunned by Hooker's audacity and Geissler's apparent acquiescence.

''Hey, I'm gonna' get out of this thing if you guys are going to pull that kind of stuff on me!'' Ruhe warned.

Geissler realized he'd offended his partner, and Hooker moved quickly to smooth things over.

''Ah mean, are you questioning this? You're not in favor of this? Bill and ah talked about it, and . . .''

Ruhe pulled Geissler aside for a chat. While both worried about having someone as brassy, flashy as Hooker as titular head of UPI, they realized they needed him; he already had introduced them to a number of potential investors.

Fearing he might alienate Hooker if he balked, and at the same time grudgingly admiring his legerdemain, Ruhe agreed: John Jay Hooker would be UPI's new ''chay-ah-man.''

Hooker quickly put his stamp on UPI. He granted an interview to an old Tennessee friend, *New York Times* reporter Wendell "Sonny" Rawls, and disclosed he had bought a 30 percent interest in UPI for $1.00.[1] The story also quoted "sources" as suggesting Scripps all but gave away UPI in the mysterious 1982 transaction.

The article angered Ruhe. When he chastised Hooker for disclosing company secrets, his new partner apologetically characterized it as an inadvertent slip. But it wouldn't be the last time Hooker's style infuriated his partners.

The *Times* story, while helping explain why Scripps's disposal of UPI had been shrouded in secrecy, raised fresh doubts about the financial resources of three owners who had invested nothing in the company.

For weeks after Rawls' story, staffers sarcastically waved dollar bills at one another and demanded the right to "buy" a piece of UPI.

· · ·

Hooker's first order of business was to help minimize the fallout from the departures of Rob Small and Overgaard. Bill Small had agreed to remain as president, but Ruhe and Geissler feared that with his most enthusiastic supporters gone, Small might be less than wholeheartedly loyal. Hooker volunteered to talk to him. Chatting over lunch at the Grand Hyatt Hotel, Hooker told Small he would have to accept the fact that his role would be diminished, that he no longer would be a "big fish."

Small listened noncommitally. Hooker reported back to his partners that he doubted the president ever would willingly take a back seat, always would consider himself a big fish. Behind Small's back, Hooker jokingly began calling him "The Tuna."

Hooker haunted UPI's thirteenth-floor executive offices like Banquo's ghost, steeping himself in the business and the lore of UPI. He read and digested the report by Dick Farkas that recommended UPI demand union concessions and make profound cutbacks in its scope and mission. Having dreamed for years of owning UPI, Hooker was shocked to find things far worse than he imagined. Searching for someone knowledgeable who could give him the straight financial scoop, Hooker settled on controller Fred Greene. Hooker animatedly would ask Greene, "What d'ya think?

---

[1] A third of Ruhe's and Geissler's stock, or 20 percent of UPI's shares, was put in a blind trust for Hooker, to be controlled by and voted in a block by Ruhe and Geissler.

Are we gonna make it? . . . We're committed to the journey. Ah want to know how much gas it'll take to get from point A to point B. We've got to stop the bleedin'.''

Traipsing UPI's hallways took its toll. When Hooker burst into somebody's office, plopped down on a chair, and propped his feet on the desk, he revealed holes in the soles of his expensive shoes.

A virtual perpetual motion machine, Hooker seemingly had no difficulty juggling multiple activities. Once he phoned UPI public relations man Bill Adler from Nashville. Listening to the noises in the background, Adler surmised Hooker was chomping a raw carrot and speaking on a portable phone—all while playing tennis.

Despite Hooker's quirky nature, he was a savvy businessman with far more experience and credentials than his new partners. He saw the obvious problems at UPI but also envisioned enormous potential.

Always ready with a folksy analogy, Hooker was fond of declaring that UPI had to discover its ''razor blades''—its cutting edge. Spin-offs, diversifications from UPI's main product could be the ''blades'' that helped the company into the black, Hooker thought.

''We've got to find the blades,'' he'd intone. ''We've got to find the blades.''

He also told and retold his favorite yarn about the chairman of Greyhound, who, concluding that travelers with battered kidneys would leave the bus and head straight for the restroom, hatched the idea of pay toilets.

''We've gotta find UPI's pay toilet,'' Hooker would declare.

• • •

Like Rob Small and Overgaard, Hooker soon grew frustrated by the owners' strange, casual, management style. He found communication with Ruhe and Geissler sporadic and unsatisfactory. His new partners seemed oblivious to the urgent need for hard decisions, oblivious to the cash draining every day from the embattled company. Looking for ways to diversify, they were spending on costly projects and consultants that seemed of dubious value. When other executives questioned Ruhe about UPI's financial status, he airily brushed them off.

''Don't worry,'' he would say. ''We'll take care of it. . . . We're working on it. . . . We've got a handle on it. . . . Money's no problem.''

Fred Greene knew money was a problem, a deadly problem. He groaned as he realized in December that the $5 million Scripps provided already was gone. Indeed, auditors would determine that, for the seven months from the sale date until the end of 1982, UPI's cash flow was even worse than Rob Small and Overgaard had guessed. Operating losses were $5.95 million, almost a million more than the start-up capital Scripps had provided in June. Its cash exhausted, UPI was beginning to rely on delaying payments to vendors and on hand-to-mouth collections from clients.

Seeing the company's financial condition deteriorate, Greene and chief financial officer Tom Haughney began to openly challenge Ruhe.

"We're running out of money," Greene warned Ruhe on one occasion.

Ruhe shrugged nonchalantly. "Looks like I'm going to have to throw another $5 million into this outfit."

Greene would not sit still for that kind of braggadocio, even from his boss.

"Wait a second," he shot back. "You never put the first $5 million in!"

Haughney, who earlier had confronted Ruhe about his plans to borrow money from UPI, soon found himself in his boss's office, stunned to hear accusations that he had been an indifferent manager who had failed to produce monthly financial statements.

Haughney told Ruhe that, despite the bookkeeping nightmare that was UPI's accounting system, he had regularly produced monthly financial statements. He angrily gathered up the past statements, circled Ruhe's name to show it had been on the distribution list, and plopped them on his boss's desk. Nonetheless, Ruhe continued telling other UPI executives that Haughney had been derelict.

Haughney was reassigned, his financial duties turned over to treasurer Bill Ahlhauser. Ruhe's loyal Baha'i friend would be far less an obstacle on future money decisions.

• • •

During Scripps's paternalistic reign, no matter how sick or unproductive veteran Unipressers became, the company always had found ways to keep paychecks coming. Employees soon would learn that such generosity had ended June 2, 1982. No longer able to ignore imprecations from Dick Farkas and Fred Greene, Ruhe and Geissler responded to the worsening cash situation by purging forty-five nonunion employees, saving $1.5

million. Nearly all of those who suddenly were booted out the door were veterans, mainly low-paid office managers, mailroom workers, and secretaries. Six months removed from Scripps's protective embrace, the layoffs sent a stark message to Unipressers worldwide.

Ken Braddick, never a favorite of fellow Unipressers, knew he was viewed as lord high executioner. Unipressers had few doubts from the list of layoff victims that old scores were being settled and imagined slights redressed. Ted Marks, former assistant to Rod Beaton and Braddick's successor as Northeast Division vice president, had treated Ruhe with cool diffidence in their first meeting. He was fired. So was John DePrez, the satellite chief who had sharply disagreed with Ruhe on communications.

Dorothy Ohliger, sixty-two, a thirty-seven-year veteran who earned less than $15,000 a year as UPI's Washington office manager, sat in stunned disbelief as vice president Grant Dillman imparted the news. For all her years with the company she would receive thirteen weeks' severance pay. Ohliger finally found refuge with the "old family," securing a clerical job in the Scripps Howard bureau in Washington.

Southwest Division vice president Travis Hughs flew to Denver and, at Stapleton Airport, fired regional sales executive Lee Hamann. Returning to Dallas, Hughs spotted Bill Lyon, vice president for newspictures, standing in the first-class passengers' line at the American Airlines counter.

Lyon, talented but blunt, opinionated and prickly, had racked up a lot of enemies, among them Braddick, and, more recently, Ruhe.

"Did you get it too?" Hughs asked, almost rhetorically.

"I got it," Lyon snapped, "and if they can fire me, I can fly back first-class!"

Ruhe and Geissler, still in their thirties, reportedly had mocked the "grayhairs," longtime Unipressers they felt were blocking needed changes. Shortly after the firings, Lyon, who later would become a top photo executive at AP, joined thirteen others in an age discrimination suit against UPI.

George Muldowney, a twenty-eight-year veteran union activist who supervised the New York mailroom, watched warily as fellow clerical workers were dismissed.

Just when he thought he had escaped, he was summoned to Greene's office. Greene was badly shaken as he delivered the news. Muldowney, though for years a thorn in the company's side because of his union activities, was "family."

Never had there been such a housecleaning. Times sure had changed at UPI.

• • •

Enthralled with being in the limelight again, John Jay Hooker was determined not to fail—not after Minnie Pearl, not after his aborted political career. His ego just wouldn't permit it. He began to pump the telephones, contacting old friends and acquaintances and searching for potential investors who could save UPI.

He faced an immediate obstacle. Hooker knew it would be nigh impossible to attract cash unless investors could be assured of a major voice in UPI's destiny. When Hooker asked Ruhe and Geissler if they would be willing to sell their controlling interest, he was dismayed at the response.

"We'd rather not," Ruhe said. "There might be circumstances under which we would, but we'd rather not."

Ruhe told Hooker that UPI's savior would be acclaimed a hero, and he'd rather not share that with an outside investor.

"Doug, it doesn't make any difference whose capital you use," Hooker said. "Just get it done."

"Look," Ruhe replied, "I think in order to get full credit for a turnaround, you gotta' do it yourself."

At Ruhe's insistence Hooker agreed to seek investors on the owners' terms, but doubted he would succeed. He believed UPI needed an infusion of between $8 million and $15 million. Who would risk that kind of money and take a back seat to men who hadn't invested a dime?

As UPI's cash position worsened, Ruhe decided to sell off assets. He and Geissler directed Braddick to draw up a possible shopping list. It would have made veteran Unipressers cringe. Included were some irreplaceable services, threads of UPI's very fabric that were vital if the company ever hoped to diversify: The photo library of 11.5 million negatives dating back to before the Civil War; its cable TV news service; UPITN, a television news service for independent stations; its partnership with Knight-Ridder in a commodity news service; its stock-price quotation service; and its enormously prestigious worldwide photo service. Braddick and others already had begun shopping around pieces of UPI's kingdom. In their single-minded determination to hang on to UPI, Ruhe and Geissler seemed willing to risk long-term damage for short-term expedience.

Ruhe wanted the best of both worlds. He believed that by negotiating joint venture deals for UPI's assets he could raise vital cash, maintain a piece of the action, and turn over to someone else responsibility for developing new products. That philosophy was evident in his dealings with Jim West, who almost three decades earlier had begun to provide newspapers with ready-to-print TV program listings. Ruhe first met West on Friday, August 13, in his office, and when the two hit it off, Ruhe hired him on the spot as a $7,500-a-month consultant assigned to help shave UPI's communications costs. In the ensuing weeks their relationship flourished. At times it seemed Ruhe was closer to West than he was to Bill Geissler.

On November 18, during a visit to Dallas, West told his old Unipresser friend Travis Hughs that Ruhe had encouraged him to spin off assets to set up joint ventures that might lead to new profit centers.

"Let's figure out what we can spin off," West told Hughs. "Doug is absolutely convinced that the only way to make money out of UPI is to spin off the good parts. And he doesn't mind splitting the profits."

• • •

Although Hooker abhorred Ruhe's plans to sell off UPI's assets, his efforts to sway his partner were gentle, not confrontational.

"You know, Doug, you're like Charles Lindbergh," Hooker said. "If you crossed the Atlantic, you'd want to get a couple of chocolate bars, load the plane with gas, aim it east, and stick your head out.

"But me, I'm a first-class guy. I would have gone on a 747 and been up in the first-class section."

Hooker felt if he could start Ruhe thinking "first-class," the owner might begin to comprehend that only big outside money could end UPI's twenty-year drought.

Hooker's preoccupation with going first-class came so naturally that he would motion, almost subconsciously, to UPI executives to fetch his bags as he headed for a hotel or an airport. Despite their efforts to avoid becoming his high-priced redcap, one or another always seemed to find himself trekking resentfully behind, carrying Hooker's luggage.

Hooker usually traveled by limo, UPI footing the bill. On one occasion, in the lobby bar of the Hotel Harley, he realized he was late for an appointment. Hooker paid for both his wine and the glass, climbed into his waiting limo, and instructed, "Driver, drive on."

He carried the first-class joke to extreme, mocking Ruhe and Geissler for taking economy flights between New York and Nashville and having to fold their lanky frames into the narrow coach seats.

"Doug, us entrepreneurial-type guys have to fly first-class. You meet a better class of prospects. Let me tell you a story. When ah was in the chicken business ah was taking the Red-Eye from Los Angeles to New York. There was only one other guy in first-class. By the time we were over Kansas City, ah had sold him eighteen franchises. Ah knew the only way ah wasn't gonna sell that guy was if he jumped out of the plane."

To silence Hooker, Ruhe and Geissler finally tried a first-class flight. But on the bigger issue of relinquishing control of UPI to new investors, Doug Ruhe would not budge.

• • •

Trying to solidify his position and pump life into UPI, Hooker turned to old Tennessee friends and business acquaintances. Just two weeks after Sonny Rawls interviewed him for *The New York Times*, Hooker sounded Rawls out about replacing H.L. Stevenson as editor.

Many newspaper executives remembered the collapse of his Minnie Pearl fried-chicken empire and the SEC probe. Hooker felt hiring a respected editor might allay the industry concerns over his involvement with UPI.

Ruhe and Geissler, anxious to be rid of the independent-minded Stevenson, liked the idea. On March 16 the three met with Rawls for half a day at the Hyatt Regency in Atlanta. Rawls seemed interested, and they agreed to talk further.

Urgently looking to lure big investors, Hooker began discussions with Marvin Josephson, a successful businessman whose company owned the *Captain Kangaroo* kiddie television show. John Jay also approached old friends Karl Eller of Gannett and Raymond Mason of Charter Company, Inc., both of whom had earlier joined him in talks with Scripps about buying UPI.

Mason and his son-in-law, Tom Moody, seemed more than casually interested. Hooker felt Mason, who had bought the Philadelphia *Bulletin* through a division of his high-flying Charter Oil Company, was the kind of high-rolling entrepreneur UPI needed. At a Kentucky Derby party at Churchill Downs, Hooker had witnessed Mason casually borrow $100 million for a business venture.

After introducing Ruhe and Geissler to Mason at New York's posh Pierre Hotel, Hooker soon grew convinced that Charter's insurance subsidiary was seriously interested. But Mason got negative reports from a financial analyst he sent to look over UPI, and his enthusiasm further waned when he learned Ruhe wanted to use his money but was adamant about retaining operating control.

Hooker was frustrated. He felt the owners were being unreasonable in refusing to consider an outright sale. But he did not give up. He also phoned Marty Davis, chairman of Gulf and Western, which had gone into the publishing business.

"The problem here is, UPI could go down the drain. We need more than one wire service," Hooker said. "This is something you could do for your country." Unfortunately, Davis's business acumen prevailed over this fervent appeal to patriotism.

Fred Greene handed Hooker yet another prospect, Thomas Wise of the New York investment banking firm Lazard-Frères. Wise, who himself had tried to get UPI from Scripps, introduced Hooker to senior executives of the prestigious firm.

As winter's snows began melting, Hooker grew increasingly distraught over Ruhe's intransigence. One weekend at a party in New York, Hooker cornered Geissler. Later relating the incident to associates, Hooker said he tried to gently sound out his partner.

"Look, Bill, what are we going to do? Doug has one view, ah've got another. If we don't change our course, we are going to be like the *Titanic* and run into an iceberg. We got a chance now to solve the problem before it's too late. How do you feel about it?"

"I want to save it," Geissler said, "regardless of what steps we have to take."[2]

Hooker was surprised. Perhaps Ruhe and Geissler did not always walk in lockstep. Still, he sensed Geissler would not turn against his domineering partner.

Finally, Hooker took his concerns to Ruhe.

---

[2]Geissler denied making the remark.

"What we need is a navigator," Hooker said. "We need to know where we are and how far it is to safety. Who's navigator?"

"I'm the navigator," Ruhe replied.

Hooker's heart sank. With Ruhe at the helm, he believed, UPI would always founder. Why was Ruhe so obdurate, unwilling to listen to reason? What was driving the man?

Hooker was torn. He could see UPI deteriorating by the day, and he was making little headway with his partners. Yet, Hooker reveled in being chairman of UPI, and his obsession with succeeding was beginning to overwhelm logic. He saw this as a chance, at last, to compensate for his political and business setbacks with a triumph that would preserve an important journalistic institution. And, even better, if he could pull it off he might make some money.

Cash was growing perilously short, and Ruhe pressed ahead with his efforts to sell some UPI assets. Hooker protested that would be akin to "cutting the cat's tail off an inch at a time." Nonetheless, Ruhe arranged a meeting with Reuters, which long had coveted parts of UPI's international operation. The booming, British-based news agency particularly wanted UPI's newspictures service; it had none of its own.

More than three decades earlier, the United Press had pioneered the concept of transmitting newspictures from around the world to match its stories. Now Ruhe was suggesting a possible retreat to cover the annual $3 million cash drain from UPI's European operations.

In March a four-member UPI contingent met with top Reuters executives Mike Nelson and Peter Holland at the Parker Meridien Hotel overlooking Central Park. Hooker seized the moment to describe, in flowery full-drawl, his vision for UPI. The Brits sat bemused. Never had they encountered his like.

"This is a $100 million company now, but it's going to be a billion-dollar company," Hooker boasted.

Then, without warning, he launched into his story about the Greyhound chairman and the pay toilet.

Nelson, a proper Englishman who might have come straight from central casting in London, was baffled until Holland explained, "He means a loo, where you have to pay to get in."

Not missing a beat, Hooker declared, "Well, that's what we're lookin' for here. We're lookin' for UPI's pay toilet."

If Hooker's down-home analogies precipitated minor culture shock, the Brits were not dissuaded from offering $5 million for UPI's foreign picture service. Back at the office to brief Geissler and other executives, Hooker paced the room, asking, "What do you think? What do you think?"

Bill Small and international vice president Claude Hippeau said they were unalterably opposed, arguing that a picture wire could give Reuters a foothold on the U.S. market. Yet everyone knew UPI was struggling to meet payroll and that Ruhe and Geissler had yet to pull off any of their promised deals.

"Look, it comes down to this," Fred Greene said. "You can get maybe $12 million from these people if they're really serious."

He also suggested UPI could probably work out some cost-cutting arrangement to swap pictures for foreign news coverage.

"But you heard everybody. It's not the thing for us to do. We'll lose control."

Pointedly, Greene asked Ruhe, "Do you have money to put into the company? Because we're out of money."

Ruhe dusted off his standard reassurance.

"Money's not a problem."

"If money's not a problem," Greene said, "then don't do it."

"I can come up with $10 million any time I have to," Ruhe said.

"All right, fine," Greene replied, skeptically. "But if you can't come up with the money, we're about not to be able to pay our bills."

Reuters was politely turned away—for now.

• • •

Soon after at LaGuardia Airport, Hooker spotted a potential answer to UPI's dilemma—his older brother, Henry. Hooker felt his brother had the business experience and background to raise the kind of money needed to bail out UPI. Sharing a cab into the city, he told Henry he had bait dangling at Lazard-Frères and with other potential investors and urged him to become involved. Next morning Henry found himself listening to Ruhe and Geissler enthusiastically pitch UPI's turnaround prospects.

When Henry returned from a trip to Europe, he found John Jay even more pumped up about bringing him into the deal.

"Wait a minute, John Jay," Henry said, cautiously. "Let's find out what's happening."

He asked to see UPI's financials, concerned that although Ruhe and Geissler raved that their treasurer was a genius, Bill Ahlhauser had yet to produce a business plan.

Henry sought out Greene, keeper of the books.

"Has anybody here really got a handle on this thing? I've been hearing only happy talk on the cash flow."

"No," Greene replied bluntly. "It's a real mess."

In fact, Greene told Hooker, he was so disillusioned with UPI's aimless foundering that he was job hunting.

While Ruhe and Geissler were out of town, the Hookers also met with Tom Haughney and Jim West, who told them they felt UPI needed a big investor to help finance the switch to satellites.

The Hookers asked Fred Frick, their friend from the Nashville office of Price Waterhouse, to check UPI's books and prepare a business plan while they continued to search for possible investors.

When Ruhe learned of the behind-the-scenes meetings, he was irritated. Just as he had been suspicious of Rob Small and Cordy Overgaard, even of Richard Farkas, now a few weeks later he feared the Hookers were trying to seize control of UPI themselves.

Actually, Henry was less than enthusiastic about John Jay's determined attempts to tap his business skills and money-raising prowess. At a dinner with Ruhe, Geissler, and Henry in early April at the Belle Mead restaurant in Nashville, John Jay bluntly urged the owners to split their 60 percent stock four ways and bring Henry in as a partner.

Ruhe was cool to the idea. Even Henry was taken aback. After dinner Henry pulled his brother aside and told him UPI was a lousy risk.

"Look, John Jay, don't get me any of this stock, and you'd better start considering whether you want to be there yourself."

Underscoring Henry's concern was a bleak assessment from Fred Frick. "We like to say 'nothing's hopeless,' " Frick told Henry in a phone call from New York. "But these guys are hopeless, and you've got to get out."

Frick complained he couldn't come up with sufficient numbers to determine exactly what was happening at UPI, much less construct a business plan.

Frick also cautioned John Jay: "Don't do this. This thing is too far gone."

John Jay Hooker was shaken by the warnings. He loved his new high-profile role, but respected Henry's business judgment and Frick's numbers-reading ability. And he had no intention of presiding over another failure. He was starting to lose sleep. During a visit to Washington he sought counsel from John Seigenthaler, who doubled as editorial page editor of *USA TODAY*. After breakfast at the Watergate Hotel, Hooker and Seigenthaler strolled along the Potomac.

"Look," Seigenthaler said, "you can't let this drive you crazy. You're going to have to go on with your life. Either it's going to work out or it's not going to work out. But you have no business losing all this sleep when you have absolutely nothing invested in it except a helluva lot of time."

But for Hooker, the prestige of his job as chairman and his deep feelings for UPI meant more than just money.

"Goddammit, ah just love it," he told his pal. "Ah just absolutely love it, and ah would like to be able to do it."

Soothingly, Seigenthaler assured Hooker that even if he had to leave UPI, time would heal the scars.

• • •

During the second week of April, with Ruhe and Geissler again out of town, the Hookers once more converged on Fred Greene. Henry, who couldn't bear to see his brother wounded again, was determined to get all the answers about UPI's finances.

Greene held nothing back. "If you look at the numbers, there are savings that can be made," he said. "But you need about $25 million for new equipment."

Greene said UPI could save on ribbons, paper, and printers by delivering its news directly into subscriber computers. But that would mean shelling out millions to help clients upgrade receiving systems, to replace UPI's own dilapidated equipment, and to invest in expensive new photo transmitters and printers.

Ruhe was angry when he learned of the meeting. Increasingly impatient with Greene's candor about UPI's precarious finances, he marched into the controller's office.

"I heard you talked to the Hookers."

"Yeah, John's the chairman," Greene said. "He called me in."

Glowering, Ruhe asked, "Do you mind telling me what you talked about?"

Greene said, straightforwardly, that he had thoroughly briefed the

Hookers about UPI's dire straits. Ruhe stomped out without another word. Soon after, Henry phoned Ruhe to tell him he had urged his brother to resign. Henry told Ruhe he was skeptical that an investor could be found, and that he felt his brother had joined without fully comprehending the severity of UPI's problems. Further, if UPI were added to his brother's litany of business and political failures, John Jay might be left an emotional wreck.

Seeing that John Jay still was clinging to his dream, Henry leaned hard on him to quit.

"You know, John, you've gone under once before, and this outfit's going to go under. You don't want to be connected to this."

Ruhe was hardly dismayed by the prospect of Hooker's departure. Good riddance, he thought. Hooker had failed to produce on his boasts that he could bring in investment capital, and he seemed to be angling to take over UPI himself. He felt the "chay-ah-man" had become more trouble than he was worth.

Ruhe told Geissler, "I think John Jay's going to split. I think he's frightened and he wants to get out."

Geissler was distressed. Hooker's departure, so soon after Small and Overgaard, would underscore UPI's instability.

* * *

On Wednesday, April 13, the Hookers sat in John Jay's suite at the Grand Hyatt, debating well into the night. Trying to persuade his brother to step down, Henry said he was worried that Ruhe and Geissler did not understand the depth of UPI's financial miseries. Besides, he told his brother, you'll never be more than a figurehead.

Suddenly the phone rang. It was Warren Beatty, about to leave for Europe.

"Ah probably ought to go over there and get you some attention," John Jay teased his Hollywood pal. "Look, Warren, you're just a local movie star. Ah'm the chay-ah-man of United Press International."

The line crackled with their laughter.

But when Hooker hung up, reality again closed in. Should he remain the "chay-ah-man" or should he quit?

Even after Henry left, Hooker wrestled with his problem. Finally, awake in bed at 3 a.m., he remembered his December promise to Ruhe and Geissler:

"You'll make more money and have more fun with me in the deal than without me."

At last he had his answer. It was their deal, not his. They weren't having much fun, and certainly weren't making more money. At dawn he rang Henry and Tom Haughney and invited them for room-service breakfast.

"You know, it's not do-able," he told them. "These fellows have let me in the deal. It's their deal. It's so complicated. . . . Ah think ah'm going to leave."

Before informing his partners, Hooker decided to close a deal he had worked out for UPI to pay a quarter million dollars to economists John Naisbitt and Michael Evans, authors of the best-seller *Megatrends*, to write columns for the wire service. He joined Ruhe and Geissler in Washington on Thursday, April 14, to sign the deal.

Later, over a glass of wine in a Washington restaurant, Hooker informed his partners he was leaving.

"Fellows, ah appreciate what y'all have done for me. You've sold me a third interest and you've made me chay-ah-man of the board of a great company, and ah deeply appreciate that.

"But ah don't want to stay and be a divisive influence. You've been partners for a long time. We have serious differences of opinion as to how to make the company survive. And since y'all were the ones who let me in, ah feel if somebody has to go it should be me."

Geissler, who liked Hooker and understood the effect his quick and sudden departure would have on UPI, grew emotional. But Ruhe just listened quietly.

Hooker excused himself and went to the men's room, leaving the owners to ponder the implications. When he returned Ruhe said, "If that's the way you feel. that's the way you feel."

Then, as he had with Overgaard and Small, he bluntly asked Hooker to return his stock.

"Sure," Hooker, southern gentleman to the end, replied without hestitation.

The three agreed to write a joint statement declaring the parting amicable. Hooker also promised to continue to be alert for possible investors. Then he phoned his brother in Nashville.

"The deed's done, Henry. On to the next subject."

Although he had made his decision, Hooker still couldn't resist one last approach.

"Look, ah still love it and would like to buy it," he told Geissler over the phone. "Ah think ah could raise a few million dollars."

But Geissler had closed ranks with Ruhe. "We're not interested," he replied curtly.[3] Trying to forestall adverse publicity, Geissler persuaded Hooker to allow UPI to include in its press release announcing his departure his offer to buy a 51 percent interest.

At day's end Hooker and Seigenthaler went to National Airport to hop a plane for Nashville. They arrived to discover the flight was full, and Hooker had no ticket. He would have to await the next flight.

The last thing Seigenthaler saw before the plane took off was a devastated John Jay Hooker, close to tears, standing alone at American Airlines' Gate 9.

• • •

Hooker, back in New York a couple of days later to fetch his belongings and say good-bye, knew well the crisis looming for UPI. The company was out of money, the life raft needed air—and, worse yet, Doug Ruhe was still the navigator. Hooker summoned Bill Small and Fred Greene, feeling obliged to at least warn them of what might lie ahead.

"Fellows," Hooker said,"ah've been bankrupt and ah'm gonna tell you, you as the president and you as the controller are goin' to be in deep trouble if you're not careful. Because, sooner or later, they're not going to pay their payroll taxes."

Small and Greene shuddered. Hooker was warning them that they could be personally liable if UPI did not pass on to the IRS the income taxes it was deducting from employee paychecks.

Hooker also bade a warm farewell to Bill Adler, UPI's publicity man.

What went wrong, Adler asked? Why are you leaving?

Hooker shrugged and drawled enigmatically:

"The room was too warm, and the soup was too cold."

---

[3]Ruhe and Geissler denied that they ever rejected a serious offer for a controlling interest in UPI. But other UPI executives said most sale talks in 1983 and 1984 never reached a serious stage because the owners insisted on retaining control.

8
· · ·
Limping Badly

No one ached more over UPI's cash squeeze than Fred Greene. In the spring of 1983 the depressing evidence was piling up, day after day, in the big double drawer of his desk.

The company's computerized accounting system was programmed, as bills became due, to print payment checks to hundreds of creditors. Now, with the tank perilously close to empty, Greene put a hold on the checks that had spewed from the computer. Each day he carefully wrapped them in envelopes, marked the date, and tucked them in the double drawer, where they would remain until he was certain they would not bounce.

The drawer filled rapidly—$100,000, then $500,000, then $750,000 worth of unmailed payments. Before long the painful arithmetic hidden in Greene's desk totaled hundreds of checks worth some $1 million. The veteran controller, recalling the "good old days" when Scripps paid the bills on time, agonized as the vendors who provided vital equipment, supplies, and services began pressing for payment.

He thought about approaching Bill Ahlhauser, treasurer and chief financial officer, to discuss the problem. But Ahlhauser, even with his Harvard business degree and experience with the Big Eight accounting firm of Touche Ross, did not seem overly concerned about UPI's financial plight. In fact, while bills languished he had ordered Greene to earmark scarce funds for Ruhe's pet projects. Greene decided to brace Tom Haughney, now charged with trying to arrange loans and find investors willing to accept minority partner status.

"Tom, are you coming up with new money or making any plans for bankruptcy?" Greene asked.

"What are you talking about?"

"Tom, we can't mail these," said Greene, brandishing a fistful of the past-due checks.

Struggling to stay optimistic, Haughney hollowly reassured Greene it was inconceivable UPI could go bankrupt.

An outside auditor advised Greene and his staff to reprogram the computer so it would stop producing checks when there were no funds. Greene knew that, with or without the damning evidence in his desk drawer, UPI was in deep financial trouble. No matter how you juggled and finagled, the bills kept inexorably pouring in.

• • •

Despite John Jay Hooker's announced departure in mid-April and although he had cleaned out his desk, even now he couldn't quite bring himself to cut the umbilical cord. Bereft of his title and working from his suite at the Grand Hyatt, he continued to operate as a sort of offstage apparition, seeking investors and hoping Ruhe and Geissler would relent and sell him the company. Still deeply depressed, Hooker would visit Tom Haughney's office or join him for lunch to exchange frustrating stories about UPI's slide. Like Don Quixote, he sought new windmills, even though he sensed his cause was hopeless.

Several times, without success, Hooker asked Ruhe and Geissler to reconsider his purchase offer. When they encouraged him to continue seeking investors, Hooker took Ruhe to the midtown Manhattan office of Marvin Josephson in the Squibb Building. Josephson, whose talent and literary agency represented news commentators, also owned eight radio stations. He had indicated to Hooker and Bill Small that he might be willing to invest $15 million.

Again, Ruhe made it abundantly clear that he had no intention of relinquishing control. Josephson told Hooker privately, "Look, this is a troubled situation. I'm just not prepared to invest unless I am in charge of my own money."

Once more Ruhe's intransigence had frightened off a potential investor.

Hooker also talked to Nashville businessman George Gillett and fielded a few phone calls from New Hampshire entrepreneur Max Hugel, who had resigned as CIA covert operations chief amid allegations from two former associates that he had engaged in insider stock trading.

Finally, late in May, Hooker acknowledged his maverick quest was lost, closed the book on his UPI fling, and headed home to Nashville. Eccentricities and showboating aside, his departure so soon after Overgaard and Rob Small underscored UPI's continuing chaos.

Less than a year after acquiring the company, Ruhe and Geissler were embattled. Hooker's leave-taking left them alone at the top, isolated and worriedly watching UPI's debts soar. They had stubbornly ignored repeated warnings from Hooker and, before him, Small and Overgaard, to bring in fresh money and to impose severe austerity measures. By refusing to loosen their grip on the company, the owners had sharply narrowed their options. The tighter and longer they would cling to UPI, scraping for cash, the dimmer would be the company's hopes.

• • •

In UPI bureaus, ignorance was bliss. Ruhe and Geissler were maintaining an optimistic facade that convinced most of the work force their company was on a turnaround course. The owners opened several new bureaus and cranked out press releases hailing $8 million in "new business" in the first quarter of 1983. Indeed, UPI had signed Newhouse to a five-year, $9 million contract that increased from thirteen to seventeen the number of its papers subscribing. With the *Philadelphia Inquirer*'s signing the year before, UPI now was serving the nation's twenty-three largest papers. Ruhe and Geissler talked glowingly of not only stemming the erosion of UPI's critical newspaper client base, but even adding to the total of about 800 dailies.

Unipressers around the world were doing more than their share. Unaware of the crisis gripping the executive suite, staffers cheered a string of triumphs on major news stories, victories that were helping the sales push. Over the years it had not been uncommon for UPI to break ahead on major stories, only to be overwhelmed in succeeding days by AP's sheer numerical advantage. While that still was a problem, UPI's

enthusiastic coverage was grabbing the attention of the nation's editors
—even the top brass at AP, who liked to pretend there really was no
wire service rivalry.

On September 14, 1982, reacting instinctively on opposite sides of
the Mediterranean, UPI correspondents pounced almost simultaneously
on two breaking stories. First, a bulletin interrupted the UPI wires announcing that Princess Grace of Monaco, the former Grace Kelly, had
died of a brain hemorrhage after her car plunged down an embankment
on a steep mountain road and burst into flames. Moments later came
another bulletin. Lebanese president-elect Beshir Gemayel had been as-
sassinated in a bombing that demolished the Christian Phalangist headquarters in East Beirut, flinging his nation into turmoil. UPI broke well
ahead of AP, its victory even sweeter because the competition first reported Gemayel had survived the blast.

Three days later the Christian Phalangists retaliated for the bombing.
Sweeping through Sabra and Chatilla, two camps in southern Beirut, they
massacred 700 to 800 Palestinian refugees. UPI foreign correspondents
Walter Wisniewski and Jack Redden, both dispatched to Beirut, were
among the first journalists allowed into the camp. But like the rest of the
reporters who had converged on the scene, they were stymied by a communications cutoff. For hours the world was ignorant of the bloodshed.
Wisniewski finally reached an Israeli command post and a telephone and
dictated a story. UPI's scoop was exclusive for so long that newspapers
and networks doubted its accuracy. But it was true, and for their work
Wisniewski and Redden won the coveted Overseas Press Club Award.

UPI's Washington bureau early in 1983 swarmed over allegations
that the Enviromental Protection Agency was awash in political appointees
closely tied to industry. As the scandal enveloped the Reagan White
House, Bill Small exulted. The TV networks and major newspapers were
chasing underdog UPI on stories exposing the activities of EPA chief
Anne Burford and her top lieutenants.

Unipressers, convinced their news report was competitive and delighted with the promises by Ruhe and Geissler that they soon would
attain pay parity with the AP, had no idea that the owners were struggling
to cover their paychecks.

Fred Greene knew the truth. And he became more alarmed when he
dissected some of the group sales agreements and found that the new
contracts fell far short of the owners' boasts. The addition of four New-

house papers would increase revenues only toward the end of the contract. As an enticement to get Newhouse to sign a long-term agreement, UPI had agreed to rewrite the existing contract and give the other thirteen papers a short-term rate cut worth hundreds of thousands of dollars. Greene considered that sheer folly. UPI didn't need money down the road. It needed it now.

Further, while such "sales incentives" were helping bring aboard new clients and contributing to the illusion that UPI was humming right along, they also had triggered controversy. Angry editors at two important clients, *The Dallas Morning News* and *The Denver Post*, protested the low introductory rates, which they said violated UPI's promise of a uniform pricing structure. They announced they were abrogating the contracts they had signed in the Scripps years at much higher rates than newcomers were paying. Will Jarrett, editor of the *Post*, in a slap at the owners, declared, "I didn't sign a contract with these gentlemen."

Jarrett was hardly alone in expressing discomfort with Ruhe and Geissler. In signing the group contract with UPI, Newhouse executive David Starr had even tried to avoid being photographed with them. To his dismay, they elbowed their way into the picture.

UPI executives were reluctant to further alienate the Denver and Dallas newspapers, but knew they had to take a stand or face a run of cancellations. Lawyers prepared breach-of-contract suits, and UPI vocally defended the discounts as merely an introductory offer.

• • •

On May 10, seated on a platform in a large room in a Denver hotel, Ruhe and Geissler peered out at the powerhouses of the newspaper business attending the annual convention of the American Society of Newspaper Editors. Many delegates eagerly awaited their first close-up look at the enigmatic men who had controlled UPI for almost a year. Ruhe and Geissler faced perhaps their biggest test: they could win over a skeptical audience or fail miserably and prove their detractors correct.

In the crowd sat H.L. Stevenson, UPI's editor for a decade, a seasoned veteran who greeted editors by their nicknames. But Ruhe and Geissler, who were quietly looking for a new editor, did not even bother to invite Stevenson to join them on stage. Also absent was president Bill Small, back in New York with the flu. Recently departed chairman John Jay Hooker was in the audience but relegated to the sidelines. Without those three, who could have helped immeasurably, Ruhe and Geissler were sitting ducks.

Creed Black, ASNE president and editor of the Lexington, Kentucky, *Herald-Leader*, opened with this zinger: "I wish I could say our speakers need no introduction. Unfortunately, they do."

That would prove the high point for UPI's owners.

A panel of questioners included David Starr of Newhouse and *Denver Post* editor Will Jarrett.

Jarrett pulled no punches.

"What can you provide newspaper editors that the Associated Press cannot?" he asked.

That gave the owners a golden opportunity to score a touchdown with a fervent defense of their wire service. But while Stevenson and many UPI loyalists in the audience watched in horror, Ruhe fumbled on the goal line.

"Well, I think that's one of our problems, that when you study the services they're very similar," he said.

The editors, particularly those spending money on both AP and UPI, couldn't believe their ears. These guys couldn't articulate the unique qualities of their own company! Ruhe and Geissler tried, with even less success, to answer questions dealing with their reasons for buying UPI, Hooker's departure, and the wire service's mounting losses.

Up popped Paul Janensch of Louisville, executive editor of the *Courier-Journal* and the Louisville *Times*.

"I don't want to appear antagonistic toward UPI," he said. "As a matter of fact, I used to work for UPI some years ago in Chicago. I think you blew an opportunity in failing to answer Will Jarrett's first question, which was, in effect, why should a paper . . . take UPI? I'll give you another opportunity to answer."

Rarely do the condemned receive such a reprieve. It did Ruhe and Geissler no good.

"Well, the, uh—60 percent of the copy is different between AP and UPI," Ruhe said. "They're actually different. There's different information, different news is covered on the two wires. . . . That study was done awhile ago. I don't know exactly what it is presently. I think that the, that the answer to that is that—a—either for competitive reasons to be able to cover, to have coverage of everything—b—to uh, to uh—

you know, we beat AP—of course, it doesn't make any difference. . . .
In many cities it's a one-newspaper town, the fact that, uh, it's later or
earlier coming in on one wire or the other makes little difference. It's a
tough question to answer, and to be honest with you, it's one of the
reasons UPI has lost business.''

Geissler, plagued by a slight stutter, sprang to assist his faltering
partner.

"I'd like, uh, I'd uh, I'd like to take a crack at that,'' he said.
"Actually, it is, uh, a complex question. . . . I mean, uh, obviously we
think that we, uh, have a strong and competitive service. In many states,
we are, we are stronger. We have, uh, we have our state reports, and
our regional reports are stronger, and they're known to be stronger. We
have market share in those states—''

Black interrupted, mercifully ending their public humiliation. Leaving
the room, the editors who provided UPI its lifeline were abuzz. The
owners had fallen smack on their duffs.

Three days later a *New York Times* report on the meeting noted,
"Without exception, editors interviewed after the session said they were
convinced that Mr. Ruhe and Mr. Geissler did not know enough about
newspapers to make it worthwhile to subscribe to the service.''

Robert Maynard, editor and publisher of *The Oakland Tribune*, was
quoted that UPI's new owners had "shot themselves in all four feet with
one bullet.''

• • •

UPI executives, including Bill Small, found themselves fielding calls
from editors across the country. Some were angry, some curious, some
solicitous.

Tony Insolia, editor of the prestigious Long Island newspaper *Newsday*, summoned his old friend, UPI vice president Mike Hughes.

"Jesus Christ, Mike, who are these two turkeys you've got running
the company? How in God's name can we be supportive when your own
owners don't know why we should be buying your service?''

Hughes knew his pal was right, but tried to put the best face on
things.

"Look, these guys are new to the business. They don't know their
way around. Geissler is very shy in public. He stutters a lot and stammers.
He's not good in public. But they have good brains.''

"They have no brains, to go and make a statement like that!" Insolia shot back. Indeed, Ruhe and Geissler had felt uncomfortable throughout the meeting. As Baha'is, neither of them drank, nor were they good at making small talk with strangers at cocktail parties.

While they knew they had bobbled their chance to gain credibility, predictably they shifted much of the blame to UPI's client editors. Ruhe and Geissler were annoyed that, as owners of a private company, they could be subjected to the same scrutiny that might be directed toward the heads of the giant AP cooperative.

Small, who mingled easily in the clubby newspaper atmosphere, saw the need for speedy triage and persuaded them to put him in charge of damage control.

It was Bill Small's big chance to rebound. He had been all but frozen out of the loop since joining UPI, his stature further diminished by the departure of Rob Small and Overgaard. He publicly had kept his distance from the owners, even tweaking them in an interview shortly after his arrival for their habit of working at their desks through their lunch hours.

"I don't eat lunch at my desk," Small disdainfully told a reporter from an industry publication.

Small, whose background was news, not business, generally had been denied all but the skimpiest financial information. He concentrated on decisions affecting the news report, working diligently on budget control while lobbying to reopen bureaus in North Dakota and Alaska to once again give UPI a presence in all fifty states. But he recognized his primary duty: to somehow give Ruhe and Geissler credibility.

Small spent much time on the road, courting major subscribers. He drew up a list of UPI's thirty largest newspaper clients and vowed to visit them all. He also made trips to Europe and South America, taking his wife, Gish, at company expense, under a provision he had negotiated into his contract.

He also visited the *Denver Post* and diplomatically told disgruntled editor Will Jarrett that, no matter how angry he was with UPI, he could not walk away from a valid contract. And in an interview with *Editor and Publisher* he accomplished what the owners had failed to. Under the headline "Judge us by our product, not by our personalities," Small touted UPI's editorial successes and vigorously championed the concept of competing wire services. Slowly, the wave of negative publicity from the Denver fiasco ebbed.

• • •

Tom Haughney was busy searching for a loan to tide UPI over for a few months, but he faced a major hurdle. He needed an accountant's vote of confidence.

For several years the annual outside audit of UPI for the E.W. Scripps Company had contained the explicit qualification that the wire service could stay in business only with aid from Scripps.

Despite the way it sounds, an unqualified audit—that is, one that does not carry an accountant's reservations about the company—was needed or potential lenders and investors might be frightened away. After all the years of receiving only "qualified" ratings under the Scripps regime, auditors now were reluctant to give UPI a clean bill of financial health for fear they might face legal liability if the company failed. Haughney and Ahlhauser knew they needed an "unqualified" rating in the 1982 annual audit in order to attract a loan. So they simply stalled closing the 1982 books, hopping from one Big Eight accounting firm to another searching for someone willing to risk such a rating.

Tom Sinton of Arthur Young and Company seemed the most receptive. But he quickly became nervous when he interviewed Greene, who acknowledged UPI was out of money and revealed that the owners were embellishing in the company's press releases the importance of the new business being signed. When Sinton raised concerns, the owners again were angered by Greene's candor. The controller was unrepentant.

"Tell them to stay away from me," he declared, "but I'm not going to lie to an auditor." Ruhe later denied that Greene ever was pressured to put the best face on UPI's financial difficulties.

The problem with the audit and the delay in closing the books on 1982 prevented the issuance of monthly financial statements at a time when UPI executives desperately needed to track cash flow.

The situation was becoming so tense that UPI's survival at times seemed a week-to-week proposition tied to Braddick's success in selling off parts of the company. A couple of million dollars already had been raised through the sale of two money-losers: the rights to manufacture UPI's Unifax 2 photo transmitting machine and its 25 percent interest in UPITN, a service for non-network television stations, which was sold to joint-venture partner ABC.

Sinton finally was comforted by these stopgap deals and assurances in a series of letters that other assets could be sold. Arthur Young issued an unqualified audit on May 12. Ruhe, now confident that UPI could land a loan, told colleagues that the way things were going the company was just a deal or two away from salvation. The tune would become very familiar.

• • •

UPI's position was disintegrating before the very eyes of its balding, veteran controller. Fred Greene also was disturbed to learn that when Rob Small and Overgaard departed, Ruhe and Geissler had given themselves small pay hikes and had sharply increased the "management fees" they billed to UPI. In March of 1983 alone the owners had transferred more than $100,000 to their Nashville company, Focus Communications, an amount far exceeding their salaries or those of other Focus employees serving UPI.

And at a time when UPI was strapped for cash, Ruhe and Geissler told their top aides they wanted the company headquarters moved out of New York City. Ruhe and Geissler did not like New York or the cost of doing business in Manhattan, which meant they had to shuttle back and forth to Nashville by plane. Besides, UPI was paying $1 million a year rent at the Daily News Building. The owners decided to move corporate headquarters to a Nashville suburb, where it would share office space with Focus, and editorial headquarters to Washington. Ken Braddick had told the owners the Washington move could be accomplished for $1 million, but Greene figured it would cost at least $2.5 million, and communications chief Bob Kelly was even less sanguine.

"If it isn't closer to $4 million, I'll kiss your ass," Kelly told Greene. He knew the complexities of realigning the delicate computer system that carried UPI's news around the world.

Greene knew it was absolutely the worst time to move. Employees would be uprooted, operations disrupted, and huge cost overruns were inevitable.

A UPI loyalist to his very core, Greene could stomach no more. He ended his twenty-seven-year career to accept a job with Reuters, a company he knew had a future. The man most knowledgeable about UPI's finances had defected to a competitor.

• • •

Luis Nogales, watching developments with interest from Los Angeles, where he was now vice president of a big public relations firm, had no inkling things were going downhill at UPI. He was only seeing the outwardly good news in the media and getting gung-ho reports in occasional telephone calls from Doug Ruhe, who had stayed in touch although preliminary job discussions a year earlier had proved fruitless. Shortly after Hooker's departure, Ruhe phoned again.

"I want you to come out again and talk to us, and, hey, join us," Ruhe said.

More than a year since his associates had begged him to find an experienced manager, Ruhe finally was making moves to recruit one.

But this time Nogales was wary. He remembered how he had been kept cooling his heels when he flew to New York the previous summer.

"I want some definition. Like, what am I going to do?"

"Well, you can do whatever you'd like to do," Ruhe replied, casual as ever with his job descriptions.

"Well now, you have a president, so what are we talking about?" Nogales demanded.

"You could be in charge of Latin America . . . or you could come and be kind of the chief administrative guy."

As they talked it became clear to Nogales that Ruhe had little regard for Bill Small. Ruhe also described himself and Geissler as idea men and deal-makers who would set UPI's overall policy direction but had little stomach for the nitty-gritty details of daily management.

Nogales agreed to fly to New York in May. This time he was not kept waiting. Ruhe asked Nogales to meet with Small as a courtesy, warning him that the president probably would eye him as a potential rival.

Indeed, during their forty-five-minute chat, Small made clear he planned to check all Nogales's references. Nogales found it amusing that Small was positioning himself as the one who would decide his fate.

"My relationship is with the owner," he thought, deciding to humor Small.

As the meeting ended, the two shook hands and Small said, "I'll get back to you."

Meeting again with Ruhe, Nogales discussed a title and how to deal with Small. They agreed Nogales would be an executive vice president, reporting directly to Ruhe.

Ruhe had mailed Nogales financial figures that overoptimistically projected UPI's revenues would surge from $100 million to $120 million, and the company boasted of millions of dollars in new sales. Hearing only positive news, nothing about UPI's harsh realities, Nogales theorized that when Ruhe's plans to convert to cheaper satellite transmission bore fruit, UPI could become profitable simply by pruning expenses.

Expediently, Ruhe did not tell Nogales that things were so dismal he had begun stripping assets to meet payroll.

Nogales found Ruhe's job offer seductive. He liked the salary of $85,000 a year, plus a $50,000 incentive bonus should UPI become profitable. The wire service seemed a lively, challenging opportunity, and Nogales persuaded his wife, Mary, to leave California. He phoned Ruhe.

"Great," Nogales said. "Let's go."

* * *

Even before Nogales had come to terms, Ruhe and Geissler intensified their efforts to find a big-name editor in chief to replace thirty-year veteran H.L. Stevenson. Stevenson had never recovered from the poor first impression he made with the owners at the opening meeting at the Harley Hotel. Besides, he had at least three strikes against him: he had his critics, he was too independent to suit Ruhe and Geissler, and he was long an archenemy of Ken Braddick.

Through media consultant Ruth Clark, Geissler had become interested in Australia native Maxwell McCrohon of *The Chicago Tribune*. As the paper's editor, McCrohon had helped the *Tribune* shed the virulent right-wing image of its founder, Colonel Robert McCormick. He boldly had eliminated the *Tribune*'s daily Red-baiting, front-page editorial color cartoon and dropped from the masthead the shameless slogan "World's Greatest Newspaper."

Although the *Tribune* captured several Pulitzer Prizes under Mc-Crohon's stewardship, he had been criticized internally for devoting too much time to special projects. In 1981 he was kicked upstairs to make room for the *Trib*'s brightest young star, *Orlando Sentinel* editor James Squires.

Despite his lofty new title, vice president for news, McCrohon, a former reporter, missed the daily bustle of the newsroom. When Geissler phoned him in the spring of 1983, McCrohon listened receptively as UPI's owner bubbled enthusiastically about the wire service's resurgence.

Finding McCrohon a bit hesitant, Ruhe and Geissler asked Bill Small to help. Small flew to Chicago, and the UPI president, who had developed a reputation for dodging the tab, was treated by McCrohon to lunch. McCrohon had been watching UPI's latest ad campaign in *Editor and Publisher*, with the slick new logo "UPI: One Up On the World." He was impressed by Small's enthusiasm.

"By golly, they *are* beginning to move again," he thought.

McCrohon wheeled a lucrative UPI contract offer past his lawyer and agreed to come aboard for a salary approaching $200,000 by the third year—more than double what Stevenson was paid.

Ruhe and Geissler wasted no time making room for McCrohon. Borrowing a page from the *Tribune*, they created an executive vice president's post for Stevenson. Stevenson, a first-rate newsman who had poured his heart and soul into UPI for three decades, was bitter but hardly surprised to find himself shunted aside.

In a news release on June 28, 1983, Small announced that Stevenson had been named executive vice president/editorial, a post in which he would be involved in expansion and new services.

"We hope to name a new editor in chief soon to free Stevenson to deal with these vital projects," Small said in a burst of corporate double-talk.

• • •

By early summer the company's cash shortage had become so perilous that Ruhe assigned treasurer Bill Ahlhauser to rush the sale of UPI's interest in UNICOM, a British-based financial newswire whose losses were costing UPI tens of thousands of dollars a month.

Ahlhauser and Ken Braddick had put together a deal that would turn over UNICOM to the wire service's partner in the venture, Knight-Ridder Newspapers, for $1 million cash. Racing furiously, Ahlhauser and Braddick sealed the deal on July 13, just in time to cover a payroll.

The outside world, UPI's own employees, and Ruhe's two hot new recruits—Luis Nogales and Max McCrohon—had no idea how close the bullet had come. Ruhe and Geissler had brilliantly shored up UPI's image, even as the company was sinking.

• • •

Nogales arrived at UPI's New York headquarters on schedule in August of 1983 and began educating himself on UPI's complex worldwide operations.

He had been in Manhattan just a week when he was invited to a dinner party at the home of Mary Bundy, wife of former Kennedy White House aide McGeorge Bundy. Mrs. Bundy and Nogales had served together on the board of the Levi Strauss Company.

Also a guest at the Bundys' elegant Manhattan apartment was former CBS executive Fred Friendly, who had recommended his close friend for the UPI presidency.

"Do you work for Bill Small or does he work for you?" Friendly asked bluntly.

Nogales was taken aback. He managed to evade a direct answer, but Friendly persisted.

"Do you report to Bill Small or do you report to somebody else in the company?"

"It all depends on the project and the assignment," replied Nogales, artfully dodging again.

Nogales, no pushover, was not intimidated. But he was struck by two things: Bill Small had some mighty powerful friends and UPI's executive suite seemed a hornet's nest of infighting and intrigue.

• • •

Nogales never had shied from hardship, challenge or confrontation. His had been an extraordinary rise, from migrant fruit picker to the top echelons of the world's second-largest news agency.

No doctors or hospitals were nearby when Nogales was born October 17, 1943, on a dusty roadside near the central California town of Madera. His grandmother acted as midwife.

By age six Nogales was picking grapes with his parents, two sisters, and a brother. The family lived in tents, abandoned stables, or under boxes stacked to form crude lean-tos. In early years he attended a one-room schoolhouse in the tiny town of Manteca, struggling with his broken English to keep up with classmates.

By the time he started high school, his father, Alejandro, had purchased a small house in the border town of Calexico.

Alejandro Nogales made his children's schooling a top priority. He lectured young Luis that not all Mexicans were doomed to die fruit pickers—that one only had to peek across the Mexican border to see Latino doctors, lawyers, and other professionals.

Emily Wogaman, Nogales's teacher when he was a high school freshman, found him shy and timid on the surface, but a boiling cauldron inside. In class Luis decried the working conditions of migrants and demanded to know why Hispanics were treated so poorly.

Like Doug Ruhe, Nogales had learned early about racial bigotry. Towns along the migrant circuit barred Hispanics from swimming pools, restaurants, and service-station restrooms. In Delano, where Cesar Chavez's farm workers union was later born, Nogales as a child was perplexed to be shunted to one side of the movie theater with other Hispanics, blacks, and Filipinos.

Each summer of high school he followed the trail of ripening fruit from Yuma, Arizona, to Huron and Mendota, California. A three-sport star in high school blessed with huge hands, he packed cantaloupes so fast that other workers grew to resent him. Neatly plucking six different sizes from separate bins to place in their proper boxes, he could fill 100 crates in an hour and earn $15. One summer he salted away $4,000 for college tuition.

Towering over most fellow packers, Nogales, a strapping young man, did not shy away from fisticuffs. Working alongside poorly educated whites who taunted his heritage, he often pummeled rednecks who accosted his compadres.

Nogales had decided in high school to become either a teacher or a lawyer, in part because—besides doctors—he knew of no other professional jobs. Pulled toward activism, he decided law was the best way to effect social change.

Nogales enrolled at San Diego State and each year was named best cadet in his Air Force ROTC class. His commencement speaker said, "Here is a name I want you to remember. Luis Nogales. Watch and listen for that name."

While Nogales continued working as an itinerant fruit packer during summer vacations from college, he got his first taste of union activism —a fight to improve the lot of underpaid Hispanic workers. He and other vegetable packers were arrested in Yuma while picketing on a farm, a tense work stoppage that lasted a week as unpicked melons rotted. Finally Nogales and a couple of dozen equally stubborn cohorts were hauled off by sheriff's deputies to spend a night in jail.

At San Diego State, Nogales earned such extraordinary grades that he became the first Rhodes Scholar finalist in the school's history, missing out by one vote. He was accepted at Stanford Law School, fulfilling a lifelong dream. In the Portola Valley, in the shadows of Stanford, his grandparents had picked prunes for twenty-five years on ranches owned by gringos.

Arriving at Stanford at the dawn of the civil rights era, Nogales wasted no time getting involved. He and two friends established the Chicano Student Union and soon rounded up 150 members, although they couldn't recruit Stanford's star Chicano quarterback, Jim Plunkett.

Disturbed at the paucity of Hispanics at Stanford, Nogales also helped form a statewide student group that drafted a plan for pressuring California universities to increase scholarship aid for his people.

Confrontations with school officials were peaceful but blunt. Nogales visited the admissions officials at the Stanford schools of medicine, education, and law, urging more financial aid to Chicano undergraduates.

He composed impassioned treatises on why Stanford should lead in expanding educational opportunities for Hispanics—as one of the foremost private colleges in America, it was an educational treasure that must be racially blind.

The entreaties worked. By the time he received his law degree, Nogales and his cohorts had extracted from Stanford a pledge to grant Hispanics 100 scholarships a year, worth millions of dollars.

Picking and packing summers throughout law school, he graduated in 1969 and took a job as an assistant to Stanford president Dick Lyman, continuing to champion the Hispanic cause. By 1972, when he was selected as a White House fellow under Richard Nixon, Hispanics held 300 scholarships, five faculty posts, and positions in nearly every phase of Stanford's administration.

After his stint at the Interior Department as a White House fellow, Nogales took a job in Los Angeles with Golden West Broadcasters, a rapidly growing media company owned by old cowboy movie star Gene Autry. Nogales worked at the Golden West headquarters in Hollywood on the old Warner Bros. movie lot on Sunset Boulevard. Named director of business affairs, he was the station's lawyer and oversaw personnel decisions. A year later he was named a vice president of Autry's TV station, and soon climbed the corporate ladder. He became a vice president of the entire corporation, then a senior vice president, and finally—still in his mid-thirties—executive vice president and a member of the board.

Nogales continued his social activism, serving on the Los Angeles Community Redevelopment Agency, the California Commission on Higher Education, and on the boards of the Mexican-American Legal Defense Fund and a drug clinic in a Los Angeles barrio.

Perhaps he had risen too quickly to suit John Reynolds, president of the Autry company that had mushroomed to include a dozen radio stations. Reynolds appeared resentful that Nogales, not he, routinely was invited to serve on such major corporations as Levi Strauss and the Bank of California. And it couldn't have helped that Autry, who also owned the California Angels, took a shine to the tall, handsome Nogales and often invited him to Anaheim Stadium for ball games.

Nogales had begun to sense Reynolds's antagonism. When a seat on the board opened with the death of Autry's wife, Ina, Autry summoned both men to his office and told Nogales, "I want you to take Ina's seat." Nogales felt Reynolds stiffen.

So Reynolds promptly turned over to Nogales Golden West's troubled pay TV project. When it continued to lose money and Reynolds was on the hot seat, he responded by firing Nogales. Autry invited Nogales to stay on as a personal assistant, but Nogales was shaken at being terminated. It was the first real setback of his career. Politely declining Autry's offer, he became a partner in a Los Angeles advertising and public relations firm.

Nogales, always an aggressive personality, frequently found himself at odds with his partners and left after two years. He had been working in Los Angeles at the big PR firm Fleishman-Hillard when Ruhe invited him to New York.

Nogales would be stunned to learn that, Doug Ruhe's puffery aside, he was joining a company scrambling to stay alive. Ruhe had managed to conceal from most employees and the outside world a most ominous situation. With their company mired in debt, the owners had alienated much of the publishing industry, committed UPI to enormous expenditures, and repulsed approaches from businessmen who had the experience and the capital to save it. UPI's time was short.

Luis Nogales was about to face the challenge of his life.

9
. . .

Problems, Problems Everywhere

Hardly had Nogales settled into his thirteenth-floor office at UPI's New York headquarters than he began to suspect things weren't as Ruhe had promised.

The company exhibited the ill effects of having operated for fifteen months without any real manager. It would fall to Nogales, as executive vice president, to repair the damage. He easily slipped into the role of day-to-day manager, and Bill Small stirred no fuss when he learned Nogales would chair meetings of the Executive Committee. Small relished being UPI's chief industry emissary, mingling with publishers and broadcast czars, lunching with the likes of CBS anchorman Dan Rather, and patching troubled relations with *The New York Times* and *The Denver Post*.

Nogales learned quickly that UPI had severe cash problems and that things would be even rougher in 1984 with the enormous expenses of covering the presidential campaigns and two Olympics that recurred every four years. He also discovered that, despite the fact that UPI generated $100 million a year in revenues, nobody seemed to have a handle on what was happening to the cash. Small groused that he had not been receiving financial figures at all. Nogales learned to expect optimistic projections from Tom Haughney and conservative ones from Bill Ahlhauser. The waters were further muddied by contracts administration chief Christobal Tortosa, who projected UPI would be making money within a year.

In addition, Nogales found the company was in utter disarray over moving from New York to Nashville and Washington. The poorly planned moves were languishing way beyond schedule and, as Fred Greene and Bob Kelly had feared, were costing far more than Ken Braddick's estimates.

Nogales also discovered that nobody seemed to be monitoring either the fees or performance of the multitude of outside consultants wandering around the executive suite. Some were friends or colleagues of Ruhe and Geissler, earning salaries double and triple what UPI's senior news staffers were paid; others had found entree in other ways.

For men who had been reluctant to accept advice from any quarter, Ruhe and Geissler in late 1983 seemed fair game for almost anybody who came knocking with a bright idea. The owners were captivated by the vision of using UPI to wheel and deal, forging new horizons in the exciting world of mass communication.

When Ruhe wanted to replace UPI's antiquated stocks transmission computer, he had turned to longtime friend and fellow Baha'i Riaz Khadem, a member of the Atlanta consulting firm owned by former NFL quarterback Fran Tarkenton. To design the software for the new system, Khadem hired computer programmer Sy Go. While awaiting arrival of a new computer, Go was being paid $15,000 a month. Though UPI got little benefit from Khadem's consulting team, Ruhe had ordered the accounting department to give top priority to paying his old buddy.

Jim West had been hired by Ruhe for his communications expertise at a rate equal to $90,000 a year. Ruhe also had put Steve Pruett, who had helped him with Focus's pay television ventures, on UPI's payroll as a consultant on broadcast sales and services.

Then there was Harry Coin, a Stanford University computer whiz kid who at sixteen had helped automate the circulation department at Rob Small's *Moline Daily Dispatch*. Ruhe had hired Coin as UPI's "director of computer research" for $1,000 a week to find ways to deliver the news report over a computer screen. Thanks to $100,000 from UPI, Coin had transformed a campus apartment into a high-tech laboratory.

Nogales also wondered why the owners' former partner Joon Chung, now in Hawaii, was getting regular $15,000 payments for laying out the floor plan for the new headquarters. Couldn't they find a cheaper, closer architect? Save for a couple of visits by Chung, executives had to send drawings and design changes via expensive express mail or over UPI's photo network between Washington and Honolulu.

The consultants seemed to proliferate. While UPI scrambled for cash to just maintain current services to subscribers, Ruhe and Geissler were diving into expensive projects and joint-venture deals that might not bear fruit for years—if ever.

To the outside world, a stream of announcements about their speculative new ventures created the mirage of a bustling, aggressive front office, a far cry from the last days under Scripps. Few could guess the owners' frantic and expensive activities, however well intentioned, were bleeding the company dry. Even when Ruhe's ideas seemed feasible, his attention span was too short to push a project through to fruition.

For example, UPI had paid a total of $350,000 to economists John Naisbitt and Michael Evans for a regional economic service and weekly business column, a deal put together by John Jay Hooker. The ill-conceived arrangement, which called for pulling UPI's hard-pressed reporters off news coverage to gather economic data for Naisbitt and Evans's projections, flopped.

Network News, Inc., a Washington firm that wanted to use the UPI wires to syndicate articles by free-lance writers, got $75,000 from Ruhe and Geissler. But the material was boring and turgid, Network News soon collapsed, and UPI lost its investment.

The owners chose a Baha'i friend, Seward Rist, to head a new subsidiary, UPI Real Estate, Inc. Rist was supposed to try to negotiate an ownership share of the buildings housing UPI bureaus. Once again Ruhe's ambition far outstripped his means. Only with the lease for the new Washington bureau would UPI gain an ownership interest.

Ruhe and Geissler brought another old Baha'i pal, Dwight Allen, former education dean at the University of Massachusetts, where they got their master's degrees, into a joint venture with market researchers Arthur Shapiro and Edward Keller. UPI ASK, Inc., was formed to measure consumer preferences via portable "polling poles" to be placed in shopping malls, airports, and other public places, with customers billed for the services. In this deal and some of the others, a new element entered the equation. Ruhe and Geissler, who had not invested a cent, took 49 percent of the venture for themselves and saddled UPI with $360,000 in up-front money and any losses. When Allen, Shapiro, and Keller failed to deliver a money-maker, UPI lost its investment and a promised slice of the profits.

Although Ruhe's efforts to have UPI install its own satellite dishes had failed miserably, now he decided he could save money by forming UPI Service Company to handle the Herculean task of repairing UPI computer terminals and client news printers. Ruhe merged it with the satellite installation company headed by his Baha'i friend Lee Moynahan, and gave her and UPI communications experts Bob Kelly and Don Burks a half interest as incentive to market the service outside of UPI. Ruhe and Geissler kept for themselves 40 percent of UPI Service Company and gave UPI just 10 percent of the stock, although the wire service was responsible for all liabilities. Later, when the venture rang up $1 million in losses, the owners transferred their share to UPI, which had to pay off all the bills. The former anti-establishment idealists were demonstrating how well they had learned their corporate lessons—cover your ass and cut your losses.

Meanwhile Geissler, fluent in Spanish, came up with an excellent idea to tap America's rapidly expanding Latin market with a new Spanish-language radio network. "Nuestras Noticias"—"Our News"—a joint venture with the Spanish news agency EFE, was unveiled October 4, 1983, offering five-minute Spanish newscasts in return for a share of advertising revenue. But although the network ultimately made money, the more than $1 million in start-up costs came at a most inopportune time for UPI.

In early December the company rolled out UPI Custom Data, a marketing coup that had been in the works for years. It permitted subscribers to use a sophisticated computer program to customize the news they received and eliminate unwanted stories. The service was particularly attractive to small clients anxious to avoid sifting through millions of words a day.

The fertile minds of Ruhe and Geissler were hard at work on still other ideas to capitalize on their "international communications highway."

Unipressers could barely keep up as the owners unveiled new products, cut new deals, and made high-blown press releases fall like April rain. Although some ventures might eventually prove profitable, Luis

Nogales and other executives worried that the huge expenditures were mortgaging UPI's future. Yet when they voiced concern Ruhe often trotted out this philosophy:

"If you have enough balls in the air, one or two of them are bound to come through."

To their credit, Ruhe and Geissler were a fount of energy and ideas, and did not take lightly their commitment to maintaining UPI as a complete news agency. But the owners were failing to adopt traditional financial controls and seemingly spending on impulse. They were gambling that UPI would last long enough to profit from their grand dreams.

● ● ●

Ruhe had enticed him with rosy financial projections, but Nogales soon discovered UPI hardly seemed ripe for a turnaround. He knew his work was cut out for him.

Particularly distressing was the realization that Ruhe and Geissler not only had hired their buddies as consultants but also had put inexperienced cronies in key managerial jobs.

One was Bill Ahlhauser. With Fred Greene gone and Tom Haughney off seeking loans, Ahlhauser was left alone to manage UPI's tangled money problems even while he doubled as chief financial officer for Focus, umbrella company of Ruhe and Geissler's other business ventures.

"Who's in charge of accounts receivable here?" Nogales asked Ruhe. "Who's in charge of accounts payable?"

Ahlhauser, replied Ruhe.

So Nogales asked Ahlhauser why profit-and-loss statements came quarterly, not monthly. The answer came back: "We are transitioning." Ahlhauser told Nogales that UPI's books were a shambles because no new computerized accounting system had been developed to replace the interim service Scripps had been providing.

Nogales was not trained as a money man, but he was aghast at the inability of the financial people to generate accurate, timely reports. How, he wondered, could any company be so ignorant of its financial condition? UPI didn't even know how much it was losing!

Ahlhauser seemed dreamy and distant. He never had run a financial department, yet he continued to brag that UPI simply could not fail.

Worried by reports that cash was running out, Bill Adler had cornered Ahlhauser one day in early 1983.

"Bill, what are we going to do?" Adler asked.

"It's not what are we going to do, it's what the AP's going to do. I feel so sorry for the AP."

"What do you mean?" asked an astonished Adler.

"They're going out of business. We're going to put them out of business!"

Adler's heart sank. Could anyone truly believe UPI would drive AP out of business?

Prodded by Nogales, Ahlhauser finally began hunting for someone to fill the controller's position that had been vacant for three months. In September he summoned Charles Curmi, London-based UPI controller for Europe, Africa, and the Middle East, to New York.

Curmi arrived at UPI headquarters promptly at nine o'clock on a Tuesday morning, weary from jet lag but eager to talk about a promotion.

"Hi, just give me two minutes," Ahlhauser said, motioning him to wait outside.

Nearly three hours later Ahlhauser reappeared and said he had to fly home. He suggested Curmi meet him in Nashville the next day. When Curmi arrived there he again found himself camped outside the treasurer's office. Curmi, a somewhat volatile native of Malta, fast was losing patience. When Ahlhauser appeared in the hall, he rushed to intercept him.

"Excuse me," Ahlhauser pleaded. "Just give me five minutes and I'll be with you."

Again, the minutes turned into hours, and Curmi, exhausted, at last checked into a hotel. Next day, after another interminable wait, Ahlhauser invited Curmi to spend the night at his house.

"On one condition," Curmi said. "We talk business tonight."

After dinner, with Curmi expecting his host to bring up the controller's job, Ahlhauser yawned and said he was heading to bed. He handed Curmi some Baha'i religious tracts to read.

Curmi was stunned. How could you deal with this strange character?

After breakfast they returned to the Focus offices, Curmi certain they finally would have their talk. Instead, he was stalled again.

After several more hours Curmi reappeared at his door and said, "Unless you see me immediately, I'm going to return straight to London."

"Okay, Charlie. Let's have a hamburger."

Curmi grudgingly accompanied Ahlhauser to a luncheonette where they talked of many things, but not the controller's job. Heading back home, Curmi heaved a sigh of relief. The bizarre events had convinced him he never could work for Ahlhauser.

• • •

Another upper-management figure that Nogales found of dubious worth was Ken Braddick, whose far-reaching responsibilities had included negotiating deals to sell company assets and overseeing the relocation of world headquarters to Washington. Braddick had become Geissler's right-hand man in sales and personnel matters, but his prickly personality and arbitrary decisions had incurred the animosity of almost everyone, including Doug Ruhe. Ruhe told Geissler that Braddick lacked competence and maturity to be making crucial company decisions. Geissler disagreed, and their frequent arguments over Braddick began to drive a wedge between the partners.

For his part, Braddick felt Ruhe repeatedly had thrown him into no-win situations for which he would be left to take the blame. The owner, he felt, had to shoulder a large part of the responsibility for the tangled move to Washington because he had dragged his feet in selecting new offices until just a few weeks before Unipressers in New York were to report to the nation's capital. Braddick had several long conversations with Geissler about his status, including one at LaGuardia Airport early in the summer of 1983. There he complained that he was tired of being the scapegoat for nearly everything that went wrong in the company.

"I want out of UPI," he said. "What I'm getting real nervous about is, I'll never be able to work in the news business again if this keeps up. I just keep taking these hits. If somebody gets hit by a truck, I'll be held responsible."

Geissler, also feeling the heat from Ruhe, agreed to put somebody else in charge of the move.

The damage already had been done. The moves to Washington and Brentwood, Tennessee, were colossal debacles that exacerbated UPI's financial crisis. Until Nogales arrived, Braddick had been making many decisions on the Washington move without consulting key executives. When Nogales summoned him to a meeting at the Grand Hyatt with Geissler and Bobby Ray Miller, vice president for labor relations, Braddick seemed ill-prepared for the new executive vice president's demands for the specifics of his planning. Braddick fumbled through his pockets for notes scrawled on scraps of paper, bristling at Nogales's suggestions that he had screwed up. Where did this guy get off acting like UPI's savior, Braddick wondered. Finally, he blew.

"Well, I guess you think that everybody at UPI is a fucking asshole!" he shouted, snapping to his feet and heading out the door. "Well, I'm sorry you feel that way, but with this attitude, *you're* an asshole!"

Braddick later returned and apologized for his language—not for his sentiments—much the same way he had handled his blowup at Charles Scripps two years earlier.

Nogales was convinced that Braddick's handling of the move would cost UPI dearly in both aggravation and money.

UPI had not decided on its new quarters on Vermont Avenue until May 13, 1983, less than three weeks before the Washington staffers were supposed to vacate the National Press Building, where UPI's lease was expiring. There was no chance the new bureau would be ready by June 1, and if UPI were evicted, its ability to cover news in the capital would be crippled. Braddick negotiated a monthly lease extension. But then, with New York staffers already beginning to dispose of their residences in preparation for the move, the Vermont Avenue deal fell through. Ruhe, Braddick, and real estate man Seward Rist frantically resumed their search. They settled on a new, unfinished high-rise at 1400 Eye Street, in the middle of Washington's seamy porn strip.

Counting the days to the move, Unipressers in Washington tolerated the intolerable. The National Press Building itself was undergoing total renovation, and demolition crews unearthed dust and mice and disrupted building services. When the move finally occurred after Labor Day, Washington staffers who had worked without air-conditioning through the summer found their desks consisted of folding tables placed on barely dry concrete floors. But for UPI it was either feast or famine. Acting as if UPI were thriving, Braddick had ordered expensive modern furniture, including plush "ergonomic" chairs costing up to $879 apiece.

In New York, Unipressers angry about being ordered to move to Washington wrestled with profound decisions. Lucien Carr, a die-hard New Yorker and a legendary veteran editor, abandoned his Greenwich Village loft and moved to Washington "for the good of UPI." Yet sidekick Don Mullen, who needed the income from his wife's Long Island day-care center to support his family, joined the financial desk that remained in Manhattan. Others simply quit.

As the delays dragged into late autumn, Nogales found that Braddick had communicated poorly with union leaders representing the scores of employees whose living arrangements would be affected. New York staffers who had sold homes or surrendered apartments in anticipation of the original target date had been forced to check into Manhattan hotels with their families at company expense.

Another expensive foul-up resulted from Braddick's failure to consult veteran radio staffers before ordering construction of the new audio studios in Washington. The walls were not soundproofed and background noise so disrupted newscasts that the studios had to be rebuilt, a waste of hundreds of thousands of dollars.

When Braddick had finally insisted somebody else be placed in charge of the move, Geissler didn't hesitate.

"I know just the guy!" Geissler said. It was Luis Lizarraga, a tiny, cocky Mexican Baha'i and brother-in-law of Ruhe's secretary, Lana Bogan, who had joined Focus in the spring of 1983 after his Mexican restaurant failed. Hired to handle special projects for Ruhe, including some at UPI, Lizarraga already had antagonized all too many UPI executives with his abrasive egocentricity.

Lizarraga had taken it upon himself to offer direction to the likes of Ted Majeski, UPI's vice president for newspictures who was a forty-year company veteran, and even to Kurt Weihs, artistic director for UPI's New York PR consultant, the firm of Lois Pitts Gershon. Weihs had designed the famed CBS television "eye" logo, but when Bill Adler introduced Lizarraga to him, the soft-spoken, well-mannered Austrian promptly found himself on the receiving end of a Lizarraga lesson on graphics. Adler cringed during the lengthy lecture, wishing for an excuse to duck out. Finally, Weihs plaintively pulled Adler aside and said, "I've never had to ask this before. But, Bill, please don't make me work with this man."

As Lizarraga cultivated new enemies, Nogales quickly realized Ruhe's crony was the wrong man in the wrong place at the wrong time. He decided to take command of the move himself, but it was too late. All the bungling had exacted a heavy toll—moving would cost upwards of $6 million, eclipsing by as much as sixfold Braddick's pie-in-the-sky estimate.

• • •

Staffers around the world hadn't a clue in the fall of 1983 that Ruhe's ambitious projects were producing neither revenue nor savings, and that bills were going unpaid even as UPI spent money like a land-starved sailor reaching an exotic port of call.

Important vendors like AT&T and RCA Service Company were pressuring the company to pay its tab. With UPI adroitly and creatively dodging the demands, an embattled Tom Haughney tried to nail down financing to help keep the wire service afloat. As UPI lurched from paycheck to paycheck, it seemed that heroic new gymnastics were needed every two weeks to ensure that Unipressers would get paid.

Haughney, UPI's point man for raising funds, was acting more Willie Loman than Wharton School MBA. And if that meant he occasionally had to portray UPI's creaking jalopy as a Rolls-Royce, so be it.

Haughney seemed perfect for the job. Short, lively and at once both impish and sincere, he needed all the disarming charm he could muster. For Haughney was a salesman with a flawed product.

In midsummer Haughney had wrung a $3 million loan from Barclay's International, but the deal required so much collateral that UPI never could draw more than $1 million. To a company with soaring losses, that was a drop in the bucket.

Searching for financing to complete Ruhe's languishing satellite conversion, Haughney stumbled on a Los Angeles-based company that specialized in high-risk lending. Officers of the Foothill Capital Corporation looked at UPI's hefty monthly income and concluded it was an acceptable risk. They offered $4 million at 14.25 percent interest, more than three points above the prime lending rate. It was steep, but UPI had little choice.

In Foothill, Haughney saw a temporary savior, a way to both pay off the Barclay's loan and to cover UPI's payroll for awhile.

• • •

By October 27, 1983, Haughney was close to completing the loan agreement with Foothill. That day, he was on the road pursuing the latest proposed gimmick for wringing additional cash from the information humming over UPI's wires. At the Marlton, New Jersey offices of TeleSciences, a manufacturer of telephone equipment, Haughney was trying to hold together a deal for a high-tech system to deliver automated stock-price quotes to customers over the telephone.

But while TeleSciences chairman Fred Cohen, whose company had developed the needed technology, was excited by what would have been a pioneering venture, UPI owed his firm $800,000. Haughney, sales executive Jim Buckner, and general counsel Linda Thoren had brought some financial statements to the meeting, hoping to convince Cohen that UPI had both money and bright prospects and would pay its bills.

Haughney was interrupted by a call from treasurer Bill Ahlhauser. The two frequently chatted by phone as they scurried to fulfill the latest demands by Foothill loan officers for information, and the serious threat of missed payrolls lent their efforts a kind of madcap urgency. This time Ahlhauser startled Haughney. How, he asked, would UPI's monthly payments to Focus Communications affect the Foothill loan?

At first Haughney assumed Ahlhauser was referring to the fees UPI paid Focus for Ruhe and Geissler's "management services." But he quickly learned much more was involved, something potentially dangerous.

Ahlhauser said that Focus had, for some time, been drawing $150,000 to $200,000 a month from UPI—far more than the owners' salaries.

Haughney froze.

Why the hell was Focus charging UPI all that money? He jotted himself a note: "No wonder we're not getting financial statements."

Haughney informed Ahlhauser that all cash transfers to Focus needed to be documented, promptly and properly, if they weren't already. He hung up, then scribbled, "Consider resigning from the board if things aren't right."

Were Ruhe and Geissler, whether by design or naiveté, diverting UPI assets to their other business ventures? Haughney was upset, too, that the large cash transfers were occurring even as he scrambled to hatch financing schemes and deals to keep UPI afloat.

Unless the money to Focus were declared as personal income, the Internal Revenue Service might cause trouble. And Haughney feared Rob Small and Cordy Overgaard, who remained minority shareholders, might file suit if they found out about the transfers.

Haughney later told associates he was frightened that the cash transfers to Focus would endanger the Foothill loan, and that when he returned to Washington he had confronted Ruhe. Choosing his words carefully, Haughney reportedly cautioned Ruhe that, in his experience, the IRS would be on the lookout for "dividends" to company officers disguised as something else. Haughney said the IRS might tax the transactions as Ruhe's and Geissler's personal income.

However, Haughney told Ruhe he thought that if the transferred funds were loans, the money could not be considered income.

Haughney said that when presented with this option, Ruhe responded, "Oh, yes. It's a loan."

Somewhat mollified, Haughney said he advised his boss that UPI's board of directors had to approve any loans. Ruhe later denied discussing with Haughney the propriety of the cash transfers to Focus.

Although he did not mention his conversations with Ruhe and Ahlhauser to Luis Nogales, Haughney resolved to resign from the board lest he be held responsible for any possible financial improprieties.

The revelations presented Haughney a moral dilemma. If he divulged—as he should—that Ruhe and Geissler were transferring large sums from UPI to Focus, would Foothill get jittery and back off?

Wrestling his conscience, Haughney chose to keep secret from Foothill the large amounts being moved from UPI, mentioning only the smaller monthly management fees Ruhe and Geissler were taking.

Before closing the Foothill loan for an unrestricted $4 million line of credit and another $1.2 million in satellite financing, Haughney fielded several more frantic phone calls from Ahlhauser. UPI was on the verge of missing a payroll. Haughney, under the gun, knew what was at stake. On November 2 he signed the deal at Foothill's Century City offices.

It was just in time. UPI was sinking in debt, swamped by its staggering communications burden, by the costs of the moves, by fees to a proliferation of highly paid consultants, and by costly joint-venture deals. Compounding the problem was the owners' secret transfer of cash from UPI to Focus. During 1983 it would total $1,434,000.

The loan Tom Haughney wrung from Foothill bought UPI some desperately needed breathing room. Yet, incredibly, by the first days of 1984 the money would be gone.

• • •

In the first week of February 1984, UPI was preparing for a party unparalleled in its history. Despite their financial woes, Doug Ruhe and Bill Geissler were unveiling the bright and shiny new world headquarters in lavish style.

Painters scurried to put finishing touches on the spacious new bureau, and staffers unaccustomed to such amenities watched wide-eyed as a local nursery festooned the reception areas with plants and trees.

On February 29, the big day, reporters and editors were ordered to police their work areas and unclutter their desks. Late in the day the brilliant magenta vans of Ridgewell's, the capital's most elite caterer, pulled up incongruously at the curb in Washington's porn corridor, in front of the twelve-story building suddenly bearing the big brass letters "UNITED PRESS INTERNATIONAL."

Tuxedoed caterers unloaded trays of fancy hors d'oeuvres and cases of booze and champagne, setting up shop in the ninth-floor executive suite amid fresh-cut, out-of-season flowers.

Among the hundreds of guests were members of Congress and media bigwigs. A string quartet in formal attire played classical music outside Doug Ruhe's office. White House press spokesman Larry Speakes read a congratulatory telegram from President Reagan. UPI photographers battled the crowd, snapping pictures.

Unipressers accustomed to eating brown-bag lunches at their desks sipped bubbly, munched chocolate-dipped strawberries with whipped cream, and marveled at the transformation of UPI from tightwad to wastrel.

"I've never seen anything like it," cried Dan Rapoport, one of the dozens of ex-Unipressers in attendance who had moved on to greener pastures. "These guys must be *made* of money!"

The Washington Post "Style" section wrote glowingly of the three-hour bash, which cost upwards of $10,000.

For years the news fraternity had swapped rumors of UPI's impending demise. Now it had sparkling new, well-appointed headquarters. Sales reports were glowing, expectations never higher. UPI's world seemed bright.

How could Unipressers guess the company was whistling in the graveyard?

UPI's owners were spending money like they had it.

10
· · ·
Descent into Hell

While partygoers sipped champagne and nibbled canapes at the grand opening in Washington, 700 miles away in the Nashville suburb of Brentwood UPI's accounting department was under siege.

Unpaid vendors flooded the corporate office with angry calls. Cash was so short that every afternoon an emergency meeting was convened to decide which creditors provided services so crucial that their bills could be ignored not a moment longer.

In the first weeks of 1984, unbridled chaos reigned. The books were in the worst mess ever, a situation aggravated because Scripps finally had stopped handling UPI's accounting functions on December 31, and because Ruhe's expensive consultants had failed to deliver a new computer system to track customer accounts. With no monthly statements being produced, the accounting staff could only guess that UPI had lost $3 million in 1983. The bookkeeping labyrinth was profoundly damaging—a whopping $6 million in billings for January 1984 could not be mailed as scheduled.

When Arthur Young and Company balked over providing another clean bill of health in the 1983 audit, Ruhe asked Haughney to again try his charms on auditor Tom Sinton.

Poring over the mess during a meeting with Haughney, Sinton simply couldn't believe his eyes. For months UPI had failed to keep track of even the most basic bookkeeping function—cash receipts. For all practical purposes, the accounting staff had thrown in the towel.

"It's out of control," Sinton bluntly told Haughney, categorically refusing to lend his company's name to another clean audit.

To try to restore order, UPI brought aboard a new controller, Peggy Self, a Nashville accountant from the Baptist Sunday School Board; and Jack Kenney, a money man from a Murfreesboro, Tennessee, computer manufacturing firm.

Like Nogales and McCrohon, Self and Kenney had been misled. UPI headhunters had told them expansively—and wildly inaccurately—that the company was completing a turnaround and should be profitable by the end of 1984. Instead, Self and Kenney arrived to find chaos. Self was appalled by the crush of debts for everything from consultants to Ruhe's myriad new projects, and baffled by the inexplicable monthly cash transfers to Focus.

Equally perplexing was Ruhe's decision to hand out UPI-imprinted American Express Cards, for the first time, to reporters and editors. Ruhe had seized on the idea of purchasing department head Linda Miller as a way to closely monitor expenditures. An unballyhooed side benefit was that the Amex cards, in effect, gave the owners a new short-term line of credit—and another way to stave off bankruptcy.

Haughney had tried to convince his boss that issuing credit cards was a terrible idea that would lead to widespread abuses. "Why don't you just give everybody blank checks?" he told Ruhe sarcastically. "You've got great record-keeping if you give everybody blank checks. You can see who it was made out to."

Watching Ruhe's blood pressure surge, Haughney decided to drop the matter. His original assessment, however, quickly proved accurate. Unipressers accustomed to fighting to get expenses reimbursed suddenly owned a great new toy for travel, for business entertaining—even, on occasion, for treating colleagues to expensive lunches. Their vouchers rarely were challenged, and UPI was saddled with yet another large cash drain.

The company simply could not keep up with the mounting bills. Each day Self and her staff found themselves overwhelmed by phone calls from irate creditors. Among the most impatient was American Express, which requires payment in full in thirty days and now was owed months of back debts. Creditors wearied of the excuse that moving corporate headquarters to Brentwood had fouled up UPI's payment schedule.

At last Self and Kenney simply stopped answering the phone. Instead, Self installed troubleshooters Terri Lavelle and Emily Hudson in a small room dubbed "The Crisis Center." The two spent their days pacifying creditors with the reassuring but oft-broken promise "We'll call you back."

Lavelle and Hudson arrived each morning at eight o'clock to ringing phones that never stopped. Pacific Bell and New York Telephone threatened to cut off service to key bureaus, landlords leveled eviction notices, consultants lined up to be paid, and Western Union demanded reimbursement for emergency cash advanced to traveling staffers. Juggling as many as 400 calls a day, Lavelle and Hudson went home unnerved and exhausted.

Some callers were abusive.

"Pay us or I'll break your knees!" threatened a Chicago car rental agent named Dino.

The frenzied atmosphere bred in Lavelle and Hudson the camaraderie of soldiers in a foxhole. They learned not to take things personally and to roll with the threats of physical violence and legal action. When creditors threatened strong-arm tactics, they retorted with a favorite challenge: "Shoot your best shot, sucker!"

Some callers were shocked and angry to find that a company as famous as UPI was stiffing them. "What kind of organization is this?" cried one creditor. "This is UPI! This is America!"

By 1 p.m. daily, Lavelle and Hudson compiled a priority payment list, often taking pity and setting aside a few thousand dollars for small mom-and-pop vendors. The list generally totaled almost a quarter million dollars, the minimum they felt needed to keep the wolves at bay.

Self took the list to Ahlhauser, who routinely whacked the suggestions down to $25,000 or $50,000. Lavelle and Hudson would type checks and rush them to Federal Express for overnight delivery. Before UPI's account was cut off for nonpayment, it had racked up huge debts to Federal Express.

Lavelle, a savvy, cheerful woman being paid only $18,500 a year, frequently found comfort from this sign over her desk:

"I've been lied to, kicked, spit on, and slapped in the face, and the only reason I hang around this place is to find out what happens next."

Self, who had abandoned a low-key job heading a sixty-person accounting department at the Baptist Sunday School Board, was ill-prepared to deal with such pandemonium. She frequently awakened at night in a cold sweat, jolted by dreams of Unipressers at the Winter Olympics in Sarajevo, Yugoslavia, being stranded behind the Iron Curtain when Amex yanked their cards.

Haunted by her nightmares, she would go to Ahlhauser and stress the urgency of UPI's plight. "I'll talk to Doug," he would promise.

Ruhe then would pop into her office and say, soothingly, "It'll be okay. We've got these deals going, and one of them is going to come through."

Ruhe's "don't worry about a thing" brush-offs did not satisfy Self. One night in early March she phoned Nogales in Washington.

Somewhat shielded from the financial operations, Nogales was surprised to learn the depth of UPI's cash problems. Like Ruhe, he had no experience that would brace him for what lay ahead.

• • •

Seemingly certain he could maneuver his way out of trouble, Ruhe continued to rebuff suggestions that he find a buyer. Instead, he said, he would sell off assets—some of the very products needed to realize his dream of turning UPI into a diverse communications highway with gold-paved off-ramps.

UPI already was selling data to computer libraries, newspictures to publishing houses and other commercial customers, and beaming a special news report onto TV screens in the rapidly expanding cable market. Ruhe planned for UPI to retain a stake in the peddled assets so it could share in any future profits.

Perhaps he had forgotten the old business axiom—bargain from strength, not weakness. For reality never could match his dreams. In a series of rapid-fire deals beginning in the late fall of 1983, Ruhe and UPI were about to get skinned again and again, making his "joint venture" strategy look like a fire sale.

Before Haughney could close the Foothill loan, and with a payroll looming, Ruhe rushed through a deal to sell UPI's news service for cable television viewers. Denver businessman Clinton Ober, a friend of consultant Jim West, initially offered $1.4 million for a 49 percent stake, but sensing Ruhe's desperation, lowered the offer to $1.1 million. Ruhe instructed West, "Make it happen." Ober's Telecrafter Corporation wound up with the lion's share of the new venture. Blithely sugar-coating the details, Ruhe hailed it as a UPI breakthrough in tapping the blossoming home cable market.

Next on the block had been UPI's invaluable electronic data base. Again seeming to operate the company out of his back pocket, Ruhe had begun negotiations without consulting Luis Nogales. When marketing chief Jim Buckner took Ruhe to the Manhattan office of an old friend, Graeme Keeping, president of Comtex Scientific Corporation, Ruhe immediately saw a perfect fit. Comtex had money and staff but no product, and UPI had no money and a huge product. When Keeping expressed interest in a partnership, Ruhe instructed Buckner and Haughney to work out a deal giving up the rights to the data base in exchange for cash and a piece of Comtex.

Haughney later told associates that, walking back to the UPI office, Ruhe said excitedly, "The data base business is the wave of the future. I want you to work out a deal. Try to get a million bucks for it, and see if you can't get part of Comtex."

"Sounds good," Haughney replied.

"Do it," Ruhe snapped, employing a favorite phrase.[1]

In early December, Ruhe finally informed Nogales of the deal. UPI would get $1.2 million cash and 45 percent of Comtex's common stock in return for a twenty-year license to market the data base. Nogales was not at all happy. Ruhe was turning over an irretrievable asset—and getting less than the $1.3 million the data base would earn during 1984 alone.

The preliminary agreement announced December 12, 1983, was a lovely Christmas present for Graeme Keeping. Ruhe boasted UPI would reap $7 million, playing down that most of that was in 2.5 million shares of highly speculative Comtex stock.

Once again Ruhe's deal-making had been driven by a company payroll. While working out final details in early January, Haughney slipped into a cloakroom at the offices of Comtex's New York lawyers to take a phone call from a panicky Ahlhauser urging him to hurry or the next paychecks would bounce. Haughney donned his best poker face. If Comtex discovered UPI's desperate straits, it might demand an even more favorable deal.

---

[1] Another source said that the preliminary discussion of a sale price and other financial terms occurred spontaneously at the meeting earlier with Keeping.

On April 1, just a few months after giving Keeping entrée to a lucrative deal, Buckner became a Comtex vice president and continued to market UPI's data base.[2]

Within six months Comtex informed its shareholders that annualized revenues from the data base had risen to $1.8 million. UPI would not see a penny.

Doug Ruhe, self-professed deal-maker extraordinaire, was running amok.

• • •

Next, Ruhe took aim at UPI's historic library of 11.5 million photo negatives that dated back to the Civil War. It included shots of virtually every famous person and event of the 20th century, such as Clarence Darrow and William Jennings Bryan at the 1925 Scopes "Monkey Trial" in Tennessee. UPI sold historical pictures for modest prices to commercial customers, and even with only four salesmen the library generated more than $1 million a year. But the owners decided they couldn't afford to modernize the obsolete retrieval system. In early fall 1983, vice president Mike Hughes was at a meeting in Nashville when Geissler disclosed the photo library was on the block. Hughes was stunned. He felt that with the right commitment revenues could be tripled, but Geissler made it clear the decision was irrevocable.

"Who cares about a damn picture library?" he said. "You probably only need to go back about twelve months for pictures. We should donate it probably to Harvard. It's of no use to us."

Ted Majeski, photo chief whose advice never had been solicited, told Geissler that UPI was sitting on "a gold mine," and should do all possible to upgrade the retrieval system. When Ken Braddick, who had been placed in charge of negotiations, smugly disclosed one day that a deal had been signed to turn over the library to Bettmann Archives in Manhattan, Majeski glared venomously and cried, "That's just stupid!"

Ruhe and Geissler had dealt away another potentially big money-maker.

On February 2, 1984, Ruhe announced a joint venture, yielding to Bettmann, which itself owned 5 million negatives, exclusive control and

---

[2]Buckner said his move to Comtex had nothing to do with his giving Keeping entrée to the deal.

marketing of UPI's library for ten and a half years in return for 25 percent of gross revenues, including $1.1 million up front. Braddick had not even protected UPI's access to its own file photos—the wire service would have to pay a fee to Bettmann, too. Even worse, Bettmann was unprepared for the immediacy of the news business and missed deadlines. Service declined, and UPI bore the brunt of the criticism.

● ● ●

Consultant Jim West had been assigned to upgrade UPI's stock-quote service. Like others Ruhe had dealt with, West soon found he had struck a mother lode. Discovering that UPI's delivery of stock quotes was hobbled by an antiquated, fifteen-year-old computer, West persuaded the owners to order a new $684,000 Stratus system. When it arrived at the Dallas communications headquarters in January 1984, senior technicians who had begun to learn of UPI's cash-flow problems because of the difficulty in getting equipment dared not uncrate it for fear it would be repossessed.

With the computer gathering dust, Ruhe decided to turn over the stock-quote service to West, whom he considered a technical genius. The newest joint-venture deal would be called Fintext, and Ruhe and West promised newspapers in the spring of 1984 "the most complete and comprehensive financial feed available." West envisioned improvements allowing UPI to update stocks for newspapers twenty-five times a day, and projected a fivefold increase in subscribers that would boost revenues to $7.2 million a year.

West paid a token $100 for his 50 percent interest in Fintext. He only had to reimburse UPI for its costs in producing the market data and got to keep any surplus revenues to finance his research. Without having to put up any cash, he had won himself a $96,000-a-year job as Fintext president and revenues of several hundred thousand dollars a year.

To worsen matters, Ruhe's announcement of a technological "breakthrough" may have been good publicity, but it tipped UPI's hand.

Three months later UPI newspaper marketing chief John Mantle wrote in a confidential memo, "I believe we are facing a disaster unless we act decisively now. For the third time, we have announced a new product prematurely—with catastrophic results. AP has reacted with an announcement of 'AP Digital Stocks-11,' which will be ready this fall.

"What has happened, of course, is that AP has reacted with characteristic alarm when faced with a threat to their newspaper membership. It looks as though UPI will be beaten on our own idea. We'll be lucky to hang on to what markets we have now, let alone start taking stocks business from the AP.''

When West failed to deliver his promised new technology, Mantle's warning proved hauntingly prophetic. The episode dramatized a decades-old problem. Dating to the days of Scripps, UPI never had invested enough resources to fully develop its hottest new product ideas. AP, slower to conceive but quick to mimic, promptly would seize on the ideas, pour in vast money and manpower, and beat UPI to the marketplace.

And unlike most of the other assets transactions, Ruhe's Fintext deal didn't even give UPI a big money infusion—only the vague hope of future profits. Instead, Fintext was a cash drain. West, not the company, now was reaping the revenues from UPI's stock-quote service.

Doug Ruhe had boasted he was cutting a bunch of swell joint-venture deals that would brighten UPI's future. Nogales and other top executives saw it far differently.

In selling the company's cable TV service, electronic data base, picture library, and stock-price service, Ruhe had shrunk UPI's revenues and disposed of some of its most valuable assets. Luis Nogales realized the wire service's plunge was accelerating. If Ruhe kept selling off large chunks, he feared, soon there wouldn't be any UPI left. True, the "deals" had raised several million dollars, but the money was evaporating like dew under the hot sun.

• • •

By late spring 1984, Ruhe's world was starting to collapse around him. His go-it-alone determination was backfiring. He was slowly disman-tling a major media institution viewed by many as nothing less than a public trust. Ruhe had reason to feel cornered. His sale of key assets had begun to alienate Nogales, the man he had brought aboard to help run the company, and other UPI executives. Rather than seek their advice, he increasingly turned for help to outsiders. And there was no shortage of bright, hungry people willing to offer their services—for a nice price.

Shortly after announcing the Fintext deal, Ruhe jumped at a call from associates of former Treasury Secretary G. William Miller, touting that his small investment banking firm could help find a buyer or cash partner.

Miller was an international figure with easy access to the biggest names in the financial world.

Ruhe still showed no interest in selling UPI. He instructed Haughney and Braddick to draw up a sales prospectus aimed at raising $12 million cash from a minority investor. The document contained financial projections so wildly optimistic that George Orwell would have blanched at such a scenario. The unsigned solicitation depicted a UPI poised on the brink of almost inconceivable financial success. While the 1983 audit was expected to show losses of $8.3 million, the company was ready to reduce that to $1.6 million in 1984. By 1985 the profit would be $6.3 million, and by 1987 new information services would send revenue soaring to $164 million and pretax profit to almost $37 million. The figures were trumpeted as "conservative."

Haughney, who held 5 percent of UPI's stock in his wife's name, attributed the glowing projections to giant strides made by Ruhe and Geissler after two decades of benign neglect by Scripps.

Although anyone knowledgeable about UPI would have found these forecasts preposterous, G. William Miller circulated the document in a hunt for a long-shot minority investor. Miller assigned the husband-wife team of Alice Rogoff and David Rubenstein, a former adviser to President Jimmy Carter, to pitch UPI. Among those approached were Warren Buffett, a Nebraskan who owned Berkshire Hathaway, Inc., the shirt company that held stock in the Washington Post Company; the Italians who owned Fiat; and Hong Kong shipping magnate Y.K. Pao.

Miller's team discovered that such big-league players were deeply skeptical of UPI's glowing business projections and loath to play second fiddle to men who had invested no money and were unknown in the worlds of high finance and communications.

While Miller searched, several new characters found their way onto UPI's gravy train. One was smooth-talking West Coast attorney Rinaldo Brutoco, who had helped Ruhe and Geissler during their pay TV escapades in the late 1970s. While Haughney was trying to tie up the Foothill loan, he had run into Brutoco, who offered to intercede with the lender.

When Ruhe bridled at the mere mention of Brutoco's name, Haughney politely brushed him off. Still Brutoco continued to meddle, finally so annoying Foothill officials that they told him to butt out. Even so, when the deal was done Brutoco bragged to Ruhe what a big help he had been. Easing into the owners' good graces, he soon signed on as a highly paid consultant for their Focus television operations.

In early 1984, Brutoco got Ruhe together with Jerry Hillman, son of a wealthy Boston lawyer, who talked glowingly of ways to help UPI. Jerry Hillman's credentials seemed impressive: Harvard graduate, Rhodes Scholar, and former partner in the consulting firm of McKinsey & Company. But Hillman was a strange man who also had conducted meditation and consciousness-raising seminars for harried businessmen. A short, bearded enigma, Hillman had ended his meditation phase and now was positioning himself to be UPI's "guru." Ruhe put him to work on UPI's ninth floor at a cool $20,000 a month. Unipressers who never had heard of Hillman would have been outraged to discover he was being paid more every six weeks than they earned in a year.

Hillman was perhaps the quintessential consultant. When vice president Don Brydon decided to retire to enter the consulting field, Hillman applauded, telling him one day as they shared an elevator, "You'll work half as hard and make twice as much."

Hillman was full of ideas. Identifying the company's major illness as cash anemia, he boasted to Ruhe that he could find the long-sought minority partner and also persuaded Ruhe to let him negotiate a plan to defer or stretch out payments to AT&T. UPI already owed its biggest creditor $6 million and was adding half a million dollars to that tab every month.

In April, Hillman turned for help to a friend and business partner, Ray Wechsler, who had valuable contacts as former chief financial officer for AT&T International. Wechsler agreed to come aboard as a consultant and approach his old friends at AT&T about extending credit.

Wechsler grew concerned, though, when Bill Ahlhauser could not give him concrete financial information. When he flew to Brentwood to examine UPI's books, he was astounded to learn no reliable figures were available. This internationally famous company had no systems, no controls, no procedures, no financial reporting—and, apparently, no money!

Although he had reservations about getting involved, $7,000 a month in consulting fees was enough to make Wechsler gulp hard and swallow his misgivings.

• • •

Nogales and other executives, distressed by the garage sale of assets, hadn't seen anything yet. A year earlier Ruhe had agreed with his senior executives that UPI should not sell its foreign newspictures operation to Reuters unless the cash situation were desperate. Reuters officials had continued, however, to hover like birds of prey, convinced desperation was just around the corner. Their patience was rewarded. Now, in the spring of 1984, Ruhe quietly was negotiating to sell one of UPI's prized parts, the award-winning newspictures service, to his rival.

Reneging on a pledge to join European news agencies in a newly formed newsphoto cartel, Ruhe had secretly decided a sale to Reuters was necessary to dig UPI out of its financial hole. He did not even disclose his decision to European vice president Gene Blabey, to whom fell the awful task of informing Thilo Pohlert, head of the German news agency, that Ruhe had inexplicably changed his mind about joining the cartel. Blabey had known the incendiary former German tank commander for years, but never had he seen Pohlert angrier.

"This man is dishonest!" Pohlert raged. "In Europe when a man gives his word, it's his bond. Mr. Ruhe is not a gentleman."

Pohlert predicted to vice president Mike Hughes that Ruhe would further betray his loyal European supporters by selling the foreign picture service to Reuters. Most European agencies detested Reuters, considering it aloof and uncooperative.

Pohlert, one of UPI's biggest subscribers and staunchest supporters, also distrusted and disliked Ruhe. Perhaps it was because UPI's egalitarian owners seemed oblivious to the fact that most European publishers are elitists who expect to be treated almost like potentates. When Pohlert had visited UPI in 1983, he was deeply affronted that the only refreshment he was offered consisted of tea in a Styrofoam cup and tiny finger sandwiches fixed by a secretary.

Pohlert returned to the States in 1984 to discuss renewing his agency's $55,000-a-month contract with UPI, and Hughes was determined to redress all previous slights. He wined and dined Pohlert, renting a limo and even purchasing a new set of fancy china to serve him tea. And he swore UPI would keep its foreign picture service.

"I absolutely guarantee you, Thilo, that all this talk you've heard about our service being sold to Reuters is absolutely untrue."

Trusting his old friend, Pohlert renewed UPI's lucrative contract and reassured his directors the Reuters rumors were false. Hughes was unaware that Ruhe was secretly talking to Peter Holland of Reuters, who had sized up the cash-starved UPI owner as a juicy target. So certain was Holland a deal would be made that Reuters, in a June 4, 1984, public stock-offering prospectus, predicted it would soon close a five-year joint-venture arrangement in which it would obtain UPI's overseas picture service for $7.5 million. In early June, Holland flew to Nashville to work out details.

One Saturday morning Hughes got a call from Blabey in London. Blabey always was ready to spread the latest gossip about Reuters.

"Mike, a deal is being done between Reuters and UPI on pictures," he said.

"For Chrissakes, Gene, you're up the crick again, giving me bullshit," snapped Hughes.

"I'm telling you, I have it from the horse's mouth. You can't quote me, but Peter Holland told me the deal is done."

Stunned, Hughes dialed Ruhe in Nashville and implored, "Doug, tell me it ain't true." But Ruhe confirmed his worst fears. With Reuters and the French news agency AFP poised to start their own picture services, Ruhe concluded UPI soon would be squeezed out of the foreign market.

"Who's the weakest guy out there?" Ruhe asked, rhetorically. "Whose lunch are they going to eat first?"

Ruhe was betting UPI's traditional clients, particularly those in Latin America and Asia, would continue to buy its news wires even though Reuters controlled foreign pictures.

Hughes insisted he join the negotiations so UPI didn't get steam-rollered. Ruhe told him to be at a meeting in New York on Tuesday, and Hughes summoned Blabey.

Arriving at the negotiating table they quickly realized the deal lacked only final signatures. Ruhe planned to sell UPI's foreign picture rights for $3.3 million in cash and $2.4 million in monthly installments over five years. The total package was nearly $2 million less than what Reuters had just projected in its stock offering.

UPI would turn over its foreign photo staff and all overseas picture contracts, and would provide Reuters pictures of American news events. Reuters, in turn, would provide foreign pictures for UPI's domestic clients.

Hardly had Hughes heard the details when his bile began rising. Each time he and his colleagues tried to extract concessions, Holland would reply, "Well, that's not what I agreed with Doug Ruhe."

Finally, Hughes erupted at his old acquaintance. "Peter, I consider this goddamned rape!" he shouted, contending that without UPI's foreign service it would cost Reuters $25 million to start its own photo network.

"Well, Mike, a deal's a deal."

At day's end Hughes told Blabey, "Well, mate, we've been sold down the river. Let's go back to Ruhe and see if we can undo some of this stuff."

Next morning, over breakfast, even general counsel Linda Thoren and the normally pliable Bill Ahlhauser questioned the deal. Ruhe brooked no criticism. Another payroll was breathing down his neck.

"Look, the deal is done! Just get the thing signed!" he snapped, and stormed out.

Later that morning Holland delivered what Hughes and Blabey considered the final insult. Almost as an afterthought he asked that Ruhe include a clause permitting Reuters to independently market its own pictures in the United States to big papers such as *The New York Times, Washington Post*, and Baltimore *Sun*.

"Yeah, okay," Ruhe agreed.

"Doug, you can't do that!" Hughes cried.

Pulling Ruhe aside, Blabey argued that the clause would give Reuters a competitive foothold in the U.S. market and could eventually knock UPI out of the photo business altogether. He said UPI must demand the same rights abroad.

"Look, all they want to do is serve these few papers," Ruhe said, brushing aside his protests. "They're not about to set up a competing service in the United States. Go ahead and do it."

"Ruhe-the-deal-maker has been suckered," Hughes thought despondently as he headed back to Washington.

Hughes could not know the constraints Ruhe was under. UPI had exceeded its $4 million line of credit, and Foothill was pressuring for a prompt resolution. Even while the complex deal was being set to paper in marathon meetings in Reuters' London boardroom, Ruhe slipped into another office to phone Los Angeles and beg Foothill for a little more time.

As the deadline approached, European controller Charles Curmi urged Ahlhauser to hold out for a higher price. Curmi's contacts had suggested Reuters was prepared to go as high as $8 million to $10 million.

"Don't rock the boat," Ahlhauser warned. "We need the money."

When the deal was announced on June 25, Thilo Pohlert furiously phoned Hughes.

"What kind of an idiot are you?" he shouted at his old friend. "I am very disappointed in you, Mike. I have been made to look a fool before my directors.''

"Thilo, on my honor as a gentleman, I never knew," Hughes protested, embarrassed.

Little outcry had been voiced at Ruhe's earlier deals, whose impact few Unipressers grasped. But now he had sold off a crown jewel. Nogales, Bill Small, McCrohon, and Hughes complained bitterly. This time no amount of bravado, no flourish of press releases could hide the fact that, to keep UPI afloat, Doug Ruhe was emasculating it. Even as he boasted of the company's growth potential, some of its most valuable assets were gone.

If he thought the $3.3 million cash bonanza from Reuters would revitalize his limping wire service, Ruhe was sadly mistaken.

Once the cash transfer was made, Jack Kenney began paying off angry creditors and setting aside funds to cover UPI paychecks being distributed that week. When Ruhe returned to Nashville four days later, he threw up his hands in anguish.

The Reuters money was already gone.

• • •

In the six months since Foothill had agreed to finance UPI, its officers had grown increasingly concerned that the wire service was continually flirting with its $4 million credit limit. In the spring of 1984, Foothill officials summoned Luis Nogales and other executives to Los Angeles, and were upset to learn that UPI's projected $3 million loss for 1983 suddenly had more than doubled. They were also astonished when Ahlhauser fumbled their questions, seeming to lack even the most rudimentary understanding of UPI's finances.

Privately, Foothill vice president Peter Schwab demanded that Ahlhauser be removed from day-to-day control over the accounting department. Ruhe had no choice. Newcomers Peggy Self and Jack Kenney assumed Ahlhauser's responsibilities.

Self had already become frustrated by UPI's lax accounting and unhappy that the owners were ordering her to skip over more pressing bills in favor of paying their consultant friends. Still given priority was Ruhe's longtime Baha'i buddy Riaz Khadem. UPI accountants had sneeringly dubbed him "Ream Khadem," convinced he was reaming the company, pulling down large fees without delivering results.

When Khadem and a Canadian subcontractor, Probe, Inc., had failed to produce an automated accounting system for UPI's complex, worldwide operations, the firm of Touche Ross was brought in. UPI ended up paying nearly $1.5 million on the two consulting contracts—without materially improving its accounting procedures.

Whenever Khadem phoned Brentwood to inquire about his fees he insisted on talking to Ahlhauser or Self, both of whom took pains to dodge his calls. Accounting staffers once kept Khadem waiting on hold for two hours, then left for the day with the phone button still lighted. Usually, though, Ruhe would intervene, ordering Kenney and Self to pay his friend.

In early summer 1984, with UPI's cash squeeze again reaching crisis proportions, Self got a bill for $100,000 from Probe. She, UPI lawyer Bill Bowe, and others decided to sit on it. They were not surprised when Ruhe directed that they "Go ahead and pay Probe." Watching her authority wither, Self resigned in July after six hellacious months, returning to her less exasperating job with the Baptist Sunday School Board.

• • •

Editor in chief Maxwell McCrohon had boldly demonstrated money would be no object if UPI could make a splash with a big story. McCrohon, editor of *The Chicago Tribune* when it won a string of Pulitzer Prizes, was something of a soft touch for investigative stories.

When former Kentucky television reporter Sally Denton sought help in her crusade to expose allegations of money-laundering and drug-trafficking against former Kentucky Governor John Y. Brown, Jr., McCrohon quickly hired her. Sensing an opportunity for UPI to win its first Pulitzer in more than a decade, he summoned a score of reporters and editors from across the country to Washington. The slim, blonde Denton titillated the gathering with videotapes of her TV reports and recent disclosures that a courier for Brown had withdrawn more than $1 million in cash from a Miami bank, money Brown said was for gambling debts. Although her evidence was circumstantial, McCrohon launched a full-scale investigative effort. Dreaming of another Pulitzer, he assigned half a dozen reporters to follow the twisting trail spun by Denton. Cost of the initial planning meeting alone exceeded $10,000.

Reporters crisscrossed the country for five months, feverishly chasing a blockbuster that never materialized. The focus of the story changed repeatedly as Denton and her colleagues fought to save the project, ringing up big travel expenses on corporate American Express Cards in pursuit of her hunches.

The project, launched without any source who had firsthand knowledge of wrongdoing by Brown, fizzled. Faced with rapidly mounting expenses and zero prospects of a juicy exposé, McCrohon finally shut it down when Denton and UPI Kentucky editor Brian Malloy tried to turn the Brown story into a yarn about CIA drug-dealing in the 1970s.

Tens of thousands of dollars had been blown, and not a single decent story to show for it.

• • •

Since Peggy Self's worried phone call in early winter, Nogales had carried through his resolve to inject himself more vigorously in financial affairs. Perhaps Nogales had been a bit slow to grasp UPI's enormous problems, perhaps he had felt shackled by Ruhe's and Geissler's single-minded determination to run the company their way. By early spring he had come to the conclusion that, before it was too late, the owners must expose their deep financial problems to employees and openly seek their help.

Union president Bill Morrissey, secretary-treasurer Dan Carmichael, and the union's accountant already were complaining that the company was far behind in reimbursing staff expenses, that employees were subsidizing their own work assignments. In March, the union leaders were given a rare look at the books. They were astonished to find red ink everywhere. Ruhe agreed to their demand for a meeting, but no expense checks were forthcoming.

Nogales, however, found the union quite cooperative. While assisting Ruhe in negotiations with Byers Communications in Atlanta over the possible sale of UPI's international computer network, he had persuaded the guild to agree to sacrifice the jobs of some technicians to help close the deal.

Nogales began to privately urge the owners to seek major union concessions, much as Dick Farkas had a year earlier. The guild's April 15, 1984, automatic pay increase was drawing near and UPI was having trouble enough meeting the current payroll. Nogales pressed the owners to ask the union to accept a wage freeze for the rest of the year and to cut the staff by 200.

Despite the company's precarious position, Geissler adamantly opposed such stern measures and grew angry when Nogales insisted. Finally, while home in Tennessee one Saturday in May, he fired off an angry letter to Nogales removing him from negotiations with the union.

Soon the Byers deal collapsed and the owners found themselves in even deeper trouble. It was now clear that the 1983 losses, rather than the latest projection of $6 million, would be a staggering $14 million. Ruhe and Geissler owed $15 million to creditors and were losing more than $1 million a month. Not only was Ruhe out of cash to cover expenses and running out of assets to sell, but UPI was also exhausting the list of substitute vendors willing to float credit for vital goods and services.

Even Geissler had set up a committee to consider austerity measures, but he stubbornly stuck to his belief that UPI could solve its financial woes without major layoffs.

"All you MBAs think the only way to solve problems is pay cuts and layoffs," Geissler snapped at Nogales. "The way to do it is sales and marketing, and increasing revenues."

By mid-July, such thoughts were merely a pipe dream. One day Ruhe poked his head into a meeting of Geissler's committee and declared, "We've got to have 200 to 250 staff cuts. We're not going to make it without them."

Geissler, absent at the time, returned to hear the news and stomped out to angrily confront Ruhe. Returning a half hour later, he said sheepishly, "Well, we've got to go through with the cuts."

On July 31, Nogales issued a confidential memo to senior officials freezing hiring and management salaries and slashing operating budgets by 10 percent.

Nogales at last convinced Ruhe to seek union concessions. Nogales knew such a move was fraught with danger, for the depths of UPI's woes would now become public, and the industry reaction would surely be swift and perhaps devastating.

He also knew there was no alternative. UPI's employees must be told of the dire straits. Without a buyer, only they could save the company.

Late on the afternoon of Friday, August 10, Nogales called Morrissey at the union offices in New York. Solemnly, he begged for help. He could not solve UPI's problems alone.

The seventy-seven-year-old wire service was on the brink of extinction, he said, quietly detailing the company's plight.

Morrissey sat motionless, silent so long that union officer Kevin Keane thought his boss had been placed on hold.

But Morrissey was listening to every word. He was silent because he was dumbstruck.

11
• • •

The Unkindest Cuts of All

Amerika yawned as delegates to the Republican National Convention, gathered in August in steamy, sweaty Dallas to crown Ronald Reagan for a second term.

During this hectic summer, scores of UPI staffers descended on Dallas, on San Francisco for the Democratic Convention, and on Los Angeles for the Summer Olympics. The "quadrennials"— the time every four years when politics and sports converge to bore or enthrall America—are rough financial sledding even for affluent media companies. For UPI in 1984 the multimillion-dollar drain was horrendous.

Dallas was the homestretch. In a few days Unipressers, struggling to extract any tidbit of news from the largely somnambulant GOP convention would return to their bureaus to prepare to cover the general election campaign. As the proceedings cranked up, the seventy-five UPI employees working out of the Dallas Convention Center were abuzz with the rumor that the company faced a financial crisis. There was talk that secret negotiations were under way in New York between union and management teams and that pay cuts were inevitable. Some convention staffers grew panicky when they discovered that American Express had canceled their company credit cards. Reporters and editors steeped in the wire service's tradition of gallows humor donned Federal Express "Don't Panic" promotional buttons—and taped over the "Don't."

If UPI's future hung in the balance it was hard to tell by watching the company's president, Bill Small, whose patrician, almost diffident exterior never changed around the staffers. Small, frozen out of virtually every key operating function by Ruhe and Nogales, carried out his self-appointed role as UPI's ambassador of goodwill. He stalked the convention workroom, often with longtime assistant Sylvia Westerman at his side, offering small talk and encouragement to the UPI staffers.

Small seemed as relaxed as ever. He enlisted a college student from UPI's convention motor-pool staff to drive him to early morning tennis dates, and he hit the VIP parties that highlight national political conventions. Despite his six-figure salary, Small seemed preoccupied with his love for political souvenirs and freebies.

At the Olympics the previous week, Small had groused repeatedly that he had been deprived of a portable radio cassette player given to reporters by Sanyo. Finally, executive sports editor Milt Richman wangled an extra for him. Out of earshot of his president, Richman muttered to colleagues, "That ought to hold the little baby!"

Watching Small occupy himself with ceremonial functions and UPI's political crew scurrying to cover the conventions, casual observers would never have divined the company's peril.

• • •

During his August 10 phone plea to Morrissey, Nogales had requested an urgent meeting. Morrissey, who had spent his career with the rival AP, quickly passed the word to Dan Carmichael, a UPI reporter who served as the union's firebrand secretary-treasurer.

Two days later, at 1:15 p.m. on Sunday, August 12, Nogales brought the company contingent of Ray Wechsler, Max McCrohon, labor vice president Bobby Ray Miller, and financial officer Jack Kenney to the hotel room of international union representative Dick Pattison at the Anthony House in Washington. Pattison, Morrissey, and Carmichael were waiting.

Wechsler, with the best handle on finances, told the glum-faced union leaders the company was, in effect, already bankrupt. It owed $20 million and each month was losing $1.5 million more. Nogales said that since a bankruptcy filing might frighten subscribers, the company wanted to avoid such a formal declaration and instead lay off 300 employees and cut all salaries by 10 percent.

Carmichael's stomach dropped as if he were aboard a speeding elevator. A man who rarely passed up a chance to antagonize, this time he sat quietly. He was beginning to believe things actually might be as dreadful as management claimed.

McCrohon, an innovative, visionary editor, seemed as stunned as anyone. Trying to shape the editorial report to his philosophy of hunting down big-impact stories, he had just days earlier announced an editorial staff expansion and, anticipating the industry's preoccupation with graphics, had greatly enlarged the art department and hired a new graphics chief. Now he realized that major manpower cutbacks were inevitable for his already lean operation.

The two sides talked for nearly ten hours, the gravity of the situation nurturing uncharacteristic harmony. So convinced were the union leaders of the urgency for quick action that they agreed on the spot that concessions were imperative. In return for a promise from management to reduce planned layoffs from 300 to 200, Carmichael and Morrissey tentatively agreed to a package that included a year of deep wage cuts for all employees, starting at 25 percent for three months. The union also won a promise that its accountant could review UPI's books. In an attempt to compensate for the draconian concessions, Nogales offered union employees stock in UPI.

Being told that Ruhe and Geissler had approved the deal in principle, the union negotiators staggered out for a post-midnight snack at the Howard Johnson's across from the Watergate Hotel. The agreement was anything but final—and even with the concessions, there was no guarantee UPI would survive.

On Monday, Carmichael phoned fellow union officer Drew Von Bergen at a Delaware beach house rented by a group of Unipressers. "This is Dan. Do not say a word. Just listen to me. You've got to get back to Washington. The company is about to go bankrupt. We're going to have to give concessions."

"Oh, shit," Von Bergen groaned. "I'm leaving now."

The next day guild accountant Chuck Kurtz began poring over the books and the union team converged on UPI's corporate headquarters in Brentwood to start formal negotiations.

Knowing that unless management made a full confession UPI could kiss the union's support good-bye, Nogales directed that the guild be made privy to the company's most intimate secrets. During an eleven-hour opening meeting UPI general counsel Linda Thoren diagrammed on a blackboard the bewildering maze of companies that Ruhe and Geissler had spun off from the wire service and their Focus television operation. The union delegation sat transfixed, fighting back anger as they pondered what shenanigans the owners had perpetrated.

In an unprecedented appearance, Nogales and his team next described UPI's predicament to the union's twelve-member executive committee in New York. Shortly after the presentation ended at 1:30 a.m. on August 16, the union for the first time disclosed the company's fragile condition to its members, announcing in a bulletin carried on UPI's internal message wires that layoffs and pay cuts were likely.

At 2 a.m., McCrohon invited the union negotiators to join him for a drink at Ryan-McFadden, a Second Avenue bar near the office. McCrohon looked a wreck. Sallow cheeks further sunken, thinning hair disheveled, he implored Morrissey and the union to help him save as many editorial jobs as possible. The wire service was already lagging badly behind the AP and the supplemental services being marketed by the big newspaper groups, and the inevitable cuts in staff and salaries would be even more disadvantageous. Every ounce of resourcefulness and luck was necessary if UPI were to survive. Together, McCrohon and the union leaders wrung their hands.

The chilling financial news at last was public. As Unipressers read the union bulletin in bureaus around the world, they were badly shaken, numbed. How could they pay the rent, buy groceries, send their kids to college?

The news media quickly picked up on the story. Now, after all of Doug Ruhe's optimistic press releases boasting of a turnaround, the industry on which UPI depended knew the truth.

• • •

After reviewing the company's books, union accountant Chuck Kurtz delivered a shocking appraisal to Morrissey:

"I can tell you one thing. They're losing money. If you ask me how much, or where, or in what detail, I cannot give it to you. All of their accounting records are in boxes, in envelopes, and there are no books in the sense that you would understand books. And they don't know how much they're losing.

"I don't know how they're in business. The best I can tell they haven't done their taxes in three years. Of course they don't owe any taxes. They haven't made any money.''

The union began asking hard questions. If employees already paid below industry standards are asked to sacrifice, what about UPI's $220,000-a-year president, Bill Small? What about the battalion of high-priced consultants? And when are the owners going to invest any of their own money? Indeed, beyond signing loans and leases, Ruhe and Geissler had never financially put themselves on the line for UPI.

The harmony from the initial Sunday meeting between union and management quickly dissolved into bitter stalemate as each side battled to salvage what scraps it could. The negotiations were like none the veteran combatants ever had witnessed. Everyone knew what had to be done, but union leaders were determined to accomplish two things: make sure that if employees sacrificed to save the company, management would accept parallel cuts, and second, to emerge with some token measure that would allow employees to keep their self respect and maybe even benefit in the future.

To secure something tangible for the rank and file, guild negotiators settled on Nogales's offer of stock. Though they knew the shares now were worthless, it seemed the very least the company could do for veteran employees who, during the first phase of the cuts, would be paid at the paltry rate of $22,500 a year. Stock ownership soon became a rallying point for union members across the country.

The union demands for 12.5 percent of the company's stock versus the 6 percent that had been offered put Nogales in a real bind. There was not enough stock to go around. Ruhe and Geissler had insisted on retaining at least 51 percent. Other blocks of stock were controlled by minority owners Tom Haughney and Bill Ahlhauser and by former partners Rob Small and Cordy Overgaard, who had never relinquished their shares. If the union got a piece, there would be little left to offer a minority investor or possibly to creditors in exchange for forgiving debts.

As the negotiations continued, Nogales's strong hand was evident everywhere. It was clear that Nogales, who on August 16 had been appointed general manager, was running UPI, not Bill Small. Nogales was listening closely to the advice of Wechsler, a savvy, highly competent financial man who was pressing for as many union concessions as possible. However, some of the proposals from Wechsler and his buddy, consultant Jerry Hillman, were outrageous. One day, Hillman appeared at the negotiations and spent an hour flashing numbers to show how the union could terminate its $12 million pension plan, purchase annuities to cover its obligations, and invest up to $3 million in UPI.

"You know, your math is fascinating," guild attorney Sidney Reitman told Hillman. "But it is illegal for us to do that."

Carmichael added snidely, "When we see three million dollars from Ruhe and Geissler, we'll think about it."

During the negotiations Morrissey was catching catnaps on a sofa bed in Dick Pattison's cheap room at the Iroquois Hotel. One night he was in the bathroom shaving, preoccupied with the company's future and the grave responsibility he felt for hundreds of workers. Suddenly he walked into the bedroom, overcome with emotion.

"Dick, I just don't know what to do," Morrissey sobbed, tears streaking his cheeks.

Pattison, who during thirty years of fighting management had been a close witness to a number of newspapers folding, grabbed a table to steady himself. "I don't know, either," he said, tears welling. "I don't know if I've ever faced anything like this. I just don't know what to do."

• • •

Nogales continued to be a buffer during the delicate negotiating process, a shield for Ruhe and Geissler. Emotions ran high, the seemingly endless meetings and terrifyingly high stakes fraying nerves and tempers. For, whatever the outcome, incalculable hardship would be visited upon more than 1,000 Unipressers.

Late one night, as union leaders privately caucused, Pattison began weeping openly.

"UPI's probably not going to make it anyway, and I am crying for your innocence," he said. "I've been through this before, but none of you are ever going to be the same person after this is over."

His emotional outburst cut right through Carmichael, Von Bergen, and Morrissey. They struggled to fight back tears. When they finally composed themselves, the four men began to seriously discuss whether it would be more humane to just pull the plug and end UPI's misery.

• • •

The workers' plight even occasionally drew sympathy from the management team. During a particularly eloquent discourse by a guild bargainer, company representative Hugh Cullman was transported. "I agree with the union!" He blurted. Morrissey swiftly extracted his guild membership card from his wallet with a flourish, crossed out his own name, and substituted "Hugh Cullman." It was Cullman's last bargaining session.

At 4 a.m. on Friday, August 17, after three days of marathon talks brought no end to the deadlock, tempers boiled over and the union stalked out. Negotiations dragged for days, often ending when the first gray garbage trucks clanked noisily on Manhattan's streets. The guild's stock demands fluctuated wildly, at one point reaching a 25 percent share of the company.

Ruhe and Geissler lay low during the talks. Only once, when Nogales was pressed by Morrissey, did Ruhe appear. He passed through the conference room en route to an adjoining storeroom, self-consciously inquired, "Everyone okay?" then headed for the door.

"Aren't you going to sit down, Doug?" Carmichael called out.

Ruhe flashed a quick smile, then ducked out.

Ruhe proved elusive. At one point Nogales and McCrohon spent hours trying to track him down for consultations. When they finally found him in the wee hours of the morning, union negotiators who had delayed their dinner to await the owner's response had fallen asleep on the conference-room floor.

With no break in the impasse, Nogales and McCrohon decided they must announce to employees a scenario to "bring UPI into the black." The company would lay off 100 workers, sixty of them part-timers or newcomers who had not lost their "probationary" status and could be dismissed without a legal challenge. Wage concessions would give way after thirteen months to a "regular program of raises."

"The effect of these measures will be immediate and dramatic. During the last quarter of this calendar year, United Press International will be operating in the black for the first time in twenty years."

Unipressers could read between the lines. The "profit" would be wrung from their pocketbooks.

Still the guild wasn't bending, and union lawyer Sidney Reitman challenged Nogales.

"Look, why are we going through all this? Chapter Eleven is the legal remedy available for a company in your kind of trouble. Why aren't you availing yourselves of it?"

The mere hint of filing for Chapter 11 protection under the Federal

E.W. SCRIPPS CO.

Portrait of United Press founder E. W.
Scripps.

CINCINNATI ENQUIRER

Above: Charles Scripps, the eldest of E. W.'s
grandchildren.

Below: Semi-retired CBS journalist Walter
Cronkite; Cronkite as a UP war
correspondent in 1944, talking to a Russian
air attaché in London.

UPI/BETTMANN NEWSPHOTOS

UPI/BETTMANN NEWSPHOTOS

UP White House correspondent Merriman Smith dictating a story after an all-night vigil covering President Dwight D. Eisenhower's illness in September 1955 at the summer White House in Colorado.

Below: UPI White House correspondent Helen Thomas with President-elect John F. Kennedy in 1960 and with President Lyndon Baines Johnson in 1964.

At the signing ceremony for the ''sale'' of UPI by Scripps on June 2, 1982, are (*seated*) Douglas Ruhe and (*standing, left to right*) Scripps executives Edward Estlow and Lawrence Leser and Ruhe partner Cordell Overgaard.

Below: UPI's new co-owner, William Geissler (*left*), and former CBS and NBC executive William J. Small, hired in 1982 as UPI's new president.

Above: Departing UPI president Rod Beaton (*seated*), sharing a joke with minority owner Len R. Small, Jr., days after the sale.

Left: John Jay Hooker, who would later become UPI's chairman, sharing the limelight in 1975 with Muhammad Ali.

Luis Nogales (*left*) and Doug Ruhe shake hands on March 7, 1985, after a bitter all-night negotiation resulted in Nogales gaining operating control of UPI.

Below: The signing of an early union concessions package in the spring of 1984. *Seated, from left*, are Wire Service Guild president William Morrissey and co-owner Bill Geissler; *Standing, from left*, are union secretary-treasurer Dan Carmichael and UPI vice president Bobby Ray Miller.

Above: Two of UPI's succession of presidents: Ray Wechsler (left) and Max McCrohon.

Left: U.S. Bankruptcy Judge George Bason.

UPI's chief lender, president John Nickoll of the Foothill Capital Corporation, surveying a display of Pulitzer Prize-winning photos at UPI's world headquarters in Washington, D.C.

Below: In one of UPI's most famous photos, a joyous President Harry S. Truman crows over an erroneous Chicago *Tribune* headline on November 4, 1948.

Left to right: UPI winning bidder Mario Vazquez Rāna kids with Luis Nogales and minority partner Joe Russo on November 12, 1985.

Below: Earl Brian (*right*) addressing a news conference shortly after taking control of UPI in February 1988. With him is new UPI president Paul Steinle.

Bankruptcy Code brought shivers to the owners, who knew that if they turned UPI over to court supervision they almost certainly would lose control of the company. Although many firms had successfully reorganized under Chapter 11 protection, they also feared the stigma of bankruptcy might be lethal to UPI.

"Bankruptcy would seal UPI's fate," Nogales told Reitman. "We could not survive."

In fact, Hillman already had taken the initiative to find UPI a bankruptcy lawyer. He persuaded Ruhe to retain Richard Levine of the Boston firm of Hill and Barlow, who had headed the Justice Department's office of U.S. bankruptcy trustees in the Jimmy Carter administration.

• • •

The stalemate finally broke. Ruhe and Geissler agreed to give to the union stock in Media News Corporation, UPI's parent—shares theoretically more valuable than those in UPI. Nogales and his management team were able to bargain the union down to a 6.5 percent share of Media News. In return, the union gave tentative agreement to concessions that would bring UPI a $10 million bonanza.

Hours later the union joylessly announced "a package designed to protect UPI employees to the maximum extent possible while keeping the company in business."

The steep pay cuts were made even more difficult by the elimination of three substantial pay increases over the next thirteen months. For three months top-scale reporters who would have begun receiving $580 a week in October instead would be earning less than $420. Beginning journalists would make only $250 a week. As a sop the union was awarded two seats on UPI's Executive Committee.

"The Wire Service Guild did not cause UPI's financial mess—it was caused by years of mismanagement and neglect," the union bargainers somberly told members. "Unfortunately, it is the employees who are being asked to pay the price."

The union had decided, reluctantly, that "part of a paycheck is better than no paycheck."

In a separate statement Morrissey said, "This has been the most traumatic, gut-wrenching assignment of our lives. We cannot assure you that the employee concessions alone will keep UPI in business. But we feel we must try to do so. . . . The team felt unanimously that it, alone, could not decide whether UPI would live or die. That is too big a decision. It is now up to the members of the union to decide.''

• • •

Nogales and the guild held a joint news conference at the Grand Hyatt Hotel, then fanned out separately to major bureaus across the country to rally support for union ratification. The angry staffers they faced were feeling abused and misused.

On August 27, en route to talk to workers in Nashville, Carmichael was outraged when he spotted Wechsler flying first-class. Wechsler, now pulling down $20,000 a month, would not alter his life-style even after two weeks of extracting financial concessions from the union.

In Nashville the union's ''truth squad'' got a look at UPI's loan agreements with Foothill. They were astonished at the high interest being paid and furious to learn even the name ''United Press International'' had been mortgaged—Foothill owned its rights if UPI defaulted.

As the informational meetings continued, morbid humor abounded. Wags distributed ''25 reasons why the 25 percent cut is good,'' including:

—Sex lives will improve. We cannot afford to do anything else.

—We'll have more living space once our furniture is repossessed.

—We won't worry about keeping up with the Joneses.

—You won't feel guilty about refusing to give money to bums. You'll be one.

On August 30, Nogales faced hostile staffers in New York barely surviving at even full salary in one of America's most expensive cities, and later in Washington, where the housing market was going through the roof. Carmichael and Morrissey were openly pessimistic, beginning the meetings by saying the concessions only would buy staffers a little time to update resumés and hunt for new jobs.

Waiting his turn to speak, Nogales steamed. The union leaders were posturing, covering their own political rumps and trying to insulate themselves from blame if UPI collapsed. To stand any chance of winning ratification, Nogales decided, he had to turn unabashed cheerleader.

''This company is gonna' make it. . . . We can do it. . . . We're gonna do it,'' he exhorted employees seated on the floor in the jam-packed graphics department in Washington.

He, McCrohon, and chief UPI White House reporter Helen Thomas, always the company's biggest booster, implored ratification. The wire just must keep humming, they said.

Nogales was a refreshing change from Ruhe and Geissler, who rarely ventured into the newsroom. He openly discussed UPI's financial condition and enjoyed bantering with the staff, even when the questions were harsh and direct. At this hortatory staff meeting, however, he wasn't having much fun. If the union accepted the package, he rashly declared, "I promise we will never have to come back to you again."

Privately, Nogales was worried about more than whether the union would ratify the cuts. Still steadfastly clinging to control, Doug Ruhe seemed irreconcilably opposed to even the possibility of seeking a buyer for UPI. Nogales, inviting Morrissey and Carmichael to dinner that night at the Georgetown Inn in Washington, suggested to the surprised union leaders that they seek to convince Ruhe to sell. But they were in no mood to lead such a challenge. They had an agenda of their own. If guild employees had to take pay cuts, they wanted big heads to roll—starting with Bill Small's.

• • •

Awaiting the verdict on the pay cuts, Nogales each day fended off calls from dozens of angry creditors. Under pressure from American Express, Nogales was forced to eliminate the corporate credit cards. That meant UPI had to put out cash in advance for all employee travel.

Nogales imposed the same salary cuts on UPI managers and required them to forgo a two-week paycheck, promising to replace it when cuts were restored in 1985. Employees had no idea, however, that consultants like Wechsler and Hillman were spared. So were employees of most of the subsidiaries set up by Ruhe and Geissler.

Ruhe and Geissler accepted the pay cuts, but had their own private way of softening the blow. When they missed the September 1 paycheck, former officials of Focus Communications said, the owners directed Focus accountants to write them replacement "loans"—loans that never were repaid.

• • •

Near panic swept the company as the September 17 date for the counting of ballots approached. Many staffers, including a number of the most talented ones, feared the concessions package might be rejected and began searching for new jobs. While it seemed obvious that ratification was the employees' best option, many, weary of the enervating treadmill of low pay and underappreciation, spoke bitterly of simply letting the company die. Management clearly had to dramatically demonstrate its own commitment.

Bill Small never had been Ruhe's favorite. In June, just when UPI's fortunes were sinking to historic depths, Small had cleverly negotiated a five-year contract extension. Now the union was after Small's scalp, feeling him an expensive appendage at a time when members were facing wage cuts or dismissal. Guild leaders thought Small might be a valuable trophy to present the membership.

Ruhe, who thought Nogales deserved the title of president, was determined that Small should go. He overcame fierce objections from Geissler, who argued that firing Small would be a terrible public relations move amid the financial turmoil.

On September 4, Small arrived in Nashville for a management meeting, and instead found himself alone with Ruhe.

"I've decided that I can't work with you any longer," Ruhe said, offering a partial settlement of Small's new $1.25 million contract.

"I've got a contract," Small said coldly. "My lawyer will be getting in touch with your lawyer."

"Hey, that's fine with me," said Ruhe in Clint Eastwood, "make my day" style. He told Small to negotiate with UPI lawyer Linda Thoren.

Small stalked out. Back in New York he consulted his lawyer, who advised him to continue reporting to work.

Finally, on Saturday, September 8, Ruhe announced publicly he was promoting Nogales to president and chief operating officer, and that Small had been "terminated." In the announcement carried on the UPI wire, Ruhe praised Nogales as "a strong leader."

While Small had his detractors, the firing scarcely could have been more badly bungled. Only when *Washington Post* reporter Sari Horwitz called did Small learn his dismissal had been officially announced.

"What makes you think I've been terminated?" Small asked.

Spokesman Bill Adler acknowledged to Horwitz that Small had not been formally notified of his firing before the story ran, and that UPI had belatedly sent a telegram to his home on Central Park West. Still, Small's attorney, Lawson Bernstein, advised him to honor his contract and continue reporting to his thirteenth-floor office in New York.

On Tuesday, September 11, Small received a certified letter from Ruhe confirming his firing for "breach of your employment contract."

"I regret this action, but I feel there is no alternative under the circumstances," Ruhe wrote.

Small ignored this as well. Stripped of authority, he sat each day at his desk, used the phone, and generally conducted "business as usual."

Thoren and her assistant, Bill Bowe, phoned Small to ask him to stop coming to work.

"See you in court," Small said breezily, and hung up.

On Wednesday, Thoren wrote Small, directing him to "immediately discontinue using the offices of the company" and warning him to clear out his belongings by the next day or UPI would "make arrangements to accomplish this."

Small's intransigence had UPI executives worried that the protracted public dismissal might jeopardize client relations. It would be embarrassing if Small were still around when TV reporters came to cover the September 17 vote result. So, on Friday, Bowe ordered the locks to Small's office changed.

When Bill Adler arrived at work Monday, the day of the big vote, he saw a shiny new knob on Small's office door and was relieved when fellow executive Al Kaff told him Small had come and gone. It seemed the crisis was over.

Walking by Small's office at 11 a.m., Adler did a double take. The door was open and Small sat, feet propped on his desk, reading a newspaper. He was grinning like a Cheshire cat, teeth clenched around his pipe. Small had arrived to find his door locked and his treasured collection of pipes and paperweights in a box outside his office. Small had glared at the door a minute, then remembered a side entrance through the adjoining office and slipped inside.

Adler dashed to a phone and called Bowe in Nashville.

"What do I do?"

"How did he get in there?" asked Bowe, shocked.

"I don't know."

Bowe told Adler to have building security guards remove Small before the media arrived to cover the vote count. "Let me talk to him," volunteered John Mantle, vice president for newspaper sales.

Mantle walked into Small's office wearing a friendly smile.

"I've always liked you, Bill, and respect you," he said. "I'm sure you understand that this is a very sensitive situation. I'm asking you, as a friend and as a colleague, to do the sensible thing and call it a day."

Expressionless, Small sucked on his pipe.

"Mantle," he said evenly, "I always knew you were an asshole."

Mantle, speechless, turned and left.

Two building guards then entered Small's office, but it was only after UPI's executives met Small's demands for yet another letter confirming his eviction that the ousted president departed, leaving no doubt he would sue.

On his way out he phoned switchboard operator Catherine Downey.

"This is Bill Small," he said. "I'm leaving now for lunch, and I'm never coming back."

• • •

Nogales and Wechsler had expected to comfortably win the union vote, but the owners almost upset the apple cart. With inconceivably bad timing, Ruhe and Geissler announced they were joining a consortium undertaking a direct-broadcast satellite television project. Ruhe and Geissler said they planned to take out loans to finance their portion of the joint venture with Communications Satellite Corporation and Prudential Insurance Company. Although the deal was not directly related to UPI and would never be consummated, employees were furious. Why were Ruhe and Geissler out borrowing money for other projects while trying to finance UPI through sacrifices by employees?

In the days before the votes were counted, UPI had continued to trim its management payroll. Vice presidents H.L. Stevenson and Tom Haughney, an original partner, both had left on September 14. Including Small, the departures of top managers would save more than $1 million.

The vote was announced hours after Small's departure. By a margin of 3 to 1, UPI's employees had given their company the kiss of life.

Sullen Unipressers around the world went about their business as usual. That week Democratic nominee Walter Mondale doomed any chance to upset President Reagan by outlining a plan to raise $85 billion in new taxes; and in Beirut, staffers, exhausted by endless sectarian violence, sprang to action when a station wagon loaded with explosives blew up outside the U.S. Embassy, killing eight people.

If staffers generally shrugged off the results of the union vote, there nevertheless could be no arguing that Nogales had pulled a tremendous coup. Seizing the initiative and appealing to the loyalty and dedication of Unipressers, he had somehow made palatable the most onerous of employee sacrifices.

In a thank-you to the staff, Nogales said, "The vote demonstrates the special character and resolve of the people who work for UPI. The company now has the best chance it has ever had to succeed within its own resources."

Even as the memo was being circulated, Doug Ruhe had stunning news that would have enraged his employees. Not long after the vote was announced, Ruhe summoned Mantle and Adler to his office. The owners, who had never invested any money in UPI and had just begged the workers to carry the company, were about to become beneficiaries of a financial windfall.

"Hey, man, I'm in big trouble," Ruhe said. "I've just cut a deal for $40 million to sell a TV station in Chicago. It's a sweet deal. What am I going to tell the union?"[1]

---

[1] Ruhe later denied making the remark.

12

Focus Pocus

Even before the shock of their first truncated paychecks wore off, Unipressers learned a sale of Channel 66 might indeed be in the offing. The staff was buzzing over a blurb in the September 29 issue of *Editor & Publisher* saying the UHF station Ruhe and Geissler had built virtually from scratch was on the block for $40 million.

Ruhe had exaggerated the proximity of a sale, though, in suggesting in his chat with Mantle and Adler that a deal had been all but consummated. Ruhe had signed a preliminary agreement for Channel 66 with Milt Grant, owner of Grant Broadcasting in Miami, under which the owners would be paid as much as $5 million in up-front cash. But Grant, like Taft Broadcasting before him, had second thoughts and pulled out. The near misses only strengthened Ruhe's resolve.

Unipressers desperate for any crumb of good news were cheered by the *E&P* article quoting spokesman Dave Wickenden that the owners intended to use funds from a sale of Channel 66 for "UPI ventures that are aimed at developing specialized information businesses for new markets." However, the statement UPI spokesmen extracted from Ruhe fell far short of a commitment to invest money directly into the wire service.

Luis Nogales kept his disappointment to himself. He knew that the pay cuts had bought him only a little breathing room, a temporary operating profit. The cash crunch would soon reappear when wage restoration began right before Christmas. Perhaps the owners really would sell Channel 66 and maybe they then could be persuaded to at last invest some of the money they always seemed to be promising.

Nogales realized he somehow had to rekindle the faith of UPI's greatest asset—its employees. As autumn wore on it was clear that Unipressers who for years had been dismissing UPI's going-out-of-business rumors were heeding the counsel of their union leaders to search for new jobs. Scores resigned. Over two months, seven of eight staffers in North Carolina departed. Nor were high-level managers immune to the panic —in four of UPI's five domestic division headquarters, the top editor quit.

Underscoring management's new openness, Nogales frequently chatted informally with employees in the Washington newsroom, describing the latest steps to save the company and exhorting them not to lose faith. At one meeting he declared Ruhe had told him the sale of Channel 66 was imminent.

"The owners have pledged to put $10 million into UPI—whatever it takes," Nogales said.

Despite deep misgivings, the vast majority of Unipressers stuck it out. Some stayed because the job market was tight, others out of idealism and their affection for UPI; some were persuaded that Nogales could indeed turn things around. They could only hope their own financial commitment would be matched by Ruhe and Geissler, men toward whom many Unipressers now directed growing distrust and even open antagonism. Employees were beginning to resent that these two entrepreneurs had invested nothing in the company yet continued at the helm, making decisions that would affect UPI's future.

Ironically, it was the talk about a Channel 66 sale that gave UPI executives a chance to test the level of the owners' commitment. Financial officers and consultant Jerry Hillman had been frantically searching for a way to convince Tom Sinton of Arthur Young & Company to give UPI a third straight unqualified audit so they would be in a better position to search for capital. With the losses over the past two years totaling nearly $23 million, Sinton had balked for months at signing off on the 1983 year-end audit, concluding the pay cuts alone were not enough to ensure solvency.

Seizing on the Channel 66 rumors, UPI financial officers pressed Ruhe and Geissler to back up their talk by signing a letter pledging unconditionally to lend UPI $2 million "upon written demand." The owners signed the pledge on October 22 and Sinton issued the clean audit.

Sinton, more than a thousand Unipressers, and even top managers were ignorant of the full extent of Ruhe and Geissler's financial troubles. In truth, the owners had to sell Channel 66 because, awash in debts, they could barely make payroll at their Focus operations.

• • •

In pursuing their grand vision of a television empire, Ruhe and Geissler had constructed a quivering financial house of cards. Not only had they invested no money from their other ventures into UPI, but privately were transferring millions from UPI to Focus Communications, flagship company of their television operation. Ruhe and Geissler had aimed too high, spread themselves too thin, and devastatingly miscalculated the market.

Their entry into the high-yield, high-risk world of television had begun favorably enough in the deal in which they snared 70 percent of Channel 66 in negotiations against some of the biggest, shrewdest players in the business. Focus Broadcasting Company soon was collecting $2 million annually to run the station and Ruhe and Geissler were plunging deeper into the pay-TV business.

Recruiting Baha'i buddies and other minorities, among them at least three former officials of their alma mater, the University of Massachusetts, Ruhe and Geissler peppered the FCC with applications for minority-preference licenses. By 1982 they had obtained rights to build about 150 low-power neighborhood stations in places like Minneapolis, Washington, Cleveland, and Waycross, Georgia, and had licenses pending for high-powered channels in Providence, Rhode Island, the Nashville suburb of Murfreesboro, and in several other cities.

Full-power licenses, like beachfront property, were particularly hot commodities. But each one required large outlays of cash and would not begin to return the investment until the station reached the air. At any given time Ruhe and Geissler juggled as many as a dozen license applications, running up hefty legal fees.

Ruhe and Geissler had charged ahead even though the emergence of cable was putting the squeeze on pay television. In 1982 they hired Steve Pruett, a Chicago-based industry consultant who proved a valuable acquisition, finding investors so Ruhe and Geissler did not have to put up money of their own.

Pruett concentrated first on financing construction of the new Channel 39 in Murfreesboro and on the purchase of struggling pay-tv Channel 64 in Providence from Dallas Cowboys owner Clint Murchison. After hunting for six months for venture capital, he chanced upon Jim Moore, an Atlanta investment banker with lots of contacts, and they began drafting a business prospectus. The search for investors suddenly became easier when Ruhe and Geissler gained credibility with their acquisition of UPI.

Nashville investment banker Henry Booth was instrumental in finding thirty-five investors to put up almost $3 million—$83,000 each for a 1.4 percent interest in Channel 39. When Ruhe showed up for meetings wearing a business suit and tennis shoes, Booth ducked investors' nervous queries by shrugging and saying, "You know as much as I do." Pruett and Moore packaged a similar deal to raise $3 million for the Providence station.

In April, Ruhe and Geissler created UPI Media, Inc., named Pruett executive vice president, and put him in charge of the two new stations and of Channel 66 in Chicago. Pruett raised yet another $1 million to cover operating costs of the new management company. For use of its name, UPI got a 10 percent stake.

The Murfreesboro and Providence deals were closed the last week of September 1983, the ventures structured so that Ruhe and Geissler received total operating control without having to put up money or share detailed financial information with investors. UPI Media retained controlling interest in each station.

By late 1983, as subscription customers turned to cable, the owners' would-be empire, even its centerpiece, Channel 66, began to crumble. In early 1984, United Cable, which provided programming, pulled out of the Chicago station. Ruhe and Geissler were forced to fill air time with music videos and soft-core sexploitation flicks, a far cry from their idealistic dream of an Independent Quality Network.

Deep in a hole, the partners switched course, attempting to sell more stock in Channel 66 so they could convert it to a regular commercial station. With Murfreesboro and Providence still not on the air, bills mounted and cash transfers from UPI to Focus began to mushroom.

In 1982, while Rob Small and Cordy Overgaard were still around, UPI had transferred $250,000 to Focus Communications, largely management fees for Ruhe, Geissler, and Ahlhauser. But on March 1, 1983, one month after Small and Overgaard left, the owners began transferring $90,000 a month, and sometimes much more. UPI's 1983 financial statement showed transfers to Focus of $1,434,000, and accountants would trace a similar amount in 1984. By early 1985 the total wire transfers would well exceed $3 million.

Some UPI executives felt that sum was far more than what reasonably could be charged for the kind of "management services" being provided by Ruhe, Geissler, and Focus.[1]

• • •

Woody Sudbrink, the Florida broadcaster who flirted with joining the owners' consortium, had bolted when he learned Focus would be involved in managing the wire service. Sudbrink had feared Ruhe and Geissler might be tempted to amass a "slush fund" of UPI money for their other projects.

Ruhe and Geissler may never have believed they were creating a slush fund with the cash transfers from UPI to Focus, but accounting people in both companies were bothered by the constant smudging of the financial lines. Rarely were the transfers accompanied by detailed invoices.

Some accountants began to worry that the owners were making UPI their private toy. Since Ruhe and Geissler owned both UPI and the various Focus companies, they seemed to see nothing wrong with sharing money and facilities as if all were one big family.

In hiring friends and Baha'is, they often bypassed more qualified candidates. And, in the tradition of the religion, they offered financial support to Baha'is outside their companies. Ruhe ordered employees in the Focus accounting department to draw checks for tens of thousands in "loans" to Baha'is such as Octavio Neri, who wanted to start a TV station in his native Venezuela, and Pepe Banchero, a would-be partner in a Peruvian pay TV venture who got $50,000.

When Nogales questioned why Banchero and Neri were given com-

---

[1] Ruhe maintained the money transferred to Focus was for legitimate management services, but offered few details of what those services were.

pany credit cards to cover their travel expenses in the United States, he was told they were acting as consultants to assist UPI's conversion to satellite news delivery in South America. Nogales shrugged off his misgivings, reasoning that since Ruhe and Geissler owned UPI, they were free to make such decisions.

In addition, Ruhe gave some Focus employees interest-free loans of up to $3,000. The owners took loans themselves, too, recording them simply as "Loan to Ruhe" or "Loan to Geissler." Most later were written off, although employees familiar with the books said Focus issued no IRS W-2 forms reporting that the "loans" had turned into bonuses on which recipients would owe taxes. Accounting department officials said that between 1980 and 1984 the loans from Focus totaled more than $200,000.

Ruhe and Geissler also were generous in loaning money to fellow Baha'is struggling with their own business ventures. Focus employees said one friend received as much as $50,000 for a clothing store.

Geissler and Ruhe, whose father was on the Baha'i world governing council, did not ignore their religious brethren. They sent checks to Baha'i groups totaling up to $2,000 a month, some directly to the Baha'i Fund at national headquarters in Wilmette, Illinois.

Another $12,000 was sent to the Baha'i fund earmarked for Dean Stephens, an engineer working in Puerto Rico, to devise a decoder box for pay-TV customers. Focus also sent $500 a month to a Baha'i missionary in Africa, and made regular $500 payments to another "pioneer" in South America—Ruhe's older brother, Chris.

The owners sometimes portrayed themselves as philanthropists with few material ambitions. One year when there was talk of small bonuses for Focus employees, Ruhe declared, "I don't need it. I'll give my share to the Indochinese relief fund."

Although they were not high-livers, Ruhe, Geissler, and Ahlhauser each took company cars, new Honda Accords. Ruhe and Geissler also availed themselves of the travel opportunities offered by an international company, ringing up $138,169 in corporate credit card charges in the first seven months of 1984. Geissler took business trips to his native Venezuela and to Bolivia and Brazil, and visited Mexico and Cuba a couple of times. Ruhe went to Europe and to Mexico. Their wives, Diti Geissler and Beverly Ruhe, sometimes had the use of UPI corporate American Express Cards, company sources alleged.

UPI's move of corporate headquarters to Brentwood Commons, near Nashville, enabled the owners to merge UPI and Focus offices. UPI wound up footing the Focus bill for tens of thousands of dollars for rent, telephones, fancy new furniture, and even some postage costs.

It wasn't the first time UPI had subsidized Focus. In November of 1983, Ruhe made Vanessa Drucker, a college friend of his wife, vice president and director of programming for Focus. For two years she sat in a rent-free office in the UPI New York bureau and screened movies for Focus television stations.

Despite the way UPI funds were handled, most of those who worked closely with Ruhe and Geissler did not feel the owners were out to enrich themselves at UPI's expense. Rather, they treated the resources as one big pot from which they could draw funds as necessary. In doing so, Ruhe and Geissler were sapping the lifeblood of an international institution.

• • •

Even as losses mounted at Channel 66, Ruhe and Geissler found ways to squander nearly $6 million in investors' money on the Tennessee and Rhode Island stations. Once again inexperience and perhaps ingenuous idealism helped sabotage their dreams.

Channel 39 in Murfreesboro had been doomed almost from the start because Ruhe's and Geissler's technical wizards misgauged the hilly terrain in situating its 1,000-foot antenna. The signal was so weak that many viewers in the big Nashville market didn't even know about the station, whose programming was by any measure, mediocre. Arbitron ratings, which determine advertising rates, never reflected a blip. Compounding the disaster, the station faced competition from a new, better-financed channel with an antenna that worked. Losses mounted, and investors, who would be left with little more than tax losses, sizzled.

In Providence, Channel 64 was plagued by growing friction between Pruett and Geissler, who stymied the former's efforts to hire experienced hands by demanding that half the staff be minorities. Geissler also insisted on putting an inexperienced black woman in charge of Channel 66. Open warfare erupted in the summer of 1984, even as UPI's employees were being asked to accept huge pay cuts. Geissler decreed Pruett had to hire the owners' minority candidates as managers at Channel 64 until a 50 percent quota was reached. Showing Geissler's memo to Jim Moore and the Channel 64 investors, Pruett said, "This is what these guys have on their minds. I don't want to be part of this deal."

Pruett had also balked when the owners tried to tap UPI Media's cash reserves as things got tight at UPI. Conceding he was concerned about UPI's "cash-flow problems," Ruhe in late 1983 asked Pruett to loan the wire service as much as $100,000 from the funds put up by television investors. Ruhe also wanted UPI Media to spring for $30,000 a month to finance his new joint polling venture, UPI ASK.

When Pruett sought the advice of Linda Thoren, general counsel for both UPI and the owners' TV interests, she warned it would be improper to divert investors' money and that he could face personal liability if such loans were not repaid.

Ruhe succeeded on one occasion in persuading Pruett to loan UPI $50,000. It was quickly repaid, but as the wire service's cash squeeze worsened Pruett resisted Ruhe's subsequent entreaties.

"No, that's commingling funds," he said. "That's not the purpose of the limited partnership. We're not a bank."

Pruett began to ignore Ruhe's phone calls, sometimes succeeding in avoiding him for days on end. Finally, Ruhe told bookkeeper Cathy Balthrup that when he ordered loans she'd better not tarry. Ultimately, over Pruett's objections, UPI Media loaned UPI more than $200,000 of its investors' money.

Angry at the continuing raids on UPI Media funds, Pruett and Moore delivered an ultimatum: unless Pruett was guaranteed operating control they would raise no more money for the struggling TV ventures. When he got no such assurances, Pruett submitted his resignation on August 14. While he agreed to stay until a replacement was found, on Labor Day weekend Ruhe and Geissler abruptly fired Pruett and ordered the locks on his office door changed.

They replaced him with Rinaldo Brutoco, the California lawyer who had resumed consulting for them months earlier. Brutoco was paid a whopping $50,000 a month to try to salvage something by selling their tottering television operations. It was too late. By the fall of 1984, with UPI employees pinning their hopes on the sale of Channel 66, the market for television stations ranged from lukewarm to cold.

Nogales's own illusions about the TV sale were short-lived. Not long after he had delivered to employees the owners' pledge of a cash injection, he recalled later, he was chatting with Ruhe when the subject of the owners' investing money from Channel 66 came up.

"I wouldn't risk a dollar in UPI," Ruhe said firmly.

Nogales couldn't believe what he was hearing. He had just put his reputation on the line for the owners.

"Doug," he said, bristling, "I went down and told the staff after clearing it with you that you would put $10 million or $12 million from the proceeds of the [TV] sale into UPI."

Ruhe stiffened. "No, I'm not going to put in a dime," he declared.

On many occasions Nogales had gone out of his way to excuse the shortcomings of the owners, who had hired and promoted him. But now, he thought, Ruhe had betrayed him. And betrayed UPI.

13
A Dangerous Gamble

UPI owed so much money to so many creditors in the fall of 1984 it feared any three could band together and attempt to plunge it into involuntary bankruptcy. The new president, Luis Nogales, and his management team shook their heads in dismay as they kept stumbling upon debts long hidden by UPI's botched record-keeping.

They began drawing up a blueprint for dealing with $20 million in short-term debts to more than 5,000 creditors. Only if they could persuade those creditors to cooperate might UPI's cash flow turn positive. Otherwise, financing costs and payments on the crushing debts would swallow the temporary operating profits brought by the employee pay cuts.

Fortunately, none of the big creditors wanted to be remembered as the one that pulled the plug on UPI. Indeed, giant conglomerates like AT&T and RCA were fellow media companies—and felt a special kinship and responsibility.

Ray Wechsler had negotiated a secret deal in the spring of 1984 with his old colleagues at AT&T. In an arrangement the phone company wanted to conceal from its other clients, it permitted UPI to delay paying its $6 million debt and to defer part of its $500,000 to $600,000 monthly bill for six months. Wechsler and his buddy Jerry Hillman, like other consultants spared the wage cuts borne by lesser-paid Unipressers, cashed in handsomely on the deal. Besides their regular fees, they shared a $100,000 commission funneled by UPI to Masters and Company, a subsidiary of Hillman's firm, Chareeva Productions.

The agreement with AT&T would be a model UPI would try to follow with other creditors. On September 18, the day after the union accepted the concessions, Nogales, Wechsler, Bill Adler, Jack Kenney, and Steve Spritzer, a newly hired financial consultant, fanned out to beg big creditors to let UPI stretch out payments.

In New York, Adler visited the Fifth Avenue offices of Lois Pitts Gershon, still owed $400,000 for its highly imaginative advertising campaign. He promised that if UPI's debt was frozen for a couple of months, it would be paid by year's end.

"I wouldn't still be here if I didn't think it's going to work," Adler told Dick Gershon, one of the company's partners.

"We can't afford not to have you pay," Gershon said, "but I believe you're serious." Within weeks a deal was sealed.

Wechsler scored similar successes, capitalizing on the warm feelings UPI still engendered to win payment grace periods or discounts for products and services. But some smaller firms, operating on tiny margins, had read about employee wage concessions and assumed the company was flush again. They were not so sympathetic, saying, in effect, "Pay or I'll see you in court."

The pressure still was immense. On October 22, the day Ruhe and Geissler pledged to lend $2 million, a meeting of the executive committee in Brentwood was consumed by efforts to juggle finances.

Dan Carmichael, given a seat on the committee as part of the deal with the union, for the first time got a frightening inside look at the machinations necessary to keep the company running. Despairing, he phoned guild president Bill Morrissey after the meeting and briefed him.

"Danny," Morrissey said, "the place is going."

• • •

More than once advisers had suggested Ruhe and Geissler seek shelter from creditors under Chapter 11 provisions of the Federal Bankruptcy Code. That option seemed to offer UPI precious time to reorganize: payments on all past debts, even interest charges, would be frozen until the company was either liquidated or restructured. UPI could work out a deal with creditors to pay just a fraction of what it owed, could cancel oppressive or unwanted contracts, and could shop for a buyer flush with money.

With a sound reorganization plan under Chapter 11, and employees working for reduced wages, UPI would be instantly profitable.

Boston bankruptcy lawyer Rick Levine, who had begun advising UPI in September, was convinced that even the huge employee pay cuts fell far short of a cure. Despite all the financial legerdemain, massive debts soon would drown the company. Foothill officials were demanding evidence that the financial mess was being tended to. UPI's salvation, Levine counseled, lay in Chapter 11.

Ruhe and Geissler were unalterably opposed. They feared the very word "bankruptcy" would send clients fleeing to the AP. Besides, they had a deeper worry. When Ruhe asked Nogales' opinion of Chapter 11, the answer touched a raw nerve.

"I think that if you go into bankruptcy," Nogales replied frankly, "you will not survive as an owner."

Ruhe's refusal to consider bankruptcy had profound negative ramifications for the company. First, in Chapter 11, the money from the pay cuts could have gone directly toward turnaround efforts rather than to creditors. Second, under court supervision, Ruhe and Geissler almost assuredly would have been shunted aside. That would mean scrutiny of all money transfers to Focus and payments to consultants, no more stripping of assets. UPI would have been on the sales block, and, with more than $90 million in annual revenues still pouring in, might indeed have proved a tempting takeover target.

Ruhe quickly demonstrated just how far he was prepared to go to avoid Chapter 11 and keep control of UPI, whatever the consequences. At a meeting in late September, consultant Ray Wechsler brandished the latest dire financial figures. Then, executives attending the meeting said later, Jerry Hillman made a suggestion that shocked Ruhe, Nogales, and advisers Kenney and Spritzer:

The short-term solution to the financial crunch would be for UPI to delay turning over to the federal government the fourth-quarter employee withholding taxes. Witnesses said Wechsler then supported the idea, although Wechsler later labeled such assertions "absolutely insane."

In any event, the proposal was greeted with stunned silence.

Finally Ruhe spoke.

"That would be illegal," he said.

The desperate search for a solution to the money woes had taken a dangerous and foreboding turn. In the Internal Revenue Service, UPI would be flirting with a most formidable opponent. Failure to remit payroll withholding taxes could even bring criminal prosecution.

According to witnesses, Hillman and Wechsler tried to reassure their colleagues, saying they had talked with Sigmund Balaban, a specialist in IRS matters who also was the accountant for New York Mayor Ed Koch. Balaban reportedly expressed confidence that, because UPI would be a first offender, the government would agree to a lenient repayment schedule. All but ignored was the fact that if the gamble failed and UPI were unable to quickly repay the debt, its officers would be risking personal liability not only for the tax money but also for any penalties.

Ruhe then recalled that once or twice his small companies had missed withholding taxes without being prosecuted. This gamble would be far more serious; UPI's quarterly withholding taxes exceeded $1.5 million.

He quickly calculated the worst-case options. Surely he could find ways to pay the taxes and the probable 5 percent penalty. By January, Channel 66 should be sold, and in a pinch he could always sell UPI's remaining interests in Comtex or Fintext. Ruhe, the riverboat gambler, gave the go-ahead.

The decision to divert Uncle Sam's money to creditors gave Kenney the chills. He declared nervously, "I always say, there's two things you don't fool with—Mother Nature and the IRS."

About a week later he sought out Nogales and stressed that everyone who had attended the meeting faced the risk of personal liability for the withholding-tax decision. Nogales was startled. He had assumed that Ruhe, as an owner, would be responsible. He tried to reassure himself Ruhe could come up with the money, but he began to grow nervous.

Nogales had found it difficult to object to the tax scheme. He had placed his reputation on the line in pushing for the wage cuts and promising employees the owners would invest $10 million in UPI. Now he agonized about his support for his bosses. Had he blundered in placing his confidence in the owners? Was the decision to skip fourth-quarter taxes indicative of how reckless and feckless Doug Ruhe was?

Nogales decided to try to limit the damage by insulating the editorial department from the tax decision. He intentionally kept editor Max McCrohon away from the discussions.

When McCrohon heard what was going on he consulted his Chicago attorney, Jack Levin, who told him he was not liable. He instructed McCrohon to type a letter disavowing involvement in the decision and always to carry it with him. Thereafter, whenever a discussion of the tax decision arose, McCrohon would unfold and brandish his letter, then march out of the room. Behind his back other executives disparaged him as a wimp. But deep down they wished they, too, were letter carriers.

On the advice of his own lawyer, Nogales insisted that Ruhe and Geissler agree in writing to absolve him of liability for "any obligation or debt" owed by UPI. The owners signed the letter, but ignored Nogales's request that they also pledge, in a second letter, that since they had made the tax decision "the proceeds from the sale of Channel 66 . . . will be invested in UPI, including the payment of moneys owed to the IRS."

Nogales doubted, however, that such letters would carry much weight with the government. He told himself the best protection for everybody was to make sure UPI did not fail.

• • •

Nogales, McCrohon, and the UPI sales force attempted in the fall of 1984 to put the best face on a terrible situation. They worked the telephones and visited editors and publishers of powerful newspaper clients like *The Los Angeles Times* and *Chicago Tribune*. Somehow, UPI's management team had to persuade its customers that, despite the loss of 200 staffers and 25 percent pay cuts, the product had not suffered and the worst was over.

Amid this intense effort, Bill Small, a man widely popular with industry leaders, struck back and further roiled UPI's troubled waters.

Just a month after his stormy ouster, Small filed a lengthy suit in U.S. District Court in Manhattan accusing UPI's owners of breach of contract and demanding $10.2 million in damages. Small alleged his airtight contract permitted his firing only for "fraud or gross malfeasance or other improper conduct resulting in substantial injury to UPI."

Small also charged UPI had sullied his reputation, particularly when the Nashville *Tennessean* quoted an anonymous company official assailing him for "spending too much time jet-setting around the world and hob-nobbing with royalty," traveling first-class while other top executives were making substantial sacrifices during UPI's financial crisis. Small called the statements false and libelous, noting he "almost never traveled first-class on UPI business trips" even though that specifically was permitted by his contract.

Process server Herbert Perry later said in a deposition that when he delivered a notice of the suit to Ruhe at the Nashville airport on October 18, the owner shouted, "And you tell that Bill Small that we're going to get him!"

• • •

The more he had seen of the owners' stewardship, the more Nogales felt impelled to cast himself as UPI's guardian, growing increasingly assertive in questioning the activities and motives of Ruhe and Geissler. He particularly was upset when Ruhe tried to transfer UPI's 5 percent ownership of the headquarters building in Washington to himself and Geissler—even as employees were accepting pay cuts. When Nogales challenged the move, Ruhe said they merely wanted to use the building for tax losses, which he said were of no value to UPI. Nogales informed him that transferring one of UPI's sole physical assets would enrage employees, and Ruhe dropped the plan. But he was beginning to resent Nogales's interference.

Hardly had that confrontation abated when Nogales threw a roadblock in Ruhe's efforts to sell company assets. Ruhe was discussing a sale of UPI's half ownership of Fintext, the stock-quote joint venture, for $1 million to Colorado businessman Clint Ober, who a year earlier had purchased rights to distribute UPI's cable TV service. Nogales, telling himself Ruhe already had made enough lousy deals, demanded the owner let him negotiate with Ober. Reluctantly, Ruhe consented. When Nogales and Ober met in Denver in late fall, their talks and the deal collapsed. Ruhe was furious. The money might have helped extricate him from the IRS mess.

Perhaps Ruhe's displeasure with Nogales made him receptive when adviser Jim West introduced him to a former Scripps Howard executive who had the know-how to run UPI and was admired and respected in the industry. Bill Payette, seventy-one, former head of Scripps's giant, highly successful United Features Syndicate that had once been part of UPI, had retired to Palm Desert, California. West suggested Ruhe hire him as an adviser.

In early December, at a lengthy meeting in the courtyard of the Palm

Springs Sheraton also attended by marketing chief Thomas Beatty, Ruhe, who had been serving as chief executive officer, asked Payette to take the post and help Nogales run UPI. Ruhe did not mention his disenchantment with Nogales.

Payette, although fearful of the pounding of a full-time management job, was tempted by the challenge of returning to help his troubled company. He agreed to think about it.

• • •

With the company limping along and employees' anemic paychecks stretched to the breaking point, along came a December evening that restored company pride. Nogales, other executives, and reporters from the Washington bureau rented tuxedos and donned ball gowns to honor their colleague Helen Thomas as she was presented the National Press Club's prestigious Fourth Estate Award.

Even as UPI's fortunes had declined, Thomas's star had gained luster.

She had been a Unipresser since the war-torn summer of 1943, easing into a Washington bureau depleted because many males had been drafted. Fresh out of Wayne State University journalism school, Thomas spent a dozen years reporting to work at 5:30 in the morning to pound out tedious local radio stories. Her big break came in November 1960, when she was dispatched to Palm Beach, Florida, to keep an eye on Jackie Kennedy while her famous colleague Merriman Smith handled the more important business of covering President-elect John Kennedy.

Thomas, who had never before seen an ocean, couldn't believe life in the fast lane. "God, this is fun. They pay for all your meals." What more could a young reporter want? Covering major stories with the whole world as your audience—this was the big time at last! On January 21, 1961, the first full day of the John Fitzgerald Kennedy presidency, she squeezed into the cramped UPI White House booth between Merriman Smith and Al Spivak. "I assigned myself," she often said proudly. "I decided it was my beat, and nobody could pry me out."

Nor would they try. Through Kennedy's assassination; through Lyndon Johnson's forced retirement; through Nixon reopening the door to China, then falling to disgrace and resignation over Watergate; through Ford and Carter and Reagan, the one constant at the White House was Helen Thomas asking the hard questions. She was an institution unto herself, her renown the antithesis of the faceless, unknown wire-service reporter. Blazing a path for women journalists, she collected most of her profession's top awards and honors. But perhaps most important for UPI, she visibly bore high the banner of her struggling company.

In winning the Fourth Estate Award, Thomas joined some of the biggest names in journalism history: Walter Cronkite, James Reston, Herb Block, Vermont Royster, Theodore White, and Eric Sevareid.

Two of her best friends, Abigail Van Buren, who wrote the widely syndicated "Dear Abby" advice column, and ABC Television correspondent Sam Donaldson, alternately roasted her and praised her before a packed house of journalism luminaries.

• • •

By early January, Jack Kenney, facing the daily nightmare of running the accounting department virtually alone, was losing sleep. UPI continued to be deluged by dunning calls from many of the thousands of creditors who had been fighting for months to get paid.

Ironically, Nogales's attempt to reassure creditors by announcing in late October UPI's first monthly operating profit in more than two decades only fueled demands for payment. Vendors did not understand that a modest operating profit barely dented the enormous debts.

There were so many pressing bills that UPI's life-support systems began to falter. Occasionally, finding its phones dead, a bureau would send a frantic SOS on the internal wires to Washington. Managers there would call the accounting department in Brentwood to plead for an emergency payment. The trick was to try to restore service before subscribers could discover the phones had been disconnected.

Harried editorial managers with such pressing bills learned to phone the accounts payable department in Brentwood early in the morning or forget it. Kenney had assumed Ahlhauser's old job of informing his assistants how much cash they could disburse each day. When an aide one morning routinely inquired how much was available, she stopped cold when Kenney replied, "None."

By January, with employees having received the first round of wage restorations returning them to 85 percent of their old salaries, the money crunch was even tighter. Kenney concluded there wasn't enough to send Focus its monthly "management fees," which Ruhe and Geissler had been politic enough to reduce to $33,000.

When she didn't receive the January check, Focus controller Sharon Sherman phoned Kenney.

"We need our money," she said.

"I don't think we can get it for you. I can't make payroll."

"I can't make payroll, either," Sherman replied, voice rising in panic.

Ruhe came to her rescue. On his orders, UPI transferred $33,000 to Focus.

It wasn't just creditors who besieged the accounting department. Employees also peppered the Brentwood switchboard asking after long-delayed expense reimbursements. Current crises aside, the company's traditionally closed-purse attitude toward employee expenses was legendary. Each Unipresser had a horror story.

Reporter Matt Quinn laughed about a tiff he had with the company after covering a Ku Klux Klan rally in a pasture in Plains, Georgia, on Independence Day 1977. A crazed Vietnam veteran drove his Jaguar XKE through the rally, hitting Quinn so hard it knocked his shoes off. Later, from his hospital bed in nearby Americus, Quinn joked over the phone to Atlanta bureau chief Bill Tome, "I'll be putting new shoes on my expense account." Tome, hoping to forestall a raid on the company treasury, quickly dispatched two Unipressers to hunt for the shoes. To no avail. Quinn submitted a $55 expense item for a new pair of Clarks Wallabees, and won. But when he quit a year later he was informed the cost of the shoes was being deducted from his final check.

Even with such a tightwad tradition, getting expenses had never been this bad. Unipressers had been waiting months for reimbursements that for some exceeded $3,000. Union leaders Morrissey and Carmichael came under heavy pressure to do something about hundreds of thousands of dollars in unpaid expenses. Receiving no satisfaction from the National Labor Relations Board, Morrissey secretly directed guild lawyer Sid Reitman to assemble legal papers that could force UPI into involuntary bankruptcy. "I want you to lock the papers up in your safe," Morrissey told Reitman. "If this is not resolved fast, we are going to file."

• • •

Nogales, Wechsler, and Kenney hardly were surprised when the owners failed by early January to come up with the money they had pledged— or any funds to cover the unpaid payroll withholding taxes. They had grown accustomed to Doug Ruhe's raised expectations and broken promises.

As financial men, Kenney and Wechsler feared the wrath of the IRS. Taking a step to ensure no one would be tempted to continue the folly of diverting IRS money, Wechsler broke the news to Foothill vice president Peter Schwab that fourth-quarter withholding taxes had not been paid. Schwab reacted as though a rocket had been ignited inside Foothill's vault. As the prime lender, Foothill always had been first in line for payment in case the company failed. An IRS lien likely would jeopardize that most-favored-lender status.

Furious, Foothill president John Nickoll contemplated pulling the plug on UPI's loan but decided that shutting down such a legendary company might prove a public relations disaster. Instead, he directed a separate payroll account be formed so that Foothill, before advancing any more loans, could verify that taxes were being paid.

By the first weeks of 1985, factions were forming in UPI's executive suite. The owners' failure to deliver a cash infusion had spawned a dark, mutinous mood among Nogales, Wechsler, and Kenney, the three men overseeing the company's day-to-day struggle for survival. Wechsler, who had won Foothill's trust and had rapidly gained influence since arriving the previous spring, had seen enough to conclude the owners were on a path toward certain destruction. He was not bashful about sharing his opinion with Nogales.

For his part Nogales was being hounded from all sides: the union wanted expense money and was angry the owners never had turned over the promised 6.5 percent stock in Media News Corporation; major creditors wanted money; Foothill wanted austerity steps; and UPI bureaus wanted assurance that things ultimately would turn out all right.

Wechsler's complaints about Ruhe and Geissler reinforced Nogales's skepticism. He felt the owners had deceived him with their promises of capital. And, having accompanied Ruhe to wasted meetings with potential investors, he was convinced the owners had no real prospects of finding a minority partner.

Following a meeting with union leaders on January 10, Nogales again goaded Morrissey and Carmichael to persuade the owners to step aside. Later he phoned Morrissey and said he doubted UPI could survive more than four months unless they somehow could be convinced to relinquish control. But, once again, the guild leaders decided against risking a confrontation with Ruhe and Geissler.

• • •

On Tuesday, January 15, 1985, Unipressers got more distressing news. United Press Canada, a joint venture between UPI and several big Canadian papers, had shut down. UPI lost the services of some fifty journalists and also faced the impossible task of covering the gigantic nation with single staffers in Montreal, Toronto, Ottawa, and Vancouver.

Despite reassurances from Nogales that the shutdown would have little effect, many staffers and outside observers alike considered it another harbinger of impending doom.

The next day Nogales, by now aware of the union's threat to file a bankruptcy petition, told Carmichael he had come up with enough cash to cover the previous September's employee expenses. For now, the union kept the bankruptcy papers locked in its safe.

Nogales had grown short-tempered over what he felt was the union leaders' continued sniping. He resented their complaints about the cash shortage, particularly when they seemed to have no stomach for confronting Ruhe. Urging them again to take a lead role in persuading the owners to relinquish operating control, Nogales arranged for them to meet with Ruhe.

Carmichael and Morrissey, who had heard the Channel 66 sale had fallen through, asked Ruhe if he was going to put money into UPI. Although his response was vague, as usual, they chose not to press the issue. When they described the meeting to Nogales, he was furious.

"I can't believe it! You guys are real pussies! You come to me angry and you confront me about the lack of capital. And then you meet the guys really in charge, who are responsible, and you're bowing down."

• • •

During his chats with employees in the Washington newsroom, Nogales continued to brief them on the company's progress—or lack of it—toward a secure future. Some staffers began to notice Nogales seemed less ebullient, a trace disheartened. Although he marshaled a brave front, inside he was seething. Over and over he was being forced to defend owners who apparently had no compunctions about letting him be the fall guy for their shortcomings.

At one of these late-afternoon sessions in early winter, with dozens of Unipressers jamming the eighth-floor lunchroom and spilling out into the hallway, Nogales encountered sharp questions about UPI's perilous financial state.

"If the owners are refusing to give up control and are looking only for a minority partner," one staffer asked, "and if outside investors feel Ruhe and Geissler lack credibility, how can this company have a future?"

Nogales hesitated, then in a moment of striking candor said softly, "That's a good question."

Unipressers were stunned. There, for the first time bared for all to see, was a stark and dangerous rift between UPI's owners and its president.

Quickly the meeting broke up. Across UPI's world the news leaped from bureau to bureau like an autumn brushfire.

14
. . .

The Mexican's Revolution

Through his boyhood days as a fruit packer, through his path-blazing civil rights battles at Stanford, through high-ranking jobs in the worlds of broadcasting and public relations, Luis Nogales had never shied from conflict, had always taken a stand.

Now it was time to take a stand again.

In normal circumstances at most companies, disgruntled managers simply quit. These were not normal circumstances, UPI was no average struggling enterprise, and Nogales was hardly a typical company president. He recognized that the wire service simply was too important to let die and knew it was on the brink again. A new financial crisis loomed with the restoration of the previous September's pay cuts. Besides, he was worried about his tax liabilities. He had to find a way for UPI to pay some $3 million in employee federal and state withholding taxes owed for the fourth quarter of 1984.

In early winter of 1985, Nogales wrestled with his dilemma: he owed allegiance to his bosses, Doug Ruhe and Bill Geissler, but believed they were destroying the company. Beginning to feel a bit like Fletcher Christian in *Mutiny on the Bounty*, Nogales had sought the counsel of his New York lawyer, William Josephson.

Listening carefully as Nogales outlined the financial and tax problems,

Josephson agreed that the wire service was an insolvent mess and that, based on what he had seen and heard, Ruhe and Geissler had been largely to blame. Then Josephson made a stunning declaration. He said Nogales's responsibilities as president had changed; now his first duty was to ensure UPI's survival, even if that meant Ruhe and Geissler were forced out.

Nogales knew such a course was perilous. If he failed to act in the owners' interest, and things got messy, they might fire him, sue him, or both.

By mid-February there was daring talk in UPI's executive suite. Nogales and his aides plotted ways to convince the owners to step aside or, in the worst case, to squeeze them out. Nogales joined in frequent conspiratorial chats in the ninth-floor corridors with consultant Ray Wechsler and controller Jack Kenney, their voices dropping whenever someone approached. They knew what they were discussing amounted to mutiny.

The seeds of rebellion had been planted weeks earlier, when Nogales dined with Wechsler and Jerry Hillman. Hillman had praised him and Wechsler for holding UPI together and suggested they form their own venture capital company, shove aside Ruhe and Geissler, and make a financial killing off the wire service. Nogales brushed aside suggestions he align himself with Hillman, a man he had never liked nor trusted.

In February they again went to dinner, at La Marimba restaurant in Manhattan. Nogales, himself a mean trencherman, sat astonished as he watched the bearded Hillman wash down course after course of Mexican food with a pitcher of Sangria. That night Nogales was listening, not eating. Hillman had changed his tune. Rather than urging Nogales to join in a revolution against the owners, Hillman assailed him for allowing UPI's financial problems to fester, and bluntly suggested he resign.

Eating little, Nogales concentrated on sizing up this enigmatic, troubling man. He wondered whether the $240,000-a-year consultant was trying to position himself to wrest control of UPI, carve up its assets, and profit handsomely as it collapsed. Nogales vowed to himself that, if there was an insurrection, he would do whatever he could to protect UPI from predators like Hillman.[1]

---

[1] Hillman declined to be interviewed about his experiences with UPI.

While Hillman no longer played a direct role, he continued to have an entrée to the company because Wechsler, a financial whiz, had rapidly risen to power in his few months at UPI. Wechsler had become one of Nogales's most important allies, and he was lobbying the hardest to force the owners out. Nogales needed Wechsler's business acumen. A graduate of Columbia University's business school, Wechsler had fallen in love with numbers as a kid, advising his father on financial matters by his early teens, and by age twenty dabbling at the racetrack, where he would always remember winning $129.50 on a $2.00 bet on Manassa Mauler in the Wood Memorial and, after once picking five straight winners, missing the Pick-6 jackpot of $18,000 when his horse lost by a nose.

Now, Wechsler had made some sense of UPI's financial tangle had and won the trust of Foothill officials, easily outshining the rest of UPI's lackluster financial staff. That enhanced his influence with Foothill officials, whose concern about the company's financial predicament grew daily. In the fall Foothill had jacked up the interest on UPI's $4 million line of credit to a whopping 5.25 percent over prime. If the interest rate was high, Foothill officers were finding their headache rate from UPI even higher.

Wechsler saw Foothill as the perfect avenue to put the squeeze on the owners. He moved to capitalize on his close ties with the lender, asking bankruptcy lawyer Rick Levine whether he could use Foothill to help force out Ruhe and Geissler. With his legal obligation to the owners, Levine would have no part of such talk.

Nogales sensed that confrontation with Ruhe and Geissler was inevitable. Again and again they ignored suggestions that they sell UPI and step aside. Normally energetic and effervescent, Nogales grew increasingly introspective and morose.

One night he sat alone in his dark office, enveloped in despair. As if UPI's problems and his potential tax liability were not enough, his twenty-year marriage was disintegrating. Nogales was commuting constantly to California, seeking to mollify Foothill, trying to convince his friends at the *Los Angeles Times* to step in and buy UPI. His wife, Mary, pushed beyond her limits, made it clear he would have to choose—their marriage or UPI. Nogales decided then and there that there was no turning back. He had made a new commitment to another family, the hundreds of Unipressers around the world.

• • •

By late February the tidal wave of red ink threatened to drown the company. Any benefits from the withholding-tax decision and the employee pay cuts had all but disappeared under the crush of back debts. Supplies were so short that the Washington bureau sometimes had to send a messenger racing to the airport to ship emergency rolls of printer paper to bureaus or newspaper clients. So much money was owed photo suppliers that they stopped floating credit for the chemicals needed to maintain high-quality newspicture reception. News, sports, and photo stringers who had patiently waited to be paid hundreds, sometimes thousands of dollars now knew the depths of UPI's problems and many refused to take any more assignments unless they were paid up front. It was a daily battle for UPI to function.

Amid the storm signals, Ruhe and Geissler packed up their wives and Rinaldo Brutoco and headed for the placid, aqua waters of Hawaii, a week-long vacation several company sources said was substantially charged to UPI.

If Ruhe and Geissler thought they could find respite on the island of Maui, they were sorely mistaken. Nogales, Wechsler, Kenney, and now even editor Max McCrohon were demanding a solution. There wasn't enough money to cover the next payroll. It was time for a summit meeting.

It seemed every time the owners tried to dunk a toe into the Pacific or lift a cool tropical drink, Nogales or McCrohon would phone from the mainland and interrupt their idyll. The message never differed—Ruhe and Geissler must sell control, even if it meant offering UPI to the likes of sensationalist tabloid publisher Rupert Murdoch.

Ruhe, not taking kindly to the interruptions, talked with Brutoco, now his top adviser. Why not just fire Nogales and his team? While the move would likely have serious repercussions with Foothill, there was at least one suitable successor, Bill Payette. At Ruhe's request, Nogales had had a poolside chat with Payette earlier in the month in Altadena, California, but since Payette had not formally agreed to come aboard, Ruhe realized he was not yet in a position to fire Nogales. Finally, the owners consented to meet with their managers at the airport Marriott in Los Angeles on Sunday, February 24. Wechsler and Nogales had been summoned to brief Foothill the next day on the company's strategy for solving its money problems.

Ruhe, Geissler, and Brutoco showed up on time for the airport meeting, but McCrohon, dubbed by Unipressers "the late Max McCrohon" because of his habitual tardiness, again arrived late and blamed the airline. Nogales and Wechsler were irritated. They had counted on McCrohon providing the support of UPI's editorial forces at the crucial confrontation. When McCrohon did arrive it was apparent he did not plan to drop his posture of studied neutrality.

As it turned out that didn't matter. Ruhe fired a pre-emptive strike almost before opening pleasantries were exchanged, introducing Brutoco as UPI's new chairman. Brutoco said his strategy would be to immediately institute new cost-cutting measures to save the company.

Nogales and Wechsler were aghast. Short of enormous staff layoffs, there was no way an austerity drive could address UPI's problems. Nor could the owners expect employees, who already had sacrificed from their paychecks, to agree to give more. The owners had lost credibility with UPI's staff, its prime lender, its creditors, and the newspaper industry. Yet, Nogales and Wechsler thought, here they were languishing in a dream world, convinced they still could save themselves. Foothill officials never would stand for this latest charade.

Barely an hour into the meeting, without giving Nogales a chance to respond, Ruhe rose and announced he was going home to Nashville.

"We've got some really important decisions here," Nogales protested. "This is life and death for the company."

"Sorry, I've got to go," said Ruhe, declaring he needed to get back to his family.

McCrohon, who had been staunchly loyal to the men who hired him, had sat quietly through the meeting. Now even he concluded Ruhe was acting like a pig-headed child. The owners either were insensitive or oblivious, he felt, to the fact that the company was crumbling around their shoulders.

Leaving their shocked subordinates behind to ponder the next step, Ruhe and Geissler blithely winged their way east. If they thought they had dodged the issue, they were sorely mistaken. They were only delaying the unavoidable. Doug Ruhe was trying to figure out a way to get rid of Luis Nogales, and Nogales a way to be rid of Ruhe. Which one would get there first?

• • •

The next day Wechsler briefed top Foothill officials John Nickoll, Peter Schwab, and Dennis Robinson about the meeting with the owners and said UPI would have trouble making its next payroll. Wechsler said he was so fed up he was considering quitting. His words did little to soothe the lender's worries.

Nickoll knew something must be done to remove Ruhe and Geissler, but his position was ticklish. While UPI's survival was in Foothill's best interests, should a bankruptcy court conclude he had interfered his firm might lose its favored-creditor status. Nickoll had to walk a tightrope.

"You'd better get the owners back out here," Nickoll said. "We're at a crucial point. You guys don't own the company. You're managers, not owners. Owners need to make the decisions."

Artfully, Foothill had joined the fray. Ruhe could not ignore Nickoll's summons. On Wednesday, February 27, a day before UPI had to meet its twice-monthly payroll, he, Geissler, Brutoco, Nogales, Wechsler, and McCrohon assembled in the Foothill conference room on the sixth floor of the gleaming Century City Towers near Beverly Hills, a stone's throw from the Twentieth Century Fox movie lot.

Joining his Foothill colleagues was the company's aggressive, ego-centric chairman, Don Gevirtz, who loved dealing with high-risk, high-profile companies like UPI. Gevirtz, who had been an adviser to President Carter on business issues, had urged Ruhe the previous summer to create a UPI advisory board comprised of serious businessmen. Rarely bashful or modest, Gevirtz volunteered to serve.

As the meeting began, Ruhe and Brutoco launched into their standard glowing generalities, trying to dazzle Foothill with expansive claims of impending deals and business ventures. They trotted out again the chestnut that they were close to selling Channel 66 in Chicago and expressed confidence that money from the sale would fuel a UPI comeback. Nogales seethed. Ruhe was up to his old tricks.

Foothill officials had heard such spiels from borrowers all too often. They sarcastically had coined the phrase "terminal euphoria" to describe borrowers perpetually boasting of impending bonanzas. With every word from Ruhe and Brutoco, it was clear that here was a bad case of the dread disease.

Gevirtz, a tall, gray-haired, starkly handsome man, interrupted their happy talk with uncharacteristic vehemence.

"We've heard what you're saying. There's nothing different from what you've told us before. What the hell is going on with this company? You're not adding anything to the party."

Ruhe sat stiffly. The words were a blow to his solar plexus. But that was a love tap compared to what Gevirtz and Nickoll were about to deliver.

"We don't have confidence you can turn it around. We're not going to fund the company with its present ownership. Often, in situations like these, management takes over. If you want to work out an agreement where management takes over, we'll work with you."

Foothill demanded an agreement under which Ruhe and Geissler would give up control and allow their stock to be swapped to creditors agreeing to forgive debts. In a few brief sentences, Gevirtz had thrown Foothill's support to Luis Nogales and lowered the boom on Doug Ruhe.

"Okay," Ruhe replied soberly, "we'll talk."

The Foothill contingent quickly departed, leaving UPI's owners and managers alone to wage a high-stakes war of words and nerves. Nogales and Ruhe eyed one another distrustfully. Their rift had simmered for months, but now there was no concealing it.

"Before we start," Nogales said, "I want you to know that if I go across the table from you, I'm no longer your employee and I will negotiate for what is best for UPI."

"Fine," Ruhe replied, familiar smirk playing at the corners of his mouth. Geissler sat scowling. Nogales, he thought, was a Benedict Arnold.

With UPI's fate in the balance, the two sides plunged into intense negotiations about the terms under which Ruhe and Geissler would yield control of the company and most of their stock. How much they would surrender became a critical issue. Wechsler emphasized that he and Nogales needed a substantial block of stock to offer creditors and a potential buyer.

Nogales and Wechsler knew they had the stronger hand. Playing their powerful cards, they proposed setting aside 35 percent for creditors and 25 percent to Foothill for continuing to float the high-risk loan. Management would get a hefty 20 percent and the union 10 percent, leaving the owners a mere 10 percent.

Ruhe and Geissler, who had clung to their stock like barnacles to a rotting ship, were outraged. They had diluted Rob Small and Cordy Overgaard's stock months earlier, and now owned 84 percent of Media News Corporation, UPI's parent. They could not bear the thought that the very managers they had hired would own twice as much stock as they.

The owners also didn't like the prospect of setting aside 25 percent for Foothill. Ruhe believed Gevirtz had an ulterior motive, that he ultimately hoped to win UPI for himself.

As the meeting wore on, McCrohon took pains to stay out of the line of fire. He said later he had hoped to shield the editorial department from the open warfare between owners and managers, but he also was vaguely uncomfortable about any move to oust the owners. McCrohon found it particularly difficult to sever his ties to Geissler, his patron, with whom he continued to talk privately. He also was developing an intense dislike and distrust of Wechsler, the former AT&T executive who he felt regarded journalists as just so many interchangeable telephone installers. Ever the politician, McCrohon gave Nogales and Wechsler the impression he was their ally. One night he shared popcorn with them at a Los Angeles theater where they saw the hilarious foreign farce, *The Gods Must Be Crazy*. For the three the movie's lunacy was an example of art imitating life.

UPI employees, few of whom had been able to accumulate nest eggs on their munificent salaries, were unaware of the secret negotiations in Los Angeles. On Thursday, as they received paychecks that without an agreement would begin bouncing, the California talks took on the air of a fast-paced Monopoly game. The owners now had set a fancy price tag on yielding control of UPI, dispelling any lingering suspicion that their motives were entirely altruistic. In return for their shares they demanded a 25 percent liability-free interest in UPI, $200,000 each in consulting fees over two years, and commissions if they were able to sell such assets as the audio service, business wire, or domestic newspictures service. Nogales and his team scoffed at the suggestion that these entrepreneurs, who had invested nothing and had rung up nearly $30 million in debts, should be paid handsomely to fold up their tent—or even more to continue carving up UPI.

Once again Ruhe's tenacity won him some concessions. Thursday night the two sides agreed that the owners, management, the union, and Foothill would receive equal 15 percent blocks of stock, leaving 40 percent to be offered to creditors. Nogales would take over as chairman.

Wearily, the combatants shook hands and marched across the plaza to Jade West, an Oriental restaurant. Dinner was a melancholy affair.

After struggling nearly three years to make UPI a winner, fiercely resisting all entreaties that they sell, the owners appeared to have thrown in the towel and seemed resigned to their fate. Seated next to Geissler, Nogales was careful not to gloat, fearful of further poisoning the atmosphere. Privately, he exulted. He was UPI's new chairman, and, for the first time in the eighteen months he had been aboard, he felt he had control of the company's destiny.

As Ruhe and Geissler headed home, Wechsler phoned Kenney in Nashville and told him to hop a plane to Los Angeles. Kenney, in turn, called new general counsel Bill Bowe and excitedly broke the news.

"I've made reservations for you to fly to Los Angeles," he told Bowe. "An agreement has been reached that will result in a change of control, a sale of the company, and a working out of the creditor problem."

Bowe's assignment was to put into ironclad writing, for presentation to Foothill Sunday night, the agreement removing the owners from control of the company. Nogales should have known it wouldn't be that easy. Although they had shaken hands on the deal, Ruhe and Geissler were bitter that the men they had hired had just dictated the terms of their surrender. Flying back to Nashville, they craftily plotted strategy.

• • •

While Nogales and Wechsler assembled their team in Los Angeles to put final touches on the agreement, the ever-cautious McCrohon did not want to be perceived as participating in a management coup. Borrowing a typewriter from the desk clerk at the Century Plaza Hotel on Friday, he dashed off a confidential memo to Nogales.

"I have very strong feelings about the practicality of what we are doing, about the priorities of the negotiations, and about the ethics of it all," he wrote.

Defending the owners, he stressed that while UPI had cost them nothing, "The fact is that the publishers of America didn't put even fifty cents on the table during the two years the company was for sale."

"However Ruhe and Geissler did it," he said, "the fact is they have kept UPI alive for more than two years. We owe them something for that."

Nogales and Wechsler, who felt the owners had shown a pattern of irresponsible behavior since acquiring UPI, were disgusted by the memo.

They considered it just another example of McCrohon wimping out, protecting his options with the company's survival at stake.

But, the deal done, they shrugged it off. Much work remained before the banks opened Monday morning, or Foothill would not cover the 1,300 paychecks employees had already cashed.

• • •

Returning to Nashville, Ruhe and Geissler groped for ways to exact revenge, salvage pride, and perhaps get a better deal. They had to sell the company before circumstances beyond their control took it out of their hands. They told Porter Bibb, now with the New York investment banking firm of Ladenburg, Thalmann and Company, to find a buyer.

Among those Bibb contacted was Don Kummerfeld, Rupert Murdoch's top associate. UPI had been hesitant to approach Murdoch, the Australian publishing magnate famed for magically changing staid newspapers into lurid tabloids pushing stories of murder, rape, and pillage.

Kummerfeld and Bob Page, former UPI general manager who now was publisher of Murdoch's *Chicago Sun-Times*, had in the past tried unsuccessfully to round up media partners to purchase the wire service. Page, who had dreamed of the day he would run UPI, had reluctantly concluded purchasing the company was too big a risk. Hearing anew from Bibb and separately from Australian McCrohon, Page and Kummerfeld took another look. But, with the numbers even worse, the answer still was an emphatic no.

Ruhe also phoned Jim West at Fintext headquarters in Glens Falls, New York, and told him Foothill had turned off the spigot.

"There isn't any cash," he said. "It's very, very serious, but I don't think it's fatal."

Ruhe talked of firing Nogales and replacing him with someone acceptable to Foothill, or finding an investor and paying off the lender. West agreed to try to help Ruhe put together a fast deal.

By Saturday, March 2, Ruhe had abandoned any thought of honoring the Los Angeles agreement hammered out two days earlier. He talked again with West, who had flown to Denver, and asked him to once more approach Bill Payette about running UPI. Payette was still interested but unwilling to commit pending another talk with Nogales.

That hardly was an option. Doug Ruhe had decided to fire Luis Nogales.

* * *

In Los Angeles, Nogales and his team were plowing ahead with plans for a transition. Wechsler had been working with Jeff Peterson of the investment banking firm of Bear Stearns & Company to put together a business plan under which UPI could restructure. Wechsler also summoned bankruptcy lawyer Rick Levine from Boston to discuss how to deal with creditors and whether to file for Chapter 11.

Unaware of Ruhe's planned turnabout, general counsel Bill Bowe arrived in California to formally draft the agreement. He found himself in a most awkward predicament. He had been working for Ruhe; now, with control about to shift to Nogales, so would his allegiances.

Worse yet, Bowe found no written account of what had been negotiated. He sensed trouble. He knew he had only until Sunday night to turn an ill-defined verbal accord into a document that Foothill would accept. Bowe persuaded Lisa Greer and John St. Clair of the law firm of Lawlor, Felix and Hall to help him, although they knew UPI's position was so precarious they might not get paid.

At the Lawlor, Felix offices on the thirtieth floor of the Broadway Plaza Building on South Flower Street, the lawyers had no time to enjoy the spectacular view of the San Gabriel Mountains north and east. They worked all day Saturday and Sunday morning, consulting Nogales on the fine points of the agreement. When Bowe phoned Ruhe in Nashville to hash out final details, he was stunned to discover the owners did not intend to sign the agreement.

Feeling like a shuttlecock in a badminton game, Bowe instinctively concluded that Ruhe and Geissler had become his clients again. Hanging up, he informed Nogales, Greer, and St. Clair that Ruhe was balking.

Nogales and Wechsler knew if they couldn't present a package satisfactory to Foothill Sunday night, the wire service might be forced to shut. Foreign correspondents could be marooned in remote outposts and hundreds of clients might be left without news until the AP got around to installing its service. . . probably at greatly inflated prices.

But Nogales knew Doug Ruhe well enough to have expected he might try to back out. When Bowe relayed Ruhe's message, Nogales shrugged. As far as he was concerned, a deal had been struck. He remained determined to bring matters to a head that night when he met with Foothill officials at John Nickoll's home.

• • •

Just before 7 p.m. on Sunday, Nogales veered his rental car off Wilshire Boulevard in Beverly Hills and turned right on North Whittier. A few blocks up the tree-shaded, curving street he pulled into the half-moon driveway of Nickoll's mansion.

The fieldstone rambler was enormous, the immaculately manicured lawn shaded by mimosas, aspens, and five tall palms. In back, amid lush foliage, were a putting green, a swimming pool fed over lava rocks by a ten-foot high waterfall, and a redwood footbridge leading to the private tennis court.

Nickoll politely greeted his guests and led them through sliding oak doors into the dark, richly paneled den, where they fixed drinks from the bar and plopped into comfortable chairs around a coffee table. Nickoll sat in an armchair near the couch, chewing ice.

Crowding into the den, whose built-in bookcases flanked a matching oak fireplace, were Nogales and Wechsler; lawyers Bowe, Greer, and St. Clair; Bear Stearns advisers Peterson and Patrick Graham; and Foothill vice presidents Peter Schwab and Dennis Robinson.

The atmosphere was glum because word of the owners' monkey wrench had circulated, and everyone pondered aloud the next step. Wechsler, who found comfort in numbers whenever crisis struck, began laying out UPI's latest financial projections.

Then the phone rang. Ann Nickoll answered it and called Nogales into the bedroom.

Nogales's heart skipped a beat when he heard Doug Ruhe's voice.

"Luis," Ruhe said without hesitation, "you're fired."

Nogales swallowed hard in disbelief. So it had come to this. Ruhe was willing to gamble UPI's future in a spiteful demonstration of ego and revenge.

"Why?" Nogales asked.

"You just are, and you, better than anybody, should understand."

"It's a bad move," Nogales protested, knuckles whitening as he squeezed the receiver. "It's not going to work. The whole company is going to crash."

"Well, that's the way it is," Ruhe said, coolly.

"Doug, it can't end like this."

"It just did."

Nogales fell quiet as the words sank in. He knew there was no reasoning with Ruhe, no hope of appealing this ultimate folly.

Ruhe broke the silence. "May I speak with Ray Wechsler, please?" he asked evenly.

Nogales placed the phone down on the bed, padded down the hall to the den, and stood in the doorway, his suddenly pale face a stark contrast to his rust-colored windbreaker. Everyone looked up expectantly.

"Well, guys," he said, "I've been fired. We can forget this meeting."

The room fell silent. Tears glistened in Lisa Greer's eyes.

Nogales turned to Wechsler and said, "Ray, Doug wants to talk to you next."

Everyone knew what was coming, and despite the calamitous news, faint smiles curled their lips.

Even Wechsler's.

"Luis, just tell Doug I'm too busy, I'm in a meeting right now. What do I want to talk to him for and get fired?"

Nervous laughter greeted Wechsler's attempt at humor. When nobody moved toward the phone, Bowe finally acknowledged his onerous duty as UPI's counsel and headed to the bedroom. When he picked up Ruhe barked out orders.

"Go in there and fire Wechsler, fire Lawlor Felix, fire Bear Stearns, fire Levine." Bowe paled. His protests were to no avail. He placed the phone down and returned to the den.

"Ray, Doug has instructed me to tell you your services are no longer needed," said Bowe, a man whose lofty manner of speaking had prompted ever-irreverent Ruhe to disparage him with the sobriquet, "The Blowfish."

Attempting to wring some dignity from the escalating madness, Bowe then asked lawyers Greer and St. Clair to join him in the dimly lighted dining room. There, apologetically, he broke the news of their dismissal.

He took Peterson and Graham into another room and repeated the message. Levine had escaped to New York. Now, Bowe was the only one in the house still employed by UPI.

Watching Bowe uncomfortably playing the role of angel of death, John Nickoll feared for both his company's substantial investment and the fate of UPI. Nogales's leadership had inspired confidence among the very employees and clients Ruhe had so badly alienated. Nickoll, who disliked Rinaldo Brutoco and found him unstable, simply was not going to stand still while Foothill's investment was in jeopardy. He went to the bedroom and picked up the phone. Ruhe was still on the line.

"Doug, you've got to be crazy!" Nickoll said with uncharacteristic bluntness. "What's going on?"

"Nogales and I have a disagreement on management styles," Ruhe replied.

"Are you going to run the company?"

"No."

"Well, UPI has no management. Foothill has nobody to deal with. You'd better get out here immediately and talk to Nogales and come to some sort of agreement."

Ruhe was frantically trying to arrange a deal for UPI that would enable him to pay off Foothill, thereby foreclosing any leverage Nogales and Wechsler might bring to bear. He needed more time, but he could not ignore Nickoll's demand. Reluctantly, he agreed to fly back to California.

Hanging up, Nickoll returned to the den to find the shell-shocked group still milling aimlessly. Finally, Ann Nickoll graciously but firmly eased them out the door.

• • •

Shortly before Nogales was fired, he had confidently phoned UPI spokesman Bill Adler, who was in his pajamas at his Washington apartment, and instructed him to hustle to the office. He told Adler to draft an announcement that the owners had stepped aside and the company would be reorganized and sold.

Delighted, Adler began dressing. Then the phone rang again. This time it was Geissler, who told Adler to prepare an announcement stating that Nogales had been fired. Geissler warned Adler that if he released anything other than what the owners demanded, he, too, would be sent packing.

Utterly confused, Adler threw on his clothes, rushed to the office, and summoned his assistants, Dave Wickenden and Lauren Savadel. They worked deep into the night, drafting alternate press releases to cover any eventuality, no matter who was in control.

• • •

Leaving Nickoll's home, Nogales and Wechsler headed back to the airport Marriott, where most of the UPI team was staying. Behind the wheel, trying to sort out the strange turn of events, Nogales could not imagine anyone agreeing to bail out Ruhe and Geissler. The owners had lost all credibility in the financial world. Nobody would give them a penny, he thought. They would have to face Foothill, and Foothill wanted them out.

"It isn't over," Nogales thought. "Ruhe and Geissler can't do it without us."

Jack Kenney was in his room at the Marriott, lying in bed watching Arnold Schwarzenegger in *The Terminator* on pay TV. The phone rang. It was Nogales.

"I've got good news and bad news. The good news is, I don't have to worry anymore."

"C'mon, Luis," Kenney said, demanding an explanation.

"The bad news is, I got fired."

Kenney was stunned. All he could do was protest Nogales's lame effort at levity. Nogales told him to come down to the hotel bar to discuss strategy.

Before heading for the elevator, Kenney phoned Ruhe. It was midnight, Nashville time.

"Under the circumstances," Kenney said, "there's no way I can work for UPI."

Bob Brown, a UPI consultant who recently had been named communications vice president, had been standing by in Los Angeles during the negotiations but had flown back to Dallas. Nogales called to notify him of the firings. Brown promptly phoned Ruhe and also resigned.

Bill Bowe had a pregnant wife to consider. He feared complications similar to the premature birth of their first child, which had brought medical bills totaling $110,000. Needing UPI's health insurance, he chose to stick it out.

As Nogales, Wechsler, Bowe, Kenney, and accountant Steve Spritzer sat over drinks in the bar in the Marriott lobby, the mood fluctuated between disbelief, relief, and anger that the owners would so bizarrely jeopardize UPI's survival. What if Ruhe and Geissler simply refused to negotiate?

"I can't believe they're going to trash the fucking company," Wechsler said, over and over. The group dreaded the chaos certain to come with the dawn, when paychecks would begin bouncing and UPI's internal crisis would become the talk of the news media.

As a couple of them made a move to head for a lobby phone and arrange for flights back home, Nogales waved them to sit down.

"We're not through," he exhorted. "I want you guys to stay, because it's not over. Something is going to happen in the next two or three days."

As they talked and drank until three in the morning, they decided to stick around to see what that something would be.

One thing was crystal clear. Nogales's bold power play had left Ruhe and Geissler in a real fix. They had no standing with Foothill, and Foothill was UPI's only source of cash. With four senior members of the management team gone, who was left to run the company?

• • •

Max McCrohon had flown from California to New York on Sunday. Starting Monday, he would begin the arduous two-day task of judging the Pulitzer Prizes, journalism's most prestigious awards.

McCrohon checked into the Lotus Club, a literary club on Fifth Avenue and Sixty-third Street. He was up late, his custom, when Nogales phoned about 1 a.m.

"Max, I've been fired."

"Jesus Christ, what happened now?"

Nogales explained. Despite his close ties with Geissler, McCrohon knew the consequences.

"Well, how can we undo it?" he asked.

Nogales had no answer. He was neither surprised nor disappointed that McCrohon did not offer to resign in sympathy. That would have thrown UPI's editorial operations into the same chaos.

McCrohon hung up, then tossed and turned most of the night.

• • •

Nogales was staying at the Burbank Hilton, twenty miles away from the airport, so he could be near the home of his younger sister, Florence, who did his laundry while he was in L.A.

It was a balmy, starry night as Nogales wended his way toward his hotel after saying good night to his cohorts. With dawn approaching and the city's usually jammed freeways almost deserted, it should have been a peaceful drive. But Nogales's adrenaline was pumping as he wrestled with various scenarios and replayed the events of the evening.

"What are they going to do? What am I going to do?"

He began to plot ways to rally Foothill, the union, and UPI's key managers around his efforts to reverse the owners' actions. Nogales knew it was possible that Ruhe really had found a savior to pay off Foothill, but what if the owner was bluffing? The consequences would be grave for the company, and Nogales had too much blood and sweat invested not to call the owners' hand.

Technically, he no longer worked for UPI. But Luis Nogales knew he simply could not let go.

•   •   •

Back in Washington, Adler was in a tizzy. He had finally heard back from Nogales, who apologized for having so abruptly ended their previous conversation and confirmed he had been fired.

"Is it final?" Adler asked.

"I really don't know."

"Doesn't John Nickoll have something to say about this, since he's providing our money?"

"Nickoll has been involved in the discussions, and he has nothing more to say," Nogales replied.

Adler was incredulous.

"Doesn't Nickoll realize that this is probably the end of UPI?"

Hanging up, Adler angrily dialed Nickoll's home. Ann Nickoll, who by now was beginning to regret ever hearing the name UPI, answered and rousted her husband.

Adler got right to the point.

"Do you understand that the staff and the clients and the vendors won't stand for this?"

"We're just the lender, and we have no opinion on staff changes," Nickoll said, concealing that he already had begun putting the pressure on Ruhe. "It's Mr. Ruhe's company to do with as he pleases. I'm sorry, but I can't help you."

Depressed, Adler hung up and turned to Wickenden and Savadel, still working on the assorted press releases. They discussed the possibility of a mass sympathy resignation, but Nogales had counseled against that. They decided the best course would be to ride it out.

Suddenly, the phone rang. It was Geissler, directing Adler to run on UPI's wires the owners' version of the day's developments.

"What's going to happen to Nogales?" Adler asked.

"Sorry, man," Geissler chuckled. "Nogales is history."

15
· · ·
California Chaos

In the sixteen months Ron Cohen had been UPI's managing editor, the telephone had routinely served as his alarm clock, so much so that his wife, Jill, had demanded they switch sides of the bed to save her fumbling to answer in the dark. At 5 a.m. this Monday morning, March 4, 1985, Cohen picked it up before the second ring. It was Henry Reske, manning the lobster trick in the Washington bureau.

"Ron, I think you'd better listen to what the owners just made me move on the A-wire."

Cohen was instantly awake. The owners ordering a staffer to move a story without approval of a senior news editor was a dangerous breach of UPI's editorial independence.

This is big trouble, Cohen thought. Reske read over the phone:

> WASHINGTON (UPI)—The two principal owners of United Press International, Douglas F. Ruhe and William E. Geissler, said today they would take steps to relinquish control of the news agency in a program to recapitalize the company and to guarantee its future.
>
> To facilitate restructuring of the ownership, Ruhe also announced the termination of Luis G. Nogales as president and Ray Wechsler as financial consultant. A replacement for Nogales will be named.

"The company ended 1984 with a fourth-quarter profit of $1.1 million," Ruhe said in a joint statement issued with Geissler. "We are beginning the second phase of the company's recovery program, recapitalizing the company."

There was no further mention of Nogales, Wechsler, or the firings.

Cohen threw on clothes and drove twenty-two miles from his Potomac, Maryland, home to UPI's downtown Washington office. He had been secretly told the previous Friday an agreement had been reached in Los Angeles for Ruhe and Geissler to step aside and let Nogales run UPI.

Now, Nogales was gone. Worse, the owners had slipped the story on the wire in the dead of night. Pressing hard on the gas, Cohen told himself this was the last time they would hijack UPI's news wires.

Arriving at 6 a.m. he found the executive suite deserted. As early desk staffers trickled in and learned what had happened to Nogales, a man they had trusted, they gasped in anger and disbelief and wondered if UPI could survive.

When Cohen made another trip upstairs at 8:30 a.m., he spotted sales vice presidents John Mantle and Tom Beatty. The two executives, who had worked closely with Geissler, assured him everything would be all right. Cohen replied that, so long as he was managing editor, the owners would never again put a story on the wire without clearing it with senior editorial managers. He warned that the staff was mutinous and the owners should approach the newsroom at their own risk.

More employees arrived and clustered in small groups, buzzing and swapping theories about the impact. Mantle and Beatty, who had been in touch with the owners, tried to act calm and reassuring at an impromptu staff meeting. Encircled by a crush of staffers in the newsroom, their halting answers to even the most basic questions rang hollow.

"Who's in charge?" demanded Sean McCormally, a volatile, articulate union leader who worked on the Washington copy desk.

Mantle hesitated, then replied, "We are. Everything will be all right."

Unipressers were not reassured.

Resigning himself to the worst, Cohen vowed that if the company were about to go under UPI at least would assign reporters to try to determine what really had happened and write its own obituary. He called

McCrohon at the Pulitzer office at Columbia University and read him the first few paragraphs of the story Ruhe and Geissler had sent.

"Max, we can't let this kind of shit go out on the wire," he said. "I want to cover this story from now on like a news story, and I'm going to assign Greg Gordon to do it."

"Sure," McCrohon said. "We have to."

While Geissler set up shop on the ninth floor, Cohen directed Gordon, UPI's chief investigative reporter, and veteran Unipresser D'Vera Cohn to piece together the weekend's events in Los Angeles for a story.

As they tried to assess the new shock waves, Unipressers in bureaus around the world faced another busy news day. Even as they pounded out their stories, Unipressers kept an eye on the wire, eager for news about the upheavals. By midafternoon Gordon and Cohn had stitched together enough information to conclude that UPI's management war had been brewing for some time, and that Nogales and Wechsler had been fired after joining with Foothill to try to force the owners out.

Gordon and Cohn learned from "sources close to the departing officers" that, even with UPI's survival on the line, Ruhe and Geissler had demanded financial concessions before they would agree to surrender their stock. When the reporters went to the ninth floor to interview Geissler, he seemed stunned and embarrassed that his own wire service was going to cover the turmoil. After first declining comment, he finally read Gordon a statement any bureacratic obfuscator would have loved:

"To isolate a set of numbers from a process of discussion is out of context. We obviously entertained discussions on details of this alternative. It would not be productive to comment on specifics, but rest assured our decision will be conditioned on achieving our primary purpose: the strengthening of the UPI service."

Late Monday afternoon, editors moved a lengthy story disclosing UPI's internal problems and revealing the wire service faced $17 million in short-term debts. At last, even as they wondered how long they would have jobs, Unipressers were beginning to learn the full dimensions of the company's troubles and about the shenanigans in the executive suite.

The story also riveted the attention of the news industry, and half a dozen major newspapers assigned reporters to measure the panic at UPI and assess the damage of "Blue Monday."

• • •

Nogales spent the day after his firing shuttling between the airport Marriott, where Wechsler was lolling poolside, and the downtown offices of Bear Stearns, where he found the now formally terminated Jeff Peterson sympathetic to UPI's plight and willing to help.

Newspaper reporters' calls to Nogales flooded the switchboard at the Burbank Hilton where he was staying. He returned one from *The Tennessean* and found himself peppered about allegations that he was a mutineer. Having heard nothing more from Ruhe, Nogales responded cautiously, lest he further antagonize the owners. A front page headline in the next day's *Tennessean* would say: "Fired UPI President Denies Plotting 'Palace Coup' " and quoted sources, obviously from the owners' camp, that Nogales and his cronies were trying to pirate the company.

Nevertheless, the pressure on the owners was being turned up another notch. In playing his trump card and firing Nogales and Wechsler, Ruhe had overlooked something important. Controller Jack Kenney's resignation left nobody available to transfer money from Foothill to UPI's account at the Bank of California. By Monday afternoon, even though Foothill had yet to formally cut off credit, UPI's well was dry.

For decades, whatever UPI's financial straits, employees never had missed a paycheck. Now word that checks were bouncing raced from bureau to bureau as a doomsday warning.

• • •

In Washington, Bill Adler anxiously hoped the events of the weekend could be reversed and Nogales reinstated. Discreetly, he began to help Nogales and Wechsler strengthen their hands for further negotiations with Ruhe.

Using a telecopier just outside Geissler's office, Adler and Mary Ellen Ripley, Nogales's secretary, began transmitting financial documents to them in L.A. While Ripley nervously fed the machine, Adler would divert Geissler's attention. Adler knew they both would be fired instantly should he catch on. Late Monday night, after they thought he had gone home, Geissler suddenly returned while Ripley was transmitting a large stack of documents to Wechsler.

Chatting like a frantic magpie, Adler tried to steer Geissler back to his office, but the owner turned to Ripley and asked, "What are you doing with the Fax?"

Flushed, her brain whirring, she blurted, "I'm using it as a copier." Adler and Ripley held their breaths. They knew the machine could not perform that function. Geissler paused for several long seconds, then said, "Okay."

Adler and Ripley could barely mask their relief.

* * *

Before Ruhe returned to California, the owners contacted adviser Porter Bibb in New York. Bibb felt that, if necessary, they could take UPI into Chapter 11 bankruptcy without surrendering their stock and still be able to try to sell the company. "Whatever you do, guys," he cautioned, "don't let them push you into anything."

Ruhe flew to Los Angeles on Tuesday, checked into the Century Plaza, and hurried to Nickoll's office. Nickoll repeated his warning that Foothill would continue financing only if it were satisfied with UPI's management.

"Look, you and Nogales seem to have this irreconcilable conflict. We have no confidence in what's going on. Why don't you sit down once more and see if you can't resolve it?"

Saying he would think it over, Ruhe returned to his hotel room and told the front desk he did not want to be disturbed.

* * *

Union president Bill Morrissey arrived in Los Angeles on Tuesday morning to find a worried Nogales in the lobby of the Century Plaza. Morrissey had learned of the firings when awakened by Dan Carmichael's phone call early Monday.

"You've got to be shitting me!" Morrissey exploded.

The union leaders had quickly decided the company's future was at stake; it was clear they would have to abandon their spectator's role. Electing to throw their support behind Nogales, they asked union international representative Richard Pattison to join Morrissey in Century City and keep alive the threat of filing a Chapter 7 bankruptcy petition to force a resolution.

Talking with Nogales in the lobby, Morrissey learned just how badly things had deteriorated. Ruhe was holed up in his room, refusing to see anyone even as the clock ticked toward UPI's destruction. Nogales told Morrissey he was willing to return, but only if Ruhe surrendered control.

Urging Morrissey to help him try to open a dialogue with Ruhe, Nogales declared, "We can't let this die."

"I'll talk to the guy," Morrissey said, but still Ruhe didn't answer the phone. Finally, Nogales, unable to contain his impatience, found out Ruhe's room number and took the elevator upstairs. Even though he knew he might further alienate the mercurial owner, Nogales felt he had no choice but to force the issue. Ruhe's position was precarious. If the company should crash, the owners might have no money to cover the millions in unpaid federal and state withholding taxes or other debts for which they were personally liable.

Nogales hesitated a moment outside Ruhe's door to calm himself, then knocked and called softly, "Doug, this is Luis. We've got to talk."

No answer.

"Doug, this is Luis!" Nogales said, speaking louder and knocking harder. "We've got to talk. We can't let this company go down."

Silence.

Nogales intensified his rapping. Ruhe finally cracked open the door.

Remembering that Ruhe sometimes broke a tenet of his Baha'i faith by indulging in an occasional cigarette, Nogales offered him a smoke.

"Yeah, I'll have a cigarette," said Ruhe, partially dressed and in stockinged feet.

Nogales slipped inside and stayed about forty minutes. When he returned to the lobby, Morrissey, Wechsler, Kenney, Spritzer, and Bowe rushed to find out what had happened. Nogales described a surrealistic scene:

Seated at a coffee table, Ruhe soon began talking vaguely about his days as a medic in Vietnam. His voice taking on an almost mystic quality, Ruhe said that serving in Southeast Asia had made him "ready for anything"—he was even prepared to die. Nogales was astonished. Ruhe, with his company near collapse, was rambling on about events that had occurred half a globe away almost two decades earlier.

Gently trying to ease Ruhe back to reality, Nogales said he regretted that their relationship had deteriorated so badly. But, he said, Ruhe had no option other than to reopen negotiations—UPI's survival was directly in his hands. To the relief of the others in the lobby, Nogales said he felt Ruhe had left the door open for possible compromise. Ruhe, asked to confirm this account, had a different recollection of the conversation. He said that Nogales came to his room in tears, saying his daughter had heard on the news that he was fired and called to ask if it was true. He said Nogales all but begged for his job back. Ruhe said he felt badly for Nogales and began to relent, and that Nogales later told him that he faked grief to play on his sympathies. Nogales flatly denied Ruhe's version.

• • •

UPI's own stories had raised the possibility that Nogales might be returning as president, but when there was no break in the impasse, union leaders decided to try to force a settlement. Early Wednesday morning Morrissey phoned both Wechsler and Rinaldo Brutoco and warned that if the management issue were not resolved by day's end, the Wire Service Guild would file a Chapter 7 petition, based on unpaid employee expense claims, to force the company into involuntary bankruptcy.

In New York, Carmichael issued a bulletin accusing both sides of "dangerous brinksmanship" and declaring that the union was attempting to mediate "a crisis situation." The bulletin, quickly distributed to *The Washington Post* and other newspapers covering the story, said the bickering "threatens the future of the news agency."

The pressure appeared to work. A short time later Ruhe phoned Nogales at Bear Stearns, where the ousted managers were gathered, and said he was ready to meet in early afternoon at the office of his lawyer, located in the same building as Foothill.

Struck by the sudden confidence in Ruhe's voice, Nogales was suspicious when the owner announced that he had patched things up with both Foothill and the union. He wondered what stunt Ruhe had up his sleeve this time.

"I want to meet, but just you," Ruhe said.

Nogales had no intention of meeting alone with Ruhe. He wanted witnesses in case the owner tried to wriggle out again.

"I'm not going to come by myself," he said. "I'm going to bring some lawyers. This is a very complicated deal."

"No, just you and me."

Nogales continued to resist. Finally, Ruhe gave in, but only if Wechsler—whom he bitterly blamed for poisoning his relationship with Foothill—were excluded. Nogales reluctantly agreed. He knew Wechsler would be apoplectic.

234 / DOWN TO THE WIRE

When Nogales arrived for the meeting with a full contingent of law-yers and investment advisers, he learned that Ruhe was already talking privately with Morrissey. The owner emerged wearing a big smile. Ob-viously, Nogales thought, Ruhe was girding for some big play.

Nogales approached the union president outside Ruhe's lawyer's of-fice.

"Well, you guys are back together," Morrissey said.

"What do you mean?"

"Well, Doug says you've agreed to come back to work for him."

"Bullshit! I have not! That's what this meeting is all about."

Morrissey was flabbergasted.

"That dirty sonofabitch," he growled. "He just lied to me for forty minutes."[1]

Nogales was incredulous. How could even Ruhe expect to get away with this? Ruhe was trying to assure all sides—Nogales, Foothill, and the union—that he had reached an agreement with each of the others. He seemed blissfully certain he could work three sides against the middle, yet soon he would be in face-to-face meetings with all three. How could his ploy not be unmasked?

Nogales did not have to wait long for the next installment in this crazy soap opera. In a phone call before the meeting, Brutoco had tried to verbally bully Foothill vice president Peter Schwab into keeping UPI's loan money flowing. Now, just before the session began in the law firm's conference room, word of their phone confrontation was filtering back to John Nickoll.

As the others chatted quietly, Nickoll stood at a large credenza in one end of the room, a phone to his ear. "Yeah . . . uh huh . . . yeah. He did? Yeah." Hanging up, the normally reserved and proper Nickoll spun and shot daggers across the room.

"Brutoco, don't you *ever* threaten my people! You don't have an agreement with us. You don't have financing with us, as of this minute. Don't you *ever* threaten my people!"

There was dead silence. Ruhe's smile melted. Nogales's suspicions were confirmed. Not only did the owner not have the union in his camp, he most certainly did not have Foothill.

"There must have been some misunderstanding," Brutoco protested,

---

[1] Ruhe denied misleading Morrissey.

red-faced. He quickly exited, vowing to clarify the situation. Nogales sat confidently. With the bargaining about to begin, any vestige of Ruhe's credibility and negotiating power had melted away.

Nogales, knowing Ruhe still would be a tenacious foe, resolved to hold out for the full power and authority he felt he needed.

"As long as you have those clowns in there," he told himself, "it's going to fail, because they can't do anything right and they're starting to get greedy."

Morrissey opened the meeting with a short speech.

"The company is in dire, dire circumstances. Paychecks are bouncing all over the globe, and there have been calls [to the union] from Tokyo and São Paulo, Brazil, from Unipressers saying, 'How am I going to get home?' Everybody at this table has an obligation to get sensible."

Nogales then reiterated his commitment to UPI, but demanded, among other things, that he be indemnified from personal liabilities and legal costs, including the nearly $3 million in unpaid withholding taxes.

Morrissey's eyes bugged. It was the union's first hint of unpaid taxes. On the heels of bum paychecks and owner-management slugfests, this was too much.

Talks proceeded at a snail's pace, Ruhe balking at most of Nogales's demands. Nogales frequently left the room to answer calls from an angry Wechsler demanding to know what was happening.

In UPI's bureaus the suspense was almost palpable. Unipressers were monitoring the updates moving on the wires of the Los Angeles meeting. In Washington, Gordon and Dee Cohn pounded out stories with sketchy details of the crucial talks. Los Angeles bureau chief Doug Dowie had dispatched rookie reporter Ellis Conklin to the meeting. When Conklin told a secretary he was from UPI, she assumed it was all right to fill him in. Dowie promptly relayed the tidbits to Washington to spice up the story.

Glaring across the table, Ruhe and Nogales resumed the previous week's war over distributing UPI's stock. Nickoll and Morrissey applied the prod, reminding them they could not leave the building without an agreement.

Nickoll, who needed to preserve at least the appearance he wasn't interfering, had to let the confrontation play out, although he knew the only hope was for Nogales and Wechsler to prevail.

"Doug Ruhe has crippled UPI," he often had remarked to aides, shaking his head over the bizarre situation Foothill was mired in. "It's unbelievable. There are so many consultants there, getting huge amounts and ripping off the company. Meanwhile the staff, which is really the company's backbone, is being paid paltry salaries. Ruhe and Geissler don't appreciate what they've got, and they don't know what they're doing."

Although the Los Angeles talks would stretch into the early morning hours, it was clear only a few final details needed to be worked out before the owners would sign a legally binding agreement giving control of UPI to Nogales.

Isolated a continent away, guarding the executive suite, Geissler had grown increasingly bitter. When Greg Gordon dropped by for a late-afternoon interview, the owner vowed revenge on Nogales and Wechsler.

"Whatever goes around, comes around," he said.

• • •

Max McCrohon had spent most of his time in New York fending off questions from fellow Pulitzer judges about UPI's future. Returning to Washington, he continued to get regular briefings from Geissler on the developments.

During one such telephone chat in his Connecticut Avenue condo, McCrohon learned that the boards of UPI and its parent, Media News, would be redrawn to consist of Nogales, Ruhe, and Morrissey. Just as Geissler had hoped, McCrohon was upset that UPI's editorial department had been denied representation—so upset that the Camel-smoking editor fumbled and dropped a lighted cigarette on his daughter's doll house and had to rush to douse the flames.

At 5:44 a.m. Washington time, McCrohon phoned Ruhe and Nogales and threatened to resign unless he, too, were seated on the boards. Nogales bristled at McCrohon's demand, and Wechsler was beside himself. While other executives had put their careers on the line, McCrohon had been a continent away judging contest entries. The editor, aloof and patrician, always seemed conveniently occupied with other things at crucial times. Nogales and Wechsler thought McCrohon was too close to the owners. If he were a director, Ruhe and Geissler would play him like a yo-yo to create 2-2 deadlocks.

But Nogales also sympathized with having the editorial department represented, and the last thing UPI needed was for its respected editor to resign. He agreed to McCrohon's demand. Wechsler, still furious at having been frozen out of the negotiations, erupted anew, demanding to know why he had not been put on the board. Fighting to hold together his fragile coalition, Nogales privately promised to make Wechsler UPI's new president.

Ruhe continued battling, wringing from a weary Nogales a commitment to continue paying the owners $132,000 in "management fees" over the next four months, even though their management role had been eliminated.

At midmorning Washington time on Thursday, March 7, the owners agreed in writing to yield control, making Nogales chairman and chief executive officer. The document, telecopied to Washington for Geissler's signature, was not unlike the accord worked out the week before splitting 60 percent of the stock evenly among the owners, the management, the union, and Foothill. Ruhe wangled one more concession—if Nogales did not conclude a deal to recapitalize UPI within 120 days, all stock would revert to the owners.

At 7:33 a.m. Los Angeles time, the last signature was affixed. Exhausted, Ruhe and Nogales managed to smile and shake hands for photographers. Despite Ruhe's antics, reason had prevailed. Whether he had succumbed to pressure or had no real alternative, Doug Ruhe had given UPI another chance.

Employees cheered the news. For a while, at least, Foothill would be covering their paychecks.

As noon approached in Washington, Geissler was drained and discouraged. The week that started with the owners celebrating victory had degenerated into inglorious retreat.

Geissler shrugged and invited Adler out for a burger. Digging into his pockets at the restaurant, he was chagrined to find them empty.

Adler bought lunch.

• • •

When Nogales returned to Washington on Friday, he began comparing UPI's comeback prospects to Chrysler's miracle turnaround engineered by Lee Iacocca.

"They [Chrysler] were in deep trouble and we were in deep trouble," he said. "They showed they can turn it around. I think we can too."

UPI staffers greeted him with warm applause when he strode into the newsroom. They recognized what he had risked to challenge the owners. In the conference room one floor above, managers draped crepe-paper streamers and toasted Nogales with domestic champagne.

Despite his confident exterior, Nogales knew his task bordered on the impossible. UPI's finances were a horrific mess. Besides the debts to major creditors, rents were in arrears, stringers unpaid for months were quitting, phones were being cut off. Embarrassingly, UPI's dirty laundry had been hung out in plain view of the news industry. Keeping clients now would certainly be even more difficult. As his first priority for restoring a measure of stability, Nogales announced he would call an early meeting with creditors to try to persuade them to exchange their debts for stock.

As if Nogales didn't have trouble enough, Ruhe and Geissler were not about to go gently. The very day Nogales and Wechsler were moving into the owners' ninth-floor offices, the partners paid another visit to Porter Bibb in Manhattan. Bibb could see they were devastated. They told him they had felt as if Foothill had a pistol at their heads. They could not tolerate Unipressers missing paychecks; it would have meant "the end of UPI."

Secretly, Bibb was aghast that, ignoring his imprecations, they had caved in and surrendered control of UPI. Agreement with Nogales notwithstanding, he said, they still could—and should—try to sell the company themselves.

"You guys need to reassert your positions as owners," he said. "That's the only thing you have going for you."

Ruhe and Geissler heeded his counsel. Soon, in violation of the spirit of their agreement with Nogales, Bibb's firm would be circulating a proposal to help the owners sell UPI.

• • •

Even before the fanfare over his Los Angeles triumph had subsided, reality closed in on Nogales. Besides UPI's perhaps insoluble problems, he had to worry about holding together his own management team. His chief concern was Wechsler.

Even though he had agreed to make Wechsler president, cracks already were beginning to rend their West Coast alliance, a marriage more of convenience than love. Wechsler, an ambitious young numbers genius who felt he should have at least equal status at UPI with Nogales, viewed the promised presidency as an insufficient sop, given the clout he carried with Foothill. He wanted to be co-CEO, and Nogales wanted no part of that. Wechsler also never would forgive Nogales for excluding him from the negotiations with Ruhe, and for ignoring his pleas for a seat on the board of directors.

Wechsler deeply resented Nogales hogging the spotlight. Not a man afflicted with a small ego, Wechsler felt that he, not Nogales, had forced the owners' ouster; it was his presence, not Nogales's, that had convinced Foothill to pressure Ruhe.

Wechsler also grew jealous of Nogales's easy rapport with UPI's editorial staff. He could not match it, even though he tried hard to be "one of the boys."

Yet another stumbling block was their sharply differing view of the union. Nogales understood, in a company like UPI, the necessity of peaceful coexistence. Wechsler would have loved to see the union just disappear. And although Nogales had promised there would be no more wage cuts, Wechsler was pushing hard for both staff and pay reductions.

But Nogales realized that somehow he had to try to smooth things out. Wechsler, the numbers man UPI always had needed, would be difficult to replace. Nogales had to placate him, even though he knew making Wechsler president would enrage UPI's top editors.

The storm signals were unmistakable. Nogales had landed smack in the middle of UPI's worsening cash-flow problems. Confrontation with the IRS was inevitable. Ruhe and Geissler surely would continue sniping and nipping at his heels. Top staffers were actively hunting for other jobs. Disgusted clients were fast losing patience with the foundering wire service.

UPI was headed down to the wire. Luis Nogales may have saved the company, but he was smart enough to know he had only won a reprieve. UPI still was on Death Row.

16
...
The Tax Man Cometh

Bankruptcy lawyer Rick Levine and UPI spokesman Bill Adler stood sentry at the door to a convention room at Chicago's O'Hare Hilton on March 14, 1985.

More unlikely bouncers could hardly be imagined. Levine, slight, balding, jovially good-natured; Adler, baby-faced, a bit taller than Levine but hardly mistakable for Chicago Bears linebacker Dick Butkus.

Yet there they were, guarding the sanctity of the crucial first meeting of UPI's unsecured creditors. Owing more than $17 million in short-term debts and with liabilities easily double that, UPI's only salvation was to beg for mercy.

"Security" was necessary because of fears Ruhe and Geissler might crash the meeting and panic creditors. The March 7 agreement ceding control of UPI to Nogales explicitly prohibited the ousted owners from communicating with creditors. To Wechsler, that meant they should be barred from the meeting. Thus, Levine and Adler.

More than 100 of UPI's 5,000 creditors, including representatives of the biggest vendors, streamed into the room. Many were more curious than hopeful that they might recover more than a fraction of the money they were owed.

Suddenly the tall, husky Ruhe approached. Levine stepped forward, incongruously trying to block his path.

"The request is that you not attend the meeting," Levine said.

"Are you going to bar me?" Ruhe asked, incredulous and amused.

"The request is that you not attend the meeting."

Ruhe brushed past as if Levine were a gnat.

Soon, Rinaldo Brutoco appeared. Sarcastically promising "I'll be an angel," he, too, swept in.

Ruhe and Brutoco *were* angels, sitting quietly in the back. But their presence was a reminder that, even though the ousted owners no longer controlled UPI, they would be watching Nogales's every move, stalking an opening.

Nogales gave the creditors a general overview, Wechsler detailed UPI's finances, and McCrohon pledged continued editorial excellence. An informal creditors' committee was appointed to work with the managers to restructure the company's massive debts. Nogales was delighted when the creditors agreed to consider a ninety-day moratorium on debt payments.

· · ·

Even as they mapped strategy, Nogales and Wechsler were irate over the mess they had inherited. They were suspicious of Ruhe's and Geissler's cash transfers to Focus, and Nogales was irked at the owners' sale of key UPI assets. Ruhe and Geissler had padded the payroll with consultants whose products never materialized, hired pals with dubious skills, and neglected to impose more than token financial controls.

Desperately caulking the gushing leaks, Nogales and Wechsler scurried from crisis to crisis. Besides cajoling creditors and calming Foothill, they launched a drive to scrape away the barnacles and parasites sapping the company of more than $2 million a year—firing most of the consultants, dismissing the mainly Baha'i research department, and terminating money-losing joint-venture deals.

Nogales directed that no more UPI expense checks be cut for Rinaldo Brutoco and ditched Ruhe's Baha'i secretary, Lana Bogan, and her officious brother-in-law, Luis Lizarraga, little more than a glorified go-fer who was drawing $60,000 a year. News staffers had disparagingly dubbed Lizarraga "Louie the Lizard" and "Louie Lasagna," unaware he was earning double their salaries.

Nogales had heard reports that Lizarraga, in computerizing UPI's plans for paying off debts, had antagonized creditors who phoned in. Then, after the UPI chairman fired him, Lizarraga departed with a microcomputer and the disks on which he had placed the payout plan. Lizarraga phoned Nogales and offered to sell them back to UPI for $25,000 in consulting fees. When Nogales threatened to call the sheriff, he returned them.

Nogales particularly groused about Ruhe's damaging sale of UPI's foreign pictures service and other assets, deals he feared would hinder his efforts to attract investors. The helter-skelter deals had fetched nearly $10 million to cover payrolls, but helped shrink annual revenues from more than $100 million to $93 million.

The difficulty of restoring UPI to health would be further compounded by sweeping industry changes that threatened the niche the wire service had historically carved. While UPI had declined in size, media giants such as *The New York Times, Washington Post, Times-Mirror*, Knight-Ridder—and even old partner Scripps Howard—were making sharp inroads in the newspaper market, selling their own supplemental services at a fraction of what UPI charged.

Major metropolitan dailies often received many of these services and increasingly questioned why they were paying so much for UPI coverage that was strikingly similar in content to AP's, but less comprehensive. With but a few cities still boasting competing newspapers, fears of being "scooped" by a rival had all but vanished. UPI, its revenues from newspapers threatened, would have to quickly woo non-media customers.

• • •

In the face of this predicament, Nogales and Wechsler first had to dramatically demonstrate to Foothill their commitment and competence to begin turning things around.

Wechsler, aggressive and persistent, brought to the job a tough, MBA mentality foreign to UPI. A pudgy man who sported a curly "perm," Wechsler was obsessed with numbers. He worshipped at the shrine of the bottom line. Once, Wechsler wore to an office softball game a T-shirt reading, "Happiness Is a Positive Cash Flow." Almost from the outset, however, Wechsler demonstrated little regard for UPI's history and tradition as a complete news service, an attitude that would quickly earn him enmity throughout the company.

Even before the owners had stepped aside, Wechsler had persuaded Nogales that since UPI's operations in Europe, Africa, and the Middle East were losing $3 million a year, the solution was deep staff reductions abroad. Wechsler summoned executive editor Mike Hughes, who also was UPI's international vice president, and told him the European operation had to be shut down.

"You must be joking!" Hughes said, appalled. UPI always had prided itself on outstanding coverage from Scandinavia to Saudi Arabia.

"No, I'm not joking. Europe is operating on a $3 million deficit. If we could eliminate this deficit, we could make this company run."

"Well, my friend, how do you propose for us to cover Europe, the Middle East, and Africa?"

"We'll have fifteen 'trench coat' reporters."

Hughes wondered where Wechsler had picked up "trench coats," jargon for roving foreign correspondents poised to race to the latest world trouble spot. Hughes, a hot-tempered Brit, knew fifteen reporters could not possibly handle client demands in one of the world's busiest news areas and felt such cuts would only court more subscriber losses. In a voice he was certain carried to the newsroom a floor below, Hughes shouted, "You're a fucking idiot! And you have no goddamned business being in this place! It will not bloody work!"

"Well, it must," Wechsler said, unshaken. "Otherwise, the company will not survive."

"Well, let me tell you something! If you try and pull this shit, you are going to kill UPI—no matter how much you are trying to save us. I'm not going to do it. I'm not listening to this."

Hughes stormed from the room, but for the next eight days he was closeted with Wechsler and Nogales, often in shouting matches. Nogales finally nixed the "trench coat" plan but ordered Hughes to cut seven European staffers by attrition.

Days after the Los Angeles accord, Wechsler was lobbying again for staff cuts and also urging Nogales to seek more union contract concessions. In negotiating 25 percent wage cuts, Nogales had promised not to ask the employees for more sacrifices. But with Foothill demanding evidence that UPI was taking steps to solve its financial problems, he reluctantly agreed to Wechsler's demands.

On Tuesday, March 13, just five days into the new regime, Nogales, Wechsler, and vice president Bobby Ray Miller proposed to Bill Morrissey and Dan Carmichael a laundry list of concessions, including continuing 15 percent pay cuts for another eighteen months.

"Fuck no!" Carmichael snapped.

The union leaders sensed Wechsler's hand behind the proposal and were convinced he was out to destroy the union. Employees were outraged to learn they might not get their 5 percent pay restoration on April 1.

In late March, Wechsler struck again. Max McCrohon was ordered to cut 300 domestic staffers. Although the news report inevitably would suffer dramatically, Wechsler persuaded Nogales that they had to gamble that clients, most of whom had remained loyal, would understand that UPI was undergoing a wrenching fight for its life.

They also counted on the dedication of employees to dig even deeper and pick up the slack. For decades, despite a numerical inferiority, UPI had scratched and scraped to cover everything from coronations and coups to traffic fatals and local weather. Cutting manpower without cutting services would have sorely tested employees at any company. At UPI, editors and staffers already were pushing themselves beyond reasonable limits; Nogales and Wechsler bet they would find a way to do even more.

McCrohon and Hughes fought to save every job they could, demanding parallel reductions in noneditorial personnel. Nogales finally agreed to limit the editorial cuts to ninety-five reporters and photographers and to let an "Executioners' Committee" selected by McCrohon specify the victims.

After its first all-day, bureau-by-bureau analysis of potential cuts, committee members were shocked to find that, rather than slashing staff, they had concluded that UPI needed at least a dozen more reporters to cover the news properly. Sadly, they returned to the drawing board.

• • •

During committee deliberations one day, Hughes was summoned to the phone. It was Nogales, from Los Angeles.

"I want to name Wechsler president," Nogales told the No. 2 editorial manager.

"No fucking way! There is no way in God's green earth that I'm ever going to agree to this. Luis, if he's president, there's no way this company is ever going to make it."

"Mike, I need the guy for Foothill and he won't work for us anymore unless he becomes president."

Nogales begged Hughes to meet with Wechsler and work things out. Hughes later phoned Nogales to describe a stormy, hour-long confrontation in which he demanded that Wechsler relinquish his $240,000 consulting fee and retroactively take the same pay cuts other Unipressers had accepted in September.

"Good," Nogales said. "Good. It's time you told off that sonovabitch. I support that."

Wechsler finally agreed to take a $50,000 pay cut to $190,000 a year—the same salary as McCrohon—and to then accept the company-wide pay cuts. The job of president was his.

McCrohon, uncharacteristically vehement, told Nogales, "It will be a grave mistake, Luis."

"You may be right," Nogales replied, "but I need him."

On March 27, Wechsler officially became UPI's fourth president in thirty months.

• • •

Nogales, Wechsler, and Jack Kenney had worried for months that the IRS would come knocking. Uncle Sam showed up as they prepared for a second creditors meeting.

"As you know, the company owes us $1.7 million," agent John Myers told Rick Levine in a phone call from the IRS office in Nashville. "I want to come to the creditors' committee meeting in New York."

UPI's problem with the IRS loomed large. The government could force the wire service into bankruptcy, and it also had the muscle to seize the property and possessions of those who had been involved in the decision not to pay the taxes. With little choice, Levine agreed to let Myers attend the March 29 meeting.

Wechsler, president just two days, swaggered into the meeting place at the tightly guarded New York headquarters of AT&T, his old company and one of UPI's biggest creditors. His cocky grin quickly disappeared.

There to greet the UPI contingent was a tall white man with a huge bushy Afro that seemed to shimmer even when he stood still.

"Hi, I'm John Myers," he said, flashing his IRS identification badge in the faces of the UPI executives. "I'm required by regulation to do this. I'm concerned about the taxes. Will you tell me the whole story?"

The UPI executives stood stiffly, fumbling for a response. The moment they had been dreading had arrived. Finally Levine spoke up, promising that UPI would get back to Myers with all the details—at a more convenient time.

Despite Myers's presence, the creditors meeting went smoothly. Myers actually gave a boost by announcing the company was abiding by an interim payment plan to begin reducing the back taxes. With Wechsler and UPI's investment bankers projecting a glowing financial outlook, creditors approved a ninety-day moratorium on debt payments and even agreed to discuss swapping UPI stock for back debts. Jules Teitelbaum, a tough but good-natured veteran New York City bankruptcy lawyer, was named counsel to the creditors' committee.

Wechsler remained deeply concerned about the IRS' heightened interest, fearing the IRS would file a lien against UPI—an action that would give the government first claim on company assets and could force UPI into bankruptcy. He put Levine in touch with New York Mayor Ed Koch's accountant, Sigmund Balaban, an expert in forestalling the IRS. Levine and Balaban repeatedly phoned Myers and his bosses trying to dissuade them from filing a lien.

Unfortunately, the government would not be as sympathetic as other creditors.

• • •

On April 3, Luis Nogales shook with anger when he picked up *The Chicago Tribune*. It was less than a month after Ruhe and Geissler had signed the agreement giving him sole authority to sell UPI and pledging they would not "voluntarily sell or otherwise transfer" their stock without board approval.

The *Tribune* article said that Porter Bibb was "soliciting expressions of interest in a controlling stake in the United Press International news service." The letter, circulated to thirty communications companies, did not identify Ruhe and Geissler as the potential sellers, leaving the impression it came from UPI management. To Nogales, it was a vigilante tactic that would undermine his own efforts to entice a buyer.

Further, Bibb's letter grossly distorted UPI's financial condition, ignoring the company's enormous debts and ludicrously predicting 1985 pretax profits of more than $5 million.

Without Nogales's knowledge, Bibb's scheme had gotten Ruhe and Geissler in the door at two giant media companies, McGraw-Hill and *The Los Angeles Times*. At McGraw-Hill, executive vice president Joseph Kasputys was excited by the prospect of selling UPI news and his own company's information to hotel and restaurant patrons via a nationwide network of computer terminals. L.A. Times Syndicate chairman J. Willard Colston also agreed with Bibb that UPI—or at least parts of it— might be salvageable.

However, top executives of both companies ultimately decided against dealing with Bibb. They had followed news accounts of UPI's internal upheavals, and when they learned he was representing Ruhe and Geissler they were confused about who really had the right to sell the company. McGraw-Hill officials felt that Ruhe, asking $13 million for the company, was trying to personally profit from UPI's plight. Neither firm was impressed with the owners, and neither wanted to get caught in a messy management war.

Angry by what he considered blatant interference, Nogales wrote Bibb demanding the owners stop violating "the letter and spirit of the agreement."

Later, when Nogales separately approached McGraw-Hill and Times-Mirror about buying UPI, neither was interested. Ruhe and Geissler's end-run certainly had not helped.

• • •

On April 11 Nogales and McCrohon campaigned for support from a tough audience, delegates to the annual convention of the American Society of Newspaper Editors at the Sheraton Washington Hotel.

Boasting of a fifth straight monthly profit in February, Nogales said UPI "will attract investors" once it proves it can operate in the black.

McCrohon presented a slide show of feature stories, graphics, and newspictures to demonstrate that Unipressers "are not sitting still, not wringing our hands."

In a tense question-and-answer session, McCrohon avoided discussing the looming staff cuts and assured editors that while layoffs were "conceivable," editorial quality would remain high.

When one editor asked whether "we might wake up some morning and find that UPI has gone out of business," Nogales sought to reassure him.

"UPI will survive!" he said.

• • •

For UPI's staffers and the stringers who were their lifeline, the changes in top management had little impact. It was painfully apparent there was no more money for news coverage under Nogales than there had been under Ruhe and Geissler. Reimbursement checks were nonexistent. Stringers, whose role would become more important when the staff cuts became effective, simply stopped working after waiting months for their less-than-generous stipends.

Employees, especially the volatile ones like Washington night copy-desk chief Andy Tully, had their limits about how long they would carry the company's financial burden. Late one Thursday afternoon in early spring, Tully arrived for work, sliced open his pay envelope, and blew his stack. Once again a payroll foul-up had deprived him of his weekly 5 percent night differential.

To outsiders, an extra $20 or $30 a week might seem a trifle. To Unipressers whose pay had been cut, it was serious money. And to Tully, who had jumped to the AP several years earlier and then returned at a cut in salary because UPI was more fun, it seemed the final straw. A charming New Yorker with an Irish temper and three small children, Tully had been battling UPI's beleaguered administrators for weeks.

Now he grabbed a phone, dialed the payroll department in Brentwood, and shouted, pounding the desk to punctuate his wrath, "Where's my money? I want my money!"

Not satisfied with the excuse he received, Tully slammed down the receiver, jammed his gear into his orange-and-blue New York Mets gym bag, and marched to the elevator. As he was about to disappear, a supervisor grabbed his arm and said, "Andy, you don't want to do this. It can be real trouble."

"I don't give a shit! I just want my fucking money! This company has been jerking me around long enough!"

The manager took Tully into his office, phoned Brentwood, and rectified the problem. Tully returned to work at his desk. His temper tantrum had paid off.

Every bureau in every country had problems, most not fixed that easily. Plaintive pleas barraged world headquarters. On April 5 a senior editorial manager compiled a list of horror stories in a memo to Jack Kenney.

—Please send $90 to Raine Bergstrom, our stringer in Juneau, Alaska. This is particularly dicey because he is engaged to marry the daughter of the publisher of the UPI client newspaper. (The paper later canceled, perhaps for unrelated reasons.)

—We owe $3,500 to the Cheyenne Cleaning Company, which is

cutting off the janitorial service to the Dallas bureau because there's no money to buy supplies.

—Please send $70 to Des Moines manager Alice Noble to reimburse a staffer who covered "football day" at the University of Iowa last week. (To top management worried about seven figures and the survival of UPI, such problems seemed niggling. But to Alice Noble and dozens like her, reality was seventy bucks for Hawkeye football.)

—The kid who covers the Indianapolis Indians home baseball games for $2 each has quit because we owe him $400.

—Last week the biggest snowfall of the century hit Memphis and *The Commercial-Appeal* (a Scripps Howard paper) wouldn't provide us pictures because we were behind in stringer payments. When the editor of the Knoxville *Sentinel* heard we had no pictures, he threatened to throw the UPI photo machine out the window. Only fevered efforts by state editor Duren Cheek calmed him down.

—Dallas baseball stringer Mike Stern has stopped covering because he is owed $1,400. A partial payment of $680 was mailed to the wrong address and returned to Brentwood, and no replacement check was issued. And the 1985 baseball season starts this week.

Not all UPI's problems were nickel-and-dime. In mid-April a vendor filed a $1.5 million suit against the company in Williamson County, Tennessee, for nonpayment of satellite leases. UPI got a break. Its offices in Brentwood sat about 100 yards north of the Williamson County line. On a technicality, it was temporarily spared a suit everyone agreed it could not have won.

•　•　•

On April 19, his troops' spirits sagging, Nogales gave Unipressers a pep talk that would have done Knute Rockne proud. In a three-page letter he exhorted and cajoled, sympathized and prodded and inspired. He appealed to their love of company, love of underdog status, love of a good fight. Many were moved. Some cynically dismissed it. Few would argue that it was a remarkable piece of work.

"UPI has weathered many storms in the past. Never before, however, has the spirit of this organization been so severely tested. Each of us is facing extraordinary pressures in our personal and professional lives; we are being pushed, in many cases, to the very limit of what we feel we can endure.

"Beyond our individual concerns or attachment to UPI, our mission is to ensure that this country and the world will never be without the competition and honesty of reporting that UPI provides. In a time of severe testing, individuals or groups can rise above limits previously thought impassable, or they can shrink and collapse. UPI is not ready to shrink and certainly not about to collapse. That's not who we are, not what we fought for all these years.

"If we have to stretch yet another inch, we'll grit our teeth and do it. In the next ninety days you will continue to see flurries of activity and speculation. I must ask you to take the broad and realistic view and not expect a sudden resolution or the appearance of a Deus ex machina. We're in a fifteen-round fight in which there will be no early knockouts. We've got to tough it out; there's no other way. However, while the going may continue to be tough in the short term, you should discount rumors that suggest some new drastic development is imminent. That is not going to happen.

"As we face what is in all likelihood our last major push, I ask of you again your best efforts and your renewed determination. Together, we're going to win. I am proud of UPI and proud to be your colleague."

• • •

The day Nogales's message was being distributed to Unipressers around the world, the IRS fired a shot across UPI's bow. It filed a $1.77 million lien to ensure that, if the company collapsed, the government would collect all unpaid taxes before unsecured creditors received a dime.

This was big trouble. First, the lien once more underscored to the media world that, despite all the talk of a recovery, financial problems still were staggering. Now even the government was declaring the company a deadbeat. Second, the IRS action would endanger the critical Foothill loan by tying up UPI's collateral.

Levine and Balaban leaped to action, trying to convince the IRS to lift the lien. At the same time, the company disclosed the IRS filing on its wires, trying to put the best face on a dreadful situation by saying it was "in substantial agreement" with the government on a payback schedule and the lien probably would not be enforced.

Fearful their priority lending status would be endangered, Foothill officials scurried to their lawyers and summoned UPI officials to Los Angeles. Foothill was also worried that it could drop another rung on the repayment ladder because union officials were threatening to seek a court order to force UPI to resume payments to the guild pension fund.

Feeling the pressure, Nogales phoned Bill Morrissey on Tuesday, April 23rd, to warn that unless the union made further concessions to assure continued profits, Foothill would cut off credit and force UPI into Chapter 11. Morrissey hopped a plane and arrived in Los Angeles that evening.

Wechsler and Nogales greeted him by announcing they had taken a new gamble—sending already nervous subscribers a letter begging them to accept a voluntary 9.9 percent rate increase. Seeking more money for a diminished product could trigger cancellations, but Nogales and Wechsler felt they had no choice.

At 3:30 A.M. Wednesday, Dan Carmichael was awakened at his New York hotel by a call from Morrissey, who had been persuaded the union should accept modest concessions. Morrissey had come to the guild presidency from the AP, and Carmichael, a Unipresser, always flexed extra muscle on decisions affecting UPI.

Carmichael was unwavering. "Absolutely nothing," he declared. "Not a penny more."

Morrissey knew full well the consequences. Chapter 11 now seemed inevitable, and perhaps UPI would not survive it. He met with Foothill vice president Peter Schwab and informed him the union would make no more concessions, including refusing to permit the company to defer any longer its payments to the pension fund.

On Thursday, at 2:25 p.m., the day paychecks were being distributed, Schwab emerged from a meeting of Foothill's credit committee to deliver the bad news to Nogales and Wechsler: this time, the lender would not agree to exceed UPI's line of credit.

UPI's paychecks were no good.

• • •

While lawyer Lisa Greer set to work drafting corporate resolutions approving a Chapter 11 bankruptcy filing, Nogales, Wechsler, Levine, and Morrissey agreed to discuss their options that evening at the offices of Bear Stearns. Chapter 11 would give the company months of court protection while it straightened out its financial mess, and would give Foothill first-priority repayment status in return for its continued financial backing.

Morrissey, last to arrive for the meeting, found Wechsler at a secretary's desk, pounding a typewriter. He peered curiously over Wechsler's shoulder. Wechsler, president barely a month, was typing his resignation.

"What the hell are you doing?" Morrissey demanded.

"I've failed. I've got to resign."

Morrissey tensed. As much as he and his colleagues disliked Wechsler, this was the last thing UPI needed. He yanked the paper out of the typewriter, wadded it into a ball, and hurled it into a wastebasket.

"We don't need any more shit around here!" he barked. "We've got problems to solve."

Nogales, Morrissey, and Levine agreed bankruptcy seemed the best way to protect the company's future. Not only had employees received bum paychecks, but disclosure of the IRS lien was panicking creditors. There were rumors that some vendors planned to raid UPI offices and seize leased equipment—copying machines, printers, typewriters, even satellite dishes. UPI's operations might be stripped clean.

"Okay, that's it," Morrissey said. "We're going into Chapter 11."

Nogales grimly nodded. There was no time to waste.

Late that night Morrissey and Nogales phoned McCrohon in Washington and Ruhe in Nashville to convene an emergency meeting of the UPI board. Lawyers Levine and Bill Bowe listened in from Los Angeles and Nashville.

Nogales was forced to disclose to Ruhe, his nemesis, that UPI was out of money again, and this time could not cover employee paychecks. "The best way to ensure the continuity of the company is through bankruptcy," Nogales declared.

Almost before Nogales had finished, Ruhe opened fire.

"Now, Luis, I know you've tried very hard," he said condescendingly, reveling in Nogales's predicament. "But sometimes, when you can't act like a man you've got to admit it. I think you've got to take it like a man, and admit that you're way over your head, and resign."

It was vintage Ruhe, demeaning his opponent's manhood.

Nogales was furious. What nerve! Jaw tightening, he spat out, "I'm not resigning."

Ruhe was not about to back off. He continued taunting Nogales to resign, needling in singsong fashion, "Be a man, be a man."

Struggling to control his rage, Nogales kept his voice firm and even. "I'm not resigning."

Finally, Morrissey broke in.

"Doug, I think you've asked the question a number of times, and he said no. Let's move on to something else."

As the exchanges became more acrimonious, McCrohon's discomfort grew. An editor, not a business executive, he sensed the board was about to take a step that might seal the fate of a great American institution. They must not rush. Everyone needed to take a deep breath, cool off, get their bearings.

"I don't understand the full consequences of this," McCrohon said, "and I want time to consult with a private attorney."

McCrohon's request was music to Ruhe. Any reason to delay could only help him, and he immediately agreed.

When Nogales pressed for a vote to authorize a Chapter 11 filing, Ruhe and McCrohon voted no. The motion thus failed, 2-2.

Morrissey erupted.

"You fucking sons-of-bitches have fucked this place long enough, and now you want to dillydally around while the employees' paychecks go down the tubes!"

His expletive-decorated harangue failed to break the impasse, and the four hung up. The union quickly exercised whatever leverage it had to try to break the deadlock and force a Chapter 11 filing before it was too late. At 12:15 EST Friday morning it issued a bulletin disclosing to members that UPI "has no available cash at the current time to cover payroll checks." It went on, "The company is discussing the possibility of filing a Chapter 11 bankruptcy petition. It is the union's opinion that a Chapter 11 filing at this time is necessary to protect employee rights and to protect company assets." Employees were asked "to continue working as scheduled."

As a new wave of fear swept employees, managing editor Ron Cohen and reporter Greg Gordon (D'Vera Cohn had resigned to join *The Washington Post*) raced to the office to put on the wire a story about the new developments. Despite efforts to explain that a Chapter 11 filing is meant to give a foundering company breathing room to reorganize, the word "bankruptcy" frightened subscribers. Some immediately assumed UPI's demise was imminent. During one early morning newscast, hours after the announcement, Mutual radio broadcaster Paul Henderson said hyperbolically, "It looks like the wire service may be going under."

The union's pressure ploy and the ensuing publicity had forced McCrohon's hand. He realized he had little alternative but to side with Nogales. With staff and clients gripped by uncertainty, the directors— even Ruhe—voted Friday morning to approve the Chapter 11 filing.

Chaos reigned. For many employees the warning not to cash paychecks had come too late. There would be no funds in their accounts to cover the rents or mortgages. Unipressers did not know if they were going to get paid again, or even if the company could survive.

Yet, as network television crews descended on the headquarters, Unipressers once again manned their stations, covering rapid-fire developments in Washington, Moscow, and Latin America stemming from the Central American conflict. The House of Representatives cast another vote to bar aid to the Nicaraguan Contra rebels, and President Reagan prepared to declare a national emergency to cut off air and sea links to Nicaragua. The Soviet Union, meanwhile, pledged whatever aid necessary to the Sandinista government in Managua.

As worried as Unipressers were, for dozens the worst was yet to come. Foothill, whose help UPI would desperately need as an "interim" lender during bankruptcy, was now in a position—with enthusiastic prodding from Wechsler—to press its demands for massive layoffs.

McCrohon's editorial "Executioners' Committee" had carefully drawn up a list of fifty-five editorial staffers to be cut, ensuring the most experienced national and international reporters would keep their jobs. Manpower would be slashed in low-revenue areas—ten states would be left with but a single staffer. The layoffs were scheduled to begin May 1, but Levine advised Nogales that UPI could avoid most of its million-dollar severance obligations if notice were given before the bankruptcy filing. In that event, fired employees would have to file claims with the bankruptcy court along with thousands of other unsecured creditors, hoping to collect at least a fraction of their money at some time in the future.

Nogales faced a cruel dilemma: in order to best position the company for recovery, he would have to throw veteran Unipressers out on the street without most of the financial protections they had earned under the union contract. He told himself he had no choice. He picked up the phone shortly after the board's vote and called personnel manager Bobby Ray Miller in Washington.

"I want you to fire a hundred people by midnight," Nogales said.

UPI now had decided its financial straits did not permit compassionate treatment of its loyal employees.

McCrohon was furious at the proposed timing and handling of the layoffs. He directed Miller to take no action before Monday. But Nogales overruled him, ordering Miller to consult regional editors and compile a list of targeted employees.

McCrohon and Mike Hughes departed for the evening, unaware that a few feet away Miller was dispatching impersonal telegrams. In the end, eighty employees, including fifty-five permanent and temporary editorial staffers, were dismissed immediately with four weeks' pay.

UPI's "Friday Night Massacre" had begun.

• • •

In the spring of 1985 there probably wasn't a better bureau, pound for pound, than Boise, an improbable spawning ground for talented Unipressers.

Idaho state editor Mark Shenefelt, himself only in his mid-twenties, was mother hen to Bruce Botka, Steve Green, and Nancie Katz. The four friends spent countless hours in their little bureau frantically competing against AP's seven Boise staffers. UPI's dire financial problems seemed distant indeed. Sure it was tough getting stringers paid, and reimbursement checks for expenses were rare as smog over the nearby Salmon River.

But, despite the 25 percent pay cut, living was cheap in Boise. And, ten minutes from the curious sign advertising "Fairly Reliable Bob's" used cars, they could always find the solace and tranquility of a mountain stream.

Their good life was shattered one Friday evening when Steve Green received a telegram from Washington.

"Effective today, April 26, 1985, your employment with UPI is being terminated. Yvonne Greene, United Press International, Human Resources Administration."

Green and Botka went to Shenefelt's house to try to make some sense out of UPI's decision to fire Green and Katz, cutting the Boise staff in half. The more beer they drank, the angrier they got and the less they understood. Their emotions reflected the bitterness and rage of UPI employees nationwide, both those who lost their jobs and those spared.

Watching them unhappily was Shenefelt's wife, Tammy, his high school sweetheart. Six months earlier she had given birth to their first child, Derek. UPI's distress, perhaps, was hardest on spouses and lovers. If you didn't actually work for UPI, there was no way to fully comprehend the mysterious spell that compelled Unipressers to endure hardship and anguish beyond reason.

That night, with Green deciding to return to college and Botka bitterly resolving to find a new job, Shenefelt felt his little UPI "family" collapsing. He didn't notice that Tammy was seething, first at the company that so hurt her husband; then, perhaps irrationally, at Mark himself. When the beer-and-bull sessions finally shifted to Green's house on Sunday night, Tammy held little Derek close and told her husband that unless he left UPI, she would leave him.

At 4:30 a.m. on Monday, Nancie Katz and her boyfriend, returning from a long weekend in San Francisco, pulled up to her duplex apartment on North Twelfth Street in Boise, around the corner from the Shenefelts. While Tom unloaded the car, she sliced open the envelope from Western Union.

Katz, darkly attractive with sloe, sexy eyes, erupted in rage.

"Goddamn it, that fucking company!" she shouted. Katz headed to the bureau at dawn to gather with her colleagues.

On Monday night what had been the Boise staff gathered again at Green's house, consoling themselves that the firings did not demean Green and Katz. This was simply a last-ditch effort to save UPI.

In the middle of the night Shenefelt turned restlessly in bed to check Tammy's breathing. He did it often. Tammy was epileptic. There was always the danger of an attack.

Suddenly he froze in terror. His wife was not breathing. Doctors later would say they believed a seizure had cut off oxygen to her brain. Silently, at age twenty-six, Tammy Shenefelt had died.

Green, Botka, and Katz emotionally, perhaps irrationally, blamed UPI. The strain, the anger, the uncertainty, the fear had caused Tammy's seizure. During Shenefelt's absence for the funeral, Green and Katz offered to assist Botka, now alone running the bureau.

"Don't you do anything to help UPI!" Botka spat angrily. "Nothing at all!"

In sixty hours at the end of April, the happy, gung-ho little band of Idaho Unipressers found their worlds shattered, their lives scattered to the winds.

Mark Shenefelt moved back to Utah to work on a paper. After a month Botka left journalism altogether. Katz and Green later were rehired by UPI for bigger and better jobs.

• • •

In San Francisco, Pacific Division news editor Steve Christensen, who had started in Boise and helped establish the bureau as one of UPI's most reliable and respected, was beside himself. Of the ten states in his region there were fifteen reductions in the editorial staff of 123, atop a slash of twenty-nine months earlier. Montana and Alaska had been cut to one staffer each, Idaho sliced in half. And the way it had been done! Impersonal telegrams in the dead of night before he himself could break the news to those being fired! Christensen was really pissed. A good soldier, he presided that weekend over the carnage in his division. But, he told his co-workers, come Monday morning UPI subscribers would find themselves short-changed. And he wasn't going to be a part of it.

He resigned that weekend, and pleadings from friends and bosses could not alter his decision. Steve Christensen, one of UPI's brightest young stars, was an unintended casualty of the Friday Night Massacre.

• • •

Jerry McGinn, UPI's Spokane correspondent, wasn't home Friday night to get the call from Western Union. McGinn, a twenty-one-year Unipresser, had helped roast a local high school football coach. As he lay in bed Saturday morning basking in the glow of his efforts at humor, he awaited the reward his wife had promised—breakfast in bed. She arrived with the tray, replete with flowers. Atop the plate was a telegram.

Certain it was a humorous kudo from a friend, McGinn ripped it open and read his firing notice.

Helluva breakfast, he thought.

McGinn couldn't bear to face the office that day, but on Sunday he dragged himself in and swept up twenty-one years of memories.

Before locking the Spokane bureau for good, McGinn composed a brief adieu message to his buddies, expressing hope UPI would return to glory.

"As for me, I'm going to gravitate toward things that hug back. This business never did."

• • •

About 6 a.m. on Saturday in Reno, Russ Nielsen fumbled to answer the phone.

"This is Western Union. I have a message. You are hereby terminated."

"Thank you," Nielson replied politely, too sleepy to comprehend what had just occurred. Thirty-six years after he joined the company in Helena, Montana, his UPI career was over. His reward was four weeks' severance pay.

Nielsen, getting tired after twenty-seven years of covering the busy little city of Reno by himself, already had decided to tell UPI he would take early retirement in three weeks. UPI had saved him the trouble.

Nielsen ambled into the bureau to retrieve his belongings. Like McGinn, he sat down at his terminal to compose a brief valedictory.

"My career of thirty-six years with UP-UPI ended early today. It was a great, tempestuous love affair. To so many people, thanks for the memories."

Tuesday he applied for jobless benefits. Wednesday the unemployment center called and told him that UPI was going to oppose his application. Thursday executive editor Mike Hughes called from Washington.

"Russ, mate, there's been a big mistake," said Hughes in his thick British accent. "There was a computer fuck-up and you weren't supposed to get that telegram. We're not closing Reno. You're still working."

Nielsen, afforded an opportunity many dream of but few realize, savored the moment silently. Then he stuck it to his boss.

"No way," Nielsen said slowly. "No way. I'm gone."

There never had been adequate help. There never was money to do anything. The only way to do your job well was to work twelve hours a day, and everybody seemed to just expect you would. The only time you ever heard from anybody was when something went wrong.

Russ Nielsen landed a job teaching journalism at the University of Nevada. He told his old buddies at UPI that getting fired was the best thing he ever did.

• • •

Dave Kingham, junior member of the three-person Cheyenne, Wyoming, bureau, reported to work as usual early Saturday morning, April 27. Bureau chief Scott Farris gave him the bad news.

Kingham quickly packed his belongings. When he returned home the phone was ringing. It was Western Union's termination greeting.

Three days later a form letter arrived from Yvonne Greene, UPI director of human resources, confirming his firing and his four weeks' salary in lieu of advance notice of termination.

Fittingly, Kingham's confirmation letter came postage due.

• • •

If ever a newspaper editor was a UPI loyalist, it was Norm Runnion of the *Reformer* in Brattleboro, Vermont. Runnion, who had worked for

UPI for thirteen years in Washington and abroad during the fifties and sixties, gently but firmly showed all AP salesmen the door.

His UPI bias ended abruptly the night of April 26. With no warning to subscribers, two permanent staffers and one part-timer in Montpelier got termination telegrams. The move sealed the loss of three of UPI's four newspapers and eleven of its thirteen radio stations in the state. For UPI, Vermont's lush green mountains quickly turned brown and sere.

Runnion wrote a front-page box announcing "We're with AP now," then composed an extraordinary, signed editorial noting that a few weeks earlier such a change "would have been out of the question."

"For long-time UPI supporters . . . the decline and potential fall of the UPI is sad news, professionally and personally. It was an extraordinary place to work, with immense esprit de corps, great professionalism and a sizzling sense of competition.

"That UPI no longer exists. What is in its place is a shadow of an organization dominated by almost unbelievable and childish corporate bickering at the very top, as well as mismanagement, both from a news and financial standpoint, on the national and regional levels.

"The rebuilding job is going to be monumental. In short, the story of UPI is a news industry tragedy."

• • •

The layoffs meant that in less than ten months UPI's payroll had plummeted by nearly 20 percent, to 1,218.

Besides having skirted severance obligations, Nogales and Wechsler knew each cut of twenty-five staffers would save $1 million a year in salary and fringes. Though subscribers would react bitterly, they felt they could weather the storm.

Overnight, coverage all but disappeared in the ten "nuked states." Dozens of editors, like Norm Runnion in Brattleboro, would defect to the AP, but, as Nogales and Wechsler had hoped, UPI's overall revenue losses would prove modest.

Staffers were even more enraged when they learned their fired colleagues were being denied severance pay. On Saturday, April 27, the day after the "massacre," Morrissey pumped the phones to ward off any talk of wildcat strikes.

At the same time, Nogales, Wechsler, Jack Kenney, and budget officer Steve Spritzer drove to the home of Foothill president John Nickoll in Beverly Hills to declare the deed done and to tie up Chapter 11 financing—an "interim" loan that would allow UPI to cover the bounced checks within a few days.

Rather than parking on the street, Kenney drove the rental car up Nickoll's curving driveway.

"Jack, what are you doing going all the way up here?" Nogales asked.

Kenney shrugged, slammed the car into reverse, and began to back rapidly down the incline toward the street. A number of neatly trimmed plants fell victim to one swerve. Nogales and his aides could not contain their laughter.

"Oh, hell, this is it," Nogales said. "What killed UPI is that Jack Kenney ran over John Nickoll's plants."

Inside they found Nickoll and other Foothill officials huddled in front of a TV, excited over a segment about UPI they had just viewed on Cable News Network. Vince Del Giudice, a wisecracking UPI reporter with a quintessential Jersey accent, had hung a big sign in the bureau:

"Surrender, Hell!"

The banner and the enthusiastic cheerleading of Del Giudice and other Unipressers impressed the Foothill folks.

"With spirit like that, how can you lose?" Nickoll said.

Del Giudice's banner would hang in the Washington bureau all through bankruptcy, a symbol that although the news agency might be battered and bedraggled, it was not beaten.

• • •

It was near midnight in Los Angeles by the time Nogales and his crew had worked out the final loan logistics with Foothill. Receiving the go-ahead, Levine walked up to the front desk of the Century Plaza Hotel and asked for a typewriter. While Nogales and Bill Bowe waited in the coffee shop, Levine sat by the front desk and typed out UPI's historic Chapter 11 petition. He took it to Nogales, who signed it without hesitation.

It was vital the petition be filed before Monday, before creditors could retrieve equipment or go to court to seek to liquidate UPI's few assets. Sunday morning the document was couriered by plane to Washington. But nothing was easy for the struggling company. Mechanical difficulties forced the plane to return to Los Angeles, and the petition didn't arrive in Washington until late afternoon.

Levine had arranged for the bankruptcy court clerk's office to open especially on Sunday so the papers could be filed by Frank Dicello, a bankruptcy lawyer who had been called off a Little League soccer field Saturday to assist in the case.

At 5:14 p.m. Eastern Daylight Time on April 28, 1985, Dicello filed at the District of Columbia federal courthouse UPI's petition for Chapter 11 protection.

After a quarter-century of relentless losses, disastrous mismanagement, and scratching and clawing to stay alive, UPI officially was bankrupt.

17

. . .

Here Come Da Judge!

George W. Bason, Jr., a shortish man with a wispy beard and a face like Abe Lincoln, peered down from the bench at the crowd of lawyers, reporters, and anxious Unipressers crammed into his tiny courtroom. UPI two days earlier had filed for Chapter 11 protection, and this was its first court appearance. Instinctively, Bason knew this would be his most important case. The nation's capital was home to few big companies. Most of the bankruptcies that reached his attention were penny-ante stuff.

Never had his courtroom been so packed. An enigmatic, strong-willed jurist fond of occasional flights into metaphor, Bason knew enough about UPI to realize the struggle to preserve and reorganize the wire service was a matter of grave importance.

In the short hours since UPI's filing, Bason had caught but snippets of the acrimonious corporate infighting between the owners and Nogales. So when the fireworks started almost immediately, all he could do was try to maintain order and remain calm.

At one table sat Nogales and his retinue of aides and lawyers. At another was Gary Jacobs, a Los Angeles attorney representing Ruhe and Geissler.

Without ado, Jacobs rose to tell Bason the owners had reasserted control of their majority stock and taken back their company. He said the agreement under which they had yielded operating control to Nogales had been invalidated by the bankruptcy filing.

Then, straight-faced, he revealed that the owners had held a stock-holders meeting—consisting of themselves—and once again had fired Nogales.

Unipressers in the court were stunned, but Nogales merely smirked as Levine argued the issue was moot because the Chapter 11 filing had placed UPI totally under court jurisdiction. Ignoring Jacobs's pronouncement, Bason did not even give him the courtesy of a response.

Jacobs then declared Ruhe and Geissler had been actively negotiating for the sale of UPI with Reuters and with an "investor group" headed by Pedro Lopez, principal shareholder of a Miami savings and loan. As the courtroom crowd watched in amazement, Stephen Rubin, an attorney for the "group," which consisted entirely of Lopez and his wife, Teresa Saldise, strode forward on cue and announced Lopez was prepared to buy UPI immediately for $15.8 million. However, the $2 million cash being offered for operating revenue was far short of what Nogales and his team had in mind.

Bason, startled, stared over his spectacles at Rubin and thought, "This is kind of a circus."

Then, without comment on the Lopez offer, he proceeded to the next item of business—Levine describing the shocking scope of UPI's financial mess: $21.8 million in short-term debts and total liabilities of $45 million.

Court papers had itemized 1,500 of the creditors. AT&T Communications was owed $6.1 million; Equatorial Communications Company, $2.1 million for leased satellite receiving dishes; American Express Company, $1.3 million; Scripps Howard's United Media Enterprises, $720,000 in revenues UPI had failed to pass along after marketing "Peanuts" and other features overseas; and Sperry-Univac, $637,000 for computer services.

Levine also told the judge that Unipressers had not been paid in nearly three weeks.

"The hardship on the employees strikes us as absolutely staggering," he said. "They could have quit. They could have walked out."

Bason quickly approved an interim plan under which Foothill would cover $1.38 million in paychecks frozen the previous week for 1,298 domestic employees. Unipressers in the courtroom sighed their relief.

When the hearing broke up, sparks began flying outside the court-room. Ruhe's antics had yet again set off Nogales.

Circled by reporters, Nogales forcefully dismissed out of hand efforts to fire him again and blamed the owners' "bad deals" for erecting "incredible obstacles" to UPI's survival.

"If owners can be fired for incompetence, they ought to be fired several times," he declared.

• • •

In the days after the hearing, stories began appearing in the Nashville newspapers about Ruhe and Geissler's conduct as UPI's owners. Greg Gordon was also investigating their stewardship.

Gordon, who until now had heard nothing but praise about Ruhe and Geissler from a reporter who had known them for years, was astounded by the allegations he was hearing: that they had siphoned money from UPI to Focus; had sought to benefit personally from their joint-venture deals; had broken their written promise to invest in the company.

By week's end Gordon had collected enough information for a lengthy story and had interviewed Ruhe and gotten an angry rebuttal. Managing editor Ron Cohen, aware the story would be controversial, told McCrohon he was going to run it Saturday for Sunday newspapers and urged him to review it and clear it in advance.

At 9 a.m. Saturday, before Gordon sat down to write, the two phoned McCrohon, who was flying to Milwaukee for a speech to UPI's Wisconsin newspaper editors. McCrohon, who maintained his close ties to Geissler, promised to phone in early afternoon so the story could be read to him.

Landing in Chicago, McCrohon phoned the Washington bureau and chatted with a desk editor but, curiously, hung up without asking to speak to Gordon or Cohen. At 3 p.m., with no word from McCrohon, Cohen wondered whether his boss was dodging the issue. It soon would be too late for Sunday papers. Reluctantly, he filed the 2,300-word story to UPI's clients without McCrohon's signoff. It began:

> WASHINGTON (UPI)—United Press International's chief owners reneged on a pledge to invest $2 million in the wire service and channeled millions of dollars of scarce company funds into questionable venture deals, present and former UPI officials say.
>
> According to members of UPI's current management team, several

of the deals were structured to benefit mainly Douglas Ruhe and William Geissler, principal stockholders in the wire service that filed for Chapter 11 bankruptcy protection last week, and other investors.

Ruhe and Geissler, who bought UPI for $1.00 in 1982, also paid $2.3 million to their own management company and hundreds of thousands of dollars to consultants who provided no useful products, these officials said in a series of interviews.

Ruhe was quoted in the story as charging the allegations were "smear" tactics by the "incompetent" Nogales team.

Much of the story ran in Sunday's Miami *Herald* even as hundreds of members of the American Newspaper Publishers Association converged on the city for their annual convention. The publishers buzzed about the disclosures, amazed that such material had run on UPI's own wires.

McCrohon, who had flown into Miami for the convention, was silent at first, but finally told *Washington Post* reporter Eleanor Randolph, "I don't think the story was as professional as it should have been. It was done too hastily."

Gordon and Cohen were stunned at this public criticism. Why hadn't McCrohon, as they had urged, reviewed the story before it was transmitted? As editor in chief, if the story was done hastily or unprofessionally, he could simply have killed it or ordered it rewritten.

McCrohon's criticism was a professional affront, Cohen thought. He contemplated resigning. He and Gordon were even further upset when they found out McCrohon had received a call from Geissler before he gave the interview to Randolph, his old colleague from *The Chicago Tribune*.

Outraged by McCrohon's extraordinary public criticism of one of his own reporters, Unipressers in the Washington bureau quickly collected fifty-five names on a petition assailing what they called his "intemperate" remarks. The editor returned from Florida on Thursday to find the staff on the verge of open rebellion.

Cohen, venting his frustrations on the golf course, phoned the office and learned McCrohon was taking conciliatory steps. He had called an afternoon staff meeting.

McCrohon, meanwhile, invited Gordon to lunch at the swank Hay-Adams Hotel. Listening to his small talk as they ate, Gordon wondered whether his circumspect editor ever would get to the point. Finally he pulled out a copy of the story and asked McCrohon what his problems were. Fidgeting with his pen, McCrohon finally said, "I really have no major problems with it."

Relieved, Gordon warned McCrohon about the hornets' nest he had stirred: Cohen was talking about resigning; Washington bureau chief David Wiessler and others might leave in sympathy; Gordon's own investigative staff had offered to quit in protest.

"Maybe I should go instead," McCrohon said as the two walked back to the bureau.

"I don't think that's what people are looking for, Max."

At the staff meeting in the jammed ninth-floor conference room, McCrohon delivered a gentlemanly and obviously sincere apology and gave Gordon and Cohen a vote of confidence.

The mini-rebellion was over.

• • •

Crises hit UPI almost daily in the spring of 1985, stretching from the smallest line bureaus to the White House.

AP and UPI prided themselves on "blanket coverage" of the President. It would be unthinkable for their reporters and photographers not to be on hand whenever he left the White House, even for a brief evening out at the Kennedy Center.

But that spring the unthinkable almost happened to UPI. The White House travel office at last lost patience trying to collect its enormous back debt and warned it would not let the wire service's news, audio and photo contingent travel with President Reagan to the economic summit in Europe unless it paid in advance.

Mike Hughes cringed when he learned of the threat, fearing the public humiliation when clients discovered UPI was too broke to properly cover the President. He phoned McCrohon and urged they borrow money from friendly subscribers they could count on to be discreet.

"I'll get $15,000, you get $15,000," Hughes said.

McCrohon quickly got his half underwritten by Jim Squires, who had replaced him as editor of the rich *Chicago Tribune*. Hughes caught his old pal, *Newsday* editor Tony Insolia, headed out for a round of golf.

"Tony, I need fifteen grand."

"What?"

"I need fifteen grand to get our people on the goddamned plane with the President. All I really want from you is a letter saying you're good for the money if UPI fails to pay."

After consulting other *Times-Mirror* executives, Insolia phoned Hughes that night and said, "Okay, it's done. And thanks very much for screwing up my golf game."

Insolia was so outraged by the White House attempts to exclude UPI that his paper ran a story. So much for Hughes's hoped-for discretion. Although Helen Thomas and the rest of the UPI crew covered the trip, the sight of the wire service being reduced to begging clients for money was sad and embarrassing.

• • •

The *Tribune* and *Newsday* were not the only ones willing to come to UPI's aid during coverage of the economic summit.

Anne Saker, a young editor in Washington, was assigned to be the "early desker" the week Reagan was in Europe, reporting to work at 3 a.m. Like many bright young Unipressers, Saker was hooked on the excitement, was an action junkie. She had turned down two job offers to stay at UPI, where, after only five years, she was writing regularly about the President of the United States.

Every morning on her way to work that week, Saker stopped at 2 a.m. at the 7-Eleven at Seventeenth and R Streets for the sixteen-ounce cup of coffee that kept her awake on the lobster shift. On Thursday, May 9, the store's night manager inquired why she was always out at this hour. When Saker explained that she worked for UPI, he reached for his wallet.

"I've been reading about you guys. I'm ashamed that people in your business aren't taking care of you. People with big money, like Rupert Murdoch, should come in and take care of you. It's wrong that an organization as important as UPI is bankrupt and about to go out of business."

Saker politely declined and, spirits soaring, hopped into her car and drove to the office.

In Sacramento, Unipressers found that the company's financial plight engendered sympathy even from the competition. When one of UPI's decrepit chairs collapsed one day, AP counterparts donated a couple of their new ones. And when a dictionary fell apart in the hands of bureau chief Becky LaVally, a Sacramento *Bee* reporter dug into his pocket and bought her a new one.

• • •

Jules Teitelbaum, the lawyer for the creditors, worried that the public bickering between Nogales and the owners would frighten off potential buyers and endanger the creditors' unintended investment in UPI. He told both sides that unless it stopped, he would seek UPI's liquidation. To step up the pressure, Teitelbaum summoned both sides on Thursday, May 9, to his office on East Eighteenth Street, near Manhattan's luxurious Grammercy Park residences.

If he believed a little prodding would suffice, he had woefully underestimated the depth of the rift. Although Ruhe and Geissler had paid nothing for UPI and had taken a substantial amount of money out of it, now that it was seeking to attract a buyer they refused to back off gracefully. For his part, Nogales felt their continued presence was the worst kind of obstructionism and could kill UPI.

The meeting at Teitelbaum's was no balm. Indeed, tensions escalated. When Ruhe, Rinaldo Brutoco, and their new lawyer, James Harrington, arrived they exploded in anger to discover Nogales absent. Nogales's attorney, Bill Josephson, said there was no need for his client to attend. Ruhe immediately demanded that Nogales resign. For two hours Ruhe's team taunted Josephson, insisting the owners had, with UPI's bankruptcy petition, regained control of the company and the right to sell it.

Josephson had resolved in advance not to lose his temper, lest an outburst turn the creditors against Nogales. Even so he had to restrain himself in the face of what he could only consider bullying, abusive tactics.

Finally, shortly before noon, it was Ruhe, Harrington, and Brutoco who stormed out, Josephson shouting after them that, if they wanted to talk, he would be in his office.

In late afternoon Harrington phoned, now threatening to go to court unless Nogales renegotiated how long and under what conditions he would remain.

"You can go to court all you want, I don't give a damn," Josephson said, laughing derisively. "There's nothing you can do in any court, other than the bankruptcy court, that can affect the resolution of this matter."

Before the day was out Ruhe and Geissler had filed suit in the Court of Chancery in Delaware, the state where UPI's parent, Media News was incorporated, seeking to enforce their latest "firing" of Nogales as MNC chairman. They charged Nogales had managed UPI in a "maverick and dictatorial manner," had concealed an offer of financing that would have permitted the owners to pay off Foothill, and was withholding from them financial information about UPI. It sought a temporary restraining order ousting Nogales, Morrissey, and McCrohon as Media News directors.

Josephson chose to ignore the suit. Even if the owners succeeded in removing Nogales from MNC, they could not expel him from UPI without Judge Bason's approval.

The next day a Delaware judge issued the order barring Nogales from acting as chairman of Media News. Nogales remained in charge of UPI, but Ruhe and Geissler's tactic had succeeded in triggering a new spate of stories speculating on who might prevail in UPI's executive suite war. Harrington boasted, "Up until today there have been three players— Nogales, Ruhe, and the creditors. Now there are two—Mr. Ruhe and the creditors."

In mid-May the owners got new reason to continue buzzing like angry wasps around the corporate head. Ruhe bitterly disclosed that the IRS had notified him and Geissler they were being held responsible for $1.77 million each in penalties for UPI's failure to pay its withholding taxes. It seemed to the owners that the best way to escape their huge personal liabilities would be to find a buyer for UPI—regardless of their agreement with Nogales not to.

• • •

Bill White, the Justice Department bankruptcy trustee assigned to monitor the UPI case, was appalled as he watched a difficult situation deteriorate. It was clear that Ruhe and Geissler were going to fight every inch of the way to oust Nogales. Himself no pushover, Nogales retaliated publicly each time the owners sought to subvert the Los Angeles agreement.

White knew Ruhe's and Geissler's return might jeopardize UPI's chances, but he also knew it was rare for a company's management to succeed in wresting control from its owners. Ordinarily a pleasant, nondescript man with a receding hairline, he had become so concerned about the disputatious atmosphere that, on May 16, he summoned all parties—including the union—to his Alexandria, Virginia, office for a head-bashing session.

For nine hours Nogales and the ousted owners argued about who controlled what stock and who had authority to sell the company. White left no doubt that, unless there was a truce, he would recommend that the court relieve Nogales of his duties and turn over operation of UPI to an independent trustee, a move that might mean liquidation. White already had somebody in mind.

"We'll have to shut down a venerable American institution if it doesn't reorganize," White warned. He said he did not care "how the pie is cut," but that he wanted the dispute settled.

Over lunch, Nogales's lawyer, Bill Josephson, hit on the idea of writing a court consent decree for Judge Bason to sign that would give Nogales total operating authority. Now he and Levine had to wear down Ruhe's defenses and get him to agree.

After several more hours of stormy debate, Nogales lost all patience in late afternoon and told Carmichael he was ready to resign. Harrington told Ruhe in the hallway, "Listen, Doug, hold on for another forty-five minutes and you'll have this thing won."

But by day's end the starch seemed to drain from Ruhe. He agreed to withdraw the suit and temporarily end his interference in UPI's management and sale efforts. Ruhe's only victory was an agreement under which Porter Bibb's firm of Ladenburg Thalmann & Company would help Nogales's investment bankers screen potential buyers.

Not surprisingly, Ruhe and Geissler dragged their feet in signing the documents. Nogales heard Ruhe had left town to attend a Baha'i religious activity. Steaming over the delays, Nogales publicly threatened to petition the court for a trustee to run UPI if the papers were not signed by May 24. That day in federal court in Washington, under the watchful eye of Judge Bason, final details were hammered out.

Bason, praising both sides' "statesmanship," called the agreement an important step in saving UPI. Personally, he worried that Ruhe and Geissler were going to prove an annoying stumbling block to UPI's recovery.

• • •

Just over two weeks into bankruptcy, it became clear that Judge Bason intended to make UPI's salvation his personal crusade. In mid-May a fight over medical insurance payments was played out in a remarkable courtroom drama.

UPI had fallen $300,000 behind on payments to the Prudential Insurance Company of America, which processed employee medical benefits. Prudential had severed the agreement the day before UPI formally filled its bankruptcy petition.

The decision left the company in a real fix. Employees could withstand the ignominy of having paychecks stamped "Debtor in Possession," and even might survive without pay for a couple of weeks. But howls of anguish greeted the Prudential disclosure. A medical disaster might bring an employee's family financial ruin.

Liz Wharton, a popular veteran of more than forty years with UPI, lay dying of cancer at George Washington University Hospital. When she learned her massive chemotherapy expenses might not be covered, she was distraught that the modest estate she had willed her sister in Texas would be wiped out to pay the medical bills.

Hurriedly, UPI lawyers negotiated a $190,000 settlement with Prudential to cover the month of May and the unprocessed claims filed before bankruptcy. On May 14, Judge Bason approved it.

The IRS, seeking to protect every penny of the more than $1.77 million it was owed, promptly filed papers asking Bason to reverse his decision and rule that all medical claims filed prior to bankruptcy be treated as any other debt. Should Bason side with the IRS, Prudential might back out and Unipressers' medical insurance would be endangered again.

Bason quickly squelched that possibility. In an astonishing courtroom scene, he delivered a civics lesson on the First Amendment to IRS lawyer Martin Teel. Further turmoil over medical insurance, he ruled, likely "would for many employees constitute the last straw, causing them to leave UPI." He argued that the public interest in saving the company was "rare, and perhaps unique."

Lecturing Teel like a schoolmarm, Bason said he could not recall a case with a "convergence of so many strong public interests." He said the need for a free media marketplace for ideas, for competition in the news media, and for protecting the First Amendment provide "a tremendous and powerful reason for denying the motion."

The government quickly dropped its challenge. Bason's "rare, and perhaps unique" tribute took its place alongside "Surrender, Hell!" as a UPI rallying cry.

George Bason had thrown down the gauntlet: This judge will do whatever necessary to ensure UPI's survival, so don't mess with me.

In coming months, while the complexities and pitfalls of Chapter 11 would pose a daunting challenge to UPI executives and lawyers, Bason would underscore that commitment in ruling after ruling.

When a landlord in Harrisburg, Pennsylvania, who was owed back rent shut off water to UPI's photo darkroom, he found himself in hot water with Bason. And when the landlord for UPI's new Miami bureau decided he would rather rent to someone else, he quickly faced the threat of a contempt citation.

Although UPI owed other creditors massive outstanding balances, they, too, were required to continue to provide services.

And the law even allowed a "debtor" to sue to recover assets sold at below market value in pre-Chapter 11 "fraudulent transactions." In yet another slap at the thirty-three-month Ruhe and Geissler stewardship, UPI said in court papers filed the first week of June that Nogales was investigating such "possible fraudulent transactions." It was the first hint he might try to reverse some of Ruhe's deals.

Besides the stigma attached to the word "bankruptcy," UPI had to virtually operate in a fishbowl, its weaknesses spotlighted and its soiled linen on display. Court hearings were attended by rivals AP and Reuters, *The Washington Post*, and the trade press.

Further, UPI executives realized that despite their search for a perfect buyer, the highest bidder might prevail. That could result in the company being taken over by someone unwilling or unsuited to continue its historic role.

Although past debts were frozen, UPI had to keep up with current bills or face the possibility of liquidation. In addition, it had to seek Bason's approval for every costly new project or expenditure.

UPI seemed to be in court more often than not. Legal bills skyrocketed.

• • •

To irreverent Unipressers, bankruptcy was like any other human condition—a little laughter helped you survive the rough spots.

The "little laughter" in the Indianapolis bureau consisted of bittersweet musical parodies. Over drinks after work, Indiana editor Gina Hills and her seven hardy staffers would croon into a tape recorder.

Soon after Chapter 11 came this paean to Judge Bason, to the tune of "Follow the Yellow-Brick Road":

Follow the bankruptcy code,
Follow the bankruptcy code,
Follow, follow, follow, follow,
Follow the bankruptcy code.

We're off to see Judge Bason,
The wonderful judge of Us
He is a judge, a judge, a judge
If ever a judge there was
If ever, if ever a judge there was
Judge Bason is one, is one becuz
Becuz, becuz, becuz, becuz, becuz
Becuz of the wonderful things he does
De, de, de, de, de, de, de, de, de-DEBT,

. . . Foothills and Geisslers and Ruhes,
Oh, My!
Vendors and stringers and clients,
Oh, My!

Oh, we're off to see Judge Bason . . .

Nogales had pinned hopes for keeping UPI's cash flow positive on the subscriber acceptance of the voluntary 9.9 percent rate hike. It became a litmus test of a client's commitment. By May 16 there was a typewritten list more than a page long of those who had agreed to the increase. But there was also a page of rejections as well as a page of cancellations from those contending the rate hike had violated their contracts and that UPI's editorial product was deteriorating.

Ultimately the rate hike generated about $3 million in needed cash, but the fact remained that two-thirds of the subscribers had turned their backs on UPI's appeal. Nogales recognized that the results were an indication of decreasing industry support as UPI tried to compete with the burgeoning supplemental news services. Further, as huge chains gobbled up family-owned newspapers at an astonishing rate and at outrageously overblown prices, their bottom-line-oriented accountants questioned the need for a costly second wire service—even if it meant readers might be less well served. In this depressed sales climate was UPI trying to fashion its comeback.

That wasn't Nogales's only serious problem. Monthly collections, never strong, were lagging terribly. UPI was billing clients for about $6 million a month, but April had yielded less than a million dollars in revenue. Cash-short UPI executives were beginning to panic. Were even the most loyal customers wavering?

Budget officer Steve Spritzer had an explanation. His wife had an eighty-two-year-old dressmaker in New Jersey, and Spritzer had made it a practice to be sure hers was the last bill he paid every month. If she died, he didn't want to end up contributing to her estate. Spritzer said clients probably had the same attitude. Nobody wanted to be the last to pay UPI.

Indeed, some of UPI's most important clients were among the most sluggish. *The New York Times* was three months behind on its nearly million-dollar annual contract. The Times-Mirror Company, the largest domestic client, was withholding more than $1 million because UPI owed its subsidiary for photo supplies.

Nogales plucked sales vice president Art Bushnell out of Atlanta to hammer on the laggards.

"Our intention is to keep the doors open and to provide the second wire service that's needed in the United States," Bushnell bravely told clients. "We don't intend to collect your money and then close the doors. But we need the money to survive, to keep from going into Chapter 7."

The push yielded immediate results. In mid-May, Bushnell and Spritzer discovered their insistent calls had in one day fetched more than $1 million. They rushed to tell Wechsler, and all three began shouting and exchanging high-fives like a high school basketball team pulling off a big upset. Before mid-June, UPI's collection team chalked up several days when they wheedled $2 million out of subscribers.

● ● ●

UPI did not lack for cheerleaders in bankruptcy's bleak days. Across the land editorial writers and columnists—some former Unipressers, others longtime supporters—joined a chorus of "UPI must survive."

The astonishing outpouring heartened Unipressers searching for any light in their dark despair. The editorial page of the Berwick, Pennsylvania, *News* cried that it would be ''a great American tragedy should this country lose United Press International with its different and fresh approach to major news here and abroad.''

Eugene Pulliam, in a rare, front-page ''Publisher's Memo'' in the Indianapolis *Star*, wrote that UPI's news and picture service ''has not faltered,'' adding:

''UPI may eventually be forced out of business, but a lot of intelligent effort is being made to prevent that. Should it come to pass, newspapers, radio and television stations and the reading, listening and watching public would be the poorer. UPI has a proud tradition of competent, hardworking and innovative reporting.''

Similar kind words came from editorial writers in Lincoln, Nebraska, Evansville, Indiana, and Kankakee, Illinois, where former chairman Rob Small still watched closely, hoping UPI would pull through.

Unipressers got perhaps their biggest laugh from the acerbic David Brinkley, who started his career with the old United Press.

On his *This Week with David Brinkley* show on ABC two weeks after the Chapter 11 bankruptcy, the famed television commentator closed the show with:

''This week, with some sadness, we've all watched the UPI, the United Press International, gasping for air and struggling for money. One week its employees were told that if they tried to cash their paychecks, they'd bounce.

''Well, I worked there forty-odd years ago and they behaved then as if they were bankrupt already. If I turned in an expense account for fifty cents for a taxi, they'd send a note asking why I didn't ride the bus. And it got worse. One election night I was the one and only UP correspondent in the entire state of Tennessee and was expected to gather all of the election returns alone.

''No help, no money. Impossible! So I called somebody in another bureau and said, 'How do you do this?'

''He said, 'It's easy. You steal the returns from AP, add 10 percent and send them out.'

''Well, since then things have improved, but somehow the UPI never could make any money and now it's gone bankrupt. I don't know how you could go bankrupt without ever spending anything, but they have managed it. American journalism is full of people who started out at UPI and all of us would hate to see it go. So, the welcome news this week that Reuters, the prosperous British news wire service, is thinking of buying the UPI and saving it.

"Fine. But the United Press with money? We would never recognize it!"

Brinkley's Reuters' rumor was greatly exaggerated, but his recollections of penury brought a grin from everyone who ever earned a United Press byline.

• • •

Reuters, which had never lost interest, found that in bankruptcy UPI was even more a tempting morsel. A buyer could get away with having to pay off only a fraction of UPI's total debts.

Shortly after Nogales assumed control he had been approached by Peter Holland, point man for Reuters' $5 million purchase of UPI's foreign newspictures service a year earlier. Nogales deeply distrusted Reuters, believing the British agency had suckered Ruhe into accepting far less than the photo service was worth.

However, he agreed to meet with Holland and discuss a possible sale. Joining Mike Hughes, Max McCrohon, and Holland for breakfast on the terrace of the Grand Hyatt Hotel in New York, Nogales's suspicions were confirmed when Holland indicated he wanted to discuss buying parts of UPI.

"You've wasted your time coming if all you want to talk about is buying pieces," Nogales said. "UPI is going to survive and be recapitalized. UPI's staff thinks Reuters stole the foreign picture service."

Holland said he was insulted, that the deal with Ruhe had been fair and square.

Nogales said he always had been taught that, regardless of your leverage, you always leave bread on the table for the other guy. Reuters, he declared, hadn't left UPI a crumb.

After wolfing down coffee, eggs over easy, and sausage for nine bucks, Nogales rose to leave. McCrohon and Hughes followed, sticking Holland with the check.

Days after UPI filed for Chapter 11 protection Holland came calling again, saying Reuters now was willing to purchase the whole service. When Holland proposed putting up just $5 million cash, Nogales and McCrohon shrugged at the preposterous offer and terminated the meeting, assuming Reuters once again was scheming to pluck only UPI's few remaining jewels and dismantle the rest.

In the ensuing weeks Nogales refused to cooperate with the Reuters executives, a decision that seemed to force an end to the British agency's on-again, off-again, five-year mating dance. On June 6, Reuters announced it was "unable to pursue" a bid because UPI was withholding key financial information.

• • •

Nogales's obdurate opposition to Reuters may have been fueled by a titillating phone call late in May from Alejandro Orfila, former secretary general of the Organization of American States and erstwhile darling of Washington's party-circuit hostesses.

Orfila said he knew a very, very rich man interested in buying UPI. Curiosity piqued, Nogales sat upright. He knew UPI would be a tough sell; most of the American news industry already had refused on several occasions to buy even a piece of the twenty-five-year money loser. Nogales would look long and hard at anybody who claimed to have money.

Soon after, Orfila, clad nattily in a sport coat and a shirt open at the neck, dropped by to talk further. Although both were fluent in English, they quickly switched to Spanish. Still titillated about the mysterious Mr. Moneybags, Nogales whipped out paper and drew diagrams for Orfila about his plans to save UPI.

While outwardly cordial, Nogales was troubled by controversy swirling about the dapper Orfila. A few weeks earlier Orfila had been forced to leave his job as vice chairman of Gray and Company, a high-powered public relations and lobbying firm with close ties to President Reagan. An internal Gray and Company inquiry had raised questions about Orfila's possible role in funneling a cash payment from one of the company's Spanish clients to a Spanish legislator. The allegations had led to federal investigations of possible overseas payoffs, although no charges ever were brought.

The next day Orfila phoned and revealed the name of his rich friend: Mexican publisher Mario Vazquez-Raña. Nogales agreed to a meeting.

He immediately began checking into Vazquez, phoning, among others, his longtime friend Nacho Lozano, publisher of *La Opinion* in Los Angeles. A couple of days later Lozano reported back that Vazquez seemed to be for real. One of his country's wealthiest men, he owned its largest newspaper group, El Sol, and was president of Mexico's Olympic Committee.

But Lozano also said those he had asked had given Vazquez mixed reviews. Vazquez was considered a legitimate businessman, but nagging rumors abounded that former Mexican President Luis Echeverria had helped him buy the El Sol chain from bankruptcy at a bargain-basement price, and Echeverria might even have a hidden stake in it. Nogales thanked Lozano, then kept an appointment to meet with Orfila and Vazquez in the presidential suite at Washington's elegant Madison Hotel.

Vazquez, a short, stocky, mustachioed man, meticulous in a double-breasted suit, graciously shook hands and said, "Hello." It was his last word in English. In rapid-fire Spanish he expressed a strong interest in UPI. The two struck up a quick rapport, chatting amiably for about ninety minutes. Nogales sized up Vazquez as a suitor who deserved to be taken seriously.

Before noon the next day Nogales and Vazquez met again, this time at Orfila's house near Embassy Row. Nogales brought along budget officer Steve Spritzer to show Vazquez some financial information. Vazquez was accompanied by his darkly attractive young translator and traveling companion, Linda Garcia, and a Brownsville, Texas, lawyer.

Vazquez revealed he had considered buying UPI three years earlier from Scripps, and even had discussed a possible purchase with Geissler when the UPI owner visited Mexico City shortly after taking over. Each time he had been rebuffed.

Then Vazquez abruptly announced that he wanted to send his lawyer to talk directly with Judge Bason about a purchase. Nogales was struck by Vazquez's determination and intensity, a little amused by his headstrong manner. But he also was apprehensive. Would a foreigner ever be accepted by U.S. publishers and editors, especially one from Mexico, where press standards are virtually nonexistent?

What about his ties to Orfila, the international playboy? What about the rumors Vazquez had become a successful publisher only because of his friendship with Echeverria?

Nonetheless, it was clear that Vazquez had the resources to both pay off UPI's creditors and to subsidize losses until he could drag the news agency back onto its feet. A man so eager and so rich could not be airily dismissed. Nogales decided to encourage him.

He urged Vazquez to hire lawyers expert in the specialized field of bankruptcy. Then, privately, he told Vazquez that Orfila's reputation could jeopardize any bid for UPI. He urged that Vazquez ditch Orfila and find American partners.

On a Saturday in early June, Nogales met yet again at the Madison with Vazquez and his newly hired Washington lawyer, David Rubenstein. Nogales brought Rick Levine, UPI's bankruptcy lawyer. Vazquez, a stiffly formal man, seemed unperturbed that Levine wore jeans and sneakers.

Levine patiently outlined for Vazquez the complex bankruptcy process. In America, he said, you don't just phone a bankruptcy judge and ask for a meeting.

Before the session broke up, Rubenstein joined Nogales in strongly urging Vazquez to cut loose Orfila. In a city where heroes can quickly turn into bums, they said, Orfila had become a laughingstock. Vazquez promptly sent Orfila to the sidelines.

Mario Vazquez-Raña had already had made up his mind that no obstacle would prevent him from getting United Press International.

18
The Enemies Within

As Luis Nogales began the nerve-racking task of finding the best possible buyer before the company ran out of cash, the UPI ship resembled a corporate *Mutiny on the Bounty*. As captain, Nogales found himself under siege, both from within and without. The little wars were grinding him down.

First, Ruhe and Geissler were constantly trying to undermine him, meeting clandestinely with potential buyers.

Then there was the new president, Ray Wechsler, whose financial talents made him a necessary evil but who talked as if he were bent on immediately busting the union. The guild's volatile secretary-treasurer, Dan Carmichael, could be equally troublesome. Keeping Wechsler and the guild from destroying one another, Nogales thought, would have tested even the most patient.

Nogales also suspected Wechsler was plotting with Jerry Hillman to maneuver themselves into position to try to take over UPI. In his office next to Nogales's, Wechsler was suggesting to reporters that he, not the chairman, was running things. "I'm going to get this company hot for a while," he said, boasting of his intimate relationships with world-class companies that could save UPI.

Another potential mutineer was Max McCrohon, reticent about severing ties to Ruhe and, especially, to Geissler. Nogales was irked by what he felt was McCrohon's wishy-washy allegiance, but knew he would need his editorial stature during the crucial search for a buyer.

In many ways Nogales faced worse problems than Captain Bligh did on the *Bounty*, for the various forces at UPI were fighting not only the captain but also each other. Nogales knew he had to unite or neutralize the disparate factions to ensure the sale process did not fall prey to the irrationality of the ousted owners or the unpredictability of the creditors. He never could have imagined, however, that the biggest roadblock would come from the company's most important constituency—its staff.

Wechsler's lobbying for more employee sacrifices had engendered deep enmity from union leaders, particularly Carmichael, to whom confrontation was mother's milk. The worse the company's condition, the easier it was to whip up employee hostility. Carmichael had risen rapidly in the Wire Service Guild, terrorizing and hamstringing supervisors with temper tantrums and endless nitpicking contract grievances. Nogales thought the union leader had spitefully and selfishly erected obstacles to UPI's recovery.

Now, with the company in bankruptcy, Carmichael seemed to regard himself a messianic guardian of employee rights. His world tolerated no shades of gray—the union wore white hats, management black. When Nogales had informed the union in March that the company would need more contract concessions, Carmichael's distrust of the UPI chairman had degenerated to hatred.

Prodded by Wechsler, Nogales asked his aides to draft a sweeping list of possible union concessions. In early June Nogales reduced the list from thirty to half a dozen, but they were harsh, including calling for freezing salaries at 90 percent of 1984 levels for six months, waiving more than a million dollars in company obligations to the pension fund, and slashing severance pay to a maximum of thirteen weeks. Nogales said the concessions would bring UPI a $3 million profit by year's end. Wechsler called them "essential" to attract a quality buyer.

Technically, to stay afloat the company needed only to operate on a break-even basis, but Wechsler argued that without a comfortable positive cash flow no substantial buyers would be interested. Carmichael and Morrissey were just as adamant that employees had given enough to the current management. The union leaders knew whoever bought UPI probably would ask them for more concessions, and they did not want to go through the process twice. Nogales faced a conundrum: Wechsler was pulling on one arm, Carmichael on the other, and theirs were two enormous egos. No matter what he decided, Nogales was in for big trouble. Nevertheless, although he had promised during the last round of cuts not to ask the union for more sacrifices, he had to listen to Wechsler, who knew more about the company's finances than anyone.

On Monday, June 10, Bobby Ray Miller and labor lawyer Alan Berger went to the guild office in New York and delivered the demands. Carmichael exploded like a Roman candle and immediately threatened a strike.

"Your fucking company is going to go right down the tubes!" Carmichael shouted. "We're going to be on the street!"

Everyone knew a walkout at this juncture would doom UPI.

Strike or no, Nogales's flickering hopes for internal harmony had been dashed.

• • •

Carmichael, thirty-one, short and wiry with close-cropped curly hair, had thrived on controversy since his youth when he rebelled against his conservative parents, both Marines.

Even while attending a conservative religious high school in Hawaii, Carmichael had been a firebrand. He gloried in his expulsion over an investigative story in the school newspaper, *Na Pueo*, in which he alleged the head of the cafeteria had cut a deal with a friend to recarpet the dining room at inflated prices. Democratic Congresswoman Patsy Mink of Hawaii, for whom Carmichael had campaigned door to door, intervened to help get him reinstated. Later, when four students were shot and killed during antiwar protests at Kent State, Carmichael organized a rally that briefly shut down his high school.

After serving as a UPI stringer, Carmichael landed a full-time job in the Honolulu bureau at the age of seventeen while attending the University of Hawaii. Not long after, he became active in the union.

After he was elected secretary-treasurer in 1980, he and Morrissey forged a personal and political alliance. If Morrissey was the union's long-range strategist, the incendiary Carmichael saw himself the "son-of-a-bitch hit man." He jabbed the needle until he drew blood.

Carmichael seemed incapable of passing up an opportunity to mouth off—even to respected bankruptcy lawyer Rick Levine. Levine's firm had received a $100,000 advance through the bankruptcy court, in part because lawyers frequently wind up with nothing if a Chapter 11 firm collapses.

When Levine objected to the union taking a formal role in the sale process, Carmichael let fly in traditional fashion. "Who the hell are you to talk? You know what we call you? We call you Mr. Hundred Thou." Levine, a charming fellow, was plainly affronted. Morrissey squirmed and union lawyer Sid Reitman paled.

To parry the demand for a new round of concessions, the union gadfly again donned his "hit man" hat and took dead aim at Nogales. On June 11, a day after the company proposals, union members received a scathing bulletin from Carmichael:

"UPI's 'management team' is proposing drastic new wage and benefit cuts for employees—while seeking huge raises for several top executives."

It noted the company was planning hefty boosts to bring vice presidents Bob Brown and Art Bushnell and treasurer Jack Kenney to $96,000, $52,500, and $78,000, respectively.

"The union does not know the salary of Luis Nogales and other top company officials who are seeking the contract cuts because they repeatedly have failed to provide employment contracts as requested by the union," the guild said, threatening to ask the court to order the information released.

Although the letter bomb was unsigned, Carmichael's acerbic pen was unmistakable. It would pulverize Nogales's credibility with the workers and undermine his unity efforts.

• • •

Nogales soon found he had a serious problem. Carmichael had deftly exposed his vulnerability—his determination to protect the men who had supported him during the Los Angeles coup and whose help he believed he needed to save the company. Employees were livid at Nogales's audacity in seeking to freeze union salaries while bestowing huge raises on managers such as Wechsler, Brown, and Kenney. Carmichael, in focusing attention on Nogales's salary, had succeeded in placing the UPI chairman on the defensive.

The next day the union got help from an unexpected source—Brown himself. The vice president for communications, whose peremptory dismissals of several veteran Unipressers had earned him a reputation as callous and sadistic, composed a rambling, bizarre "news story" satirically trying to justify his $24,000 raise. Bypassing UPI's editors, Brown ordered a subordinate to transmit it on the internal wires. Unipressers failed to see humor in his burlesque and were outraged at his unauthorized use of the wire. The outcry for his dismissal, even from managers, was so fierce that Nogales rescinded Brown's entire pay hike and said any recurrence would cost his job.

While UPI's executives hardly were paid outrageously compared to other top companies, Carmichael's prickly barbs had succeeded in making their salaries a union rallying cry. Try as he might to assure staffers he was on their side, Nogales found it difficult to counter the almost daily salvos.

Wechsler soon managed to immerse himself in the controversy by issuing his own message assuring the staff that the proposed concessions did not mean wage cuts. To staffers who stood to lose as much as $1,000 in scheduled pay restorations, that was just deceitful double-talk. Guild leaders Jon Frandsen and Sean McCormally led a group of angry Unipressers to Wechsler's office. There they stared at him through the window until he agreed to a meeting with several dozen staffers in the executive conference room. When Wechsler stubbornly clung to his contention that the proposed wage freeze did not amount to a pay cut, Clay Richards, UPI's blunt-talking chief political writer, summed up the Unipressers' feelings.

"Look, Ray," Richards said, beefy face reddening, "most of us have worked in Washington for a long time. You pay us to cover this town, and we know bullshit when we see it!"

Galvanized by word of Wechsler's remarks, the next day union members engaged in "informational picketing" outside UPI offices nationwide.

Seeing no end to Carmichael's hectoring about his salary, Nogales finally decided it was better to disclose that he, Wechsler, and McCrohon each was earning $190,000, minus the 10 percent company-wide cuts. Nogales stressed that Ruhe had raised his salary to equal McCrohon's when promoting him to the presidency, but that he had deferred taking the raise until March because of UPI's financial troubles.

Whatever his past sacrifice and however rational his arguments, the news of the six-figure salaries drew yelps of anguish from employees fighting to feed their families on a yearly wage of about $26,000. Carmichael seized on the momentum generated by the volatile wage disparity issue to launch new attacks on Nogales's credibility and motives.

Despite Carmichael's rancor, Nogales, the ex-cantaloupe packer, had deep empathy for UPI's employees. Instructing Miller and Berger how to approach the union negotiations, he said, "Don't tear down the morale of these people. I want this handled adroitly. Don't go in there and cut them up with a meat ax."

Wechsler and budget officer Steve Spritzer were unmoved. "That's bullshit!" they snapped, insisting professional pride always would motivate Unipressers to perform at their best no matter what their pay. Fellow executives believed Wechsler and Spritzer never would waver in their conviction that the company's salvation lay in busting the union. Years later Wechsler conceded that, in frustration, he may have spoken of breaking the union. But he denied that he ever really meant it.

With Nogales's management team now lobbying more vociferously than ever for concessions, the dispute continued to escalate for the next two weeks. When union leaders refused to budge, company lawyer Charles Dougherty abruptly announced UPI had no choice but to ask Judge Bason to void the work contract and impose the concessions. Dougherty, no candidate for a blue ribbon for tact, made the announcement while the American Newspaper Guild was holding its annual convention in Pittsburgh. Angry delegates immediately voted to give the union $30,000 to fight UPI.

Most Unipressers had for years been easygoing in their enforcement of the contract. Now, enraged by the threat that their hard-won protections and benefits would be unilaterally abridged, they began working by the book—putting in for every hour of overtime and taking vacations they had long deferred.

Only three months after Luis Nogales had returned from California a conquering hero, bad advice from his underlings and his own tactical blunders were rapidly making him a pariah.

• • •

In bankruptcy UPI offered a rare opportunity for bargain hunters, and by early summer several were window-shopping. Even as Nogales battled the union, he, Wechsler, and Kenney were escorting suitors around the eighth-floor newsroom where gossipy Unipressers watched curiously while batting out stories on their computer terminals.

Although Nogales had received a number of feelers, generally they were from rag-tag entrepreneurs with limited cash who would cheerfully bust the union and might want to carve up UPI and sell or shut down the unprofitable pieces. Among those interested were Sam Phillips, a tough-talking racehorse owner from Acton, Massachusetts, who already owned two financially ailing companies and offered only $6.5 million cash; CitiBank Venture Corporation, only mildly interested but possessed of the resources and prestige UPI badly needed; and New Hampshire race-track owner Max Hugel, who had resigned as CIA covert operations chief amid allegations from two former business associates that he had been involved in insider stock trading.

One suitor, however, seemed to have both the money to buy UPI and the resolve to revitalize it. Heeding Nogales's advice, Mario Vazquez-Raña and his advisers were hunting for American partners to lend their bid a patina of credibility. Vazquez had become acquainted with Beurt SerVaas, president of the Indianapolis City-County Council, who had purchased the moribund *Saturday Evening Post* in 1971 and transformed the venerable magazine to a health-and-good-living format. Vazquez made SerVaas a minority partner and the frontman in the bid to buy UPI; they agreed to wait for precisely the right moment before announcing Vazquez's involvement.

Although Vazquez was adamant about controlling UPI himself, his advisers also planned to grab headlines by forming an advisory committee of distinguished Americans such as Walter Cronkite, former Treasury Secretary William Simon, and U.S. Olympic head Peter Ueberroth, who himself had approached Nogales in May about buying UPI.

Vazquez, determined to move quickly, submitted his bid on July 1. Without naming names, Nogales excitedly announced that lawyers for a "very credible" investor group had submitted a formal offer in the name of New UPI Acquisition Group, Inc. It provided between $13.9 and $17.9 million to settle debts, including paying unsecured creditors 17.5 cents on the dollar.

Vazquez's Washington lawyer, David Rubenstein, immediately flew to New York to submit the offer to a creditors' meeting, specifying the bid would expire July 15. Anticipating an enthusiastic reception, Rubenstein was jolted when Jules Teitelbaum, not about to be pressured into a hasty decision smiled, coolly said "thanks," and bade him farewell.

Despite Teitelbaum's caution, Nogales was delighted. After years of unsuccessful efforts to sell the company, UPI finally could brag it had a bona fide money bid from a potential buyer interested in preserving it as a general news service. Without identifying Vazquez, Nogales warily began sounding out major publishers as to how they would react if UPI's new owner were a foreigner. No matter how great Vazquez's fortune, he would need the goodwill of the news industry to succeed.

Even as Rubenstein told reporters he doubted there would be a better offer than the one from the mysterious investor group he represented, one appeared. Two days after the Vazquez offer, the *Houston Chronicle* reported that businessman Joe Russo was talking about buying UPI for $20 million and moving its world headquarters to economically sagging Houston, where he had built a small real estate operation into an empire of office buildings. "Our interest is to develop innovative ways to fill office space," Russo said. "We're not just deep-pocket, crazy Texans."

A number of Unipressers laughed at the thought of someone with no media experience buying UPI and moving it to Texas.

Yet, with the specter that there might be more than one bidder, SerVaas's July 15 deadline passed without formal response. When Nogales did not actively pursue Russo, the Houston developer met July 16 with Ruhe, who brashly was trying to sell the owners' stock and tax losses for a "nominal cash payment"—$5 million. Nogales and Wechsler again were angry at Ruhe's quixotic efforts to sell a company he no longer controlled, and felt he hardly deserved a $5 million reward for driving UPI to the brink of bankruptcy.

• • •

Meantime, the balladeers in UPI's Indianapolis bureau continued their assault on the world of pop music. Revisiting *The Wizard of Oz*, they wrote a takeoff on "Over the Rainbow":

> Somewhere, over in debtland
> People frown.
> Creditors hold all the power
> To shut this company down.
>
> We're way in debt
> We're out of luck
> And all the creditors say is
> "Fuck Youuuuuuuuu . . ."

> We're still for sale
> Don't let us fail
> The price is right
> The staff is bright,
> Why, then oh why, not buy?

Despite his threat to ask Bason to set aside the union contract, Nogales had delayed filing the papers. In late July, the acrimonious talks foundering hopelessly, UPI finally submitted the petition. It triggered a new uproar. Bill Morrissey told *The New York Times* that if Bason granted the motion the union would urge a strike and kill UPI. UPI officials drew up secret contingency plans, but in their hearts knew their bankruptcy-weakened wire service never could survive a strike.

As an August 2 court date approached, both sides stiffened their resolve. The guild mailed strike ballots to members; Wechsler continued to urge Nogales to break the union.

Nogales still was bitter about the protests over his salary and the ceaseless personal attacks by Carmichael, who he felt was more interested in union posturing than in UPI's survival. Nogales was beginning to feel overwhelmed. He had risked his reputation to oust the owners, faced liability for UPI's unpaid taxes, and rolled up substantial personal legal expenses. On top of it all, his twenty-year-marriage was a shambles. He also had personal difficulties with the IRS, which demanded he pay $167,232 in back taxes and penalties for deducting losses from aggressive tax-shelter investments in a Utah drilling venture and a medical device called an "agglutinoscope" to monitor blood clumping in bacteria. UPI wrote a story about his IRS problem, further embarrassing its chairman.

Nogales thrived on adversarial situations—he had, for all practical purposes, successfully fired UPI's owners. Now Carmichael was beating him at his own game, getting under his skin repeatedly. In one union bulletin he had disparaged Nogales as coming from "a public relations background"—to journalists, the ultimate sin.

During negotiating sessions Carmichael would dig at Nogales. "Gee, with your salary you ought to buy us all coffee." Or, "That's a very expensive-looking suit. What did it cost?"

Nogales despised Carmichael for his taunting ways, his obdurate refusal to cooperate. And he feared the union's loose cannon would frighten away buyers. Indeed, an executive of one major company had remarked privately, "The financial community is scared to death of Carmichael. Mention his name and the litmus turns bright red."

Carmichael's carping about management salaries had stirred such controversy that Nogales felt obligated to take a pay cut as a show of good faith and felt Wechsler and McCrohon also should. Nogales was not surprised when Wechsler balked.

"I'm accustomed to a certain life-style," Wechsler protested.

Indeed he was, with UPI picking up the tab. In Nashville, he stayed in one of the city's upper-crust hotels, the Maxwell House, and drove a rented Lincoln. In Washington, Wechsler stayed at the posh Vista Hotel, patronizing its pricey restaurants. His weekly expense reimbursement checks frequently exceeded $600, more than top-scale Unipressers were earning. Once Wechsler entertained a few guests at a $260 dinner at Dominique's, famous for its exotic wild game menu. Wechsler also charged UPI for his laundry while he was traveling, soon earning the deprecating nicknames "Silky" and "S.U." from the women in UPI's accounting staff who giggled over the expense account items for cleaning of his silk underwear.

Wechsler would fast learn, however, that his high-profile job at UPI carried unusually heavy responsibilities. When the union demanded that austerity begin with management, he had little choice but to yield and take a pay cut. On July 15, he, Nogales, and McCrohon announced they would accept temporary 25 percent cuts to $142,500. To Carmichael and the union, it was a pious gesture. Trust was breaking down, also undermined because employees had seen none of the 6.5 percent stock in Media News Corporation that Ruhe and Geissler had promised almost a year earlier.

On August 2, when the two sides appeared before Judge Bason, the jurist knew UPI's future might be at stake. He took the participants to a hearing room down the hall where two federal mediators waited with Ruhe and his lawyer.

Bason said, "This is so vitally important to the nation. We cannot afford to lose one of our two wire services. These negotiations are going to be delicate and they're going to be difficult, and I want the best federal mediators to be available to help you gentlemen."

Then he left.

After five hours both sides returned to report a cease-fire: UPI would drop its bid to terminate the labor contract, the union would delay its strike vote pending further negotiations.

Delighted, Bason lauded them for avoiding "a potentially disastrous conflict" and solemnly purloined from Winston Churchill: "I hope that many of us will be able to look back and say, 'This was our finest hour.' "

Grandiloquently, he called the effort to save UPI perhaps "the most important legal proceeding that any of us are involved in in our lifetime."

• • •

As Nogales and Wechsler searched for buyers, they were confronted by expressions of concern about the assets Ruhe and Geissler had sold, particularly the losses of the electronic data base to Comtex and of control of the newspaper stock-quotation service to Fintext. Both were vital if UPI wished to create lucrative spin-off products and capitalize on the information explosion.

Nogales realized he could lose suitors unless he moved quickly under bankruptcy law to try to recover assets he believed were sold "fraudulently"—as defined by the bankruptcy code at prices below market value. Lawyers for UPI asked Bason to open the books of former consultant Jim West and his company, Fintext, half owned by UPI. After getting an inside glimpse of Fintext, Nogales was aghast. Not only had West failed to deliver, but Ruhe and Geissler had permitted him to keep most of the $1.3 million from UPI's annual newspaper contracts for stock quotes. The owners' decision left financial editor Dottie Brooks so cash-short she had to beg West for thousands of dollars for couriers, office supplies, and other services.

In late June, counsel Bill Bowe demanded that West reimburse $1.8 million UPI claimed he owed. In a stunning deposition on July 18, West revealed he had used some of the revenues to loan himself $60,000 and pay $33,000 to his own consulting firm. He also had hired his wife and son. West further acknowledged that Ruhe had pressed him to hire two Baha'i friends Nogales had fired in March, and that, at Ruhe's request, he had purchased a $14,000 van for one of them. After UPI entered bankruptcy, West disclosed, Ruhe had asked for a $30,000 loan from Fintext "because he didn't have any more money." West testified the loan idea was dropped when news stories raised questions about Ruhe's use of UPI funds.

Reading West's deposition, Nogales wondered if revelations about

Ruhe's financial machinations would ever end. Since UPI held two of the three seats on Fintext's board of directors, Nogales decided to take action without waiting for the court. Less than two weeks later he seized control of Fintext by kicking Ruhe and Geissler off the board, replacing them with himself and Bowe.

Fintext was out of cash and UPI could not collect revenues lost on West's failed project. But facing UPI's suit, West agreed in mid-August to surrender the stock-quote service in return for another $70,000 of UPI's money to cover his expenses.

Even more precious were the electronic data base sold to Comtex and the foreign newspictures service Ruhe had peddled to Reuters. Nogales had little chance of undoing the pictures deal: Reuters cannily had structured it so that if UPI wanted to sue, it would have to do it in a British court. Comtex, which he regarded a disaster, would be a more logical target. Comtex had realized a fat $1.5 million in revenues the first year, $300,000 more than it had put up to buy the service. When UPI lawyers asked Judge Bason to force Comtex executives to open their books and records, Comtex hired a prominent Washington law firm and tangled the mess in court for months.

• • •

The union's summer-long war with Nogales and Wechsler dragged on. During marathon talks federal mediator Ed McMahon tried every tactic, even putting Nogales and Carmichael in separate rooms and shuttling between them to lower the invective level. To no avail.

Nogales always had felt an edge in his knock-down battles with Ruhe and Geissler, staying in top physical condition by jogging and working out. These negotiations, however, were taking a toll. Early one morning, driving wearily back to his Bethesda apartment after another marathon day, Nogales's head nodded at the wheel of his black 1979 Cadillac. A trooper noticed the car swerving, flagged him down and asked what he had been drinking. Nogales said he was stone sober and demanded a breathalizer test.

"Why, you don't have a trace of alcohol in you!" the cop said in surprise.

"I told you, I'm just exhausted."

When Nogales related a few of the pressures and tensions of trying to keep UPI afloat, the officer sympathized and sent him home to bed.

Little did Nogales know that one reason the union was being so obdurate about further concessions—instead demanding substantial management cuts—was that Morrissey and Carmichael were stalling. They had begun to inject themselves into the sale process and were meeting with prospective buyers. They had concluded that if union give-backs were necessary to attract a buyer, they, not management, should negotiate them.

After a creditors' meeting in July, Carmichael was approached by Robert Cunningham of Pawley's Island, South Carolina, a former CIA operative who wanted to use union funds to purchase UPI and subsidize the wire service by launching a profitable new national magazine. The union leaders also met with an odd, unkempt Philadelphian named Peter Wirs, who apparently had little money but managed to involve a phalanx of investment advisers from Coldwell Banker and introduced the union over an elegant lunch to nationally syndicated muckraking columnist Jack Anderson. Wirs even got an article in the *Philadelphia Inquirer* about his newly formed media company, the Poor Richard Corporation, boasting he would buy UPI for more than $35 million, double its staff, and move its headquarters to Philadelphia. Nogales's management team dismissed Wirs as weird, and the union was put off when it learned Wirs' scheme relied on tapping its pension fund. "Weird Peter" also wanted a UPI dress code: women must wear bras and couldn't wear slacks.

It appeared the union would not be cutting a deal any time soon.

• • •

As UPI's cash flow worsened, clients continued to flee to the AP. Watching the internecine battles persist, the creditors' committee nervously began pressing for a sale deadline while there was still something to sell. Nogales agreed with the idea.

In mid-August, UPI's two investment advisers, Bear Stearns and Ladenburg Thalmann, disseminated a slick sale memorandum to about 150 interested parties. Nogales set a September 13 deadline for preliminary purchase offers, but when superstitious Max McCrohon realized the thirteenth fell on a Friday, he convinced Nogales to move the date to the following Monday.

Nogales and Wechsler, knowing there was no certainty a sale could be closed quickly, continued to press for union concessions. On September 4, in a negotiations session mediated by McMahon, Nogales told the union that without concessions the company would "go into the red in October."

"It's a desperate situation," he said, imploring Morrissey and Carmichael to reconsider. "We lose leverage if we're in the red. Who wants to buy us if we're losing money again? I know it isn't fair to ask employees for more concessions. The whole situation isn't fair. It isn't fair to employees. It isn't fair to creditors. It isn't fair to managers, who have had to make very necessary but unpopular decisions.

"It's amazing that the company has stuck together as it has. I get my ass in a wringer every week. But there is no other way. Just think of where we were last year. Carmichael told people to get out their resumés. First, you said we wouldn't make it to November. Then to December. Then you said we'd never make it to the first of the year. But we're still here. One way or another, I'll do whatever it takes to keep the company solvent."

But the union again rejected the concessions demand and offered to work together only if it had veto power over management decisions—a demand Nogales said would frighten away buyers. Carmichael was enjoying watching Nogales squirm.

"These negotiations are different," Carmichael said. "Usually we're asking the company for something, and the company can say no. This time you're asking *us* for something, and we can say no. And I enjoy it. It's fun to say no."

Nogales had had enough of Dan Carmichael even before the meeting. He had expected no more than this response and, without hesitation, announced he had "no choice" but to again seek to throw out the contract. Morrissey, who had become a father figure to Carmichael, quickly closed ranks with his union cohort.

"I want to remind you," Morrissey said, "that if you file to reject our contract, our commitment to withhold the strike vote is withdrawn. It will be a shot across the bow of the union, war to the death."

Acting as if the gauntlet had been thrown down, the union issued another of Carmichael's patented bulletins for the rank and file. Despite Nogales's assurances that he was negotiating at arm's length with all prospective buyers no matter what his own fate might be, the bulletin declared Nogales's goal in any sale was to ensure that he retain control of the company:

"Nogales wants to pluck more cash from employee pockets to finance his continuing grab for power and control."

Two days later Bobby Ray Miller sent a confidential nine-page memo to McCrohon describing the stalemate and a private conversation he had had with Morrissey. In it, he said, Morrissey had blamed Carmichael's intransigence for the stalemate.

"What Carmichael wants to do is keep using delaying tactics and then to pork the company once again," Miller quoted Morrissey. "He wants to get in a few more licks before the company dies."

• • •

There could be no selling the union short, however. In August, Morrissey read a *New York Times* story describing how two of TWA's major unions had cut a deal with corporate raider Carl Icahn that helped him wrest control of the nation's fourth-largest airline. Brian Freeman, a high-powered Washington investment banker who represented labor in restructuring troubled companies, had served as the middleman between the TWA unions and Icahn. Carmichael quickly phoned Freeman and expressed the guild's interest in retaining his services.

On September 11 the union called a news conference at the offices of the Newspaper Guild in Washington. As reporters from *The Washington Post*, AP, UPI, and Reuters trooped into the room, Morrissey and Carmichael could barely contain their glee. The union had its own hired gun.

"No longer will this union engage in a passive, reactive role, forced to choose the least damaging series of options in a scenario developed by the corporation's executives and outsiders," Morrissey declared as Carmichael watched smugly. "Beginning today, the Wire Service Guild will be a major player in the effort to sell UPI."

Hiring Freeman, fabled in the supercharged world of corporate politics, just days before preliminary offers were due was a master stroke. Nogales and his team were apoplectic. Nogales had been competing with Ruhe and Geissler, with the creditors' committee, and, he suspected, with Wechsler in searching for the best possible buyer for UPI. Now he would have to contend with the pesky union and its formidable mouthpiece. Yet he also was somehow relieved. In Freeman, he hoped, he finally would be dealing with a pro who might muzzle Carmichael and even persuade the union that contract concessions were in everyone's best interests.

In his ninth-floor office Nogales mulled over possible tactics for neutralizing the suddenly potent union during the sale process. Labor lawyer Alan Berger, as always, had an answer.

"Brian Freeman puts his pants on the same way we do. He's got only one thing to hold over our heads—a strike. That would bust UPI. Let's pull his teeth. Luis, call everybody together on the ninth floor and demand their resignations. Say you won't necessarily accept them, but you want them in hand."

Nogales's aides scurried about the executive suite soliciting, as a bargaining chip, resignations from top managers.

When the afternoon meeting with the union convened, Nogales feigned gloom.

"I've just had a terrible thing happen," he said. "I just had my entire staff resign. I have no company."

Then his voice turned hard. He said the managers had resigned because they would not subject their every decision to union veto.

"I want you to know that we in management are tired of this bullshit," Nogales said angrily. "We get to run the company under the most adverse situation of all, and we've got to take continuous crap from you. Well, we're tired of it, so you run the goddamn company. You want to sell it, then you run it! But if we're going to run it, we're going to sell it. You can participate, but we are going to sell it."

Although Freeman and the union leaders doubted Nogales was serious, they dared not call his bluff. Without hesitating, Freeman told Nogales he could live with those terms, as long as the union got a full voice in the sale process. Nogales realized instantly that if the guild managed to control a sale, as Freeman had done at TWA, it most assuredly would mean Carmichael's fervent wish would come true: that he would be gone.

Freeman also apparently recognized the chairman's predicament and his own leverage. He told the union officers that, after the meeting, he pulled Nogales aside and said:

"If you play ball with me, we'll let you out of this entire situation looking good. The second you fuck with us, we'll cut your balls off."

• • •

By mid-September, with UPI's deadline for preliminary purchase offers at hand, Nogales again was feeling alone and embattled. The chairman needed a strong team in place for his critical homestretch effort to sell

UPI, but McCrohon's support was shaky and Wechsler now was almost brazenly disloyal. Wechsler did not even bother to disguise his contempt for Nogales, telling senior colleagues UPI would be better off without him. The chairman, Wechsler declared, was a dreadful manager who was screwing up the sale process. Often with Steve Spritzer at his side, Wechsler went so far as to undercut his boss in discussions with creditors and potential buyers. He even approached executive editor Mike Hughes, apparently in a thinly veiled attempt to rally support on the eighth floor.

"I'm going to do something in a couple of weeks," Wechsler told Hughes, "and I just want you to know I've always had the greatest admiration for you."

He continued to talk in vague terms until Hughes, an impatient man under the best circumstances, lost his temper.

"Wechsler, are you trying to tell me something? Are you leaving, or are you trying to stage a coup and you want my support?"

"Oh, no, no," Wechsler protested, "I'm not looking for your sup—"

"Then why have you been wasting my time? If you're trying to stage a coup against Nogales, fuck off!"

When Hughes told Nogales, his boss was not surprised. After all, Nogales confided, Wechsler had even tried to steal away his sexy blond secretary, Eva Dillon. Having watched Wechsler operate in recent weeks, Nogales knew he wanted him out.

Entering his campaign to save the company, Nogales had been convinced he needed a team effort to succeed. Now, in the stretch drive, his alliances were crumbling. Yet he was not about to quit.

"If I have to," he thought, "I'll do it alone."

19
· · ·
Who Will Buy?

Early in the morning on September 19, 1985, Pieter Van Bennekom, UPI's vice president for Latin America, was flung from his bed like a rag doll. An earthquake was rocking downtown Mexico City, leveling hotels and skyscrapers and burying dozens of people under mountains of twisted rubble. Van Bennekom, instantly awake, scrambled up from his bedroom floor, threw on clothes, jumped into his car, and began weaving his way through the dreadful carnage. Quickly jotting notes as he drove, Van Bennekom made his way to the elegant Paseo de Reforma, where the UPI office was housed on the thirteenth floor atop an aging building that somehow had survived many shocks in the earthquake-prone capital. Van Bennekom had to make sure the building was still standing. It was—barely. Then he aimed the car north to hunt for a working phone.

Mexico City was totally cut off. The only news about the devastation that had befallen the world's biggest city was an occasional report relayed by ham radio operators. For hours Van Bennekom drove, only to find the phone lines dead in the stores and cantinas of every tiny village where he stopped. Finally, 140 miles north of Mexico City in the town of Queretaro, he managed to get through to the foreign desk in Washington and quickly dictated the first real details of the scope of the tragedy.

UPI's story arrived in newsrooms around the globe almost three hours ahead of AP's, a hugh triumph.

Brave, but perhaps foolhardy, Mexico City staffers refused to leave the bureau even though authorities condemned the tottering building on the spot. Although the monstrous quake had flung filing cabinets around the office as if they were goose down, Unipressers choking on the dust kept working, collecting every quote and shred of color. When power finally was restored and their Telex machine sprang back to life, they ignored blown-out windows and buckling walls to bang out their copy, disregarding police instructions to vacate.

A Mexican television commentator marveled at their courage. "The UPI building has been nearly totally destroyed," he told viewers, voice rising in astonishment, "yet the office continues to function, its workers refusing to abandon their places." At last police, fearful the tottering building would collapse, cordoned off the street. Shouting through bullhorns, they ordered the Unipressers to evacuate.

While colleagues celebrated Van Bennekom's "beat," newspictures chief Ted Majeski, a forty-five-year Unipresser, fumed. Clients were demanding photos, and he had none to offer. Majeski had never accepted even grudgingly Ruhe's deal that forced UPI to rely on Reuters for foreign pictures. On this, as on other big foreign stories since the merger, Reuters seemed frozen by indecision. Crusty Majeski was not about to sit silently while his rivals pondered how to cover the quake.

"If we have to wait for those assholes, we'll never get any pictures," he snarled. Even though many of UPI's best photographers and photo managers now worked for Reuters, Majeski, a no-nonsense martinet who was respected but feared and even detested by some colleagues, made no bones about his belief that Reuters hadn't the foggiest idea how to run a newspictures operation. Majeski arranged with the Dallas *Times-Herald* to charter a plane that managed to land just before Mexican authorities shut down the airport. UPI got dramatic pictures of the epic quake—and Majeski gleefully sent Reuters the bill for UPI's share of the charter.

The quake heroics were just one example of how Unipressers, swallowing the humiliation of paychecks emblazoned with "debtor in possession," shrugged off the stigma of bankruptcy, refusing to let financial woes interrupt their mission.

The months after the wire service filed for bankruptcy were the most frantic the news business had seen in years. Wave after wave of terrorist hijackers literally held the world hostage; 1985 was the deadliest year in American aviation history; the Challenger exploded shortly after lift-off in January 1986, killing seven American space explorers and plunging the nation into grief. Emergencies like these would severely stretch the resources of even rich and stable news organizations. For bankrupt UPI, the struggle to stay competitive with AP with fewer, greener troops seemed impossible.

Yet, on the biggest stories, those that commanded banner headlines, UPI scratched and clawed and frequently produced the best-written, most colorful stories—ahead of the AP. Not only was their grit winning plaudits from the news industry, but the editorial successes were hardly hurting Nogales and Wechsler in their search for a new owner. For example, UPI broke the story hours ahead of its competitors when the hijackers of the Italian cruise ship, the *Achille Lauro*, surrendered. After a Delta jet crashed in Dallas on August 2, killing 137, a Louisiana State University journalism professor hailed UPI stories as a blueprint for covering a big, breaking news event—and client newspapers praised the wire service.

The first big test had occurred on Friday, June 14, just six weeks into bankruptcy. For Peter ''Bill'' Smerdon and another staffer in UPI's Beirut bureau, the day started pleasantly enough. They pulled up to a seaside parking lot, anticipating a dip in the Mediterranean to escape for a time the rocket attacks and terrorist car bombings that now were staples of life in Beirut. Suddenly their car was surrounded by Shiite Moslem gunmen. Smerdon, a tall, wiry, bespectacled British citizen, had been through unshirted hell covering the holy war that had wrecked the beautiful capital city, but now the lunacy of Lebanon was being driven home. After letting his companion go, the five Moslem kidnappers stuffed Smerdon into the trunk of a Peugeot 504 and cruised for hours. Smerdon, with plenty of time to think in his dark, cramped surroundings, recalled that nine months earlier his bureau chief, Steve Hagey, had been seized by terrorists while dining in a French restaurant and won his release after ten hours by writing his captors $16,000 in bum checks. Hagey, Smerdon suspected, still bore psychological scars.

Finally the Peugeot stopped and Smerdon's abductors opened the trunk. After relieving him of his wallet and passport, they pointed their guns at him and ordered him to run. Terrified, Smerdon tore off, anticipating that he would be cut down any second. When no shots rang out,

Smerdon could not believe his luck. Later he would theorize that the only thing that had saved his life was his British passport, for until then British citizens had been relatively unbothered by terrorists. An American probably would not have been spared.

Out of range at last, heart racing, he hailed a cab and returned directly to the bureau. But his colleagues were too busy to celebrate. In his absence they had been plunged into the biggest story of 1985, the hijacking of TWA Flight 847 from Rome to Athens. Among the 153 hostages were dozens of Americans. Smerdon, knees still wobbly from his ordeal, dived in to help. For seventeen days he and his mates, backed by Unipressers around the world, worked marathon shifts battling to stay ahead of AP and other competitors. When the ordeal finally ended, an editor from the *Atlanta Constitution* phoned UPI's Washington bureau.

"We're sitting around the newsroom and had to call to congratulate you guys," he said. "One copy desk guy told me, 'We can't tell which one of the wires is bankrupt. UPI has been best most of the way.' "

Max McCrohon, pleased and a little awestruck by the performance of his outnumbered troops, ordered the assembling of a special twenty-page tabloid promotion highlighting UPI's stories, pictures, and graphics over the seventeen days. For its efforts the Beirut bureau also earned a special citation from the Overseas Press Club.

• • •

As the September 16 deadline for receiving preliminary offers arrived, tension between Nogales and Wechsler was tempered by the fact that they had received private nibbles of interest from more than twenty-five potential bidders, including such prestigious companies as Gulf and Western and Ted Turner's Cable News Network.

But the next morning Nogales's delight turned to rage when he opened *The New York Times* and saw a lengthy article about UPI's sale efforts quoting "sources close to the situation." It named sixteen would-be buyers. The *Times* also quoted Wechsler, ran his picture, and mentioned a couple of his contacts who had expressed interest. It was, Nogales fumed, an astonishingly brazen attempt to grab the limelight. By now he had lost patience with the president's empty boasts about luring "world-class" buyers. Nogales felt Wechsler's leaking the list to the *Times*—particularly since some bidders had demanded confidentiality—smacked of treason.

In addition, it was an open secret that, although Nogales had ordered him to have no business contact with former consultant Jerry Hillman, Wechsler routinely was in touch with the man who had recruited him to UPI. Hillman was trying to arrange deals that could ensure that Wechsler would remain a top officer, clandestinely working to assemble a consortium of three companies that had independently submitted preliminary bids: Reuters; Tele-Communications, Inc., a cable TV colossus; and EFE, the Spanish news service. He also sought to interest United Parcel Service and Bonneville Communications, the Mormon-owned broadcasting giant. Hillman, who had aligned himself with former Chase Manhattan Bank official Barry Forman, was holding out to potential investors that his old buddy Wechsler probably would be available to run the company. Wechsler later denied any knowledge that Hillman was bandying about his name.

Nogales summoned Wechsler and chewed him out for leaking the names to the *Times* and being variously villainous and insubordinate. After Wechsler departed, Nogales decided to strip the president of his authority, redrawing the company organizational chart and leaving Wechsler in charge only of himself and Steve Spritzer.

Wechsler and Spritzer were at corporate headquarters in Brentwood the day Nogales sent counsel Bill Bowe a message directing him to inform Wechsler about his reduced powers. Six months earlier, in John Nickoll's Beverly Hills mansion, Bowe had enforced Ruhe's firing of Wechsler. Now he handed the president the blunt memo Nogales had telecopied from Washington. When Wechsler finished reading it, the puckish Bowe could not resist.

"Ray," he said with a smile, "we've got to stop meeting like this."

Wechsler managed a grin, but he was angry. Determining he would not slip away silently, he turned for help to creditors' lawyer Jules Teitelbaum, with whom he had worked closely. Teitelbaum agreed to lead a committee appeal and soon flew to Washington with Tom Quinn, the AT&T lawyer who chaired the panel. They told Nogales they were afraid an ugly, public management feud would hurt UPI's sale prospects. Knowing he could ill-afford to alienate them, Nogales agreed to a compromise under which Wechsler would become a special adviser to the creditors. Although his new responsibilities would be largely ceremonial, struggling UPI would continue to pay Wechsler's $142,500-a-year salary. The creditors approved the deal on Thursday, October 3. Simultaneously, Wechsler crony Steve Spritzer resigned from UPI.

When Wechsler's new assignment was announced that afternoon, he issued a statement saying, "I believe that my efforts helped prove that UPI is a viable investment. Since my goal is, and always has been, the survival of UPI, I am stepping aside now to let the company stand with its own team."

Publicly, Nogales praised Wechsler for having done an "outstanding job." Privately, he muttered, "Good riddance."

• • •

Despite his boasts that UPI had more than two dozen potential suitors, Nogales knew deep down that the interest of the great majority of them ranged from tiny to none. UPI would need a miracle to attract a big-name, financially solid American investor.

Within a day or two after its name surfaced in the *Times* article, Gulf and Western had withdrawn. Ted Turner, pursuing a far more tantalizing target in MGM, also quickly removed himself from contention. The Colorado cable TV giant, Tele-Communications Inc., sent vice president Peter Barton to Washington to discuss a possible acquisition. But when TCI surveyed hundreds of clients and discovered a profound ennui about UPI's survival, it also dropped its flirtation.

Nogales's gut feeling about the lack of widespread interest was confirmed on October 4, the deadline he had set for "definitive" purchase offers. He found the field had narrowed dramatically to just a handful of bidders; most of those, Nogales thought, were losers.

Conspicuously absent, yet again, were the heavy hitters of the media world: CBS, NBC, ABC; *The New York Times, The Chicago Tribune*, Gannett, Newhouse, Copley, Knight-Ridder, Hearst, and even *The Los Angeles Times*, which Nogales had wooed so patiently.

Even the ardor of Reuters was waning. Controller Jack Kenney was projecting revenues of between $77.4 million and $90 million for 1986, but Reuters considered that wildly optimistic. Almost one-fifth of UPI's business was under cancellation, double its historic rate, and the British company guessed that UPI's domestic revenues that year would slide as low as $63.5 million. Deciding to bide their time, Reuters' executives felt that if Nogales could not put together a deal, they might yet wind up with UPI at a bargain price.

• • •

Unhappily watching UPI's internal wrestling matches, Judge Bason feared the company might self-destruct. Again and again, he went to extreme lengths to prevent it. Wielding wide-ranging power under the bankruptcy code, Bason had become the arbiter of last resort for settling disputes between the company and the union.

Frustrated that even a federal mediator had been unable to forge a compromise, on September 9 Bason convened a meeting with both sides in his chambers and warned that if they did not reach agreement he would impose a ruling neither side would like. Bason already had made it clear more than once that he considered UPI's employees its major—if not only—asset. Now Nogales saw little choice but to drop without fanfare his demands for further union concessions. We'll just have to gamble, Nogales thought, that UPI will be sold before it runs out of cash.

Bason had been so deeply sympathetic to the plight of UPI's employees that when Brian Freeman was hired, the judge agreed the union should have a role in the sale process. Bason had repeatedly repulsed efforts by Ruhe and Geissler to become players in the sale, reserving that right solely to Nogales and the creditors. On Friday, September 13, the judge ruled that the union, through Freeman, should also have that privilege.

Elated, Dan Carmichael hailed Bason's decision as a historic victory for the union. Nogales was keenly disappointed. Involving the union would further erode his clout. Unless he somehow could unite the disparate and cantankerous elements, there was a good chance that the judge would have to choose from three separate sale plans. The potential for that kind of confusion might cause the most reputable bidders to conclude UPI wasn't worth their time and trouble.

• • •

Freeman, working on a contingency basis with his half-million-dollar fee to come out of the proceeds of a sale, was hustling hard for his commission. Carmichael set up shop in a suite in Manhattan's once-elegant Royalton Hotel, and Freeman escorted millionaire would-be buyers up a rickety elevator to meet with him and Morrissey. Among the potential suitors was Max Hugel, who became the butt of jokes about his CIA background—allusions to the possibility the agency was using him to infiltrate the media. Carmichael could barely refrain from laughing when Hugel moaned that he "could just kill Bill Casey" for coaxing him into the CIA, creating links to the spy world that probably doomed his dream of owning a major news organization.

Union leaders were neophytes dabbling in the high-powered world of big business; not everything went smoothly. On Sunday, September 29, Morrissey, Freeman, and Carmichael arranged to dine at the Four Seasons with Texas developer Joe Russo. The union leaders showed up at the appointed time at the fancy restaurant on New York's East Side. Russo and his investment advisers also showed up on time at the Four Seasons—but they were at the ritzy hotel in Washington.

Despite the misunderstanding, three days later Russo, dressed in a well-cut suit and trademark red suspenders, met with the union. By the end of the session the engaging Texan had overcome skepticism about his earlier talk of moving UPI's headquarters to Houston and emerged as the guild's leading candidate.

● ● ●

In his quest to buy UPI, Mario Vazquez-Raña seemed to fully expect that Nogales's Mexican heritage would make him a natural ally. Nogales was assiduously noncommittal, however, encouraging Vazquez's interest while maintaining an arm's-length relationship. Under the bankruptcy code, Nogales was required to negotiate the best possible deal for UPI, ensuring its survival while providing fair payment to creditors. Although he hoped to be allowed to continue to run UPI, and despite Carmichael's allegations to the contrary, Nogales well understood that new owners traditionally bring in new managers. He knew he had to put UPI's fate ahead of his own. Besides, with two years left on his lucrative contract, he already had a "golden parachute."

Nogales had developed deep feelings for UPI. He listened avidly when veteran Unipressers described the good old days, embellishing UPI successes and lovingly portraying its legendary characters. Nogales wanted to be part of it all. On one visit to the Paris bureau he obtained a tape of "The United Press March" commissioned in 1954 by president Hugh Baillie for radio stations to use in introducing UP news. Returning to Washington, Nogales burst into the newsroom early one morning waving the tape. As copy editors strained to monitor the morning TV news shows, Nogales flipped on a recorder and shouted, "Listen to this!"

On another occasion he even proposed offering UPI's archives to a major university. He knew many retired Unipressers had troves of historical material tucked away in basements and attics, and he feared that when they died irreplaceable documents would be lost forever.

Nogales felt he had a historic assignment; he resolved to maintain his studied neutrality as Vazquez and others courted him.

One UPI executive was far less neutral. Spotting a front-runner, Pieter Van Bennekom clambered aboard the Vazquez bandwagon. He had known Vazquez for years, and when the earthquake hit Mexico and damaged the UPI bureau, it was easy for him to accept Vazquez's offer for UPI to move to his *El Sol* newspaper. When Unipressers tried to drag the decrepit furniture over from the old bureau, Vazquez insisted on replacing it. While most of UPI's Mexico City staff felt uncomfortable accepting favors from a potential buyer, there seemed no alternative. Van Bennekom, cozying up to a man who might own the wire service, soon became Vazquez's traveling companion and interpreter, blurring the line between his current employer and potential future boss.

Nogales said later that he became so disturbed by Van Bennekom's fraternizing with the Mexican suitor that he cautioned him to remember that he worked for UPI, not Vazquez.

Vazquez demonstrated his resolve to buy UPI when he learned of the spirited response to the company's search. In October he substantially raised his offer to creditors to $21 million and pledged a matching amount for working capital.

Vazquez was still operating behind the scenes, but ironically his front-man, Beurt SerVaas, chosen to deflect any criticism of UPI falling to foreign ownership, was becoming an albatross himself. One problem was SerVaas's past service in the wartime Office of Strategic Services, precursor of the CIA. Further, there had been earlier criticism that SerVaas's *Saturday Evening Post* was an apologist magazine for South Africa and that he had close dealings with the apartheid government. Former *Post* employees also told bizarre tales about the "unprofessional" operation of the magazine. Editor Cory Jane SerVaas, who like her husband had a medical degree but was not a practicing physician, nursed a reputation for eccentricity. In her fanatic campaign to increase America's fiber intake, employees said she invited them to bring in fecal samples for laboratory analysis. On an exercise kick, she also had urged staffers to roller skate at the office.

Leaders of the Wire Service Guild, made privy to Vazquez's bid, were disturbed by the reports about SerVaas and demanded that he be removed from the deal. On October 31, UPI's editors made the decision easy for Vazquez. They sent out a 2,500-word story about SerVaas's South African activities and other business interests, quoting former associates who contradicted SerVaas's recollections about his dealings with representatives of the Pretoria government. SerVaas denounced the story as scare tactics. But Vazquez, as he had done earlier with Alejandro Orfila, soon made SerVaas a historical footnote.

• • •

Seeking to woo the union during another visit to Washington, Vazquez offered to fly Brian Freeman to an appointment in Austin, Texas, in his tri-engine Falcon 50 jet. Impressed both by the courtesy and the plane, Freeman told Morrissey and Carmichael the union should look long and hard at the Mexican's effort to buy UPI.

On November 1, Carmichael flew to Mexico City to investigate the mysterious multimillionaire on behalf of the union. Before departing he had made a major miscalculation. He phoned Van Bennekom to ask where he should stay and who he should interview about Vazquez. "I don't want Vazquez-Raña to know that I'm coming," Carmichael said.

Clearing customs, he was shocked to discover that Van Bennekom and an armed bodyguard were there to drive him to Vazquez's flagship newspaper, *El Sol de Mexico*. As the car pulled up to the huge compound, Carmichael watched wide-eyed as pistol-toting guards sprang out and surrounded the vehicle. Surveying the impressive surroundings, he could see that Vazquez was a man of enormous wealth. While security guards sealed off the corridor, Carmichael was escorted to a private elevator and taken to Vazquez's suite.

Vazquez heartily welcomed him to a room the size of a tennis court, part of an office complex that included a gym, sauna, bedroom, private theater, well-stocked bar, and a kitchen presided over by a gourmet chef. In the central courtyard a waterfall gurgled amid tropical foliage and exotic birds.

Carmichael's eyes wandered. Vazquez's walls were dotted with pictures of him posing with sports figures and world leaders such as Fidel Castro. Ten telephones decorated his huge desk.

"I like to be in touch wherever I am," Vazquez joked, with Van Bennekom translating.

Over a catered lunch they amiably discussed UPI affairs, then Carmichael got a grand tour of the compound. Vazquez proudly showed off a fleet of fifteen vehicles with opaque, smoked-glass windows, including a huge van equipped with a bank of mobile phones, a bed, and a shower. For security reasons, he said, he always alternated vehicles.

Arriving at his hotel, Carmichael politely declined an offer by Vazquez's driver to stand guard at his door all night. Later Carmichael went to a cantina to meet some people who had promised to tell him about Vazquez. After a few drinks Carmichael grew tipsy and drowsy. Later, he could not recall when or how he had been relieved of $75 cash from his trousers.

Carmichael completed his "investigation" in three days and returned to Washington to tell union colleagues that Vazquez had the financial wherewithal to save UPI; there was simply no way to prove or disprove persistent negative rumors about him.

Carmichael was obsessed with finding a buyer: his hatred of Nogales and his determination to oust him were increasing his paranoia that the chairman was negotiating with the bidders to save his own job. Carmichael and Morrissey worried that if Nogales felt he was being squeezed out, he might do something destructive.

So they advised Russo and Vazquez separately to begin defending against possible sabotage. They suggested that whoever won the bidding should secretly rent offices in Washington or New York and set up a sort of "shadow government" to duplicate UPI's management functions. Then, if there was any mischief, they would be poised to seize control and have Nogales removed physically if necessary.

There was no justification for their bizarre scheme, no evidence whatever to support Carmichael's idea that Nogales was plotting to hurt the company or to assure himself a sweetheart deal.

• • •

Amid the flurry of sale activity, the bankruptcy process droned on in Bason's tiny courtroom, with matters both momentous and mundane. On two extraordinary days UPI faced separate confrontations with former owners: E.W. Scripps, accused of benign neglect, and Doug Ruhe, reproached for near-murder.

On Friday, October 5, 1985, Ruhe was summoned to testify under oath for the first and only time in the case. He had failed, as agreed, to return to UPI the stock-quote service he and Geissler had given to Jim

West. Ruhe's tactic had blocked the wire service from recovering $100,000 in monthly revenues from Fintext. During a five-hour hearing, UPI lawyers also asserted the owners had reneged on their attorney's unconditional pledge that they would resign from the Fintext board.

Repeatedly, Ruhe insisted to Bason that he did not recall seeing the resignation pledge signed on his behalf by his lawyer, Emil Hirsch, or that he had granted Hirsch the right to sign it. He said he had not understood that the Fintext agreement "was dependent upon" his resignation. UPI bankruptcy lawyer Frank Dicello poked holes in Ruhe's testimony, even threatening to call Hirsch as a witness against his own client. Ruhe scowled darkly.

After hearing more testimony supporting the company's version, Bason swiftly ruled in favor of UPI—decreeing Ruhe and Geissler must resign from the Fintext board and saying Fintext's assets must be returned to UPI the following week. Said Bason, "Regrettably, I find that Mr. Ruhe's testimony was evasive in the extreme, to the extent it was self-serving and misleading."

For months Luis Nogales had publicly challenged Ruhe's credibility. Now a federal judge had, as well.

On November 4, for the first time, UPI publicly faced Scripps. Many UPI executives still were deeply bitter that Scripps had abandoned the wire service to Ruhe and Geissler without ever offering UPI's employees the chance to buy it. Now it was Scripps that felt betrayed. UPI owed it more than $1.7 million.

For years UPI had collected royalties for selling Scripps's feature service overseas, including the "Peanuts" comic strip. During its financial crisis UPI had failed to turn over $667,382 it had collected. UPI also owed Scripps $130,000 in rent on a building housing its Dallas operations, and more than $900,000 because UPI had failed to pay rent on its New York office. Scripps, which years earlier had signed a million-dollar letter of credit guaranteeing the New York lease, got stuck with that tab.

Scripps was owed so much that it had earned a seat on the creditors' committee. Its representative rarely missed an opportunity during committee meetings to disparage UPI's management. Scripps executives never had wavered in their contention that they had done all they could while they owned UPI. Certainly they felt no obligation to prop up the company now, and refused to pay for UPI services received by eleven Scripps papers and six TV stations.

Yet, despite the bad blood, both sides wanted to settle. UPI badly needed Scripps's business. And Scripps officials perhaps were embarrassed—and a bit defensive—that their legacy had been so severely and so publicly tarnished in the last three years.

A settlement was quickly reached: UPI would waive $1 million Scripps owed for subscribing to the news service, and Scripps would remain a creditor for nearly three quarters of a million dollars; UPI would keep its computer center in Dallas and get a $500,000 bonanza—the right to represent Scripps's feature interests overseas for another six months.

Still, the damage had been done. Editors at the Scripps papers, many of whom still were loyal to UPI, soon found that the chain's Cincinnati headquarters had slashed from their budgets all funds allocated for subscribing to the wire service.

In late August, Max McCrohon had flown nine senior editorial and marketing managers to Cincinnati to try to stem the cancellations. They listened as Scripps officials groused about UPI's precipitous deterioration, particularly the quality of its state reports, then sought to reassure them the worst was over.

Lunch at the fancy Queen City Club was cordial. But in the ensuing months Scripps's relationship with its prodigal son would disintegrate entirely.

• • •

As Vazquez and Russo jockeyed for position with the union, they were unaware that Nogales was quietly being wooed anew.

Earl Brian, a California scientist turned venture capitalist who had helped finance and later taken over the blossoming Financial News Network on cable TV, had decided to bid at the last minute. Brian had assembled a seven-member consortium whose still-secret partners were said to include an arm of one of the nation's largest brokerage houses, the Wall Street firm of Merrill Lynch, Pierce, Fenner & Smith.

Nogales was intrigued. The group seemed to offer the kind of synergy that would enable UPI to trim its huge communications costs and diversify. Nogales knew that Brian, a wheeler-dealer who had formed or swallowed up more than a dozen companies, carried heavy baggage. At age thirty a member of Ronald Reagan's California cabinet in the early 1970s, he now had friends in the Reagan White House. Brian had been drawn into a national controversy during the 1984 confirmation hearings for Attorney General Edwin Meese and had himself been a subject of federal inquiries, although he had never been found liable for improprieties. Brian also had immediate advantages: he was an American, he spoke English, and, thanks to FNN, had a link to the news industry.

Nogales was glad to have another prospect who seemed serious. He knew that after ten months of operating profits UPI would have to publicly tell Judge Bason in late November that it was losing money again. He vowed that before that happened and rival media splashed it about, he would somehow close a deal.

Nogales told Jules Teitelbaum he wanted all interested parties to present their offers on Monday, November 11, to a meeting in Washington of the creditors' committee. Nogales also notified the union and each of the handful of remaining suitors.

Dan Carmichael and Bill Morrissey were not about to take a back seat in the sale process. The union leaders were confident Brian Freeman could apply their newfound leverage, perhaps both helping them choose the buyer and negotiate a favorable contract. As he had done with TWA, Freeman presented suitors seeking union backing with a "wish list" of contract demands. Quickly they reached a handshake accord with Joe Russo on an agreement in which employee pay cuts would be restored and the union would get an unprecedented voice in company operations. When Russo began having second thoughts, Freeman applied the squeeze. On November 6, he, Morrissey, and Carmichael began negotiations with Vazquez at the Madison Hotel in Washington.

Within twenty-four hours the Mexican, too, had yielded to most of their demands, including agreeing to pay the guild's mounting expenses and Freeman's half-million-dollar fee. The whipsaw strategy worked perfectly: Russo had little choice but to capitulate to similar terms.

Dismissing the FNN consortium as anti-union, Carmichael and Morrissey on November 7 rushed to pre-empt and embarrass Nogales by announcing at a news conference they had negotiated deals with Russo and Vazquez and expected to declare their choice by Monday.

Nogales was livid at what he considered a union publicity ploy. He resolved again not to let himself be pressured into a quick decision.

• • •

Although Judge Bason had praised UPI in September for its "remarkable" achievement in attracting twenty-five potential bidders, the sad truth was that only three remained in contention entering the homestretch weekend of Nogales's well-publicized scavenger hunt. All had warts that no amount of cosmetic surgery could camouflage.

Among those who had dropped out were two who had grabbed media attention by offering creditors 100 cents on the dollar in early October. Reclusive Australian magnate Robert Holmes à Court, preoccupied with a war against Rupert Murdoch over Boot Hill Petroleum in Australia, had requested an extra week. Nogales would not agree to a delay. Telecom Plus International, Inc., of Boca Raton, Florida, a large communications equipment company secretly allied with ex-CIA man Max Hugel, had backed away when creditors' lawyer Jules Teitelbaum quickly called its bluff. Teitelbaum phoned Telecom lawyer Gary Blum and declared, "I don't have to negotiate any further. Come on in. Let's get your money." Telecom didn't show, and never submitted a formal bid.

As the creditors converged on Washington for the Monday bidding deadline, the final trio of Vazquez, Russo, and FNN hardly set Nogales's heart aflutter. Yet he was convinced there was no more time to search. With UPI about to go back into the red, it was imperative that a deal be closed quickly.

Nogales, intense and introspective as the climax neared, directed financial advisers Jeff Peterson and Michael Liss to research each bidder—a tough job because there was limited information available on Vazquez, and Earl Brian was coyly shielding his partners' identities.

Seeking to lay to rest any lingering talk that he was seeking a sweetheart deal to protect his own job, Nogales named a ten-man management committee to weigh the offers and propose a new owner, and a subcommittee to interview the bidders and investigate their backgrounds.

First to be interviewed was Vazquez, short, mustachioed, stiffly formal, seemingly unawed by the prospect of being grilled by McCrohon's subcommittee. Through an interpreter, in a two-hour session, Vazquez described how he and his brothers turned the family business into Mexico City's largest chain of furniture stores. He said he had sold his share to his brothers for $26 million in 1972 and purchased from the government the bankrupt *El Sol* newspaper chain. Although then-president Luis Echeverria had approved the sale of the paper to Vazquez and was rumored to have been its secret financier, Vazquez strongly denied Echeverria ever had been involved in the venture. While acknowledging his friendship with the former president, Vazquez said:

"I have a perfect record all over the world. I have no political affiliation. Although I have been invited to get involved in politics in Mexico, I never would accept because I am in business to make money. I am the king in my business, and I do not need the President of my country to help me."

He pledged never to compromise UPI's editorial integrity and said he had plenty of money not only to buy the company but also to subsidize future losses. "I am worth $450 million, or maybe $600 million. I have not counted it recently."

McCrohon and his team also were aware that checks on Vazquez's background had been made with President Reagan's National Security Council, and that UPI staffers in Mexico City had even interviewed former movie star John Gavin, the U.S. ambassador to Mexico, about Vazquez. No smoking guns had turned up.

The UPI investigators were troubled by persistent allegations that Vazquez's newspapers were apologists for the Mexican government, and rumors that early in his career he had been connected with fleabag hotels that catered to prostitutes. How, they wondered, could Vazquez have amassed such a fortune so quickly by running marginal newspapers in a poverty-stricken country? They also had serious misgivings about the quality of Mexican newspapers. Journalism south of the border was not renowned for its ethical standards. Many Mexican reporters supplemented meager salaries by selling ads for their newspapers, a conflict that might seriously taint news coverage. The Mexican government also could buy favorable coverage through its control of the supply of newsprint paper; its generosity or penury could make a paper flourish or perish.

Despite their misgivings, McCrohon and his team listened to Vazquez with grudging admiration. The Mexican publisher underscored his reputation as a shrewd, calculating, difficult-to-best businessman, giving all the right answers. He solemnly pledged that, regardless of cost, he would make UPI the world's pre-eminent news agency.

The diminutive Vazquez's arms might be short, but they seemed long enough to reach his deep pockets—where there was more than sufficient money to save UPI.

• • •

The next day, Thursday, November 7, a supremely confident, broadly smiling Earl Brian led a gaggle of officials from the FNN bidder group for an interview with the screening committee in the ninth-floor executive suite at world headquarters. The group had prepared a bid that seemed competitive with Vazquez. Brian, tall, beefy, and imposing, shook hands all around. When he grabbed a hand, it damply disappeared.

Brian and his entourage riveted the attention of the UPI executives with a slickly professional dog-and-pony show straight from Madison Avenue, slides and charts filled with glowing financial projections for UPI over the next five years. The UPI contingent was heartened by his pronouncement that Merrill Lynch, a rich and prestigious financial institution, was part of the FNN consortium. But they were suspicious about what their background check had disclosed about Brian's business and political dealings, and were worried because he would not disclose his secret partners.

When Brian finished his presentation he was peppered with questions about his political career in California, his ties to the Reagan White House and Attorney General Ed Meese, and his fast-shuffle business empire. He was asked about a Federal Election Commission investigation into allegations that his unsuccessful 1974 Senate campaign had tried to shake down California nursing-home operators for illegal contributions in return for his influencing rate increases. Brian, who had not been prosecuted, repeatedly denied any impropriety. He also was unflappable when pressed to explain his interest-free loans of $109,900 in 1981 to his friend Edwin Thomas, a Meese crony. Thomas already had loaned $15,000 to Meese's wife, Ursula, to buy penny stock in one of Brian's companies. The loan, not declared on the Meeses' tax return, became the center of a furor over Meese's 1984 confirmation as attorney general because Thomas later got a White House job. Meese denied awareness of Brian's loans to Thomas. Special prosecutor Jacob Stein cleared both Meese and Brian of any criminal wrongdoing, but his report noted that, after the FBI conducted a background check on Brian prior to his nomination to the National Science Board in 1982, "questions raised by (the) White House Counsel's office caused Dr. Brian to withdraw his name." Brian, whose candidacy had been backed by Meese and presidential aide Michael Deaver, said later he withdrew only because a member of the selection panel was supporting a rival nominee.

Controversy had also dogged Brian's business ventures. In 1977, when he was president of Xonics, Inc., the Securities and Exchange Commission cited the firm for making false and misleading statements to stockholders. Xonics, without admitting impropriety, agreed to a settlement. Brian's myriad operations had scored unusual successes with the federal government after Ronald Reagan became president. A story in *The Washington Post* had quoted a former business associate as recalling Brian's boasts that his "direct line" to top administration officials could secure federal contracts. When the UPI questioners asked how close his ties to Reagan were, Brian replied smugly, "I don't need a pass to get into the White House."

One of his companies, Questech Capital Corporation, was among eight firms that somehow won "investment company" licenses from the Small Business Administration and multimillion-dollar loans in 1981 despite a moratorium on such financing. Stein's inquiry found no evidence to indicate that Meese had influenced the agency to lift the moratorium for eight companies. SBA audits later disclosed that Questech had breached rules restricting the amount of money it could pump into Brian's affiliated companies and had invested $100,000 that ended up in the hands of two companies operating 800 slot machines in Las Vegas supermarkets and chain stores. However, the alleged violations were not considered so serious as to lead to revocation of Questech's license.

When Brian finished talking and departed with his FNN team, the UPI executives expressed gnawing reservations about his character, financial backing, and commitment to UPI. While Brian's presentation was impressive and professional, his financial predictions seemed wildly optimistic. McCrohon's team knew Biotech had not hesitated to slash FNN's staff and budget and worried Brian might do the same at UPI.

They felt uncomfortable and vaguely soiled, as if they had just listened to a slick pitch from a carny barker.

• • •

Texas real estate man Joe Russo had no news business experience, but the UPI team found him by far the most appealing.

In a telephone call from his office in Houston, with the five UPI executives gathered in McCrohon's office, Russo came across like a genial Chamber of Commerce Babbitt. The phone line fairly crackled with his Mom, Apple Pie, and Old Glory enthusiasm. Russo, a civic leader and a patron of the arts in Houston, had built the Lyric Office Centre as the jewel in his crown of real estate ventures. The twenty-six-story, million-square-foot downtown building featured a twenty-foot statue of a cellist.

A classical pianist played at lunchtime in the courtyard, and symphonies were piped to passersby.

Despite Russo's almost corny boosterism, he was well connected. He had hired his friend, former Democratic national chairman Robert Strauss, to assist in the pursuit of UPI. Russo's bid consisted of offering unsecured creditors $14 million cash, securities to satisfy remaining debts, and $26 million in working capital.

"I have no hidden agenda," he told the subcommittee, asserting that his sole aim was to diversify into the booming information age. "I have no reason to want to slant or skew the news."

Asked where his money was coming from, he replied vaguely, "I have the resources committed. My ability to get my partners in depends on my ability to make a deal." He glibly tossed around names like Strauss, Walter Cronkite, Alan Shepard, and Jack Valenti.

Russo said his closet contained no skeletons—two speeding tickets constituted his lone brushes with the law. He had hedged his political contributions, donating to Republicans Ronald Reagan and George Bush, and to fellow Texas Democrats.

Compared to the obvious problems with Vazquez and Brian, Russo seemed fresh air—if he really had the money. That was an awfully big "if."

• • •

In the ninth-floor conference room, the ten members of Nogales's management selection committee spent sixteen-hour days Saturday and Sunday wrangling over their Hobson's choice. Weighing the finalists against one another, they found more blemishes than beauty.

Their stomachs churned from the tension of their decision and from meal after meal of Popeye's carryout "Cajun" fried chicken, the staple of Nogales's diet. Now, however, there was no time for elegant repasts. The pressure was building by the hour.

Nogales had hoped to join ranks with the union to prevent the creditors' committee from controlling the selection process. Instead, management and union again were at odds. Nogales had flown into a positive rage when he learned the details of the union's agreements with Vazquez and Russo. Christ, he thought, the two bidders wanted union support so badly that they gave away the store.

Nogales worried that the erratic Carmichael would have a disproportionate voice in company operations. Besides promising profit sharing and job security for all members until 1987, Vazquez and Russo had agreed to give the guild a role in corporate decision-making, including two seats on the UPI board.

Nogales dispatched a management delegation to Brian Freeman's office, where labor lawyer Alan Berger strenuously complained about the agreements the union had negotiated with Vazquez and Russo. "You've got a no-cut contract for you, and a fuck-you contract for us," Berger said, imploring the union to join forces with Nogales. The guild leaders, crowing over their success, rejected the entreaties.

But Nogales was not about to let the union, and Carmichael, dominate the sale process. With the crucial decision fast approaching, the weekend became a tense chess game as Nogales, the union, and each of the three bidders jockeyed for position.

Nogales maneuvered to step up pressure on the union—warning Vazquez and Russo that they had given away so much he might be forced to throw his support to FNN for the good of the company. Vazquez, impatient with the tedious process, tried to force a resolution by sending word he might drop his bid and return to Mexico. Russo, sensing management was skeptical about his ability to raise the money he had promised, scurried to impress the investment bankers from Bear Stearns. FNN's Paul Steinle met Sunday with the union team to try to secure its backing, but when he refused to match Russo and Vazquez and sign a tentative contract, the guild snubbed him.

Brian Freeman, realizing that Nogales had succeeded in planting seeds of doubt with Vazquez and Russo about the efficacy of their deals with the union, fought to keep the agreements intact.

Despite the feverish maneuverings, management committee members would not be rushed to judgment. At the end of the weekend, no nearer a decision than when they had begun, they wearily trudged home for a few hours' sleep before Monday's showdown meeting.

• • •

On Monday morning, November 11, an unmistakable electricity crackled in the newsroom at world headquarters as representatives of the three bidders arrived for the final negotiations. Unipressers around the world hung over their telephones and their newswire printers, waiting for momentous news about their company. This could be decision day, and they were more than a little nervous. Whoever won the bidding for UPI, the beleaguered company was in for major changes.

At UPI's Washington headquarters, the executive suite was declared off limits for all but the most senior company officials. In the newsroom one floor below, national editor Lou Carr chain-smoked as usual, buzzing and chattering with night editor Jon Frandsen and boisterous rewrite men Sean McCormally and Vince Del Giudice. Their wisecracks about UPI reporters writing all their stories in Spanish, moving to Houston or taking secret marching orders from Ed Meese failed to mask the butterflies in their bellies.

By midmorning, lawyers, investment bankers, strategists, and advisers were scurrying around the ninth floor like ants at a picnic. Editor Max McCrohon and other executives yielded their offices so representatives of each bidder could privately plot last-minute strategy by phone with Vazquez, Russo, and Brian at their hotels. Soon members of the committee representing UPI's 5,000 creditors began to arrive to hear the final offers, and were directed to a stuffy and cramped fifth-floor meeting room.

Nogales knew the hours leading up to a final decision would be chaotic. None of the monumental problems had been resolved, and all the same old adversaries were likely to show up to meddle. So he stationed marketing vice president Art Bushnell to guard the heavy, sliding glass door leading to the executive offices.

Doug Ruhe and Bill Geissler soon arrived with their pint-sized, white-haired investment adviser, Porter Bibb, more determined than ever to inject themselves into the snarled sale process. The owners had filed suit three weeks earlier in U.S. District Court challenging Judge Bason's decision to allow Nogales to propose a sale plan. They had accused Nogales of a classic squeeze-out, claiming they would get "no consideration whatsoever" for their stock. Now there were rumors that Ruhe and Geissler, seeking a piece of the action, were maneuvering to aid FNN.

Bushnell was slightly taken aback, but quickly concluded that as owners they might have a legal stake in the day's events. When he ushered the owners toward McCrohon's office, past the glass-walled executive conference room where the selection committee was meeting, Nogales's eyes bugged. Irate, he pulled Bushnell aside. "Get them the hell off this floor!" he growled.

Bushnell hurried to retrieve the owners, herded them into an elevator and escorted them straight through the eighth-floor newsroom to an adjoining office. Unipressers, who hadn't seen the owners for months and hadn't really ever expected to see them again, stared in wonder. Ruhe and Geissler, who had been vilified by employees, wore sheepish grins as staffers' heads snapped in their direction.

Unipressers no longer able to concentrate on their work strolled past the tiny office, peeking through the glass as if the owners were zoo animals on display. Embarrassed and angry, Ruhe and Geissler complained. Finally they were given an office on the ninth floor, far removed from the action.

Meantime, Bushnell was a busy bouncer. When Ray Wechsler penetrated the inner sanctum, Nogales angrily ordered him ejected as well. Wechsler retired to the fifth-floor sanctuary of the creditors, who had been instrumental in keeping him on the UPI payroll.

All the while the UPI selection committee continued to meet, listening to Jeff Peterson of Bear Stearns outline the pros and cons of each suitor. Peterson said he doubted sentimental favorite Joe Russo could raise enough money, but that Russo was scurrying to find a way to produce the irrevocable letter of credit that UPI had demanded. Peterson did not even have to cite Vazquez's flaw: he was a foreigner who spoke no English.

FNN's bid, Peterson disclosed, contained two unacceptable conditions that would permit it to back out of the deal later and leave UPI in the lurch. Was FNN for real? Or was Earl Brian merely "highballing" —promising the highest bid to tie up the sale process while putting nothing firm on the table? If that was his strategy, it might succeed in driving away Vazquez, a proud man already chafing at what he considered unnecessary delays. A Vazquez pull-out might leave Brian a clear shot at getting UPI for a bargain-basement price.

Nogales remained studiously neutral, warning that whatever its choice management still might find itself in a high-stakes poker game against the union and, worse yet, the creditors. It was possible the vendors UPI had failed to pay now would have the biggest say in picking its new owner—and that decision might be based on the highest bid, not necessarily on what was best for the news agency.

To Nogales, it was "us against the world." He cautioned the committee, "Don't show your hand. It's rough and we have to be rough, because we're working with people who will lie and cheat and have no scruples, no morals.''

That afternoon, one by one, the parties trooped into the dark, cheerless fifth-floor meeting room to face UPI's creditors. First, Freeman and Morrissey presented the union's case. They said Vazquez was the first choice, Russo second. Only if all else failed would they endorse FNN. The creditors also heard from veteran managers Judy Watson of New York and Jim Wieck of Dallas, who had flown to Washington carrying petitions from hundreds of managers and nonunion employees urging that the creditors give heaviest weight to the recommendations of Nogales's team. Then the bidders left their hotels to individually make their pitches. Leading off, Vazquez strode into the room, all but hidden by a phalanx of aides. Through an interpreter he grandly described his plans for UPI, offering more than $40 million, including $15 million in operating cash. Next came Russo, then FNN's Steinle, each with similar money offers.

Through the evening the creditors weighed the proposals, but they could not act without management's recommendation. Upstairs, Nogales's committee wrestled and argued, dourly contemplating what they considered three lousy choices. Finally the creditors committee, weary and hungry, decided to adjourn. It was nearly midnight. UPI's fate would wait til the morrow.

The dawn brought a startling development. At the urging of Jeff Peterson and Brian Freeman, Russo had contacted Vazquez's aides to discuss a joint bid. Russo, unable to prove he had the money to compete, now seemed mainly interested in saving face and salvaging a piece of the deal. Still searching for an American partner to ease qualms over foreign ownership, Vazquez summoned Russo to his corner suite at the Madison.

At midmorning Tuesday, with the management committee cranky and far from agreement, Nogales and Peterson materialized with the stunning news: Vazquez and Russo had agreed to be partners. Suddenly the room was abuzz, everyone excitedly talking at once. Here, at last, was a combination that might work—Vazquez's money and Russo an American.

Nogales knew it was time to vote. The shotgun marriage of Vazquez and Russo had made the managers' decision fairly easy; Earl Brian's competing bid carried unacceptable conditions. The union, which had endorsed both Vazquez and Russo, would automatically become an ally.

Further, even if the managers had favored Brian, it would be a big risk to turn away Vazquez, whose offer had no strings attached and who had underscored his determination by depositing millions in an escrow account at a Washington bank. Nogales stood before the group, a bust of Edward Wyllis Scripps benevolently overseeing the historic moment from a pedestal in the corner of the conference room.

"We are responsible for a decision that will forever affect this great company," Nogales said softly. "Whatever we do, whether it turns out good or not, we will be remembered for it forever.

"But even if we make the worst possible decision, you all know that it is a goddamned miracle that we are here to choose at all. We were on the brink of liquidation, stuck with the most incredibly irresponsible owners imaginable—yet we're here, and about to be sold."

One by one he went around the table asking their votes. "The FNN people trouble me deeply," declared McCrohon. "Their financial plan is unrealistic. And I don't like their style."

Executive editor Mike Hughes, the last to vote, said, "This is our last shot, and I think we have found the best of both worlds."

The tally was unanimous, 9–0. Nogales, who abstained, thanked them and intoned solemnly, "I accept your recommendation."

The wrenching process was over, but none felt celebratory. Joylessly, they picked at a tray of sandwiches in the conference room and discussed what they had been through.

Suddenly, Steinle appeared at the doorway, even though the room had been declared off limits. Unaware that a vote had been taken and that FNN was the only loser, Steinle picked up the sandwich tray.

"I guess you won't be needing these anymore," he said, sweeping out the door.

Watching Steinle play magician by making their lunch disappear, Unipressers were shocked and angered at his audacity. Any lingering doubts about their decision had been put to rest.

• • •

On Tuesday afternoon representatives of Vazquez and Russo went to the fifth floor and announced their merger to the creditors—Russo would hold a ten percent minority interest in the Mexican's firm, New UPI, Inc.

Jules Teitelbaum, the creditors' lawyer, was no pushover. While still in law school he had launched his own business in New York's diamond district, and now he took great pleasure from squeezing every buck for his clients in bankruptcy proceedings.

"You gots to pay your bills," he liked to say. "If you can't afford it, don't buy it."

Teitelbaum demanded that creditors be paid under terms of Russo's offer, which was higher than Vazquez's.

"Oh no, no, you see Russo is only a minority partner. It's our deal," replied Vazquez's lawyer, Dick Beatty.

Teitelbaum knew he was in a corner. There appeared no real alternative to the Vazquez-Russo offer. FNN's bid still carried two potentially fatal conditions: FNN insisted on the right to pull out after an audit of UPI's books, or if the government ruled it could not carry past losses forward as future tax breaks.

Teitelbaum figured, however, that Vazquez and Russo could not be sure whether FNN was bluffing. Teitelbaum stared icily at Beatty for a moment, then took a big gamble. "No deal," he said.

Everyone in the tiny room froze.

Teitelbaum knew that if Vazquez and Russo angrily stalked away, and if FNN didn't have the money it claimed, UPI might not have a buyer and the creditors would be left holding the bag.

Beatty and David Rubenstein departed, and Teitelbaum immediately summoned Steinle.

"Will you guys take off your restrictions?"

Not without approval from all seven partners, Steinle said.

"When will you know?"

"It will probably take twenty-four to forty-eight hours."

Teitelbaum knew he could not tie up the deal for long. He informed the committee he had told Steinle to hurry, but had emphasized that the creditors might not wait for Brian's answer.

Vazquez and Russo went for the bait. Reluctantly they agreed that, in addition to the promised $9.5 million in cash for unsecured creditors, they would double to $2 million the value of special UPI stock that creditors could redeem after five years.

Teitelbaum had wrung out another $1 million, giving creditors a payoff that could total as much as 45 cents on the dollar. It was a bonanza they would not have dared dream of when UPI first declared bankruptcy.

Beatty quickly phoned Vazquez at the Madison.

"Congratulations, you've got the deal."

It was no surprise to Don Mario. He routinely got what he wanted. "Great," he replied calmly.

UPI's bulletin story shot around the globe. Staffers exchanged cheery messages on the company's internal message wires.

Vazquez and Russo hurried over for a victory news conference. Standing before a roomful of applauding UPI staffers and reporters from other news organizations, Vazquez needled Teitelbaum for wheedling out the last million. "El Bandito, El Bandito," he said, face screwed in a tight little smile.

He pledged to safeguard UPI's editorial integrity and predicted it would take five years, until 1990, to return the company to glory.

Nogales praised the two men for their "resources, capability, desire and commitment," and took pains to generously laud UPI's employees.

"Without their tenacity, their pride, their guts, and, above all, without their love for UPI, none of us would be here today," he said.

Later, Vazquez and Russo triumphantly paraded around the newsroom, shaking hands and predicting a glorious rebirth for UPI. Nogales would have been justified in joining the celebration, but he trailed in their wake, feeling curiously detached.

Just six months earlier paychecks were bouncing and Unipressers were drowning in despair. Their company was foundering, helpless and out of options, embarrassingly forced to hide behind the judicial robes of bankruptcy Judge George Bason. Bucking incredible odds, Nogales's leadership had been a personal triumph, UPI's accomplishment perhaps a business miracle. Nogales had wrestled the company away from Ruhe and Geissler, won over Foothill, kept the other creditors at bay, neutralized Dan Carmichael, isolated Ray Wechsler, made sure employee paychecks continued to roll in, restored subscriber confidence in UPI's survival, and, through it all, helped nurture the spirit that kept the news wires humming.

Now, his own future clouded in doubt, he prepared to turn UPI over to a fabulously wealthy new owner who promised to return it to firm financial footing for the first time in a quarter century.

On this night, when he should have been savoring triumph like other UPI executives, Nogales was hounded by serious doubts. Regardless of the girth of Vazquez's bankroll, would he be up to the task of running a great international news agency? Could American publishers ever accept a mysterious foreigner who spoke no English, a man from a country where journalistic and business ethics were, to put it charitably, lax?

Nogales knew well the selling of Mario Vazquez-Raña to the American news industry would tax and challenge his resourcefulness, his determination.

For this night, however, Unipressers did not share such doubts and fears. In the Washington newsroom bottles of tequila magically appeared, and staffers clumsily improvised Mexican hat dances. They sucked Lone Star from long-neck bottles in toasts to Joe Russo, and joked that they would demand daily siestas in the next contract.

UPI had new life.

The "Tex-Mex" wire service was born.

20

· · ·

It Ain't Over When It's Over

Elated by what seemed a triumphant ending to fifteen months of chaos, Brian Freeman and the union hastily arranged a late-night victory dinner for Vazquez and Russo. At the sumptuous Montpelier room of the Madison, only great care could keep a dinner bill below $100 a person, but this was a victory to be savored, a night without care. The agreement with Vazquez called for him to pick up all the union's expenses, including Brian Freeman's half-million-dollar fee, and to protect guild jobs for a year. However, Vazquez's merger with Russo had also eliminated much of the union's leverage in the sale negotiations, forcing the guild to yield on some of its demands for a role in management decisions.

Nogales joined the celebrants, but as glasses clinked to toast the new ownership, he felt detached and somehow crestfallen. He could not help but wonder to what lengths Carmichael and the union leadership had gone to poison his relationship with Vazquez and Russo and to undermine his chances of staying at UPI. Because he had steadfastly refused to declare support for Vazquez until the climactic hours, Nogales realized he probably had squandered any chance the new owner would ask him to stay and run the company.

In the few months he had dealt with Vazquez, Nogales also had concluded that they were an unlikely team, anyway. Despite their common

Latin heritage, they were strikingly different personalities and came from vastly dissimilar worlds: Nogales, tall, handsome, Stanford-educated, traveling in lofty circles with the cream of American business; Vazquez, short, swarthy, rough-edged, modestly educated—a man who had become extraordinarily rich by bulldozing his way through the rough-and-tumble Mexican business world.

Theirs were powerful egos. Vazquez liked to make all the decisions, abhorred hearing the word "no." As badly as Nogales wanted to keep his job, he was anything but a "yes" man. Like Vazquez, he was hot-blooded and quick to anger when crossed.

While Nogales quietly wrestled with his emotions during dinner, he resolved not to dwell on his own future. He had to guide UPI to safe harbor, and it likely would take months to tie up loose ends before he could turn the company over to Vazquez.

Yet he could not help clinging to a thread of hope that he might yet survive at UPI. In his sale proposal Vazquez had pledged to keep it a U.S.-based business, with an American at the helm. With two years left on his contract and having earned the battlefield decorations and scars of the fight for survival, Nogales felt Vazquez could find nobody better.

Finally dinner ended, good nights were exchanged, and the enthusiastic chatter about UPI's new dawn faded into the midnight silence.

• • •

Few things ever came easily for UPI: for every benefactor there seemed an ogre. So it would be with attempts to close the sale to Vazquez.

The "morning after" began on a cheery note. Press coverage of the tentative sale was generally favorable. Washington staffers were surprised and pleased when a huge bouquet of yellow roses of Texas arrived courtesy of Joe Russo, with a warm congratulatory note acknowledging their fight to save the company. Then came a big tray of cookies from Vazquez. Staffers unaccustomed to such niceties at a company that never had given them even the tiniest Christmas bonus began to wonder if, after all they had been through, happy days indeed were at hand.

In midafternoon, however, Paul Steinle popped into Nogales's office and delivered a nine-page letter from FNN that would quickly dampen the rejoicing.

"In accordance with my agreement yesterday afternoon with the creditors' committee to submit an 'offer without contingencies' by Thursday,'' the letter read, ''I am pleased to submit our revised offer.''

It included a proposal to drop the two conditions that would have permitted FNN to wriggle out of the deal and a revised offer that topped Vazquez's winning bid by half a million dollars.

The letter also revealed the members of the consortium, including FNN and two other Earl Brian companies, Biotech and Data Broadcasting Corporation of Vienna, Virginia. Merrill Lynch, which had been trumpeted as a partner, was missing, but had invested in Brian's companies.

Thumbing through the offer, Nogales coolly informed Steinle the bid was a day too late.

''I wish I'd had it yesterday,'' he said.

Steinle indignantly argued that Jules Teitelbaum the day before had given him forty-eight hours to remove all conditions from the FNN bid. Nogales would not budge. Steinle finally left, but Nogales soon would learn just how hard-nosed Earl Brian could be. Steinle promptly fired another salvo, distributing to the media the details of FNN's revised bid. Questioned by staffers at an impromptu meeting, Nogales said firmly, ''The deal is done. We've decided what's best for the company, and we're not going to open the floodgates. . . . There were deadlines, decisions to be made within the deadlines. It's over.''

Bankruptcy counsel Rick Levine was there to chip in support, saying the endorsement of Vazquez and Russo by management, the union, and the creditors ''equals a contract.''

The meeting ending, Nogales abruptly grabbed Dan Carmichael's hand and raised it high in a victory gesture. As a UPI photographer snapped this unlikely alliance, the astonished union leader ground his teeth and forced a smile.

• • •

Despite his bravado, Nogales was nettled. After ten months of operating profits, another round of employee pay restorations was fast approaching and UPI was about to plunge again into the red. Nogales desperately needed to win quick court approval so he could close the deal and get $2.5 million in interim cash the Mexican had promised, including $1 million immediately. Now, Earl Brian stood in the way.

When the creditors' committee announced it wanted to look over FNN's new proposal, Nogales could but shake his head and curse. He suspected—correctly—that Ruhe and Geissler again had a hand in this latest mischief. On the day of the sale, Porter Bibb had gone before the creditors and endorsed the FNN proposal. Now Bibb announced that, on the owners' behalf, he would recommend the FNN bid to Judge Bason as "uncontestably the more beneficial offer" for the creditors.

Although in many bankruptcy cases a company's stockholders receive no money from a sale, Ruhe and Geissler were determined they would be an exception. While they had invested no money in UPI they felt they somehow should be rewarded for assuming millions of dollars in personal liability. FNN's new offer left open that possibility, specifically reserving the right to "negotiate separately" with Ruhe and Geissler "for appropriate compensation to clear the litigious atmosphere which could jeopardize UPI's future prospects."

• • •

Nogales had an even more pressing problem—selling Vazquez to the industry's press lords. If only he could get Vazquez off on the right foot when the media started seriously examining his credentials, perhaps he might mitigate the inevitable adverse publicity about foreign ownership of the "New UPI."

Vazquez already was proving less than sophisticated in media interviews. In one, to *The Washington Times*-produced *Insight Magazine*, he declared, "I am the cleanest man under the stars. I haven't the slightest fear of being investigated from every side." The article said Vazquez liked to described UPI in fairy-tale terms: "UPI is an ugly daughter with a glass eye and a limp. She is no Cinderella, so don't expect her suitor to be the Prince of Liechtenstein. I am not the Prince of Liechtenstein, but I love her, and I can care for her."

Nogales and PR deputy Bill Adler persuaded Vazquez to let them escort him on an immediate whirlwind cross-country tour to meet the most important subscribers and assure them he would guard UPI's editorial integrity. Before they left in Vazquez's private jet, Nogales, Adler, McCrohon, and newspaper sales vice president John Mantle carefully coached him on what to say to the prestigious clients.

As they headed for the West Coast, Vazquez wasted no time trying to impress his new UPI colleagues. But when he clicked on the in-flight video machine, a steamy sex scene lit up the screen. Vazquez lurched to shut it off—a sort of high-flying coitus interruptus.

Despite this inauspicious beginning, the UPI group had good meetings in California with the top brass of Copley papers in San Diego, with *The Los Angeles Times* and with the McClatchy newspapers in Sacramento. Only when the entourage hit Chicago did trouble begin. After lunch at the downtown Chicago Club with *Tribune* publisher Stanton Cook and a meeting with editor Jim Squires, Vazquez agreed to his first on-the-record interview—without the knowledge of his new aides.

Next morning Nogales, McCrohon, and Adler were stunned by the headline on the front page of the *Trib*'s business section: "UPI Suitor Hedges On Freedom of the Press."

The story, by Charles Storch and ex-Unipresser Vinnie Schodolski, said Vazquez declined to specify his position on the trend of Third World nations licensing journalists, a practice vigorously opposed by the Western media. Vazquez's gaffe occurred despite coaching by Nogales and McCrohon that he should strongly oppose licensing. The problem appeared to have been one of differing interpretations of the Spanish word *licenciado*. Vazquez quickly issued a clarification, and in Washington, UPI's publicity department scurried to defuse the first signs of an industry outcry.

Licking their wounds, the UPI entourage took Vazquez to Cincinnati to meet Charles Scripps, dean of the Scripps family; then to a meeting in New York with *Daily News* publisher Jim Hoge, chairman of UPI's newspaper advisory board; and finally back to Washington for separate sessions with Gannett's brain trust of Al Neuharth, John Curley, and John Quinn; and with Publisher Donald Graham and Editor Ben Bradlee at the *Washington Post*.

The fifteen-minute meeting at the *Post* ended uncomfortably when Vazquez offered Graham and Bradlee each a bottle of expensive tequila. Graham declined, stiffly explaining it was against *Post* policy to accept gifts. Vazquez's eyes narrowed. In his country it was considered boorish to decline a gift brought in friendship.

Perhaps sensing the awkward clash of cultures, Bradlee accepted his bottle without a fuss.

•   •   •

While UPI's road show toured the hustings, Jules Teitelbaum announced the creditors' committee had voted to stick by its endorsement of Vazquez. UPI executives sighed in relief. But Earl Brian was not a man who gave up easily. FNN audaciously sent letters to 200 voting creditors and to 1,000 UPI subscribers touting its bid and questioning the manner by which Vazquez had been selected.

Outraged, Nogales persuaded union leaders and the creditors to join him in petitioning Judge Bason to bar FNN from wooing UPI's customers. Bason agreed. Summoning the parties to court on December 2, he scolded FNN's lawyers and called the direct-mail pitch "absolutely impermissible."

Yet, again, FNN turned the heat up. Before the day was out it submitted a new bid, offering to pay creditors another $2.1 million. Suddenly Teitelbaum's attention was riveted by dancing dollar signs. Large creditors would get about 60 cents on the dollar, compared with 40 cents under Vazquez's bid. Lawyers for the creditors, contending the selection process "appears to have been overly expeditious," asked Bason to reopen the bidding.

FNN's challenge unleashed a nightmare of litigation. The union filed suit, charging FNN with tampering, and two days later Vazquez and Russo weighed in with their own suit, seeking $50 million for FNN's "intentional and unjustified interference" in the sale process. Nogales worried that FNN was gumming up the works and endangering the $1 million in quick cash from Vazquez. He was also concerned that owners Ruhe and Geissler, by joining ranks with FNN, had given the losing bidder a legal avenue to re-enter the process.

With the court battles drawing publicity, Australian magnate Robert Holmes à Court resurfaced, like a shark smelling blood, dispatching his New York agents to see if there was some way he could take advantage of the delay. UPI executives gently rebuffed him for flirting with a newly-wed, but they were anything but certain that Vazquez would ever get to take control.

Well-connected Earl Brian was a master at political hardball. He knew how—and where—to apply pressure. Former North Carolina Governor Terry Sanford, a partner in the law firm representing FNN, had long been Bason's chum. Bason had suffered from polio as a small boy, and Sanford, a student at the University of North Carolina, had taught him to swim as physical therapy. A couple of years later Bason had attended a camp that Sanford co-owned in North Carolina's Blue Ridge Mountains. Indeed, Bason had used Sanford as a reference when he applied for the bankruptcy judgeship in 1983. Now, Sanford phoned

Bason on behalf of FNN and asked for a quick hearing, saying Brian's group wanted to issue a news release promoting its latest offer. Bason troubled and uncomfortable, politely told his friend it was improper for one party in a case to privately contact the judge. At a hearing a few days later Bason stunned courtroom spectators by disclosing the phone call from Sanford. He declared he would not permit their longtime relationship to interfere in this important case.

During the hearing Sanford gave a clear hint of the thrust of FNN's strategy. Disparaging Vazquez's nationality, he told Bason it was in the public's interest for FNN to pursue the matter so that UPI's management could be maintained "along *American* concepts of a free press."

Rejecting the appeal from his old friend, Bason ruled that FNN could not distribute its news release because it might confuse creditors and further snarl the sale process. However, he scheduled a mid-December hearing to consider FNN's arguments that the sale process had been unfair. The judge would decide the wire service's fate after listening to testimony from all sides. It would be remembered as "The Trial of UPI."

• • •

On Friday, the thirteenth of December, Bason peered down solemnly from his bench in a courtroom packed with spectators and more than two dozen lawyers. He knew he held UPI's future in his hands. He would have to sift the evidence and decide whether Mario Vazquez-Raña had fairly won the bidding for UPI, or whether Earl Brian deserved another chance.

At 2:23 p.m., after the clerk called the court to order, Bason vowed to stay in session all weekend if necessary. Looking on intently were Vazquez, Russo, Nogales, and Brian. In the unused jury box sat two of Vazquez's burly Mexican aides, seemingly straight out of the fifties TV gangster show *The Untouchables*, balefully watching the proceedings.

Bason was confronted immediately with a new legal maneuver from Ruhe and Geissler, who had been thwarted a week earlier when a federal judge threw out their suit seeking to nullify the sale to Vazquez because it had been negotiated without their approval. Their lawyer, Emil Hirsch, stepped forward to announce they had signed a proxy agreement giving FNN control of UPI's parent company, Media News Corporation, for the next decade. Whatever rights the ousted owners might have to propose a purchaser now belonged to FNN.

UPI's colorful bankruptcy lawyer, Rick Levine, then likened FNN to a spurned lover and suggested the losing bidder try venting its frustration instead on "dart boards with pictures of the bad people" who had rejected its offer.

Sanford, speaking for a tableful of FNN lawyers, charged UPI's management had not "played it straight with FNN" and said Bason should decide between the two offers and "end it once and for all."

The hearing then deteriorated into a madcap, three-day legal carnival, a sort of barristers' version of the Mad Hatter's Tea Party, starring more than a score of $150-an-hour mouthpieces. Witnesses who paraded to the stand faced a dizzying crossfire of questions from lawyers for the union, UPI, Vazquez, FNN, and Ruhe and Geissler.

First, UPI tried to emphasize the dire need of quick preliminary approval of the deal so Vazquez could invest an immediate $1 million. Nogales told the court fourth-quarter losses would exceed $600,000 and predicted that despite a surge in employee morale when the sale was announced, mass resignations would ensue if the process stalled. Paul Davis, news director of *The Chicago Tribune*-owned WGN-TV, testified that if the sale were delayed he might recommend that UPI's $1.7 million contract with the *Tribune* stations be canceled.

When court reconvened Saturday morning, treasurer Jack Kenney detailed UPI's rapidly deteriorating financial picture testifying that without Vazquez's million dollars Unipressers would not be paid Christmas week. Ben Evans, accountant for the creditors' committee, told the court UPI had stopped paying bills the week before. "On a desperate measure basis," he said, hardly reassuring those UPI employees in the courtroom, "this company could probably survive until January 6."

After waiting impatiently for two days, Vazquez began his testimony. With Van Bennekom sworn in as his translator, he pledged to maintain UPI's editorial integrity, declaring he exerted no influence over the content of his sixty-two newspapers in Mexico.

Then came a moment of delicious irony—one that again proved how far Ruhe and Geissler would go to get their way. Emil Hirsch knew his client's best chance of reversing the sale decision would come if Vazquez were prevented from taking temporary control of UPI while the court fight continued. So, despite Ruhe's and Geissler's bitter feud with the man they had tried to fire, Hirsch argued that Nogales should stay at UPI's helm because he was "the glue of this company." Apparently trying to underscore his point, Hirsch asked Vazquez, "You have been able to formulate an opinion, have you not, about Mr. Nogales's competence as the manager of UPI?"

Vazquez's response was hardly reassuring. "If the court authorizes Nogales to continue as the head of UPI, then that is what will be done —but I cannot express an opinion about that at this moment, whether he is capable or not capable of managing UPI."

Nogales felt a sinking feeling. He had received a warmer endorsement from the men he had ousted than from the one he was trying to crown.

• • •

When court reconvened at 10 a.m. Sunday, Vazquez's lawyer, Leslie Nicholson, dropped a bombshell: unless Bason validated the sale, Vazquez would abandon his effort to buy UPI and return to Mexico. Nicholson argued the company's "precarious financial situation" now was public and any flip-flopping on a new owner would "do incalculable damage to UPI."

Ignoring the threat, creditors' lawyer John Battiato said his clients were intrigued by the higher FNN offer. He suggested FNN put up $5 million in earnest money. FNN lawyer Joe Levin immediately stood and said that could be done.

The drama was building, and the momentum seemed to be switching to FNN. Brian testified that his analysis showed that UPI, to survive and prosper, would need far more cash than Vazquez had offered. And, he boasted, FNN was prepared to provide it.

Sanford, despite frequent absences, somehow contrived to reappear at critical junctures, fixing Judge Bason with an unblinking stare. Late Sunday afternoon, the proceedings droning on, the judge abruptly turned to his old friend and said he was considering reopening the bidding process. If he did, and if FNN lost again, would it drop its legal fight?

The courtroom was suddenly abuzz over the development. Bason declared a short recess to give Sanford a chance to check with Brian. Lawyers from all sides rushed into the corridor to huddle over strategy. Had Brian succeeded in influencing the case with his use of Sanford, whom he said he would name chairman of UPI if FNN prevailed?

Nogales shook his head, astonished and bemused. His "sale" of UPI, he thought wryly, seemed to get more tangled every minute. Vazquez was threatening to pull out, Bason was considering reopening the bidding, and Robert Holmes à Court seemed coiled to jump back in.

When court reconvened, Sanford told Bason that if the bidding were reopened FNN would abide by the result, favorable or not. Instantly the union's lawyer, Dan Stolz, rose to warn the judge that the guild was "irrevocably opposed to FNN."

Bill White, the Justice Department's overseer of UPI's bankruptcy case, had sat quietly for three days. Now, he no longer could hold his tongue. Wondering to himself whether FNN had enough money to buy UPI, White rose and told Bason that the wire service's dire financial condition made swift approval of a sale a matter of urgency.

"Your honor, I think . . . it would be inappropriate for the court to involve itself in the negotiation process," he said. "There is obviously more to an agreement than simply the dollar amount. . . . I would urge the court not to delay a decision. I heard nothing that would lead me to believe that there's anything arbitrary, capricious, unfair in this procedure. I think, your honor, we are on perilous ground . . . something simply must be done for the benefit of United Press."

Listening to White's stirring words, UPI executives barely could restrain their joy.

• • •

The hearing continued past dinner Sunday night. Porter Bibb testified that on November 12 he had heard Jules Teitelbaum grant Paul Steinle a forty-eight-hour extension to resubmit FNN's bid. Rick Levine immediately attacked Bibb's credibility. Teitelbaum, who was absent from the hearing because of an illness, later contradicted Bibb's story, saying he had made no such gesture.

At 10:30 p.m., after hearing nearly twenty-two grueling hours of testimony, Bason adjourned court, promising to deliver his ruling the next day.

Monday morning his courtroom was packed. For one hour Bason spoke softly from the bench. He said he had concluded that UPI, its union, and its creditors had "engaged in an extraordinarily careful selection process, involving highly skilled professional investment advisers.

"I would make exactly the same decision as management has made," Bason said, characterizing FNN's argument that it had been cheated out of extra bidding time as "simply a misunderstanding."

Despite the drama of the previous three days, Bason had known all along how he would rule. He, too, doubted FNN had the money to rehabilitate UPI and worried that its anti-union posture would hurt UPI's employees. The company had a bird in the hand, Mario Vazquez-Raña, and the judge was not about to risk losing him. Bason deliberately had acted in Machiavellian fashion, flirting with FNN and building a court record that would protect the creditors' committee from any lawsuits charging it had acted improperly in rejecting Earl Brian's higher bid.

Nevertheless, in his ruling the judge refused to permit Vazquez to assume immediate operating control of UPI, leaving Nogales in complete charge until the sale was final.

Closing, Bason said, "I am very confident that UPI will not only survive, but it will be much stronger at the end of this process than it has been for at least a quarter of a century."

When he banged his gavel, Nogales, guild president Bill Morrissey, and Unipressers in the courtroom felt as if Christmas had descended a week early. Nogales hailed the decision as "a major victory," and Morrissey called it "phenomenal."

• • •

A few days after Bason's decision, in a ceremony in the eighth-floor newsroom in Washington, UPI photographers snapped for posterity a grinning Vazquez holding an enormous cardboard blowup of the million-dollar check he had just written UPI to keep the wire service afloat. Staffers cheered and clapped. They knew they wouldn't get any holiday gift more welcome.

To toast the apparent end of UPI's long nightmare, Max McCrohon invited a dozen top editorial managers to a champagne breakfast at the Prime Plus, a fancy new restaurant around the corner from headquarters.

Just three days earlier union leaders had raised their own toasts, joining Vazquez and his consultant, George Weathersby, for dinner in the Harvest Room of the Vista Hotel. During a discussion of FNN's efforts to overturn the sale, Vazquez had disparaged Nogales. The relationship between the two had continued to deteriorate. Vazquez cheerfully volunteered that he had never really trusted Nogales, a manager who had turned on his bosses. In Vazquez's simplistic view of the business world, if you don't like your boss, find another job.

The union leaders reveled when Vazquez belittled Nogales. Carmichael, especially, loved to fuel the fire. He and Vazquez ended the three-hour dinner by clinking glasses to rejoice the day Nogales would be gone.

Three blocks south, at UPI headquarters, Nogales was basking in congratulatory notes from his own champions. One hero, Lee Iacocca, the man who had saved Chrysler, sent a letter wishing him well.

"I think I know what you're going through," Iacocca wrote.

• • •

Ruhe and Geissler were tenacious, and had stumbled on a kindred spirit in Brian. Both parties immediately appealed Bason's ruling, and on January 2, FNN and Biotech Capital Corporation filed a $975 million damage suit charging Vazquez, Russo, Nogales, the union—and even the creditors' committee—had conspired to foil their group's "superior" offer. The suit, citing the federal statute designed to fight organized crime, charged a "pattern of racketeering activity," restraint of trade, and commercial disparagement.

The various legal wranglings dragged on for months. Keeping track of the many court proceedings became a full-time job. FNN and Media News Corporation searched for any legal technicality that might allow them to overturn Bason's decision favoring Vazquez. FNN also again raised its offer to creditors, this time from 60 to 75 cents for every dollar UPI owed.

Nogales and his fellow managers doubted that FNN had the kind of money it claimed. They suspected the losing bidder's fight to overturn the sale was aimed at creating such a nuisance that Vazquez would pull out entirely; or that he would give FNN a piece of the action or pay it handsomely to go away. Nogales knew that every day of delay would hurt UPI and make its recovery harder.

Equally concerned, Judge Bason donned his Superman cape at a hearing on January 28, offering to serve in any capacity to help negotiate a settlement. Bason metaphorically compared the squabbling over UPI to the endangered California condor, telling of a male and female fighting so furiously that they kicked their egg out of the nest.

"I don't care which of you folks gets UPI," he told lawyers for FNN and Vazquez in exasperation. "But I just hope you don't kill the baby in the basket."

• • •

Coinciding with FNN's onslaught was a stream of stories in conservative publications that had all the earmarks of a smear campaign. The stories were sharply critical of Vazquez, even suggesting UPI might fall under

Marxist control and citing his "special friendship" with Castro. That charge was ironic, because few Mexicans had demonstrated more deep-seated capitalistic acumen than Vazquez.

A particularly outrageous editorial cartoon in the ultraconservative *Washington Times* showed a mustachioed, cigar-chomping hood very much resembling Vazquez listening as a pin-striped gangster remarked, "We had to ice Castellano. He wanted to buy UPI."

The controversy was fueled by widespread dissemination of a report delivered at a Latin American press meeting in March in Brazil. It recounted how Carlos Loret de Mola, the author of a book critical of Vazquez, had died in a mysterious auto accident. The report mentioned Vazquez as one of several persons objecting to the scheduled publication of the book, whose other central characters were former Mexican President Luis Echeverria and Colonel Jose Garcia Velseca, founder of the newspaper group Vazquez bought out of bankruptcy.

In the report, Mexican publisher Allejandro Junco de la Vega said the author's son and a son of Garcia Velseca did not believe it was an accident that Loret de Mola's car went over a cliff. Vazquez protested, and McCrohon denounced the report as "ill-considered innuendo."

• • •

By early April the inevitable, interminable payroll crisis bore down on UPI's management like a runaway freight. Long gone was the pre-Christmas present of $1 million from Vazquez.

Nogales had finally filed with the bankruptcy court UPI's formal plan of reorganization—required before any sale could be closed—and Bason accepted it over the objections of Ruhe and Geissler.

A final legal resolution was still a couple of months away, and Nogales knew he had no choice but to ask Vazquez for more money in the interim. Nogales dreaded making the request. Since November the tension and distrust between him and Vazquez had deepened, as each tried to portray himself as UPI's savior. Vazquez had obtained a $25 million bank letter of credit guaranteeing the purchase money, but he clearly resented having to put in any more cash before he could control expenditures. If Nogales were to press for the remaining $1.5 million in promised interim money, Vazquez probably would explode in anger and refuse him.

Still, seeing little choice, Nogales made the request. He was not surprised when Vazquez left for South Korea, scene of the upcoming

1988 Summer Olympics, without producing the money. Soon the Bank of California began threatening, just days before a payroll, not to honor any more UPI checks. The company was plunging toward yet another crisis, and Nogales was in an awkward position.

Vazquez relayed word he would not address the matter until he returned to Mexico. Nogales felt he was behaving childishly and irresponsibly. He was tired of Vazquez's distrust, tired of hearing that the new owner was belittling his past efforts to rescue UPI. Without his leadership, Nogales felt, there wouldn't be any company for Vazquez to buy.

Impatiently, as the payroll crunch drew near, Nogales waited until the day after Vazquez returned to Mexico City. At seven o'clock that morning he dialed Vazquez's private number. Bluntly, the UPI chairman informed the new owner of his legal and moral obligation to provide the $1.5 million.

"I'm tired of this whole delay," Vazquez said, declaring that he would put no more cash in until he was running the company. "I'm spending money, and I'm not in charge of anything."

"Payroll checks are going to bounce if I don't get the money," Nogales protested.

Vazquez insisted his accountants first be permitted to check UPI's books. After the review, Jack Kenney told Nogales that Vazquez's representatives had agreed UPI was in deep trouble. Even so, Vazquez balked, saying he would produce only $500,000—not enough to cover payroll.

On Wednesday, April 15, the day before payday, Nogales climbed aboard the 5:50 p.m. American Airlines flight to San Francisco to attend a meeting of the board of the Bank of California. The other directors were sure to ask him embarrassing questions about their customer, UPI.

Nogales sat on the plane mulling over how UPI could survive another round of bounced paychecks.

"I've tried everything," he told himself. "We've complied with the letter of the law. He's being capricious. He's angry because he's got to put in more money and he's not in charge. Well, that's not my fault.

"If the checks bounce again, this company has had it. The employees will leave, the creditors and clients will lose confidence. And Vazquez is going to lose his $25 million because he will have failed to comply with the contract."

As architect of UPI's Phoenix-like rise from bankruptcy, Nogales had dreamed of a new owner with a fat wallet and a blueprint for success riding in on a charger to rescue the company. In the first months of 1986, however, Nogales had concluded that Mario Vazquez-Raña was no white knight.

The legal delays in turning the company over had, Nogales thought, presented Vazquez a golden opportunity to put together a comprehensive marketing and public relations campaign so "New UPI" could hit the ground running. Rather, he thought, the Mexican had been drifting through the transition period, had done precious little to prepare to run his new, complex worldwide empire. Vazquez seemed almost diffidently confident his Midas touch would not desert him north of the border.

Jesus, Nogales thought, if Vazquez doesn't start paying attention to the business at hand this could turn out to be as much a fiasco as the Ruhe and Geissler days. Just as had his predecessors, Vazquez seemed to be banking heavily on the automatic fealty of the American news industry—and Nogales had seen that philosophy utterly fail before.

He grew angry. Who the hell did this guy think he was, coming in and threatening to undo all the good things we've done, what we've sweated so much blood for? Requesting the in-flight phone, Nogales dialed Kenney back in Washington.

"How does it look?" he asked.

"It may be the end if we don't get the money tomorrow," Kenney replied, desperation creeping into his voice.

"It sounds like old times again, doesn't it?" Nogales said. "Jack, call Vazquez's lawyers and tell them to be ready for a call from me. I'm going to tell them I'm going to sue his ass tomorrow morning."

Nogales hung up, waited a few minutes, then called Dick Beatty, Vazquez's lawyer. Nogales had always kept outwardly calm in dealing with Vazquez and his team, even when he was seething inside. Now he would try a style Vazquez was familiar with.

"We've danced around long enough," Nogales told Beatty, loudly enough to draw glances from fellow passengers. "Tell the sonofabitch that tomorrow morning I'm going to sue his fucking ass for not putting in the money he's obligated to! Then I'm going to walk down the stairs of the federal court and I'm going to have a press conference. I'm going to ream his ass. He'll never do business in this country again!"

Beatty did not know Nogales was winging his way west and could not possibly hold a press conference in Washington the next morning. Beatty was stunned.

"God, are you sure you want me to tell him this?" he asked.

"You're goddamned right I do! I've got Jack Kenney standing by to accept a wire transfer, and I've got Bill Adler ready with the press releases for tomorrow morning."

Curious passengers craned to spot the source of the outburst. Before the one-sided conversation ended, Nogales had dug deep to recall the expletives from his impressionable youth in the California fruit fields. When he hung up he ordered a scotch from the stewardess. "If I had any idea I'd be at UPI any longer," he mused, "it's sure over now."

Landing in San Francisco, Nogales raced to a phone. Kenney had good news. Nogales's outburst had accomplished what temperance and reason could not.

"We got a call from Vazquez. The money will be here early in the morning."

Vazquez transferred the money in the nick of time, and UPI had survived another chapter of "The Perils of Pauline." As usual, Unipressers had no inkling about the drama being played out with their careers.

It would be months before Bill Adler could bring himself to tell Nogales how Vazquez had reacted to the power play. For the next week Vazquez had phoned Adler three or four times a day, always in a controlled rage. Never would he forgive Nogales. He wanted, he said sadistically, to pick him up like a helpless insect and tear off his limbs, one after the other.

• • •

Despite sharply reduced staff numbers, UPI almost miraculously had avoided any really colossal coverage blunders. That streak ended in terrible fashion.

On April 28, 1986, the Soviet government announced on evening television that a reactor at the Chernobyl nuclear power plant near Kiev had been damaged in an accident, that a commission had been named to investigate and that "aid is being given to those affected."

Recalling the near "meltdown" of the nuclear reactor at the Three Mile Island plant near Harrisburg, Pennsylvania, in 1979, UPI's Moscow bureau pounced on the story. With Western journalists barred from traveling to the region, details were scarce.

As winds and the earth's rotation spread clouds of radiation around the globe, pressure on Moscow to reveal details intensified. Next day the Soviets issued a statement, considered by most Western observers to be patently absurd, that two workers were dead and the radiation danger had been "stabilized." As the world waited, hungry for information and worried that tens of thousands could die of radiation poisoning, UPI Moscow bureau rookie Luther Whittington filed a story to Washington quoting a Soviet source as saying that, actually, 2,000 Russians in the vicinity of Chernobyl had perished.

The unnamed source was identified only as a hospital worker just arrived in Moscow from Kiev. The story was toned down by the foreign desk and then, with the okay from McCrohon, transmitted worldwide. UPI was taking an enormous chance using information from a single, unidentified source, but if the story were accurate, the wire service had a momentous scoop.

The Soviets immediately denounced the report and other news organizations could not confirm UPI's death toll. Whittington assured his bosses the woman was a credible source, but when he tried to contact her to reconfirm the 2,000 figure she had disappeared. UPI nervously stuck by the story for several days, but finally McCrohon ordered European news editor Barry James to fly to Moscow to investigate. James reported back that Whittington apparently had been duped in a scheme engineered by the Soviets to divert criticism to the Western media for exaggerating the disaster. UPI backed off the story, and Whittington soon was quietly removed from Moscow and reassigned to the Los Angeles bureau.

UPI had egg all over its face. For decades it had battled the largely erroneous but widely held perception that its stories might be more colorfully written but AP's were more accurate. Chernobyl had dealt that campaign a terrible setback.

• • •

The fight for control of UPI dragged into late spring. Despite frequent legal gymnastics, Ruhe and Geissler never had actually tried to submit a proposal of their own to sell the company. Indeed, their failure to do so raised fresh questions about whether FNN was stalling or was truly interested in obtaining UPI. Wearying of the owners' constant court challenges, Bason had set a May 12 deadline for their decision whether to request permission to present their own sale plan. "It's time to fish or cut bait," he told their lawyer. Bason felt the owners and FNN had been obstructing and delaying UPI's emergence from bankruptcy with their court challenges, and had run up big legal fees for the struggling wire service and sapped its resources.

On April 23 he issued a twenty-seven-page legal opinion rejecting arguments that Ruhe and Geissler had the right to propose a sale plan whenever they wished. Bason lavishly praised Nogales for demonstrating "extraordinary diligence, speed and skill, in the face of major obstacles." He said the legal struggles by Ruhe and Geissler led him to conclude the owners were "the major, if not the sole reason" for the delays.

As Bason's May 12 deadline approached, Vazquez finally decided to end the litigation with FNN that had tied up the process for months and damaged Vazquez's hopes of quickly reviving the company. Reportedly rejecting the advice of his attorneys, he flew his private jet into Dulles Airport and met with Brian. Their settlement rewarded FNN with a share of Comtex Corporation, to which Ruhe two years earlier had sold the rights to market UPI's electronic data base. In a complicated five-way settlement, Vazquez agreed to drop his $50 million suit against FNN and pay up to $350,000 of the losing bidder's legal expenses; FNN abandoned efforts to buy UPI and dropped its nearly $1 billion racketeering suit; FNN got a 40 percent interest in Comtex, and Comtex would begin turning over to UPI its data base revenue after six years.

Vazquez also lifted a gorilla from the backs of Ruhe and Geissler, relieving them of any lingering personal responsibility for UPI's failure to pay the $1.7 million in employee withholding taxes.

Vazquez had cleared away the final hurdles. With the 297 large creditors voting by mail to approve the sale, Bason set June 10 as the date for UPI, under new ownership, to officially emerge from bankruptcy.

• • •

Although Vazquez had taken pains to say publicly that he intended to try to entice Nogales to stay, the men had not exchanged so much as *buenos dias* in the six weeks since their confrontation over the $1.5 million.

UPI managers, sensing they soon would be saying farewell to Nogales, rented the grand ballroom of the National Press Club for Saturday night, June 7, to "roast" their boss over dinner and drinks. Although union leaders urged a boycott, a couple of dozen guild members also paid $25 to attend.

UPI executives came from around the country. The speech-making was forgettable, but the affection for Nogales was unmistakable. Guillermo Chao and Salvador Barros, two of Vazquez's closest aides, attended. They were befuddled by the strange Yankee custom of demonstrating friendship by heaping insults, but likely would report back to their boss the high regard Unipressers had for Nogales.

A mariachi band and flamenco dancers provided the entertainment. The party went on for hours, and Nogales was deeply touched. He had been accepted in an exclusive fraternity. Now, officially, he was a Unipresser.

• • •

On June 10 dozens of construction workers scurried frantically to put the finishing touches on Vazquez's regal suite on the eleventh floor of UPI's headquarters. Victory champagne—domestic and inexpensive—was being iced down in anticipation of the event unfolding in the federal courthouse across town.

Washington staffers slipped away from their desks to pack Bason's tiny courtroom. As the final bankruptcy hearing opened, Rick Levine announced to the judge that those creditors who even had bothered to vote had overwhelmingly approved the sale, and that more than $29 million from Vazquez to settle their claims had been deposited at the American Security Bank in Washington.

At the judge's request, Vazquez then returned to the stand to reaffirm, through interpreter Pieter Van Bennekom, his commitment to UPI.

"In the business world, if you lose money or make money, that may not be the most important thing," he said. "UPI is very rich in personal elements. There are few people in the world that would have the patience to go through this. There was not one single moment that I felt repentant about what I was doing. I will do everything I can to make UPI the best news agency in the world."

Asked if the money really was in the bank, Vazquez suddenly chirped in English, "Yeah, no problem."

IT AIN'T OVER WHEN IT'S OVER / 343

Nogales, thanking the judge, pulled out a navy blue and gold-striped "victory tie" bearing a tiny block "UPI" monogram and presented it to Bason. One of Nogales's last acts in bankruptcy had been to order 1,500 UPI-inscribed ties and scarves from Hong Kong, which he distributed to all employees.[1]

"I'm overwhelmed," Bason said, then officially issued the order and banged his gavel. After 408 days, UPI at last had erased the stigma of bankruptcy.

• • •

Back at world headquarters, Unipressers clutching champagne goblets jammed Vazquez's posh new suite, trying not to slosh on the plush white carpeting. Yet, for a victory party, the mood was strangely subdued. The judge's final decree, eight months after Vazquez had been designated, seemed anticlimactic. Staffers hardened by months of trench warfare instead wondered and worried about the changes new ownership inevitably would bring.

For decades UPI had operated on a shoestring, defying all corporate logic, staying in business year after year despite skyrocketing losses. Unipressers had covered twentieth-century events both momentous and mundane, seemingly oblivious to financial realities, loyal only to the pursuit of the news and to their indefinable, underdog spirit.

Now that laissez-faire attitude probably would change. Under the strong-willed Mexican, UPI might have to start behaving like a real business.

Sylvana Foa, the mercurial foreign editor who never minced words, seemed particularly glum. What's wrong, asked a colleague. After all, ahead lay exciting new challenges.

"We've lost control of our company," she replied, "and we'll never, ever get it back again."

---

[1]Exactly two years later, after consulting with the ethics committee of the Judicial Conference of the United States, Bason returned the tie to Nogales and a cap presented him by Vazquez, saying federal judges are barred from accepting any gifts, no matter how small.

21
. . .

Not-so-Clean Sweep

Now that he finally owned UPI, Mario Vazquez-Raña was not about to forgive Luis Nogales's outburst in April over the $1.5 million to cover the company payroll. The clash had only fed his intensifying dislike and the jealous fear that, so long as Nogales was around, Vazquez never would get full credit for rescuing UPI. The day after the big champagne bash in his office, Vazquez summoned Nogales to his suite and got right down to business.

"After what has happened," he declared, "I cannot work with you."

Nogales had known this moment probably was inevitable. Even without the bitter confrontation there would not be room at the top for the two of them. Still, Nogales felt Vazquez was being capricious and spiteful, and that his ouster would leave UPI dangerously vulnerable. He fought to control his rage.

"I wouldn't stay anyhow," he told Vazquez, jaw tightening. "But you ought to know that I saved you $25 million because this company would have died and the creditors would have sued you for all the money in escrow."

Nogales was perhaps hyperbolic, but there could be no argument that, had Vazquez not agreed to cover the payroll two months earlier, the blow to UPI would have been deep and damaging.

Vazquez knew Nogales had staunch backers in the company and in the industry, and if his departure were not handled delicately it might cause a furor. He suggested that Nogales stay a couple of months while hunting for a new job.

Nogales was in no mood to be patronized.

"You're going to pay me for the rest of my contract," he said slowly, evenly. He jotted Bill Josephson's name on a slip of paper and dropped it on the desk. "Have your lawyers talk to my lawyer. I have an excellent lawyer in New York with a Wall Street law firm. You'd better get good lawyers, too."

Seeming to ignore that challenge, Vazquez launched a monologue about the difficult task ahead of nursing UPI back to health. At last, he said, he was free of the strictures imposed by the bankruptcy court. Finally he could begin shaping the company's destiny.

"Finally?" Nogales blurted incredulously. "Finally? You've had months to study this company! You should be ready to go right away!"

Amid the company's two-year, soap opera-like fight for survival, Nogales and his staff somehow had contrived to hang on to most of the clients. Now Vazquez had a golden opportunity to capitalize on favorable publicity from the company's emergence from bankruptcy. Yet, the new owner did not have an operational blueprint and had been curiously unresponsive to the marketing and public relations proposals Nogales had directed his managers to draw up. Nogales knew UPI was on shaky ground with many clients, and that it faced an enormous rebuilding task. Yet Vazquez seemed obsessed with getting credit for the company's salvation to the exclusion of everything else, including the job ahead.

At loggerheads, the two ended their meeting by agreeing to keep Nogales's departure a secret while they negotiated. Leaving the suite, Nogales's bitterness was tinged with relief. Soon he would be free of his burden, far away from this unpredictable new owner. Well, he thought ruefully, Dan Carmichael finally was getting his wish.

The next day, at a hastily called meeting of the UPI Newspaper Advisory Board, Nogales sat quietly, grappling with his emotions as he listened to Vazquez grandly outlining his plans. Board members seemed to struggle to pay attention during the translation of the new owner's lengthy, soporific platitudes. When Vazquez finally relinquished the floor to Nogales, the room turned electric. The board members had grown to admire Nogales. He had consulted them and listened to their advice, had kept them informed about UPI's progress, had been a man they felt they could trust. They leaned forward, straining to hear. Would Nogales give a clue to his fate?

"I am convinced the transition to Mr. Vazquez will be smooth, dignified, and elegant," he said softly. "All decisions will be made with the determination that UPI shall be the best, and I will follow those decisions—whether I am internal or external. As a salesman I always thought that if it's your dime, you can call the shots. And I guess that's what I have to accept now."

Nogales had not actually said he would be leaving, but it wasn't difficult to read between the lines. When Nogales finished, Larry Jinks of Knight-Ridder offered a resolution lauding him for guiding UPI through "extraordinarily difficult times and for leading the dedicated staff of this vital wire service."

Nogales felt a rush of pride as UPI's most important allies adopted it unanimously, without discussion. Vazquez listened in silence, splenetic eyes smoldering and narrow. Everyone in the room knew the owner was taking a huge gamble in dumping Nogales.

• • •

Foreign editor Sylvana Foa had been in a blue funk at the post-bankruptcy party because she already had felt the power of the Vazquez steamroller. Although Judge Bason had ordered him to the sidelines during the transition, Vazquez's impatience had boiled over in late May, just days before he was to take control, when Foa decided to shake up the Mexico City bureau. She had obtained Max McCrohon's approval to recall bureau chief Fred Kiel to Washington and send foreign desk staffer Louis Toscano to Mexico City.

Arriving at Mexico City's Hotel Polanco, Toscano encountered Pieter Van Bennekom, not happy that his buddy Kiel had been recalled to Washington. Van Bennekom promptly challenged Toscano's Spanish.

"I'm not fluent," Toscano said, taken aback. "That's no secret."

"I don't know what we're going to do about this," Van Bennekom said, shaking his head.

Alarmed that his transfer might be in danger, Toscano returned from dinner to find his room had been ransacked, although nothing was missing.

When executive editor Mike Hughes arrived a couple of days later to oversee coverage of the World Cup soccer games, Van Bennekom told him that Vazquez himself had scotched Toscano's transfer.

Hughes knew it was not all that unusual for UPI to post overseas an American journalist not fluent in the foreign language. Besides, Toscano was taking Spanish lessons. Hughes, trying to compromise, asked Vazquez whether Toscano could have a vacancy in the Dominican Republic. Vazquez was adamant. Until Toscano was fluent in Spanish he could not work in Latin America.

Hughes and Van Bennekom took Toscano to a dingy cantina and broke the news that Vazquez had decreed he must return to Washington. Foa, Hughes explained, "shouldn't have been making transfers at this time."

Toscano, who had relinquished his Washington apartment and sold his car, was a soft-spoken man. But he could barely contain his rage. "I think you guys are reprehensible!" he spat out.

Hughes had caved in on the kind of personnel decision UPI's editorial leaders always had jealously guarded. Neither under Scripps nor under Ruhe and Geissler had owners interfered in decisions about who should work where. Yet, Vazquez, who did not even officially own UPI yet, had done precisely that.

When Toscano called Washington, McCrohon and Foa recognized the ominous portent: while Vazquez's order was not technically a directive to slant the news, the intrusion was exactly the kind of interference in the news operation that could ultimately undermine UPI's editorial integrity. Determined to win this mini-war and deliver Vazquez an important message, they told Toscano to stay in Mexico City until further notice.

On the morning of Friday, June 6, Van Bennekom escorted Toscano to Vazquez's office. Toscano was nervous. As they walked toward the little man sitting behind a desk at the other end of the long, narrow room, he felt like Dorothy confronting the Wizard.

With Van Bennekom translating, Vazquez said that until he got a handle on UPI's operations, he didn't want people transferring. Toscano could return to Latin America after things were "straightened out."

"You're the boss," Toscano replied. "You own the company. If you want me to go back to Washington, I will."

"Oh, no, no," Vazquez said. "That's a terrible attitude. This is our company. We're all in this together. Why don't you spend the weekend, see the sights and go back on Monday?"

In no mood to be patronized, Toscano said he planned to leave right away, and politely turned down a ride back to Washington on Vazquez's private plane. When he returned to the UPI bureau downstairs, Foa and McCrohon were waiting on the phone line.

"You've got to stay," McCrohon said, telling Toscano he was the symbolic focus of a struggle with Vazquez over editorial independence.

For two weeks the battle of wills raged, Toscano hanging in limbo in Mexico City while Vazquez took formal control of the company. Finally, McCrohon told Foa he had met with the new owner and the conflict was resolved. Foa, on the verge of resigning, was delighted. She sent McCrohon long-stemmed roses and a mash note calling him her hero. In truth, this time McCrohon was no hero. In the showdown meeting, he had bowed to Vazquez's demand that Toscano be recalled. Hughes had decreed that Kiel would remain bureau chief.

Unipressers had hoped the rich Mexican simply would come in, pay the bills and leave them alone. The Toscano affair left no doubt who would be calling the shots.

• • •

Nogales kept reporting to his office for several weeks as his secret settlement negotiations with Vazquez plodded along with little progress.

Nor was there a replacement in the wings. One candidate had been George Weathersby, president of Beurt SerVaas's Curtis Publishing Company, who had continued to serve as a consultant to Vazquez. Weathersby, who knew little about the wire-service business, had in late spring blown any chance to become UPI's president by demanding a $400,000 salary, a house, a car and driver for himself and a car for his wife. Vazquez, for all his millions a pecunious man, was outraged. Weathersby soon had slunk back to his old job with SerVaas in Indianapolis.

Vazquez seemed unconcerned about the impending leadership void. In early July he summoned Nogales to settle their dispute "man to man." Arriving in the owner's suite, Nogales was amazed to find him combing stacks of financial data, scrutinizing even the smallest staffer expense accounts. Even though Vazquez still had no marketing plan and client cancellations were starting to pour in, he was sweating the penny-ante stuff.

"I want to talk about your contract," Vazquez said. "I spent several hours with my New York lawyers that I hired to review your case, and they tell me that I will win on every single point.''

"That's interesting," Nogales said, indulging a small smile, "because my lawyers are the best and they tell me that I will win on everything.''

After the two haggled a while, Vazquez suddenly proposed a settlement of some $350,000, close to what Nogales's contract called for. Vazquez walked around his desk and embraced his rival.

"I will be your best friend,'' he said. "You don't know what a great friend I can be.''

Fat chance, Nogales thought. On July 8 he left with minimal fanfare. Vazquez publicly thanked Nogales for "all the work he has done for UPI,'' and accepted his resignation "with regret.''

In his own statement Nogales gave no hint of their animosity. "I believe UPI has a great future and leave with confidence, knowing it is in strong hands. It's a friendly parting.''

Luis Nogales had packed a lifetime of frustration and triumph into thirty-five months as a Unipresser. He strolled through the eighth- and ninth-floor offices, bidding friends farewell. Then he took his check straight to the bank.

• • •

Dan Carmichael was in for a shock if he believed that sharing anti-Nogales toasts had cemented a special relationship with Vazquez. Without his knowledge, the owner had begun courting Bill Morrissey.

Months earlier, while in Mexico City during the sale negotiations, guild adviser Brian Freeman had offhandedly suggested that Vazquez hire Morrissey. Morrissey at first had dismissed the idea as inappropriate. After the sale, however, his future with the union uncertain, Morrissey told Vazquez he might be interested. No more than an hour later, having obtained assurances he would not be involved in matters affecting the union, Morrissey had joined the new owner's team.

Even as Carmichael was strutting like a victorious peacock the day Nogales left, he was summoned by Vazquez and informed of his mentor's defection.

The official announcement two days later jolted many employees. They felt Morrissey had betrayed them and feared he now would be in a position to help the owner exploit the union's weaknesses.

• • •

Vazquez toiled marathon days during his first weeks at UPI. Still using Van Bennekom as errand boy and translator, he spent hour after hour questioning a small cadre of senior officials who quickly learned they could be friends with Vazquez as long as they did not cross him.

One August Saturday, Mike Hughes was summoned to Vazquez's office. For hours he listened to his boss expansively speak of his dreams for UPI. When Vazquez finished he smiled broadly and told Hughes, "We are good friends. We will work well together."

The next day, as Hughes tried again to catch up on paperwork, Vazquez called for him once more. This time Hughes was not so pliant, often challenging the owner's plans and methods. Vazquez's smile soon melted into a scowl.

"I think I liked you better yesterday, Mike," he said.

Other senior executives were disturbed by Vazquez's behavior during critical discussions about how to preserve UPI's rapidly shrinking client base. Getting a marketing plan in place was unquestionably the most important matter the owners faced. Vazquez had granted new partner Joe Russo's wish to head UPI's sales efforts, and Russo enthusiastically embraced Nogales aides Art Bushnell and Bill Adler, who for months had been drafting a marketing scheme.

On July 1, during a nearly five-hour meeting in Washington, the owners listened as Bushnell and Adler outlined their plan, then delighted the two executives by agreeing to adopt it. Before departing for Houston, Russo told them, "You'll be reporting to me."

Once Russo was out the door, Vazquez undercut his partner.

"Of course," Vazquez told Adler and Bushnell, "you still report to me."

His determination to isolate Russo not only meant Vazquez would himself be overseeing UPI's efforts to rebuild its clientele, but also suggested that he had never intended for Russo to be more than a figurehead American partner. And even after approving the blueprint offered by Bushnell and Adler, Vazquez never moved to implement it, leaving the senior executives frustrated and bewildered. It seemed in the first weeks that Vazquez's only real game evolved around dumping Nogales, perhaps the one man who could help him win the trust of the publishers.

Vazquez was an enigma. A steel-willed success story fond of calling detractors "jealous dwarfs," he refused to acknowledge the verb "lose."

Vazquez reveled in owning a respected, international news organization that historically had been the dominant service in his native Latin America. He sincerely wanted to return UPI to glory, hoping to bask in its success, yet he was obsessed with keeping tight rein on his new kingdom and was loath to delegate authority.

Vazquez was stubbornly determined to run UPI the way he ran his empire in Mexico, where he had fired 1,000 managers and centralized power in a tiny inner circle. That kind of medicine would prove dangerous for UPI. First, if this foreign owner fired more senior company officials, he might visit more uncertainty and turmoil on a company that desperately needed to demonstrate stability to the industry. Second, tight-fisted budgeting was too simplistic an approach to answer UPI's complex problems; pure austerity had failed in the past. Vazquez needed to greatly expand UPI's revenues. Yet, even as he boasted that he was adding reporters and opening new bureaus, in truth he was operating on the cheap. He thinned managerial ranks and refused to allow the hiring of experienced reporters, even insisting that raw beginners be placed in one-person bureaus where their supervisors might be hundreds of miles away.

As he struggled to impose his Mexican-style management on UPI, the media were having a field day digging into his past. Even his birthplace became an issue because, as president of Mexico's Olympic committee, he was required to be a Mexican national. Critics produced papers purporting to show he had been born in Barosso, Spain, on June 7, 1932, and had emigrated to Mexico at seventeen. Manuela Vazquez-Raña, a resident of Barosso who identified herself as a first cousin, told the Miami *Herald* she remembered Vazquez as a youth, but he insisted he had been born in Mexico.

Before his teens Vazquez was drawn into the family furniture business. Fourth eldest of five brothers and a sister, Mario kept the ledgers for Hermanos Vazquez—the Brothers Vazquez. A workaholic who labored incredible hours to build the business, Vazquez neglected his studies and he never earned a high school diploma.

At eighteen, he boasted, he was running the business. Selling on the installment plan at enormously inflated prices, he soon had built it into the biggest furniture store in the world's largest city. The brothers creatively used the new medium of television to advertise, getting free airtime one Christmas Day in return for cutting in the country's giant TV monopoly for a percentage of sales.

As he prospered Vazquez made political friends, and it was these relationships that drew the most attention from the curious American media. He had contributed to the presidential campaign of Luis Echeverria, whom he met through Mexico's Olympic program—Vazquez was captain of the Mexican rifle team at the 1972 Munich Olympics. During Echeverria's presidency, Vazquez sold out to his brothers for $26 million and began seeking new conquests. In the mid-1970s he set his sights on the bankrupt, conservative thirty-one-newspaper El Sol de Mexico chain that Echeverria's leftist government had purchased from one of its biggest critics. Vazquez bought it from the government for $12.8 million and a promise to pay off its $84 million in debts. He later denied Echeverria had helped him acquire the chain, saying the Mexican President's sole involvement was to tell him, "Hey, I hope that you can buy it."

Ensconced in a cubicle at the El Sol office, Vazquez worked eighteen-hour days, imposing severe cost-cutting measures until the red ink stopped. But by not replacing government-appointed editors with his own team, Vazquez fanned rumors that Echeverria, now out of office, was the secret power. He did nothing to allay those fears by hiring two key Echeverria aides: interior minister Mario Moya Palancia, who was named chief executive and editor; and press secretary Fausto Zapata, who had managed the bankrupt papers from the presidential palace. Vazquez continued to insist Echeverria owned no part of El Sol.

Under Mexico's arcane business climate and system of government perks for friendly publishers, the El Sol chain was smashingly successful under Vazquez, gobbling papers voraciously. Within a decade Vazquez had launched enough new journals to double his empire. Through his position as president of the Mexican Olympic Committee, Vazquez built a power base by establishing and becoming the head of the Association of National Olympic Committees, comprised of presidents of national Olympic committees.

With fortune came fame. Now a newspaper czar and sportsman of world renown, Vazquez lavished gifts and royally entertained Mexico's elite. Visitors were awed by his sprawling suburban estate, a virtual fortress awash in bodyguards. A six-foot-high fence embraced a soccer field, indoor pool, private gym, tennis courts, lush gardens, a fifty-foot indoor waterfall, fabulously expensive Louis XIV furniture, and two caged Russian black bears, Olympia and Nacho. His friend Peter Ueberroth was fond of saying Vazquez's estate would fetch $25 million in Los Angeles.

• • •

Resuscitating UPI would have daunted even one with an intimate knowledge of American journalism. Mario Vazquez-Raña would find the task nigh impossible. He couldn't read American newspapers or even UPI's own news wire, and seemed ignorant of and unresponsive to the complexities of doing business with the nation's newspaper and broadcast barons. UPI officials repeatedly warned Vazquez that the industry's patience with the wire service's struggles was wearing thin and he must seize the initiative or the remaining bits of goodwill would evaporate. Indeed, the client desertion had accelerated as Vazquez's ownership fight with Ruhe, Geissler and FNN dragged on the previous spring. Editors increasingly found they could manage with the AP and one or more of the low-priced supplemental services.

The gravity of the situation had been underscored shortly before the sale, on May 31, the day UPI's contract with *The New York Times* expired. McCrohon and Nogales had visited executive editor Abe Rosenthal and pleaded that he continue the service for another six months so UPI could prove it was serious about cleaning up its financial mess and strengthening its news report. Although Rosenthal would not sign a contract extension, UPI dodged disaster when he grudgingly agreed to keep the wire service, on approval, until the end of the year.

Further aggravating the problems with clients, Vazquez ignored the advice of UPI marketing executives and on several occasions insisted on injecting himself directly into client relations. Bypassing newspaper editors who normally make such decisions, he would meet directly with publishers, forcing them to sit through his philosophical meanderings and Van Bennekom's painfully long translations. Most publishers seemed wholly unimpressed. If Vazquez felt face-to-face meetings would assuage industry concerns about a foreign owner, his strategy didn't seem to be working.

By summer's end Vazquez still lacked a concrete plan for breathing life into his new venture, although he often audaciously bragged of making changes so dramatic that the "New UPI" never could be mistaken for its stuck-in-the-mud, money-losing predecessor. Staffers and clients alike waited in vain for specifics—and action. Instead, Vazquez seemed preoccupied with internal intrigue and political housecleaning. Now he was focusing on excising holdovers from the Nogales days.

Shortly after he left in early July, Vazquez had abruptly fired Nogales's former secretary, Eva Dillon, who had become Bill Adler's assistant and lover. In a colossal rage, Adler quit. Bushnell, also frozen out and convinced his ties to Nogales were the kiss of death, accepted a sales job with Reuters. UPI was bereft of its senior marketing brain trust.

The new owner continued to hone his ax, ordering the firing of new public relations chief Dave Wickenden, who had been Adler's deputy, and his three-person staff. At a time UPI needed to put the best face on the activities of its new owner, nobody was left to do it.

New owners often bring in their own people at the top, but another shake-up was the last thing UPI needed. Veteran Unipressers, already uneasy about the new owner, were startled by the zeal Vazquez exhibited in executing his purge. Concealing his guile with a quick smile and ingratiating small talk, Vazquez cleverly manipulated some UPI managers, eager to impress the new boss, into derogating their colleagues. With a seeming "divide and conquer" philosophy, he found it simple to exploit these grudges and ambitions.

The new owner relied heavily on the counsel of Van Bennekom and Vice President Bobby Ray Miller, both seeming masters of the smooth, chameleon-like transfer of allegiance. As UPI's top-level casualty list lengthened and new turmoil broke out, many veteran Unipressers resented the enhanced influence of Miller and Van Bennekom and suspected one or both were inspiring Vazquez's decisions.

Vazquez was being advised to replace McCrohon, who never had comfortably adjusted to wire-service journalism. McCrohon, a talented, highly principled man, was regarded by many journalists outside UPI as an editor with vision. Even his staunchest admirers, however, might have been astonished to learn where that "vision" sometimes led.

One McCrohon episode that drew snickers occurred over the long Fourth of July weekend in 1986, when Manhattan was the scene of lavish parties and gaily bedecked flotillas of tall ships filled the Hudson River for the one hundredth anniversary of the Statue of Liberty. McCrohon sent a contingent from Washington, led by features editor Andrea Herman and veteran reporter Tom Ferraro, to augment UPI's New York staff. As the clock ticked toward midnight on the Fourth, the team marked the end of a long, grueling day by unwinding with pizza and libations in the bureau. Then McCrohon phoned from Washington.

He had had this vision, he told Herman, that terrorists would strike in the middle of the night and blow up Miss Liberty in an effort to galvanize world attention to their cause. Herman, a brassy and pushy woman who long had been extremely close to McCrohon, rolled her eyes. She must, her editor continued, arrange for someone literally to "watch" the statue all night and also charter a boat on standby to speed reporters to the scene.

"Oh Max, Max!" she admonished, and, covering the phone, told her staffers, "My God, he's gone off the deep end!"

Herman, who did not hesitate to use her clout with McCrohon to win office turf fights, was always his ally, even though she was aware that when he became fixated logic and reason sometimes took a holiday.

"Andrea, if nothing happens everybody will think I'm crazy," McCrohon said, soothingly. "If something does happen, they'll think you're brilliant for being ready. So just do it."

New York staffer Seena Gressin, whose living room window afforded an unobstructed view of the statue, was dispatched to her Brooklyn Heights apartment. "Don't fall asleep," she was warned.

Thumbing the Yellow Pages, Ferraro began calling charter companies, offering a $1,000 check if they would keep a boat on standby but too embarrassed to say why it was needed. Getting nowhere, finger growing weary from punching the numbers, he finally sweet-talked someone into agreeing to the plan without requiring UPI to pay in advance.

It seemed, Ferraro mused, like a scene from Ben Hecht's madcap journalism farce, *The Front Page*—while a bunch of reporters are sitting around munching pizza, the editor calls up with this bizarre scheme.

The elaborate preparations went for naught. Dawn broke with Miss Liberty still guarding New York Harbor, beginning her second century.

Despite his occasional quirks and his largely hands-off approach to UPI's editorial product, McCrohon hardly had been passive over some of Vazquez's proposed changes. He had strongly opposed the new owner's plan to replace American correspondents abroad with foreign nationals, and had clashed with Vazquez over staffing the Mexico City bureau.

McCrohon and his top deputy Mike Hughes, a former sports editor whose knowledge of soccer helped him develop an instant rapport with Vazquez, chafed under the owner's extraordinary demands. Addicted to eighteen-hour days, Vazquez insisted that when he was in town his aides be instantly available. He ordered McCrohon and Hughes to work staggered shifts so one or the other always would be there. Since the owner beckoned day and night, that timetable quickly disintegrated.

Vazquez, who had been criticized in the media for blocking Toscano's transfer to Mexico City, surely knew removing a big name like McCrohon might be perceived as a blatant intrusion into editorial matters. Vazquez decided to isolate McCrohon by "elevating" him to president and re-placing him with Hughes. This transplant on the UPI body began on July 29 while Vazquez, McCrohon, and other company executives joined Mac Borg, chairman of the Bergen Record, for lunch in the newspaper's private dining room in Hackensack, New Jersey.

"You know, I was going to make Max president," Vazquez said loudly, gesturing toward McCrohon. "I was going to make him my right-hand man so he could be in charge when I was out of the country. But he's a weak administrator, so I can't do that."

Borg and his guests stiffened, and McCrohon was shocked that Vazquez—through interpreter Van Bennekom—had so indelicately broached the subject in the presence of an important client.

Vice president Art Bushnell said later that in the men's room, when he asked Van Bennekom what could have prompted Vazquez's outburst, the reply was, "He never says anything by accident. There's a reason for whatever he does."

McCrohon quickly read the tea leaves. He told Vazquez he could handle both jobs, president and editor. The owner demurred. McCrohon decided to accept the presidency.

On August 14, three days after Vazquez disingenuously sought from employees their nominees for the presidency, a job he already had filled, he descended to the newsroom to announce McCrohon's appointment. Hughes would become editor. Staffers applauded the elevation of men who had helped guide UPI through its most turbulent times, men who knew and understood the wire service's problems and needs. But Vazquez merely smiled at the completion of his surgical maneuver and said, "I am very happy."

Bobby Ray Miller, standing to one side, grinned and cackled, "Max just got kicked upstairs."

With one stroke Vazquez had eased out McCrohon and secured Hughes's loyalty by giving him the job he had coveted for years.

• • •

Despite his lofty new title, McCrohon found himself frozen out of the decision-making process. At Vazquez's request, McCrohon drew up and delivered to the owner a brilliant plan for UPI's turnaround. Vazquez ignored it—and ignored McCrohon, now little more than an expensive figurehead.

Vazquez then aimed at managing editor Ron Cohen, who had run the news report while McCrohon and Hughes were busy fighting bankruptcy brushfires. Hughes later would say that one summer day Vazquez told him, "Cohen has to go. It's nothing personal, I've never met him."

Hughes and Cohen had worked closely for years. On September 11, Cohen's twenty-fifth anniversary with UPI, Hughes delivered a letter to him lauding his role "in the survival of this company" and adding, "I take comfort in the fact that I have you by my side as we enter another phase of our life as Unipressers." That phase would be short-lived. Hughes soon decided to eliminate Cohen's job.

First, on September 19, Hughes fired Sylvana Foa, the foreign editor with whom he and Vazquez had clashed over reshaping the Mexico City bureau. Foa, a seventeen-year UPI veteran, also had been extremely close to Nogales. Hughes's choice to succeed her, London-based news editor Barry James, was called to Washington to meet with Vazquez. James was chatting in Spanish with Vazquez in the owner's private office when Hughes popped in and the conversation took a sudden twist.

"Mike, do you trust this guy?" Vazquez asked.

"I wouldn't have recommended him if I didn't."

Vazquez pulled out a sheet of paper and drew a circle at the top. "That's me," he said.

Then he drew a circle under it and connected them with a line. "That's Mike."

Then he drew a line from the second circle, made a third circle below it, and told James, "I'd like that to be you."

"That's Cohen's job," James remonstrated.

"Mike is going to get rid of Cohen," Vazquez said.

James was stunned. Hughes sat silently, knowing he would be caught in the middle between Cohen, a longtime colleague, and UPI's headstrong owner.

• • •

On Friday, September 26, Hughes returned from a trip to Miami to be greeted by Miller's smug announcement that, in his absence, Vazquez had reorganized UPI's editorial operations to mirror those at his Mexico newspapers. Hughes exploded. In expanding domestic operations from five divisions to twenty-one regional "profit centers," the owner, guided by Miller and former union president Bill Morrissey, had even named the new managers.

Hughes was flabbergasted that, just weeks after taking the editor's job, he already was being undercut. Cursing loudly, he rushed upstairs to confront Vazquez.

"We were in a hurry," Vazquez said apologetically. "No disrespect was intended. We fully intended to tell you."

Hughes protested that the reorganization would eliminate senior copy editors responsible for assuring the accuracy and quality of the stories from their regions. Vazquez's ill-informed assessment of the copy-editing function was, "We have too many people sitting in the office not doing anything." His stunningly puerile view of UPI's editorial operation was eerily similar to that of Ruhe and Geissler, who three years earlier also had suggested that copy editors were an expensive and unnecessary luxury.

Vazquez's reorganization plan closely resembled AP's operation, but, unlike its wealthy rival, UPI sorely lacked the managerial talent to fill the dozens of new, top editorial and sales jobs. Furthermore, a similar structure at UPI had been dismantled several years earlier because regional chiefs had tried so hard to protect the bottom line in their own budgets —and their accompanying incentive bonuses—that the company's historic coast-to-coast cooperation had begun to crumble.

Before this Friday was over Miller slipped onto the company-wide message wire the week's regular job-posting memo. It included the disclosure that, just as Hughes had prescribed, UPI would have three new executive editors. Handed the message, Cohen was shocked and incensed. It was apparent that, without his prior knowledge, his job of overseeing both national and international news was being eliminated.

Vazquez was hardly through for the day. At 8:30 p.m. he summoned McCrohon and Hughes back to his suite and announced that everyone he had consulted had told him that UPI's "problem is Washington."

"If we make a spectacular shakeup," he said, "it's going to show the clients that we are serious."

Vazquez then unveiled a hit list of employees he wanted fired, including seven top editors. Scanning the list, McCrohon and Hughes were shocked that Vazquez could believe that such a top-level editorial disruption could possibly help the company. On the list were Cohen and many of the highly capable senior managers who had stuck it out and helped hold UPI together during its darkest hours, people Hughes needed. Also targeted were Washington bureau chief Dave Wiessler and his deputy, Arnie Sawislak; newspictures vice president Ted Majeski; assistant managing editor Lucien Carr, a hard-bitten copy-editing legend for four decades of Unipressers; graphics chief Joe Scopin: and radio network editor Lou Giserman. Also on the list were Majeski's wife and secretary, Marie, and office administrator Dave Hewitt.

Hughes erupted with a stream of profanity. "This is instant bloody suicide, Mario," he said truculently. "You have only had this company for a few months. Already, it is apparent that the American newspaper industry is not supporting you."

For ninety minutes they argued fiercely, Hughes and McCrohon insisting the cuts would cripple UPI and could prompt enormous client defections. Vazquez pounded his desk, declaring, "These people must go!"

Finally, the three agreed to adjourn until the next morning. After the meeting, Hughes and McCrohon sat disconsolately in McCrohon's office, staring at each other. Hughes puffed a cigar, McCrohon his omnipresent unfiltered Camel. Both agreed the hit list was madness.

Deducing Vazquez's aim was to save money, they drew up a plan to prune a quarter of a million dollars through attrition and fine-tuned austerity moves, then went wearily home. When they returned Saturday to meet with Vazquez, Joe Russo sat in, as usual acting as cheerleader-mediator. Now, Vazquez had changed his tone.

"Whatever you put in front of me, I accept," he said sourly.

Hughes and McCrohon outlined their cost-cutting proposals.

"Whatever you say," Vazquez replied.

Hughes, worried by Vazquez's surly response, doubted his sincerity. He replied that it would be useless to go forward if the owner were going to hold a grudge.

The discussion continued. Finally, Vazquez, angry and weary, stalked out. Sweeping past Barry James sitting in an anteroom, he muttered in Spanish, "With friends like this, who needs enemies?"

McCrohon and Hughes went back downstairs, their moods dark. Both had had all they could stomach.

"You'll have to do it without me," McCrohon said, proffering his hand.

"I won't shake on that," Hughes replied. "I'm going to resign, too."

If Hughes, a Unipresser for thirty years, was wavering at all, his resolve quickly stiffened when James walked into his office a short time later. "Vazquez just offered me your job, effective in December," James said. What in bloody hell could come next? Hughes wondered. Head throbbing, he drove home to talk things over with his wife.

Throughout the weekend, the two top editors who had helped guide UPI through bankruptcy mulled over the latest crisis facing their battered company. How, with or without their presence, could the wire service be turned around under someone so headstrong, so capricious as Vazquez? What would the media world say when it learned of these developments?

Despite their deep misgivings about what Vazquez was trying to do, Hughes and McCrohon reflected further on their vows to resign. The professional futures of too many people were at stake, and as many jobs as possible had to be saved. Somehow, they had to figure out a way to get Vazquez to relent.

At home that weekend, Cohen, too, had pondered his options. He seemed to have little recourse but to counter-punch. In his office at 7 a.m. Monday, he typed a letter to McCrohon and Hughes.

"I may be an incurable optimist, but even I can read the handwriting on the wall when it's printed in letters ten feet high," he wrote. He proposed resigning in exchange for a year's salary.

Cohen showed the letter to McCrohon at midmorning. The president paled and warned softly, "Make sure you really want to do this."

Rumors of a "hit list," triggered by a late-night call from Hughes to sports editor David Tucker, were sweeping UPI's bureaus. There was talk of Hughes and McCrohon fighting to save the jobs of as many as twenty top managers. Reeling Unipressers wondered what plot Vazquez could be hatching. Who could be advising him? Did he have some nefarious scheme to control the news product and erode editorial integrity? The upheavals of the Ruhe-Geissler era and the tensions of bankruptcy had faded, only to be replaced by a new, different panic.

McCrohon and Hughes spent much of the day jockeying over how to avoid the ouster of virtually every top editorial manager in Washington. In late afternoon Hughes met privately with Vazquez. Emerging, he gave this account to his old confidant, Barry James.

Hughes said that when he demanded to know why Vazquez had offered his job to James, the owner brushed it off with "Oh well, I was mad at you, Mike, and I knew if I told Barry, he would tell you."

Hughes replied, "Mario, I've thought very hard about what you've said. In all conscience I cannot be party to this. As much as I love UPI, I cannot stay."

Vazquez sat stiffly in his chair, picked up a cigarette, flicked his gold lighter, and said, in English, "No, no, Mike. What is the problem?"

Vazquez had suddenly turned conciliatory. It would be most embarrassing if, after just six weeks, he had to replace Hughes as editor.

Switching to Spanish, Vazquez reminded Hughes that he had beaten usually fatal lymphoma and said, "Your love of UPI helped you fight your cancer. Of all the people I've met in America, you're the one I love the most."

Hughes was unmoved. "You're a very successful businessman who's used to having his own way," he said. "Today you forgive me, but the next time I cross you, in three months, or six months or one year, you'll get me. I don't believe our relationship will ever be the same."

Vazquez swore that, if Hughes agreed to stay, he would hold no grudges over this battle of wills. Vazquez summoned McCrohon. Once again, as he had been so many times before, the gaunt president was thrust into the role of peacemaker. Chain-smoking, he soothed Vazquez, finally asking:

"Mario, are we agreed that the [hit] list is withdrawn?"

Vazquez hesitated. "Yes," he replied at last.

The crisis seemed over. But while Hughes agreed to remain, he left the meeting feeling sullied. What was it that Vazquez really wanted? He doubted Vazquez really had thrown in the towel, and he was sure his own UPI days were numbered. Contemplating the matter at home that night, Hughes decided to offer Cohen, who did not figure in his long-range plans anyway, as a sacrificial lamb. Perhaps that would soothe and satisfy Vazquez.

Unipressers across the country still were rattled and angered by the rumors and the uncertainty. On Tuesday morning, as a joint meeting of UPI's newspaper and broadcast advisory boards began in Washington, union leaders delivered to Vazquez, at a time calculated to most embarrass him, a petition signed by hundreds of employees demanding details of the rumored purge. Accustomed to pliant employees in Mexico, Vazquez never could have anticipated such a stunning challenge to his authority. Trying to put the best face on the situation as influential clients sat watching, he shrugged off the petition, calling it an inconsequential matter.

At 4 p.m. Tuesday, Hughes summoned Cohen to his office and closed the door.

"Sorry, mate, I'm not going to make you one of the new executive editors. You can stay through the election, do some writing, have some fun while you're looking for something else. I won't insult you by offering you something below your stature. The one thing I want to do is make sure you walk out of here with honor and dignity."

Cohen walked out, angry and bewildered. He decided to keep his firing a secret. Perhaps there yet might be a way for him to save his job. Besides, this was no time to fuel further staff turmoil. Still, word of UPI's reorganization began to reach the press, stirring speculation in *The Washington Post, The New York Times*, and trade publications about Cohen's future and prospects of a major management shake-up. Vazquez's public avowals that there was no hit list did little to calm the speculation swirling inside the company and out. Vazquez had hoped his reorganization would breathe new life into UPI, but instead it was becoming a disaster. The impression grew that UPI had become a morass of internal turmoil and inept leadership.

Vazquez tried to quell the controversy by publicly attacking what seemed an easy target, Luis Nogales. He charged that UPI's revenue base was "$8 million less" than he had been led to believe, hinting that the departed chairman had inflated the figures to lure investors—and had stuck him with a loser.

In Los Angeles, Nogales fired back. He angrily told reporters that UPI had been required to file monthly financial statements with the bankruptcy court. "I had no incentive to lie and a lot of incentive to make sure the information was accurate," he said, suggesting that the real reason UPI was floundering was that Vazquez had failed to put a marketing plan in place.

In his public blasts at Nogales, Vazquez made no mention that on May 27th, two weeks before the sale closing, the accounting firm of

Deloitte Haskins & Sells had privately told him contract cancellations in the first quarter of 1986 would lower UPI's revenue projections from $82 million to $76 million. The report also said UPI was losing upwards of $1.5 million a month.

In the first three months after the sale, on Vazquez's orders, UPI managers also had conducted a more extensive internal audit and discovered that billings were still in astonishing disarray. They suggested that the company not even try to collect up to $20 million listed erroneously as client debts; accounting records showed that UPI had continued to bill a number of subscribers well after they had dropped the service. There also were murkier problems, such as whether to continue billing customers who had unilaterally abrogated their contracts on grounds the staff cuts had damaged UPI's news report.

One California client, the *San Mateo Times*, exhumed a 1937 contract clause stating that UPI could not unilaterally impose a rate increase. *Times* publisher J Hart Clinton declared the paper never had approved any of the increases over the last fifty years. Since the paper was canceling anyhow, UPI lawyers chose not to contest his claim. The paper's weekly rate immediately plunged almost tenfold to the 1937 level, $75 a week. It was costing UPI more than that to deliver its service.

* * *

Nogales and McCrohon, to persuade *New York Times* editor Abe Rosenthal to continue subscribing through 1986, had promised to beef up foreign coverage by adding a half dozen correspondents in Latin America, Africa, and the Persian Gulf, flashpoints for conflict.

Amazingly, Vazquez and his new team were dragging their feet on implementing the promised changes. The owner would pay dearly for his delay.

On October 27 the *Times*, whose syndicated news service in fact was a competitor of UPI, announced it would drop the wire service at year's end. James Greenfield, an assistant managing editor, said in a statement that the *Times* felt it could "better invest our resources in the continued improvement of our own news-gathering network."

Although the *Times* had canceled before, the release of a public statement made it clear that this time it was not merely a contract bargaining ploy. Unipressers worldwide were stunned and bitter that such a bellwether paper, whose credo "All The News That's Fit to Print" adorned its front page, would abandon the concept of competing wire services, deciding it could live without UPI's hundreds of stories and photos each day.

Media analysts suggested that publicity about the decision would cause a ripple effect that would reach to smaller, less profitable subscribers, damaging UPI far beyond the loss of $822,380 a year in revenue from the *Times* and perhaps threatening the company's very future. McCrohon was left with the distinct impression from *Times'* executives that the decision was a direct reflection of their lack of faith in UPI's new owner.

Vazquez didn't need an interpreter to tell him that any honeymoon was over. It had ended with a thud. Just five months after promising a new beginning, he and his company were in serious trouble with the American news industry and with UPI's own employees.

• • •

McCrohon was fed up. He felt that his credibility had been undermined when Vazquez failed to back up the promise to the *Times*. He also was tired of being frozen out of company decisions. On Monday, November 3, McCrohon told Vazquez he was quitting and that his artfully worded contract stipulated he could leave and still be paid in full if UPI's ownership changed. Vazquez protested McCrohon's money demand at first, then turned conciliatory. While not once expressing regret that his new president was departing, Vazquez said he was "not one to quibble over a few dollars." The irony could not have been lost on McCrohon that Vazquez would in the end pay more than $350,000 to be rid of him, yet had hopelessly delayed the addition of six new foreign correspondents to placate the *Times*.

In truth, Vazquez had dreamed of making a dramatic splash by replacing UPI's management and editorial team with a new set of big names. Without McCrohon's knowledge, Vazquez had weeks earlier assigned consultant Milt Benjamin, a former *Washington Post* foreign editor and assistant to chairman Kay Graham, to discreetly hunt for a new president. Now, with McCrohon leaving precipitously, things were spinning out of control. In a jam, Vazquez asked Benjamin to take over as president. Benjamin had during the sixties and early seventies worked as a UPI reporter in Boston and Washington. While at the *Post* he had helped polish Bob Woodward's and Scott Armstrong's book about the Supreme

Court, *The Brethren*. His ties to Mrs. Graham had helped give him entrée to the most prominent editors and publishers.

On Thursday, November 6, Vazquez released a long story heralding Benjamin's appointment and disclosing McCrohon's departure. The reaction from UPI employees was cool. Benjamin had not won any popularity contests, either at UPI or later at the *Post*, where he had gained a reputation as being stiff, awkward, and lacking in interpersonal skills. Many veteran Washington staffers recalled him failing on one of the biggest assignments of his UPI career. At the 1972 Republican Convention in Miami, he had been yanked from the plum job of writing UPI's main stories when, on the first day, he had sat paralyzed over his keyboard.

If Vazquez thought that the news of Benjamin's appointment would head off controversy, he was mistaken. A few minutes after the announcement, McCrohon's farewell message was sent on the internal wires. "I have never seen such dedication to an institution and an ideal," he wrote. "You're a bloody fine outfit."

It was followed by a message from Cohen. Confirming he had been fired, he wrote, "I am confident that, in UPI's continuing struggle for survival, you will bear the torch proudly and high, and never quit reaching for the dream always just beyond your fingertips."

Almost immediately UPI employees clogged the message wires with emotional farewells. Calls from reporters from *The Washington Post* and other news organizations lit up the UPI telephones.

Shortly afterward Vazquez stood in the Washington office and introduced Benjamin—UPI's sixth president in four years and third in four months. The government of Italy seemed more stable. Vazquez and Benjamin were surrounded by hostile staffers.

Later in the day Benjamin vigorously denied being behind the latest departures and said he had not even learned of Cohen's firing until a few days earlier. (Shortly before Cohen announced his departure, he was summoned for a meeting with Vazquez, who denied any role in his ouster and agreed to give him six months' salary as severance pay.)

The shake-up was not quite over.

As the gathering broke up, Vazquez assured Hughes, "Whatever that man Milton decides, you will always have a job in UPI."

Hughes, alarmed, responded with a frown. "What is that supposed to mean, Mario?"

Vazquez told Hughes he had given Benjamin total operating control, but that he would protect Hughes and veteran assistant managing editor Lou Carr. The message was clear enough to Hughes. He had risked friendships and alliances with Cohen and McCrohon to accommodate Vazquez. Now he would be the next to go.

• • •

Benjamin, a towering man at six feet eight inches, stepped confidently into the UPI presidency, ensconcing himself in Doug Ruhe's old corner office on the ninth floor. He had reason to feel secure. Exploiting Vazquez's predicament, he had extracted a handsome contract that included a $27,000-a-month fee to his consulting firm and the kind of sweeping powers Luis Nogales could never have gotten. Benjamin felt he had authority to assemble his own team, fashion a marketing strategy, and negotiate with subscribers. In addition, through his company, he controlled UPI's public relations apparatus.

Benjamin, accustomed to *The Washington Post*'s rarefied, moneyed atmosphere in which there were ample resources for specialized reporting, had his own vision. He felt that wire-service stories still lacked depth and perspective, lagging behind a trend in many newspapers toward explanatory and analytical journalism. Further, he believed that low wages and constant turmoil had driven away some of the company's best talent. Convinced UPI could be saved only by a complete face-lift, Benjamin envisioned focusing on coverage of "premium" stories, exclusives that could not be matched on the AP wire nor in the nation's top newspapers. It would cost money, but Benjamin presumed Vazquez would bankroll his plans.

However, Benjamin proved a tactless and somewhat haughty leader at a time when staff morale had sunk once again and many Unipressers were updating their résumés. He managed to offend the staff by remarking in a *Los Angeles Times* interview that UPI had no journalists from first-rate news organizations. Benjamin's comments, by inference, suggested that UPI itself was second-rate. That characterization was most unfair; despite its plight, the company had somehow managed to retain many journalists who could compete with the best in the business.

It was the second time in a month that beleaguered staffers felt publicly insulted by management. Defending himself against reports of an impending shake-up in an interview in *The Washington Post*, Vazquez had declared that he wished "UPI was as good at producing the news as it is at making up internal rumors."

Seeking a new way to vent their anger and frustration, many staffers protested Cohen's ouster by staging a byline strike, refusing for several days to allow their names to appear on their stories.

• • •

Editor Mike Hughes, fretting in limbo, returned from vacation in mid-November determined to clarify his status. He marched into Benjamin's office and confronted UPI's president. Hughes said later that Benjamin told him, "Mike, I think UPI needs a big-name editor."

Hughes, wondering just where Benjamin planned to find one at this stage, gritted his teeth. "Fine," he said. "In that case I probably will have to leave."

Benjamin gave a different version. In sworn testimony in a suit later filed by Hughes, he said he never told Hughes he planned to replace him and that Hughes simply informed him he was resigning.

Whatever precipitated Hughes' decision, Benjamin realized that his departure would leave UPI with its top four editorial jobs vacant. The next morning he asked Hughes to reconsider, to spare UPI the adverse publicity of yet another high-level departure. According to Hughes, Benjamin promised him a retroactive pay increase and $44,000 in back expenses and sales commissions. Hughes said that when he asked whether Vazquez had approved the offer, Benjamin replied, "You have to understand, Mike. I *am* Mario Vazquez-Raña. Whatever I say goes."

Hughes agreed to stay for the time being, but when Benjamin failed to put his promise in writing, the editor grew angry, remarking privately to friends, "I'm not going to be pushed around." On November 24, heads turned in the newsroom as Hughes abruptly switched off his office lights and, carrying a bag filled with personal effects, walked out on thirty years as a Unipresser.

Benjamin scrambled to recoup. Ten minutes after Hughes left he phoned Cohen at home.

"The craziness that has been going on since I joined this company won't stop," Benjamin said. "Mike Hughes resigned this afternoon."

Cohen, who already had been informed of Hughes's departure in breathless calls from ex-colleagues, feigned surprise.

"Would you consider coming back as managing editor?" Benjamin asked. "I didn't have anything to do with the decision to dismiss you. Now that Mike has left—it was his decision to let you go—I wish you'd consider coming back to your old job."

Cohen said he wasn't interested, but agreed to sleep on it.

The truth was, Benjamin was hardly in hot pursuit. He seemed more interested in seizing the moment for a public relations coup. The headline in *The Washington Post* the day after Hughes's departure read, "UPI Seeks Return of Fired Editor." Cleverly, Benjamin had neutralized some of the bad publicity surrounding Cohen's firing.

Benjamin could only hope, however, to try to minimize the damage. For if the departures of McCrohon, Hughes, and Cohen had been an orchestrated housecleaning, it had been botched, further tarnishing Vazquez's image. Publicity from the shake-up caused major subscribers to openly wonder whether anyone at all was managing the UPI news report. Within days Benjamin received a cancellation from *The Houston Post*, and other big papers would follow. The escalating negative media publicity seemed to be feeding upon itself. Soon *The Washington Post* and others reported that acting foreign editor Barry James, a close friend of Hughes, had handed Benjamin a letter during a meeting of the Washington staff charging that, despite Vazquez's denials, the owner himself had ordered Cohen's ouster.

It seemed that whenever things were gloomiest in UPI's newsrooms, a scandal or big story would come along and get the adrenaline flowing. Thrust into the job of acting managing editor to fill the editorial void, Billy Ferguson, a crusty but charming rogue who was UPI's Chicago-based broadcast chief, benefited from just such a fortuitous circumstance as he tried to lift sagging morale in the late fall of 1986.

The day after Hughes departed, President Reagan fired Oliver North and triggered the Iran-Contra scandal. Setting aside their concerns about the company's problems, UPI's staffers went back to work.

The squat, silver-haired Ferguson showered praise on his hustling crew like a coach at a pep rally, and privately told a colleague, "This scandal couldn't have come at a better time."

Looking in the mirror one day in mid-December, Benjamin found his "big name" editor. He would, he announced, serve as both president and editor in chief while continuing to search for outside talent. His announcement hardly soothed UPI clients and staff looking for some sign of stability.

• • •

UPI's latest upheavals could not have come at a worse time, for the company desperately needed to cope with monumental changes in the news business. More than 80 percent of newspapers now were controlled by giant chains, most of them public companies bent on wringing out every nickel of profit for shareholders. Often their top executives' compensation was linked to the company's bottom-line performance. In the stampede to maximize profits, it was becoming easier to abandon UPI and its endless problems.

Further, the demise of street sales and "extra" editions and vastly improved production technology had reduced the value of the wire services' most marketable commodity—speed. No longer were seconds and minutes precious to most papers; without daily competition they often could afford the luxury of picking the best story—not necessarily the first. In 1986 a twenty-minute UPI "beat" over the AP was much more important to Unipressers' egos than it was to clients. While UPI still could boast it had correspondents around the globe, other big news organizations also maintained bureaus and stringers in numerous foreign countries who could quickly file stories back to the home office via computer terminals. Improved air travel also helped major newspapers dispatch correspondents to remote sites to cover breaking stories that heretofore had been the sole domain of the wires.

Fighting to differentiate themselves from TV newscasts, newspapers had also moved inexorably away from speed to quality, depth, perspective. Free of the wires' burden to cover everything, the newspapers and supplemental services were devoting more time and resources to in-depth, perspective and investigative reporting. While the conservative AP also was sluggish to change, it had added tens of millions of dollars from defecting UPI clients and now was triple UPI's size. It had resources to cover stories far and wide and also to produce more exclusive copy and special packages than its rival. UPI editors and reporters found themselves, increasingly, in a no-win position. To satisfy the diversity of broadcast and newspaper clients, they faced the nigh impossible task of covering most every story of significance, including chasing the daily scoops of the major papers and supplementals. While it was hardly uncommon for UPI to outshine the AP on major stories, it was an increasing struggle to produce the kind of quality and exclusive copy that would make the smaller service indispensable. The steady departure of veteran UPI reporters weary of the continuing internal upheavals made the job that much tougher.

Although UPI was hemorrhaging clients by the score, Vazquez had given short shrift to the marketplace and the product. Nobody had been paying attention to the clients, and the clients didn't much like it. For years UPI had overcome many of its handicaps by cultivating and nurturing close personal relationships with its subscribers. Now, with the senior marketing executives gone, many clients were being forced to deal with total strangers—on the increasingly rare occasions when anybody from UPI visited at all.

In the weeks and months after the *New York Times'* announcement, UPI's depleted, leaderless sales force watched in horror. Cancellations cascaded in from Times-Mirror papers in Dallas, Denver, and Hartford; from the Newark *Star-Ledger* and seven other Newhouse papers; from the San Jose *Mercury-News*, CBS, *The Chicago Tribune, The New York Daily News, The Portland Oregonian, The Milwaukee Journal, The Chicago Sun-Times*, and most of the remaining Scripps papers. Threatening to join the tidal wave were *The Wall Street Journal* and *The St. Louis Post-Dispatch*.

Hoping to entice a change of heart, Vazquez had left UPI machines temporarily running in some newspapers that had canceled, such as the *The Tennessean*. Now, with every day's mail carrying stop orders, that option had become too expensive.

Even had Vazquez understood the complex challenges facing his new company, he might have been too preoccupied to address them. The first half-year of his stewardship had been squandered trying to extinguish the internal brushfires he had started and fanned with his obsession for cleansing the company of Luis Nogales and his top aides.

Losses were climbing toward $2 million a month, scores of subscribers were under cancellation, a number of influential publishers were openly contemptuous of the Mexican owner, and the executive suite seemed paralyzed to do anything about it.

Entering 1987, UPI once again was a shambles.

22

Reign of the Post Toasties

Milt Benjamin knew he needed something dramatic to reverse UPI's slide. Quietly, amid the editorial shake-up in the fall of 1986, he began to plumb his Washington contacts, offering fat salaries to bright media stars who might help return the wire service to glory.

On January 6, 1987, the word went out: Unipressers in Washington were invited to a cocktail party in an elegant private room at the International Club, where Benjamin and Vazquez would unveil the new editorial leadership. Morale was so low that only a couple dozen staffers showed up. Curious but subdued, sipping drinks and nibbling nuts courtesy of Vazquez, they met their new bosses. Benjamin had reached back to his recent past to hire three new managing editors whose talents he felt had been overlooked or underused by *The Washington Post* family: Ben Cason and Barry Sussman of the *Post*, and Kim Willenson, a former Unipresser who wrote for *Newsweek*, which was owned by the *Post*. Benjamin also promoted Bill Ferguson to managing editor and said one of the four would "emerge over time as first among equals and become the editor of UPI for the 1990s."

Surrounding Vazquez in a large half-circle, even the most battle-weary Unipressers politely applauded and permitted themselves a glimmer of hope. For the first time in months the news seemed positive. Could it

371

be the company's editorial chaos at last had ended? Would Vazquez leave these new editors alone and let them do their jobs?

Had they been privy to the behind-the-scenes maneuvering, staffers might have contained their enthusiasm. Benjamin had not fully consulted Vazquez before negotiating contracts for the three newcomers, assuring them of the owner's commitment to rebuilding UPI as a worldwide news agency.

Vazquez smiled for the benefit of the staff, but underneath he was absolutely furious. Cason, Sussman, and Willenson, represented by the famous Washington law firm Clifford and Warnke, had commanded contracts that would cost Vazquez almost $2 million over five years. Having watched the company's door revolving, the newcomers extracted assurances they would be taken care of should they—or UPI—become historical footnotes.

Quickly dubbed the "Post Toasties" by irreverent staffers, the three were risking successful careers to join UPI.

Cason, forty-four, a steady, amiable, shambling man, seemed as likely a candidate as anyone to hold his own with the mercurial Vazquez. As an assistant managing editor at the *Post*, Cason had been highly popular. While extremely capable, for a decade he had been passed over when top-level jobs came open.

Sussman, fifty-two, had directed Bob Woodward and Carl Bernstein's Pulitzer Prize-winning coverage of Watergate. A 21-year *Post* veteran, Sussman was an expert on public polling techniques and was considered a talented editor, if at times prickly and aloof.

Willenson, forty-nine, also intelligent but volatile and tempestuous, was more of a gamble. Despite a lack of management experience, he would head UPI's vital foreign operation.

Sitting across the table from his friends, with no company lawyer present, Benjamin had been more than generous. He gave Cason, Sussman, and Willenson sweeping control over editorial operations and shielded them from interference by Vazquez. The contracts, secured by irrevocable bank letters of credit, included lucrative "golden parachutes."

When Vazquez returned from a trip to Europe, Benjamin presented him with the signed contracts. The owner felt cornered and betrayed. If he did not consent to the terms by adding his signature to Benjamin's, Vazquez risked touching off a legal wrangle and stirring up yet another round of controversy in the media. After all, the new editors already were on board. Benjamin had all the leverage.

Nevertheless, for several weeks Vazquez stubbornly refused to sign. The editors grew edgy and angry. Vazquez had given Cason personal assurances UPI would be transformed into a news operation second to none. Would he dare renege before they even got started?

At last they delivered an ultimatum: without Vazquez's signature on the contracts by February 17, 1987, they would walk. Hemming and hawing, Vazquez finally capitulated, convinced that Benjamin and his crew were holding a gun to his temple. He would not soon forgive this raid on his treasure.

· · ·

The walls were closing in on Benjamin as he hopscotched the country in the dead of winter, trying to patch relations with disenchanted subscribers.

On the one hand he was trumpeting Vazquez's lavish promises to return UPI to glory. On the other he realized the billionaire owner not only was angry at him, but was beginning to nervously retrench in the face of deepening losses.

So many clients had defected that UPI was in danger of being shut off the front pages of America's major newspapers, which would further damage its prestige and drive away top staffers. Benjamin knew he could not let that happen. He was desperate. If he had to drastically cut rates, he would.

With UPI in deep trouble at *The Chicago Tribune* and the *Sun-Times*, Benjamin flew to the Windy City to try to retain the two powerhouse papers. Facing certain cancellation by the Trib, Benjamin met with editor Jim Squires and agreed to slash the weekly rate from $16,000 to $6,250 for the 14 months left on the contract—a nice $600,000 present. Then, hat in hand and worried the news of his largesse might already have crossed Michigan Avenue, Benjamin hurried to visit Bob Page, publisher of the rival *Sun-Times*. Page, UPI's general manager under Rod Beaton in the 1970s, headed an investor group that had purchased the *Sun-Times* from Rupert Murdoch.

Despite his old UPI ties, Page said there was no way that he could continue to fork over $14,000 a week. "Well, how much would you pay?" Benjamin asked.

Page suggested—and Benjamin granted—a one-year extension at $1,000 a week. Charles Hollingsworth, recruited from *The Washington Post* to be marketing chief, endorsed what amounted to a $670,000 gift, concluding UPI might win goodwill by aiding the financially struggling

Sun-Times. So old Unipresser Page would be getting round-the-clock, round-the-world coverage from UPI for about what he would pay a single top reporter. After a time Page stopped paying altogether, but the service was not yanked.

Benjamin and Hollingsworth were not through with their fire sale. At reduced rates, *The Detroit Free-Press* renewed for five years, *The Atlanta Constitution* added pictures, *The Houston Post* added a year to its contract, *The Philadelphia Inquirer* two years, *The Seattle Post-Intelligencer* extended its contract and *The Portland Oregonian* restored some service after a brief hiatus.

Benjamin's best efforts could not lift a cancellation at *The St. Louis Post-Dispatch*, and his bid to save a nearly $1 million-a-year contract with the financially ailing New York *Daily News* collapsed. Publisher Jim Hoge, a former chairman of the UPI newspaper advisory board, not only was strapped for cash but also was so angered by Vazquez's ouster of longtime executives he refused to take even a cut-rate contract. UPI found itself shut out of Manhattan, once its most glamorous and lucrative newspaper market.

Benjamin was absolutely determined not to lose his old paper, *The Washington Post*, especially after *The New York Times'* defection. So when executive editor Ben Bradlee threatened to cancel, Benjamin secretly tacked an extra year on the *Post* contract—free.

The *Post*, rolling in dough, had concluded that UPI's news report was not worth paying for. Milt Benjamin was reduced to giving it away.

• • •

Vazquez was always quick to blame others, particularly his American managers of whom he seemed innately, perhaps inexcusably, suspicious. Now, when he learned how far Benjamin's save-a-client drive had gone, he was furious. Accustomed to running things with an iron hand, Vazquez had only reluctantly granted Benjamin sweeping authority, hoping to heal the scars of his wholesale housecleaning. He felt the American had overstepped that authority and abused his trust. This was a business, not a charity; it was his money and he would control it.

UPI's latest top-level power struggle had developed into a classic clash of philosophies. Benjamin was convinced that for UPI to reverse three decades of decline it needed to shed its loser's image. That meant breaking major exclusive stories, and that meant spending money. Vazquez would just have to resign himself to absorbing substantial losses for awhile. Benjamin's new editorial team, persuading him UPI must build on its tradition as a full-service news agency, already had begun recruiting some reporters at salaries upwards of $50,000—not uncommon elsewhere but virtually unheard of at UPI. Vazquez's vision was totally different —he wanted rookies hired at less than $20,000 a year and costs cut to the bone, hardly a strategy for quickly building a powerhouse news agent. While Vazquez had reopened a few bureaus and kept his pledge that no union members would be laid off his first year, it became apparent he did not intend to pour his fortune down a sinkhole. Striking back at Benjamin, he put longtime aide Guillermo Chao-Ebergenyi in strict charge of all expenditures and talked of making him chief financial officer. Annoyed, Benjamin retorted by sarcastically telling Vazquez that his young daughter would make a better CFO than Chao.

Vazquez and Benjamin also argued over the union contract expiring in April. Benjamin urged healthy wage and fringe benefit increases to retain top staffers and make UPI a more attractive place to work; Vazquez wanted a hard line in negotiations. Watching Vazquez's eyes smolder, Benjamin, no stranger to corporate infighting, heard the ice cracking under his feet.

Like other top executives who had dared challenge the boss, Benjamin realized his predicament was hopeless. If he stayed he would, like Max McCrohon, be relegated to figurehead status. And if the wire service should fail, his reputation inevitably would be tarnished. Benjamin decided to resign and return to his consulting firm.

On March 16 he announced he was relinquishing the editor's job to Ben Cason. On April Fool's Day, his hand-picked team seemingly entrenched, Benjamin quit as president, boasting to staffers that he had led the company out of its "dark days." Because UPI was losing a great deal of money, he said, Vazquez "wanted to play a more direct role" as chairman and president.

Despite their cataclysmic differences, Benjamin refrained from publicly criticizing his boss. He had no choice. With a nondisclosure clause in his reported $250,000 settlement, the owner had purchased his silence.[1]

---

[1] Benjamin declined to be interviewed.

Another top-level head had rolled. The casualty list was lengthening impressively.

• • •

Lost in the latest upheaval was Vazquez's pledge to Bankruptcy Judge George Bason a year earlier that UPI would be run by an American. While his decision to assume total control broke that promise, it at last stopped the revolving door of UPI presidents. However, distracted by his Mexican businesses and the heavy travel attending his Olympic responsibilities, Vazquez could not devote full time to UPI. Further, if he spent more than half the year in the United States the IRS would tax him far more heavily, at the same rate as citizens.

With the first anniversary of his stewardship approaching, UPI's dreams of renewed glory had faded. The $2 million monthly losses were the worst in its history, surpassing the dreariest days of Scripps Howard and of Ruhe and Geissler.

Struggling to make the transition to wire-service journalism, the three new editors had watched UPI's sausage-grinder swallow Benjamin, their benefactor. How long could they survive against Vazquez without Benjamin as a buffer?

Cason, studious, unemotional, spent long hours secluded in his office poring over UPI's operations. He had concluded UPI must undertake a steady, long-term rebuilding program that promised to be enormously expensive. He and his colleagues chose to test Vazquez's commitment to his pledges, knowing full well that if they obligated him for further cash it likely would provoke him.

Vazquez still simmered over the the new editors' princely contracts. Now, he thought, they wanted to spend and spend while he continued to lose and lose. Vazquez wasted no time trying to wriggle free of their contractual guarantees of independent control over the news operation. Over vehement objections from Cason, Vazquez reinstituted UPI's "screening committee" to approve hiring and transfers. In early summer, the editors complained to their lawyers that Vazquez was blocking the hiring of two dozen new staffers and trying to veto Willenson's selection of new correspondents for Latin America.

UPI's editorial chiefs also were distressed by Vazquez's antics as chairman of the Pan Am Games in Indianapolis, a role in which he found it all too tempting to try to use UPI for his own purposes. A week before the games, the State Department refused a visa to Daniel Zuniga, a skeet shooter who had been a colonel in the Chilean intelligence service. Vazquez, whose allies in the World Olympic Community included some right-wing Latin leaders, promptly aligned himself with Chile and became the focus of critical stories in the media. He was irate when UPI ran a story quoting State Department officials that Zuniga was an executioner who had beaten demonstrators with rubber truncheons. As the controversy intensified, Vazquez summoned sports editor David Tucker to his hotel suite, wagged his finger and said, "I have a lot to say, and I want every word to go out on the wire."

"Well, there's no way we can do that for you."

"This is more important than you," Vazquez warned Tucker. "This is me, and this is UPI."

Refusing to be steamrollered, Tucker also brushed off a plea from Van Bennekom that UPI help extricate Vazquez from the hole he had dug himself.

It wasn't the only time Vazquez tried to interfere, although there was little evidence the owner ever succeeded in overtly manipulating the news. Usually he just wound up grumbling angrily that the American editors had refused to obey his orders. Nor was there any evidence that, as some had feared, Vazquez had a grand plan for slanting UPI's news report. Rather, most of his clashes with Cason and company centered around money; Vazquez had failed to allot an editorial budget, and the editors were subject to his whim on all but the smallest expenditures.

Cason, Sussman, and Willenson now were convinced that Vazquez never would honor his repeated public promises to make UPI the world's premier news agency. One signal, they felt, came when Vazquez opened union contract negotiations by offering paltry raises and demanding more freedom to slash staff. As the talks dragged past the contract expiration date, union members were loath to exercise their only real muscle, a strike. Vazquez might simply shut down the company and blame its failure on the employees. It was bitter irony that eighteen months after the union had cast its lot with Vazquez as the most simpatico bidder, it now was battling for its very existence.

One reason for Vazquez's seeming penury was that he felt he was spending enough on new equipment. He had committed to upgrading antiquated technology to improve UPI's performance and cut communications costs. Besides buying hundreds of new computer terminals, he announced the purchase of a new $5 million computer and the development of a dazzling, digital photo darkroom and transmission system to beam quality color pictures via satellite from any spot in the world directly to subscriber photo receivers.

The new photo system, dubbed "PYXYS," was being manufactured exclusively for UPI. Company executives hoped the system, designed from medical technology by former IBM computer whiz Tom Sudman, would prove UPI's pot of gold. In an expensive eight-page color insert in the February 21, 1987, issue of *Editor & Publisher*, UPI ballyhooed PYXYS as "the most revolutionary technology ever developed for the news media."

Concealed in the hoopla, Vazquez was secretly talking with Sudman about a deal that would secure for them the potential bonanza by placing PYXYS under ownership of a separate new company, MarTom, short for Mario and Tom. Indeed, Vazquez already had formed a new "UPI"—United Press Intercontinental, a firm chartered in the Netherlands Antilles as an offshore haven beyond the reach of creditors in the event of another bankruptcy.

Vazquez's planned smokescreen proved a waste of time. PYXYS was an abject failure. It was unveiled prematurely, before technical experts had found a way to make its innovative technology interract with UPI's outmoded communications network. When Sudman pushed for a costly switchover to a total satellite network for all UPI products, he ran into factional infighting, encountering particularly fierce resistance from communications vice president Joe Domek, whose empire would be threatened by such a change. The whole affair was a public relations disaster, first raising, then dashing, subscriber expectations. Vazquez and Sudman soon were locked in bitter dispute, both winding up financial losers. Sudman also was dismayed when his dream of computerizing UPI's photo library to make it a big money-earner was dashed. Doug Ruhe and Bill Geissler had precluded such a venture three years earlier by dealing away UPI's library rights to the Bettmann Archives.

The owner grew increasingly fretful as losses mounted and his dream unraveled. After the PYXYS fiasco, Vazquez also scuttled UPI's computer purchase, ostensibly because of a disagreement over software.

In the eighth-floor newsroom, Cason, Sussman, and Willenson continued to try to run the news report as they believed was their mandate, their obligation.

UPI editorial staffers, many of them unaware of the coming troubles, regained some enthusiasm and tried to make the news report look better than it really was. Coverage of the Iran-Contra hearings in the summer of 1987 even brought a laudatory telegram from the usually critical *Chicago Tribune*.

Still, UPI was unable to reverse the wave of cancellations. By early summer, the company dared not disclose that the number of daily newspaper subscribers had plunged below 400—less than half the client base Scripps had turned over to Ruhe and Geissler five years earlier. Vazquez, out of the country frequently and engrossed in helping plan the 1988 Olympics, reacted by yanking even more tightly on the pursestrings.

Tensions mounted. The three UPI editors felt they had contractual authority to rebuild the news agency, almost regardless of cost. Vazquez didn't want them spending anything unless he approved—and only rarely did he approve. He was losing interest in UPI almost as fast as he was losing money. The wire service he had hotly pursued two years earlier had been nothing but a headache. Now it was becoming a humiliation.

In July, determined to cut losses, Vazquez slowed the cash spigot to a trickle. Bills began mounting, conjuring an eerie sense of déjà vu. Just as they had in 1984 and 1985, UPI's accounting team delayed payments to vendors and to hundreds, if not thousands, of stringers who supplied pictures, stories, and news tips. Many suppliers were paid only when they threatened to cut services. Once again, the computer in UPI's accounting department automatically spewed out checks that gathered dust in desk drawers.

Friends tipped Cason, Sussman, and Willenson that Vazquez was asking other media groups to invest in UPI—or even to take the wire service off his hands. Vazquez was obsessed by its deterioration, railing about how Nogales had suckered him by misrepresenting UPI's financial health. He invited Reuters' vice president Peter Holland to Mexico and hinted he would like to sell. Holland expressed little interest.

In early autumn Dominic Laiti, chairman of the Washington-based high-tech Hadron, Inc., slipped into UPI's Dallas office to investigate the computer network. Laiti was a stalking horse for a potential new owner—none other than Dr. Earl Brian, the man Vazquez had beaten in the bidding for UPI.

While he searched for a buyer, Vazquez steamed about Cason, Sussman, and Willenson, but made no attempt to fire them. It would cost almost a million dollars to buy out their contracts and would bring fresh negative publicity. By fall, though, his every move seemed calculated to shove them toward resigning.

The three, convinced Vazquez was breaching their contracts, began to force a confrontation by flouting his edicts on spending and staffing decisions. Willenson was the most aggressive, deliberately ordering foreign division transfers without Chao's approval. Chao reported to an angry Vazquez that between April and October UPI had spent $250,000 on international staff transfers.

Willenson might have been the wrong person to lead an insurrection. His quirky, abrasive, arrogant nature had alienated some of UPI's best correspondents. Even before rejoining the company he had gotten in hot water with Unipressers for telling a *Washington Post* interviewer that traditional wire-service writing style was "what you call brain-dead" and blasted the standard of "absolute neutrality . . . straight factoid reporting" that had been the stock in trade of UPI and AP for decades. Having unwittingly stirred an uproar, Willenson was forced to sheepishly apologize.

Typical of Willenson's handling of his foreign staff was an incident during one of his visits to England. Willenson ordered veteran London-based reporter Bob MacKay to fly to Baghdad to update the Iran–Iraq war. When MacKay protested that he did not have a visa, Willenson, himself a former foreign correspondent, airly brushed it off.

"Don't worry about that, I'll fix things. You don't need a visa."

As MacKay had feared, when he arrived in Baghdad, Iraqi officials would not let him stay. MacKay, whose soft-spoken manner masked a fiery temper, exploded when forced to spend sixteen hours waiting for a return flight to London. Time, energy, and money had been squandered on Willenson's wild-goose chase.

As the editors battled with Vazquez's surrogates, Unipressers began to feel the three men were so preoccupied with protecting their lucrative contracts that they were neglecting the news report. Washington staffers watched in frustration through the window in Cason's office as they spent hours phoning their lawyers and plotting strategies.

So disenchanted was Cason that he frequently remarked to colleagues, "Mario Vazquez-Raña is *not* the one to save UPI," and even spoke out at UPI's Broadcast Advisory Board meeting late in September. Addressing important clients, Cason delivered a shocking portrait of a debt-riddled company floundering because its owner refused to let his managers manage.

"And I, for one," Cason declared as Vazquez glowered, "am not happy about it."

On September 29, Vazquez, forced by IRS residency requirements to operate almost exclusively from outside the United States for the rest of the year, made things even more unbearable for Cason and company. He ordered them to deliver a plan by November 15 aimed at saving $12 million by laying off 300 employees, including 250 of the 850-person editorial staff.

Cason was stunned. Such cutbacks would stagger a company already fighting a losing battle to keep a decent news report flowing around the clock. The editors' protests were met with stony silence from Mexico City. On October 6 managers were told Vazquez had taken complete control of all editorial functions, including coverage of the Olympics and the national political conventions, and managers who ignored the directive would be fired. Pieter Van Bennekom then announced guild-protected sports writers would be left off the Olympic coverage team because UPI could not afford to pay overtime. When sports editor David Tucker and other managers threatened to stay home, Vazquez and Van Bennekom backed down.

After consulting their lawyers, Cason, Sussman, and Willenson protested the new editorial restrictions in a letter to Vazquez and executive vice president Claude Hippeau:

> "Please be advised that the attached memorandum is in violation of our work agreements, it will prevent us from discharging our duties and will result in immediate crippling of UPI's editorial integrity and quality."

The editors began confiding to colleagues that their departures seemed inevitable. In mid-October, a *Boston Globe* story described their clashes with the owner, disclosures that only fed the tension in UPI newsrooms. On October 26, armed with their lawyers' assurances that even if they quit they could continue to draw on their letters of credit because of a breach of contract, the three secretly sent Vazquez a letter of resignation.

Fed up with the whole situation, middle-level managers dispatched a delegation to Washington to try to mediate a cease-fire. In the event of yet another editorial purge, how could Vazquez find replacements? Who would abandon secure jobs to join such a reeling company?

Unaware the three top editors had already resigned and that their peacemaking efforts were too late, Tucker, national editor Lucien Carr, and division editors Jim Wieck and Jacques Clafin delivered to Hippeau a warning that UPI's survival as "a viable news service or as a saleable property" was in as grave danger as it had been under Doug Ruhe and Bill Geissler.

"Ruhe and Geissler are going down in journalistic history as the guys who almost killed UPI off," their letter read. "It would be a tragedy of mind-boggling proportions if Mario Vazquez-Raña were ever to become known as the man who finished off the job."

They pleaded that Vazquez make peace with his editors, arguing, "their departure would have a tragic impact on this company by triggering major cancellations and by eliminating any chance the company has to recapture clients it has lost."

To ensure the message got through, they Faxed a Spanish version to Mexico City. They got little solace from Vazquez's written response:

"My spirits have not flagged. I am willing to continue waging the good fight, but I hope that all of you understand that I cannot allow myself to be pressured on less critical issues. I must take the financial helm of the company firmly to keep us from straying onto paths that would lead us to a sure disaster."

In truth, the owner wished to be rid of Cason and company about as badly as he wanted out of UPI.

With no solution in sight to yet another owner-management war, it seemed improbable that UPI could dig itself out of its hole. The accumulation of years of internal crisis and management failure had atrophied its storied resilience.

On November 1, with Vazquez frantically trying to cut his losses and extricate himself from the company, an "impasse" was formally declared in the union negotiations. The tactic meant the owner would be free to void the contract and impose labor concessions. A sense of impending doom descended upon Unipressers.

On Tuesday, November 3, still not having heard from the owner 2,500 miles away, the three top editors went public, announcing they would resign on November 20. They also disclosed that Vazquez was contemplating massive staff layoffs. Later they would say they had hoped a public outcry over their departures would force Vazquez to call off his plans to cut the staff.

Cason, Sussman, and Willenson distributed copies of their resignation letter in which they declared they could "no longer assure the quality and integrity of the UPI report." That parting shot, which was in the lead paragraph in newspaper stories about their decision, enraged many Unipressers. Perhaps they had chosen the harsh language because they felt compelled to explain why they had so suddenly left. Perhaps they wanted to stake out legal ground for collecting on their contracts. But questioning UPI's quality and, even worse, its integrity, was a low blow. Other high-ranking editors who had left after clashing with Vazquez had refrained from delivering incendiary valedictories. The salvo had an immediate effect—*The Chicago Tribune* pulled the plug on its UPI machine.

The bloodletting embittered everyone. Unipressers were angry over the public rending of their company. The middle-level managers who had tried to work out a compromise wondered whether the departing editors had used them to win public sympathy as aggrieved parties victimized by a capricious owner.

The three departing editors were bitter, too. As the day of their departure drew near, Sussman, sourly sitting in his office, told one veteran Unipresser: "You've been here longer than I have, and I'm sure you have many good memories about UPI. I, for one, hope I forget every minute of it." Their anguish, however, was at least partly assuaged by the knowledge they would each be drawing $10,500 every month on their letters of credit from Vazquez. The three had not lasted a year, but by citing breach of contract Cason and Sussman each claimed $345,000, Willenson $316,000.

Vazquez indignantly ordered UPI lawyers to prepare a suit charging the three had themselves breached their contracts by defaming and wounding the company with their allegations about its loss of editorial integrity. His filing it two months later would trigger a countersuit by the editors saying they had been fraudulently lured to the company by Vazquez's false promises to "rebuild UPI as a major worldwide news service."

UPI's employees could only shake their heads sadly over the latest management paroxysm.

• • •

On Friday, November 13, a few days after the departure of Cason, Sussman, and Willenson, The Downhold Club, the loose confederation of hundreds of former Unipressers, held an infrequent get-together.

More than 300 departed Unipressers and a few active employees converged from across the country on the Fifth Avenue Hotel in Greenwich Village to renew acquaintances and swap war stories.

Tugged by nostalgia, employees showed up who had departed years—even decades—earlier. They were richer and better dressed, they led lives far more stable but far less exciting. Never, most agreed, had a job been more fun than at UPI.

They had followed the company's recent depressing developments, so most were quick to recognize the tall, dark man who entered the ballroom.

It was Luis Nogales, one of the newest Downholders.

From Los Angeles, Nogales had watched the continued deterioration of the company he grudgingly had relinquished to Vazquez seventeen months earlier.

Outwardly, he had survived his departure well. Besides his handsome settlement from Vazquez, he had negotiated a lucrative, long-term contract to be president of Univision, the Spanish-language television network. Nogales also had hired departed UPI managers Jack Kenney, Bill Adler, and Sylvana Foa. Ironically, his new company was owned by Emilio Azcarraga, Mexico's television king and Vazquez's biggest media rival.

But Nogales had left a big chunk of his heart and soul at UPI, and when he learned of the Downhold party he had contrived a reason to be in Manhattan. He was fiercely proud of his efforts to keep the company alive. Although his tenure had been relatively brief, he felt he could match commitment and passion with anyone.

To all but a handful of Downholders, however, Nogales remained an outsider, an enigma. Many had left UPI long before he arrived, and unlike him, owed their allegiances to the editorial side. Cautious as a result of decades of bad or indifferent leadership, few Unipressers trusted or empathized with top management.

As he circulated, Nogales realized that, for all his brave efforts to save their beloved company, the partygoers probably always would consider him an interloper. That did little to brighten his mood, made even bleaker by the knowledge that the absence of Vazquez, who had declined an invitation, would rob him of a chance to confront his nemesis.

Suddenly he spotted Pieter Van Bennekom. Nogales needed to vent anger and frustration at Vazquez, a man he never would forgive for bumbling the company.

He strode over quickly, and, in even, controlled tones, confronted his former aide, now Vazquez's alter ego.

"What's going on Pieter?" he demanded. "Why isn't Vazquez here? Is there a reason other than that he doesn't want to get beaten up on?"

Startled, wondering why Nogales would sour a festive occasion with such a confrontation, Van Bennekom tried cheerful small talk. It failed. Nogales seemed bent on proving, by prosecutorial questions, that he was the equal of any reporter in the room.

"What's happening at UPI?" he asked insistently. "What is Vazquez doing with the company? Is there a plan? If there is, why hasn't it been implemented? Why isn't anything going right?"

Embarrassed, defensive about having to explain unpopular decisions by an absentee owner trying secretly to unload the company, Van Bennekom replied:

"I wish I could tell you what his plans are and what is happening, but I can't. I just can't. I can't tell you how difficult this is for me. But I cannot divulge the company confidences."

Van Bennekom tried to retreat gracefully, but each time he stepped backward Nogales moved forward, nose to nose, firing questions.

Finally Van Bennekom managed to slip away. Nogales wore a satisfied smirk, but to the handful of Unipressers who heard and understood the drama being played out in the midst of the throng, he seemed haunted by unexorcised demons. Indeed, his three years at UPI had exacted a heavy toll. He had gambled his professional future in a crapshoot mutiny against Doug Ruhe and Bill Geissler, the men who had hired him. People he had trusted and championed had, he felt, betrayed him. Others, distrusting his motives and driven by selfish concerns, had refused to cooperate for what he felt was the greater good.

He had risked huge personal liabilities to preserve the institution he had grown to love, often feeling alone and abandoned in his quixotic quest.

Nogales believed his efforts and his sacrifices had delivered to Vazquez a company ripe for a turnaround. Instead, UPI now was far worse off than when he had departed. In less than eighteen months Vazquez had dispatched three presidents, four editors in chief, and three managing editors.

Mingling at the party, Luis Nogales could not conceal his bitterness and emptiness. But, this time, he was helpless to prevent the inexorable deterioration of United Press International.

23

. . .

Merely a Shadow

Pieter Van Bennekom, a cagey eighteen-year UPI veteran, seemed equipped with a built-in survival mechanism that allowed him to devine the direction of company winds without having to moisten a forefinger. Perhaps it was this instinct that had prompted him, as Latin American vice president, to align himself with Vazquez during the 1985 sale process. Van Bennekom, gangly and mustachioed, served as Vazquez's pipeline to the company and soon became the Mexican's frequent traveling companion, translating his words and lighting his cigarettes.

Many Unipressers felt little affection for Van Bennekom, viewing him as distastefully opportunistic. His expensive white linen plantation suits had inspired wags in the Washington newsroom to dub him the "Good Humor Man." Yet Van Bennekom's influence had continued to grow. Vazquez trusted him as far more than just a translator: he and Guillermo Chao were the owner's eyes and ears at UPI.

In that role, Van Bennekom was perhaps best positioned to watch Vazquez grow angry, frustrated, and embarrassed as losses mounted in the fall of 1987. The proud owner seemed to sense the outside world was laughing at him, either for making a foolish investment or for badly botching the salvage job he had undertaken with great fanfare. As clients fled and losses mounted, Vazquez became even more convinced that the wire service's problems confounded solution. Although the owner continued to boast of his unflagging commitment to UPI, Van Bennekom knew the truth: Vazquez, his stewardship a disaster, was fast losing heart and casting around for someone upon whom he could dump this turkey.

Van Bennekom, who excelled at chess always was thinking several moves ahead. He knew he had to do something quickly—for the sake of UPI and to safeguard his own paycheck (only recently Vazquez had increased his salary to $65 thousand). Through the long, steamy Washington summer of 1987 and deep into fall, even during Vazquez's power struggle with UPI's top editors, Van Bennekom worked secretly to help the Mexican find someone willing to gamble on a company now taking a $25-million-a-year bath. Van Bennekom knew he also would have to dissuade Vazquez from simply selling off UPI's few remaining attractive parts. The wire service's hope lay in Vazquez surrendering control to someone credible, preferably someone who spoke English and understood the American news business. Van Bennekom faced a far worse predicament than had Scripps nearly six years earlier. Who would possibly be willing to pay for UPI now? Yet he also knew Vazquez, after plunging more than $50 million into UPI in a year and a half, would not joyfully greet suggestions that he simply give it away. Van Bennekom must persuade both Vazquez and a potential buyer that he was an honest broker with nothing but their best interests in mind.[1] It would be a delicate balancing act.

First, however, the company had to be stabilized after adverse publicity surrounding the resignations of Cason, Sussman, and Willenson. Although unaware that Vazquez was trying to bail out of UPI, staffers were so disheartened by late fall that many felt the future might be measured in months, weeks, or even days. Vazquez, who had repeatedly proclaimed he would assemble the finest journalists to run UPI, knew most of his options for recruiting a new team of editors had been foreclosed by publicity surrounding the ceaseless upheavals. So he reached into UPI's ranks and tapped graybeard Unipressers for the three top jobs. Award-winning science editor Al Rossiter was appointed executive editor, although he had scant managerial experience. Veterans Bill Ferguson and Leon Daniel were named managing editor and foreign editor.

Rossiter immediately fired a salvo in the direction of his predecessors

---

[1] Van Bennekom declined to be interviewed.

by declaring, "UPI has always stood for integrity and independence. As long as I am editor, it always will." If Rossiter hoped his words would calm anxious clients, he was wrong. Vazquez's first assignment to the new editorial team called for the firing of 110 junior staffers—the kind of massive staff cutback the recently departed editors had resisted. Rossiter's team carried out the firings in phases over several weeks in hopes of blunting negative publicity. UPI's operation in North Dakota was shut down entirely, and Montana would soon follow. Single-person bureaus were closed in other states, such as Florida, Maine, Nevada, Kansas, Illinois, and Kentucky, where UPI operated in more than one city. As word of the cuts trickled out to the media, Rossiter and his colleagues futilely offered clients the hoary assurances that UPI's news report would not suffer.

There seemed no way to keep a lid on the negative stories about UPI. On November 24, 1987, Joe Russo, his wife Sally, and two of their companies filed for Chapter 11 bankruptcy protection. They were victims of the Texas oil and real estate slump. Brought aboard to mollify U.S. publishers, Russo, despite his small share in the deal, had posted nearly $2 million to secure half his intended 10 percent interest. Russo had quickly begun to regret his investment, finding himself left to play a spear-carrier role as glad-handing good ol' boy. It had been little more than a charade to suggest that there really was American involvement in UPI's ownership. With Russo in financial ruins—he was soon to lose his entire $100 million real estate empire—Vazquez publicly expressed sympathy. Although he took pains to disassociate himself and UPI from Russo's unrelated financial problems, the development only added to the black cloud that seemed fated to envelop the wire service.

• • •

Far removed from the turmoil and controversy, Bill Geissler was living quietly with his wife, Diti, in a lovely, restored Civil War-era home in rural Murfreesboro, Tennessee. Geissler and Doug Ruhe had finally dissolved their long partnership, which had been further marred by bankruptcies in their television ventures. The strain of their UPI failures and financial setbacks at last had proved too much for their alliance. Their relationship had degenerated into angry disagreement and threats of litigation in 1987 over dividing the remaining business interests.

Once on his own, Geissler had set up a consulting business. Despite his unceremonious ouster, he never had lost interest in UPI. Perhaps he was haunted by his crumbled dreams, by the failures he just now could begin acknowledging. In a 1988 interview Geissler conceded openly, "The weight of the evidence is that Ruhe and Geissler were incompetent. They didn't have the ability, the grasp, the intelligence, the skill, the forcefulness to weld it (UPI) together and push it to health."

Perhaps seeking absolution, Geissler regularly worked the phones, tracking the company's trials and tribulations. He particularly stayed in close touch with Van Bennekom. The two had been pals since their UPI days when they had traveled to Cuba to interview Fidel Castro. During their telephone chats, Geissler learned in early fall of Van Bennekom's predicament: Vazquez was driving UPI to its grave; the owner had to be excised before it was too late. Yet, if Van Bennekom shoved too hard he risked being perceived a traitor.

In an irony that absolutely would have floored unsuspecting Uni-pressers, Geissler, according to sources, began playing a key, behind-the-scenes role in helping Van Bennekom grease the skids for Vazquez's departure. Their talks apparently centered on the possibility of rekindling the interest of Earl Brian's FNN group, which Geissler and Ruhe had supported during the bitter court fight settled 18 months earlier. There was no love lost between Vazquez and Brian, but business was business; FNN seemed a likely suitor. Geissler, who had become friendly with Jim Arnold, FNN's general counsel, made a few calls. Things soon were cooking.

Friend and foe alike knew the very thought of surrender and defeat stuck in Brian's craw. He had hated losing out on UPI and had smugly watched the wire service's health worsen, underscoring his conviction Vazquez never could make a go of it. Sensing the Mexican's resolve was faltering, Brian deduced that he might wind up getting the company for nothing. He met with Van Bennekom and made his offer. Not surprisingly, it much resembled Ruhe's and Geissler's deal with Scripps; Brian wanted all UPI's debts brought current, a demand that would cost Vazquez far more than $7 million. When Vazquez heard about the terms he was incensed; never would he allow himself to be browbeaten like this.

Brian may not have been Vazquez's only choice. UPI executives said afterwards that by late 1987 several potential deals were percolating. But with Vazquez all but prohibited from returning to Washington before the new tax year began in January, Van Bennekom seemed to be calling the shots—and his eyes were riveted on Earl Brian. Van Bennekom did meet with former president Milt Benjamin, with whom he had remained friendly, about a deal for the UPI radio network or the Spanish language network formed by Geissler, but that fizzled.

In addition, chief spokesman Christopher Smith was trying to interest three investment groups. Smith also learned from departed foreign editor Kim Willenson that two large Japanese companies had, through the Japanese embassy in Washington, expressed interest in UPI. While no firm proposal was forthcoming from any of these prospects, Smith said later that Van Bennekom was strictly controlling access to Vazquez at the time and seemed single-minded about closing a deal with Brian.

In late autumn Peter Wirs surfaced anew. Wirs' credibility had been all but destroyed in 1985 with his repeated boasts that he would buy UPI for more than $40 million and move it to Philadelphia. Bragging of financial backing and often exaggerating his connections, Wirs never demonstrated proof he was anything more than a tireless hustler. Now, he told the *Omaha World-Herald* his consortium wanted to buy UPI and base it in Omaha. Enlisting former UPI marketing vice presidents Don Brydon and Jim Buckner, Wirs approached Van Bennekom. Rumors swiftly circulated the company about this incredible new turn. Although Van Bennekom gave Wirs short shrift, cringing UPI executives began to think Earl Brian was looking better and better.

• • •

By late January, the company again was in virtual paralysis. The $4 million Vazquez had injected three months earlier was gone and the owner had snapped shut his purse. As bills piled up, Vazquez sent word that he would consider Brian's offer. Soon their deputies were engrossed in serious negotiations. Vazquez, however, had a problem. When he purchased the company he had promised to give the union first rights if it could find a way to match in 60 days any outside offer to buy 10 percent or more of UPI's stock.

Vaszquez's emissaries sought the union's cooperation in closing a deal with what they called an unidentified "investor." But Dan Carmichael and new guild president Kevin Keane were in foul humor from a months-long stalemate over negotiations for a new contract. They were suspicious that Brian, a man they considered anti-union, might be the "investor," and demanded specifics of the proposed sale before they would agree to start the 60-day clock. UPI executives warned that if the union stalled and the "investor" bolted, Vazquez might simply fold the company. Carmichael and Keane refused to budge, convinced that was just a bluff to pressure employees to relinquish their rights. For the umpteenth time an internal battle was escalating out of control.

Vazquez responded to the guild's intransigence with an even more serious threat. He instructed lawyers to draw up a Chapter 7 bankruptcy petition that, if filed in court, could mean UPI's death. On Tuesday, February 16th, vice president Bobby Ray Miller privately told guild officer Al Bruce that unless the union capitulated "the company probably will go into Chapter 7 by the end of the day." Still the union held firm, convinced the proud Vazquez could never accept the public humiliation that would accompany UPI's liquidation.

Things came to a head three days later when, after months of behind-the-scenes negotiations by their lieutenants, Brian and Vazquez met in Washington. Brian, a securities whiz, had hatched a scheme to circumvent the union's first-refusal clause. Vazquez would remain UPI's owner but in name only, ceding a "proxy" that would give Brian total operating control for ten years. This legal legerdemain would shut the guild out of the process entirely and relieve Vazquez of further financial liability. There also was speculation that it would permit Brian, if he could not make it profitable, to return UPI to the Mexican.

Aware of Vazquez's desperate need to be rid of his albatross, Brian made it starkly clear that any deal must be on his terms and must be completed that very day. Vazquez bitterly protested. He threatened to break off negotiations and recover at least some of his investment by selling pieces of the wire service to Reuters and other buyers. Barry Bavacqua, a lawyer for Brian who attended the meeting, reportedly remarked later that Brian had scoffed at Vazquez's threat, taunting, "You couldn't sell pussy to a trainload of soldiers!"[2] Brian was described as being merciless during the lengthy meeting, seemingly bent on squeezing the last penny from Vazquez.

Although proud, Vazquez was not stupid. Fidgeting in his office chair, he knew he had few alternatives that would permit him to publicly save face. He understood only too well that UPI, like a meatgrinder, had claimed another victim, sullied yet another reputation. This time it was his. Although he loathed Brian's terms and his tactics, Vazquez decided

---

[2]Brian declined a request for an interview.

to snap up the bone he had been tossed. At least the sale of a "proxy" was a way to extricate himself from his staggering financial burden while clinging to the charade that he still "owned" UPI. Just as Scripps had before him, Vazquez demanded that terms of the deal be kept secret to spare him further embarrassment.

Late on the evening of Friday, February 19, 1988, a story moved on UPI's wires announcing the company's third ownership transaction in six years had shifted control to Brian's newly created WNW (for World News Wire) Group Incorporated. Vazquez claimed to have sold control for "future considerations" totaling $55 million—money he knew he and Joe Russo probably never would see. News of the imaginative proxy deal amazed industry observers and jolted and outraged guild leaders, whose first refusal rights had been neatly circumvented. Bewildered Unipressers struggled to understand why their company was, yet again, being shoveled from hand to hand like a ball in a rugby scrum.

Vazquez hastily assembled a farewell dinner for the aides he would be leaving behind. "I hope everything goes well for all of you," he told them. "As for me, I'm happy. I'm very, very happy."

It was a brave front, but only a front. Vazquez's dream, launched with elan and braggadocio, was dead. A man unaccustomed to losing had failed, and failed miserably.

Scheduled to leave for Mexico Saturday afternoon, Vazquez could not bear one extra minute in Washington. Early in the morning he climbed aboard his private jet and, emotionally drained, headed home.

"This is the worst thing I've ever done," he told his closest associates, "the biggest mistake I've ever made in my life. This is the first time I've ever been beaten. I'm never coming back to Washington again."

• • •

Why had Dr. Earl Brian fought so hard to get his hands on this tottering enterprise? Intimates said the 45-year-old Raleigh, North Carolina, native long had dreamed of building a corporate empire to capitalize on the explosive biomedical and information markets, and figured UPI could be his crown jewel. Skeptics speculated that he hoped to reduce UPI to a collector of business tidbits to feed to his Financial News Network.

There was no way, however, of ascertaining his agenda. Brian always appeared two steps ahead of the rest of the world. His fast-moving business labyrinth was confounding to outsiders. He had reshaped his corporate umbrella drastically since his 1985 bid for UPI; even the names of some of the companies had changed. With the stroke of a pen Biotech Capital Corporation had become Infotechnology, Inc., which had a stake in some twenty high-tech companies and ventures and would be UPI's parent. Although the value of Infotech's assets at the end of 1987 was listed at $85.1 million, business associates confided that most of Brian's companies were cash-poor and struggling for survival. UPI scarcely could expect a financial bonanza from this new owner.

Rather, Unipressers were about to be confronted with a brand new management style. A former Vietnam combat surgeon, Brian could be brilliant and smooth, but intimidating both physically and psychologically. Sometimes he slouched in a chair, feet on a desk, belly distending his shirt; he addressed his aides loudly and often profanely in the folksy southern drawl that still was a trademark. He and Paul Steinle, UPI's eighth president in less than six years, were hard-nosed money men determined to operate the wire service the way others had talked of running it for years—strictly as a business. Without agonizing over it, they seemed willing to accept the fact that most of the American newspaper industry had written off UPI. Staffers listened in consternation as Brian and Steinle declared that, once things stabilized, the company would be "market-driven." It would turn out only products that would sell, even if that meant concentrating on funneling financial information to nonmedia clients and further trimming the news coverage that had earned UPI its global niche. Gone were the days when the company could operate as if it were a struggling football team blessed with an egotistical, millionaire owner.

Indeed, shortly after arriving, Steinle warned staffers that UPI faced "liquidation" without a fast million dollars to meet payroll and cover overdue rent, expenses, and other bills. Astonishingly, he asked the union for a loan. This time employees brushed off the latest threat of extinction. In a newspaper interview, Carmichael responded: "The ludicrous suggestion was met with a Bronx cheer from coast to coast. Members were calling and saying, 'Don't give them a penny.' " Unipressers had seen enough wheeling and dealing to guess Brian had not gone to all the trouble of acquiring UPI just to shut it down. They felt they had done enough. If Brian really needed the money, let him find it elsewhere. Brian, who already had cut a deal requiring Vazquez to pay off most of the company's debts, arranged for parent Infotech to loan UPI the million dollars, secured by unpaid client bills at an attractive eleven percent interest.

Steinle soon announced yet another outside study of industry attitudes to gauge the feasibility of maintaining UPI in its traditional form. Unipressers found the message clear—and depressing. Their shrunken company, founded eighty-one years earlier in the crucible of E.W. Scripps's idealism, faced more wrenching changes. It was doubtful that UPI ever again would be able to carry out its historic mission: to compete with the AP whenever, wherever news broke, The new strategy was to squeeze as much revenue as possible from UPI's client base while trying to search out any market not already gobbled up by media and information competitors.

UPI editors had expressed concerns during the 1985 bidding war that Brian and Steinle lacked sensitivity and understanding about the wire service's history and tradition. Those concerns were barely an issue now. Just keeping it breathing would constitute a major accomplishment.

At a news conference, Brian and Steinle dubbed their grandiose plan "UPI 2000." Now, UPI also would stand for "Usefully Packaged Information"—a tech-speak atrocity that made Unipressers gag. What made them gag more was Brian's flip disclosure that UPI's colorful writing style would be phased out. Stories would be judged on their "PBQ—Publishability, Broadcastability Quotient." Tailoring stories simultaneously for newspapers and broadcast would require a spare, "Just the facts, ma'am" style most Unipressers found abhorrent.

Did Earl Brian and Paul Steinle honestly believe UPI's salvation lay at least in part in abandoning its bright writing, even transforming it to the wire service equivalent of *USA TODAY*? "Yes, if that's what we need to be successful," Steinle declared. His disclosure that Unipressers would attend "retraining camps" on the new, truncated writing style drew whispered gallows wisecracks about Dachau and Auschwitz from staffers attending the news conference.

Seated beside Steinle, Brian could not resist gleefully jabbing at Vazquez. UPI at last was back in American hands, he boasted pointedly, and derided what he called the Mexican's "shoebox" accounting procedures. While predicting profitability within two years, the new bosses glossed over the big news: they had already begun to further shrink

UPI. Almost as an afterthought they mentioned that 150 veteran Unipressers, including one-third of the photo staff, had been fired the day before to save some $6 million. Combined with the dismissal of 110 staffers five months earlier, the cuts reduced all but a few states to skeletal operations and left UPI unable to cover scores of state and regional stories. The carnage was bleakly reminiscent of the infamous 1985 "Friday Night Massacre" that foreshadowed UPI's plunge into bankruptcy. Among the states left with one staffer were Arkansas and Mississippi, prompting the cancellation of the last Scripps subscriber, *The Commercial Appeal* in Memphis, which circulated in both those states.

The layoffs left scores of veteran Unipressers hunting for new jobs at just the time the industry was retrenching because of stagnant readership, plummeting advertising revenues, and soaring newsprint costs. While no one could directly blame UPI's decades-long troubles on the new management, those who found themselves pounding the pavements would have been even more embittered to learn Brian was shifting officials of his own companies to UPI's payroll, some at six-figure salaries. Dwight Geduldig, a former spokesman for Reagan in California who was named senior vice president for corporate affairs, was paid $125,000. Amber Gordon, president of the Quest Business Agency, was hired as a short-term marketing consultant at $1,650 a day. Brian also rewarded Van Bennekom by making him a senior vice president, greatly enhancing his salary to the $90,000 range, and found jobs for Vazquez holdovers Claude Hippeau and Salvador Barros.

Brian and Steinle openly acknowledged that UPI was losing $1 million to $2 million a month, but boasted they could save $10 million a year with layoffs, administrative economies, and new technology. They made no public mention of the huge amount they had extracted from Vazquez to bring bills current. Brian reportedly had demanded the Mexican pay off several million dollars in debts and indemnify his group for up to $10 million to cover any material differences between UPI's actual financial condition and Vazquez's figures. Vazquez signed lines of credit for the $10 million with his bank in Brownsville, Texas. Sources familiar with the deal said that, within months after the takeover, Brian withdrew the money over Vazquez's protestations and demanded still more. In less than two years, Vazquez's UPI adventure had cost him upwards of $70 million.

• • •

During the search for a new owner in 1985, UPI's management selection committee had been deeply skeptical of Brian, fearing his ties to Ed Meese and the Reagan administration and questions about his corporate ethics might stir trouble for the wire service. Just two months into his UPI tenure, Brian found himself entwined once again in a controversy that included Meese and none other than UPI's Chapter 11 hero, Bankruptcy Judge George Bason.

While handling the UPI case, Bason had simultaneously supervised the bankruptcy proceedings of a struggling Washington computer software company, INSLAW, Inc., which had landed a $10 million Justice Department contract in 1982. INSLAW owner Bill Hamilton charged that department officials then conspired to destroy his small company by stealing case-tracking software that would connect law enforcement computers nationwide. Hamilton openly suspected that Brian was involved.

Hamilton particularly stewed because a fired, disgruntled INSLAW employee, C. Madison Brewer, somehow was named the Justice Department's overseer of the contract and had decided to withhold payments on grounds INSLAW was not performing adequately. Hamilton's firm ultimately was squeezed into bankruptcy.

Hamilton questioned whether Meese's deputy attorney general, Lowell Jensen, who had ironically developed competing software in California in the 1970s, had been involved in undermining INSLAW's contract. He also wondered about Brian, who controlled the largest block of shares in Hadron, Inc., a Washington area high-tech firm. Hamilton said that Hadron's chairman, longtime Brian associate Dominic Laiti, had phoned him on April 20, 1983, and told him Hadron wanted to buy INSLAW and use its "very good political contacts in the current administration" to dominate the law enforcement software business. Hamilton said that when he declined to sell, Laiti replied, "We have ways of *making* you sell." Although Laiti brushed off Hamilton's allegation as "ludicrous," other Hadron officials acknowledged that the firm was pursuing INSLAW. Hamilton theorized there may have been a link between the phone call and later Justice Department attempts to liquidate INSLAW in bankruptcy court.

In December 1987, a month after Bason rejected the government's motion to shut down Hamilton's company, he learned that he would not be reappointed to a fourteen-year term. Bason, among only four of 136 bankruptcy judges so rejected that year,[3] found it all too coincidental, and wondered whether he had become a victim of Earl Brian's wrath over UPI and INSLAW.

Bason got in a parting shot. On February 2, in an astonishing ruling, he said the Justice Department had conspired to steal INSLAW's software through "trickery, deceit and fraud," and ordered it to pay Hamilton's firm nearly $8 million in licensing fees and legal costs. The ruling and Bason's ouster soon triggered a lengthy inquiry by the Senate Permanent Investigations Subcommittee.

With his picture flashing across Dan Rather's *CBS Evening News*, Brian found himself trying to minimize his relationship with Hadron and Laiti and denying that he had even heard of INSLAW before the controversy. But Laiti already had been appointed to UPI's board of directors, and Brian had rejoined the Hadron board after a three-year hiatus. It also was disclosed that, in October 1986, a Wall Street investment banking firm and its officers with long ties to Brian began buying $5 million in stock in a Pennsylvania company bidding to buy INSLAW out of bankruptcy.

For a time the episode cast a shadow over Brian—and, by extension, over UPI. But the Senate investigators could prove no Justice Department conspiracy and did not explore Brian's possible role in the affair.

•   •   •

Nobody pushed Earl Brian around. If there was any pushing to be done, he did it. One day a few months after he took control, holdover PR spokesman Christopher Smith disagreed about how to handle a press release. Smith later said Brian, nearly a head taller, pinned him to a hallway wall with a meaty hand and barked, "Don't you understand the fucking English language, you idiot? This isn't what I told you to write!" Smith soon left the company.

Brian and Steinle brought to UPI the kind of tight fiscal controls that

---

[3]Bason was replaced by S. Martin Teel, a lawyer in the Justice Department's Tax Division who also had played a role in UPI's recent past. During bankruptcy proceedings, it was Teel who had tried to block a $50,000 settlement to ensure no interruption in medical benefits for Unipressers, insisting the company first must repay its $1.8 million back taxes debt. Teel's position, which would have required UPI to be shut down, had drawn a courtroom lecture from Bason about the importance of a free press.

long had been absent, but could not entirely abandon their intimidating style. To employees, they made Scrooge seem profligate. Steinle's decree that overtime would be paid only in the most dire news emergencies handcuffed his managers' ability to cover the news the way clients had come to expect. Employees who hated to leave when the end of their shifts interrupted breaking news stories were infuriated that they would not be paid for their extra efforts. The new regime also ordered inventories of every piece of equipment, performed audits to ensure staffers got not a day's more vacation than they were entitled, and required reporters to document even the tiniest expenses. Phoning a courier to pick up important news material required prior approval by a senior manager.

Early in 1989 the new team lopped off dozens of additional staffers, cutting deeply into the already thin ranks of foreign correspondents. Gone were respected veterans like Peggy Polk in Rome, Spencer Sherman in Seoul, and Gregory Jensen in London and their combined three-quarters of a century of UPI service. The once bustling, jam-packed London bureau now became a mausoleum inhabited by three staffers, and UPI's entire European operation counted barely a dozen full-time journalists. Stringers supplanted permanent correspondents throughout Scandinavia and even in Cairo, where the wire service's last remaining staffer in the Arab world was laid off. With but fifty American journalists overseas, United Press "International" was all but a memory.

When dozens of papers abrogated their contracts on grounds all the layoffs had caused UPI's news coverage to deteriorate, Brian took the audacious step of authorizing breach of contract suits against more than a score of the defecting clients.

Nor did the Brian regime seem to have any qualms about demanding still more financial sacrifices from beleaguered employees. In early 1989, UPI froze company contributions to the management pension plan. Then after negotiating a spare, short-term union contract, Brian proposed that staffers accept a new pact including a three-year wage freeze, the elimination of vital seniority protections, and an end to all five paid holidays—even Christmas. Iconoclastic Washington bureau staffers did not try to mask their contempt. When Steinle next wandered into the newsroom they broke into an impromptu chorus of "Jingle Bells." Steinle bristled. Like many newcomers he did not understand or appreciate what passed for humor at UPI. Summoning senior editors, he demanded the ringleaders be reprimanded, but later backed off when the National Labor

Relations Board advised that caroling in the newsroom was not a punishable offense. A number of staffers sarcastically mailed Christmas-in-June cards to Steinle's home—along with copies of the First Amendment.[4]

While the latest cutbacks meant new strains for the news and photo staffs and more internal tensions, by the summer of 1989 Brian and Steinle said they had managed to nearly eradicate the $2 million monthly losses. Their efforts drew praise from industry leaders but earned little affection from Unipressers. A number of UPI's top staffers resigned. To veteran employees who already had borne hardship, Brian and Steinle seemed cold and overbearing, devoid of compassion, indifferent to their sacrifices.

• • •

The rest of the news business, which had hungrily followed UPI's twists and turns, was largely ignoring the latest "comeback" attempt. When Steinle advertised receptions at industry gatherings, turnouts were embarrassingly tiny. Even journeys to the brink of extinction, repeated often enough, become boring.

It was no secret in the industry that, however valiant the latest efforts to save UPI, the wire service now offered little that could not be obtained from the AP or supplemental news services. The company was but a gaunt shadow of its heyday. In 1982, Scripps' last year as owner, UPI boasted 1,737 employees, more than 800 newspaper subscribers and more than 4,000 broadcast clients. By the summer of 1989, UPI struggled to put out a credible, worldwide news report with roughly 650 journalists —about half the number seven years earlier. The photo staff had been cut by two-thirds, to about thirty photographers.

UPI now served fewer than 200 daily papers, the great majority small, single-service clients paying low rates. Most subscribers had decided they could get along very nicely without UPI. Fearing the 21st Century might bring electronic newspapers delivered on home computer terminals, and faced with steadily eroding circulation figures, publishers and editors sought ways to economize. Once they had dropped UPI without adverse consequences, it was well nigh impossible for the wire service to get back in. Unipressers were working as hard as ever, but far fewer customers were there to listen. When big stories broke, about all staffers could hope

---

[4]Steinle denied a request for an interview.

for was play in one or two major papers. Just a few years earlier the same stories would have streamed across the front pages of dozens of big-city papers. Things weren't much better on the broadcast side, where the number of radio and television clients also had been halved. Because the AP reaped so much more revenue from newspapers it could engage in never-ending price wars to woo away UPI broadcast clients. UPI, once dominant in the audio network arena it had pioneered, saw its clientele plunge from 1,000 to 350; now it was AP that had 1,000 audio customers.

One competing supplemental service belonged to Scripps Howard, an irony not lost on Unipressers. Building a small operation into a virtual juggernaut, Scripps now had almost doubled UPI's client base. Reuters, which so many times had considered buying UPI to get a foothold in the United States, now easily surpassed UPI in its big-paper U.S. subscribers.

Accompanying these awful, humiliating numbers was a devastating drop in gross revenue—from more than $104 million in 1984 to far less than half that five years later. As UPI had shriveled AP had grown, its budget soaring toward $300 million a year. AP had capitalized on the disarray that had marked UPI's sales effort for three years. Frightened small papers and broadcasters were often easy prey when informed that, should UPI fold, it might take AP weeks or months to install service.

However, even though its revenues had fallen drastically, a $40-million business with a seductively recognizable name like UPI still could lure entrepreneurs to search for ways to keep it alive indefinitely, even if in a vastly different form.

Indeed, even after Brian and Steinle took control, a new company, Avacus Partners, L.P., was formed by a Dutch group hoping to get control of UPI via a hostile takeover of Infotech, UPI's parent. The move stunned many observers, but few were surprised when Brian thwarted Avacus after it purchased nearly 10 percent of Infotech's stock. Brian executed a series of deals with his other companies that diluted the value of the suitors' holdings to 7.8 percent. The moves triggered a lawsuit charging him with illegal stock manipulations, and Avacus sought to have the transactions reversed so it could renew its pursuit of the wire service.

Trying to recapture some newspaper business, Brian and Steinle resorted to a gamble that had been rejected repeatedly by previous administrations: selling the wire service's various news, sports, and photo wires separately. There had been fears that this technique, called "unbundling," would open the door for many clients to cut back on the number of services they received. Now, with few full-service clients remaining, Brian and Steinle felt they had no choice. But when the salesmen hit the streets, many newspapers rejected UPI's new prices as exhorbitant. *The Washington Post*, told it would have to again start paying for UPI, promptly dropped the sports, national, and international wires, keeping only financial and local news and sports photos.

Especially mortifying was the decision by the *Philadelphia Inquirer*, whose president and editor Gene Roberts headed UPI's Newspaper Advisory Board, to keep only the sports and photo wires. Roberts blanched when UPI executives told him that, despite the wire service's staff cuts and truncated product, the $280,000 a year his paper was paying for UPI's full service would be doubled. His defection was a bitter pill. The highly regarded *Inquirer* had been one of the few big clients still prominently displaying UPI stories. While unbundling may have allowed UPI to retain some key clients, newspapers in places like Boston and Seattle so curtailed their service that UPI stories became a rarity.

Gloom pervaded newsrooms as employees watched more major newspapers drift away and the company continue to shrivel. Unipressers always had struggled against two-to-one staffing odds in battling their rival. Now the numerical imbalance astonished and disheartened even the staunchest staffers and all but made that competition an exercise in futility, a relic of bygone days. At times AP had as many people in Topeka covering the Kansas legislature as UPI had covering Congress. UPI's Louisiana staff dropped from nine to two. State editor Royal Brightbill in New Orleans found himself rattling around alone in what had been a spacious, bustling, brand-new eight-person bureau. In the state of Washington, AP outstaffed UPI twenty-six to eight. In 1982 Pennsylvania had boasted thirty-five UPI staffers, thirty-eight newspaper clients, and 150 broadcasters. Now, the operation had shrunk to sixteen staffers, thirteen papers, and sixty stations. Between November, 1987, and April, 1988, manpower in Georgia dropped from nineteen to eight. Southern division news editor David Mould, refusing to go down as the first Atlanta manager to close the bureau, often pulled double tricks and worked the weekend lobster shift.

To save money during the 1988 presidential election campaign, UPI slashed from four to one the contingent traveling with the candidates, in the process all but abandoning photo coverage. Veteran reporter Vicki Barker was forced to do double duty and work double shifts, frantically alternating between dictating notes for newspaper stories to the Washington bureau and providing voice reports for radio clients. By mid 1989, she had quit for a less frenetic job at *NBC*.

Yet many employees, who thrived on the head-to-head competition with the AP on all the big stories, found it difficult to surrender. One who wouldn't was Lori Santos. On the final three days of the 1988 presidential race, Santos was the UPI reporter assigned to a press pool following Democratic candidate Michael Dukakis on his hectic last-ditch bid to claim the White House. For fifty-three hours straight the Massachusetts governor criss-crossed America in a Lear jet, campaigning in Denver, San Francisco, Los Angeles, and snowy Des Moines. Finally Dukakis led his exhausted staff and the trailing press plane back to Boston early Tuesday morning. Santos yearned for sleep, but weary as she was she knew her bosses would flinch at the $200-a-night rates at the luxurious Four Seasons Hotel where the other campaign reporters were staying. So she dragged herself over to the more modest Lenox a couple of blocks away. An hour later the jangling room phone ended her deep slumber. It was her editors with the news that Dukakis had decided to make a last-ditch national TV appeal for votes. Because his press aides couldn't find her at the Four Seasons, Santos now had just fifteen minutes to get to the governor's home in suburban Brookline. She bolted downstairs and told the cab driver an extra tip would be his reward for rushing her there in time. That incentive produced a harrowing ride that further numbed her senses. Running the last block, she breathlessly climbed into a campaign car as the caravan was pulling away—only to discover she was the only reporter who made it.

Another who wouldn't give up was Marie Okabe on the foreign desk in Washington. At 5 p.m. on January 7, 1989, she learned that a Japanese news agency was reporting Emperor Hirohito's death. Okabe phoned Tokyo, where the day was just dawning and UPI's correspondents had not yet arrived at the bureau. When a local television cameraman picked up the phone, Okabe alertly directed him to turn on the bureau television set and place the receiver down beside it.

A few moments later came the official announcement over Japanese television: Hirohito was dead. Okabe, once posted in Tokyo and fluent in Japanese, understood every word. She slammed out a bulletin to clients and quickly added background from her files until correspondent Stewart Slavin arrived in the Tokyo bureau and took over the story. UPI, covering by phone off an unattended television set half a globe away, somehow was able to match AP on the big breaking story.

Yet another who clung to the spirit that made UPI special was Bob Lowry, talented bureau chief in Austin, Texas. Concerned about the company's future early in 1988, he approached AP and was offered a job in the Dallas bureau. Barely had he submitted his resignation than the agonizing second thoughts set in. The day before he was to report to the AP in Dallas, he knew he couldn't leave UPI.

When his longtime boss, Dallas-based news editor Jim Wieck, arrived for work Monday morning, bureau chief Phil Magers was waiting to pop the startling news.

"Lowry's still in Austin," Magers said. "He just couldn't leave."

• • •

As UPI sank, the irony was inescapable: AP was again becoming a virtual monopoly in many markets—precisely the condition that had prompted E.W. Scripps to launch the United Press in 1907. Even as UPI clients fled, the AP was restructuring its rates to pass along increases to most subscribers. In states where UPI had pulled out, AP clients faced a $160-a-week rate hike. There also were complaints that, just as many had feared, with the lack of a strong UPI presence the AP was losing its incentive to excel. In New York state a number of editors groused that the quality of AP's news report had deteriorated badly and its staff frequently was unresponsive to their coverage requests.

Hearing such complaints circulated, Unipressers' frustration levels soared. They feared their company was unable or unwilling to fight for its rightful place among the giants of journalism.

The wire service had fallen victim not only to its own internal failures but also to radical industry transformations over which it had far less control. Historians groping for answers to UPI's decline cannot dismiss these fundamental changes that wrought immeasurable damage:

- The crucial structural difference between the two news agencies left UPI at a terrible disadvantage. UPI was a private concern supposed to earn its keep, while AP was a co-op "owned" by media members, the chummy establishment that kept its scruffy competitor rapping in vain on the country club window.
- The 1945 Supreme Court decision reversing AP's historic policy of exclusive franchises had been an early spike in UPI's coffin. The

decision, which required the AP to serve all who could pay market price, ultimately also forced UPI to divert dwindling resources into expensive coverage of state and regional news. Generally for UPI this was a losing proposition, both in revenue and in terms of the quality of the news report.

- Faster and more colorfully written, UPI had amassed a loyal following among afternoon papers. But the ability of television and radio to instantly deliver news ended the era of big-city newspaper street sale battles, and most major afternoon papers folded, merged with morning papers, or themselves became morning papers. Speed was far less important, and AP's larger staff offered quantity and, in many cases, higher quality.

- The advent of huge, monopolistic chains in the 1970s had all but snuffed out the family-owned newspaper. By the late 1980s chains owned nearly nine out of every ten dailies in America, and some of these publicly held giants appeared less interested in supporting a second wire service than amassing enormous profits for stockholders. When subscribing to two similar news services became an expensive redundancy, UPI invariably was the victim.

- Many powerful names—*The New York Times, The Washington Post, The Chicago Tribune, The Los Angeles Times*, Knight-Ridder, Scripps Howard, Copley, Hearst, Cox, Newhouse—marketed first-rate supplemental news services at far cheaper rates. In truth, the very clients UPI needed to stay alive were competitors for shrinking industry dollars and stood to benefit from the wire service's demise.

There was no single reason for UPI's plunge from robust competitor to cowering dwarf. But if the wire service indeed had any chances against these outside forces, they were squandered repeatedly by owners and managers either inept, ill-suited or unwilling to rise to the challenge.

Scripps and UPI's own top managers had been ponderously unresponsive to the opportunities of the information age, and then Scripps committed an even greater transgression: dumping the news agency on two entrepreneurs deficient in skills, temperament, news industry background, and business experience.

Doug Ruhe and Bill Geissler had proved dismally inept in grasping the wire service's complex dynamics. They had lurched from project to ill-conceived project, from crisis to interminable crisis. Their reign, in which they amassed nearly $30 million in debts and sold off irretrievable assets, all but ensured that no buyer of substance and stature would risk fortune or reputation to rescue UPI from bankruptcy.

Thus the wire service was saddled with a foreign owner, Mario Vazquez-Raña, wealthy to be sure but no more capable than his predecessors of restoring the beleaguered news agency to prosperity. He utterly failed to comprehend that UPI and the business climate in the United States were not conducive to the kind of dictatorial management style that had helped make him a billionaire in Mexico. Although boasting he would spend whatever was necessary to make UPI the dominant news agency, he proved a sprinter, not a marathon man. In the eighteen months that preceded his sudden departure, the company's image was further battered by incessant internal political intrigue and upheaval.

By 1989, no one could blame Earl Brian and Paul Steinle alone for abandoning attempts to restore UPI to the competitive, full-service news agency that had been E.W. Scripps's dream. There were too many fingers of blame to point elsewhere. But the effect of UPI's decline on the flow of public information was incalculable, and the rest of the news media seemed strangely unconcerned that the nation's competitive wire-service system was unraveling, that an important alternative voice was being stilled.

• • •

For eight decades Unipressers had battled the odds, made huge financial sacrifices, stuck with their cause when things seemed hopelessly lost. Their efforts had engendered sympathy, goodwill, and encouragement from thousands of outsiders who marveled at UPI's daily struggle for survival. Yet it was a campaign few outsiders could truly comprehend. One who tried was American poet Stephen Vincent Benet, who in *Fortune* magazine in 1933 attributed the UP's morale and grit to "fearless independence."

"UP is neither a charity nor a philanthropy. It is a business concern and its members work for profit. But there is another motive which drives them quite as strongly. You can call it pride of profession or professional zest or enthusiasm or self-hypnosis. But whatever you call it, it is as common to the stockholding executives as to the lunch money copy boy. And what it boils down to, when the sentiment and the wisecracks are both skimmed off, is an actual and genuine love of the game.

"Unipressers are bound together in an unusual esprit de corps, hard to define but nonetheless real."

It was that fragile, seemingly indestructible thread that had allowed the company miraculously to survive despite more than $135 million in losses over nearly three decades. The rest of the news industry had been run as a business. Proud, fiercely independent United Press International had been a crusade.

But now UPI limped toward the Twenty-First Century, staggering under the burden of decades of management stupidity and cupidity; of neglect, low pay, miserable working conditions; of astonishing lapses in leadership and foresight; of a succession of owners who had exploited Unipressers' love of company and professional pride.

Their numbers ever-shrinking, Unipressers still raced for phones to call in their breaking stories, still hunched over computer keyboards pounding out copy as if somehow, by sheer willpower, they could turn back the clock.

They continued to fight, praying for a miracle. Yet, deep inside, the sad reality could not be ignored: their wire service could never again be what it once was.

UPI's days of glory were gone forever. The old dream was over, the crusade lost.

Why They Stuck It Out

Several veteran Unipressers put into words exactly what about UPI engendered loyalty almost beyond reason and led them to shun more stable, perhaps more lucrative employment.

Herewith their comments:

· · ·

"When I was a little kid, Errol Flynn in *Captain Blood* and *Robin Hood* seemed to me to represent the ultimate in noble adventure. When I grew up a little, I found working for UPI could simulate the life of a buccaneer or an honest outlaw—challenging and sometimes besting a richer, more 'respectable' opponent. The reason I stayed so long was, simply, it was exciting."—Arnold Sawislak, Washington news editor, a Unipresser for forty years.

· · ·

"It's an addiction to chaos. Every day you walk into the bureau, or you get a late-night phone call, and you're faced with multiple choices on what to cover and how to do it. Sometimes it's routine and mundane, sometimes the biggest story of the day. You're always outgunned by AP, so you rely on wits, intuition, and experience. Rarely are you second-guessed, and when you happen to guess right there is a tremendous feeling of accomplishment.''—Jim Wieck, Southwest news editor, a Unipresser for twenty-two years.

• • •

"Freedom. From division news editor down to the newcomer reporter, there is freedom and responsibility. Few people peer over your shoulder. You do things and worry later. Rule number one at UPI: 'It's a lot easier to get forgiveness than permission.' And the history. A Boston bar, The Front Page, is decorated with famous headlines, including a 1927 newspaper heralding Lindbergh's landing, with a Paris dateline and UPI logo. I get a tremendous sense of pride every time I see it.''—Charles Goldsmith, Northeast news editor, a Unipresser for nine years.

• • •

"The camaraderie and the bonding is very similar to a sports team. We pull together toward a common goal, very much like a family where teamwork is vital for survival. As in a family there is pain and anger, too, but the thing I cherish most is the laughter I've shared. UPI has always been *fun*, hard to find in most lines of work.''—Fred McMane, sports editor, a Unipresser for twenty-five years.

• • •

"We've survived bankruptcy, bounced checks, a strike, mass layoffs, and management blunders. I've questioned my sanity many times staying with a company on the edge of collapse. But UPI has provided a front seat for history, an almost daily chance to pit my skills against others. The results come quickly—is your best good enough or has the other side kicked your fanny? It's underdog UPI against the world. We groan and complain and criticize to each other, but an outsider had better stay out. Adversity has brought us closer—like the Bataan Death March. I've never regretted the roller coaster ride.''—Cy Ryan, bureau chief, Carson City, Nevada, a Unipresser for twenty-nine years.

• • •

"Why is UPI hypnotic? It is the love of the game, the challenge of winning despite the most adverse conditions. UPI becomes part of your self-identification and your desire to write a fast, accurate daily sentence in history while remaining loyal to the ideals and ethics of your profession. You march to an exciting, urgent beat, challenged by a kaleidoscope of subjects and characters. You understand how David felt when he slew Goliath, and hope the next day your trusty slingshot still works.''— Myram Borders, Las Vegas bureau manager and Nevada state manager, a Unipresser for thirty years.

• • •

"UPI is a fraternity of journalists who think beating the AP is the most fun you can have standing up. To belong to that fraternity you have to learn to think fast on your feet. You figure odds of six AP types to one Unipresser is about even. One minute you're punching the hog markets. The next you're telling the world Elvis is dead.''—Duren Cheek, Tennessee state manager, a Unipresser for thirty years.

Where Are They Now?

In the years after he left UPI, Luis Nogales appeared to be searching for an identity, perhaps yearning to regain the high public profile he had achieved as chairman of an international news agency. In late 1986, he took a job as vice president for news of Univision, the Spanish-language television network largely owned by another Mexican media baron, Emilio Azcarraga Milmo. Nogales soon recruited former UPI treasurer Jack Kenney, spokesman Bill Adler, and foreign editor Sylvana Foa to join him, and by August, 1987, had risen to the Univision presidency. However, a couple of months later the firm was sold to Hallmark Cards and Nogales was fired. When Hallmark refused to honor his contract, he sued and won a handsome settlement. He then set up offices in New York and Los Angeles and searched for companies in turnaround situations, honing his deal-making skills by helping facilitate the sale of a large cosmetics company. He was named to the board of trustees of his alma mater, Stanford University, and religiously kept abreast of the latest developments at UPI.

After their UPI battles ended, Doug Ruhe and Bill Geissler operated separately in the Nashville area, alienated from each other by, among other things, a rift over how to divide the remnants of their failed ventures. Ruhe became involved in a computer software firm, while Geissler, operating under the name Americom, pursued the polling operation he and Ruhe had tried unsuccessfully at UPI.

In New York, Ray Wechsler became an independent venture capitalist specializing in taking over and turning around trouble companies. He talked of someday making another try at UPI.

Not long after resigning the UPI presidency, Max McCrohon became editor in chief of the *Los Angeles Herald-Examiner*, where the parent Hearst company charged him with another uphill journalistic battle— competing with the hugely successful *Los Angeles Times*. In mid-1989, Hearst threw in the towel and put the paper up for sale.

Mike Hughes, who followed McCrohon out the door, filed a $4 million damage suit against Mario Vazquez-Rana, who had offered him the bare minimum compensation when he resigned after thirty years with the wire service. The case was settled out of court in late 1988. After a stint teaching at Baylor University, Hughes returned to the Washington area and joined the staff of the American Press Institute, which organizes seminars for professional journalists.

Bill Small, first in the long succession of UPI presidents after the sale by Scripps, was named to a special business journalism chair at Fordham University and continued to press his bitter, multimillion-dollar litigation alleging breach of contract in his 1984 firing by Ruhe and Geissler.

Finally surrendering his UPI dream, John Jay Hooker returned to Nashville, where he continued to hobnob with celebrities and was a camp follower in Jesse Jackson's 1988 presidential campaign. He also launched another fast-food operation, Hooker's Hamburgers, offering home and office delivery in gaudy vans bearing a blowup of him doffing a homberg.

Tom Haughney and Ken Braddick teamed for a time to form a company that sold satellite communications delivery services.

Bill Adler, who got a decade's worth of grooming in a few years as UPI spokesman, soon left his Univision consultancy to become manager of corporate relations for The New York Times Company.

To the surprise of UPI managers, Dan Carmichael did not run for re-election as a guild officer in 1987, dropping his quest after union president Kevin Keane and others, weary of his confrontational tactics, advised him they would support his opponent. Carmichael and several other leaders resigned from the guild in 1988, arguing it had turned into a patsy for management. He became a productive, if outspoken, member of UPI's Washington news staff.

Bill Morrissey, who had given up his union post to take a job with Vazquez in 1986, remained in a low-profile management role after Earl Brian took over the company.

Bobby Ray Miller, the UPI vice president who had survived repeated management shake-ups, was fired shortly after Brian's arrival. He landed a job offering businesses better ways to manage information.

Mario Vazquez-Raña returned to Mexico, where he resumed his stature as a powerhouse media figure and tried to forget UPI. He reportedly refused to communicate with lawyers representing him in litigation against several of his former UPI editors. However, a few days before surrendering control of the company, Vazquez did appear for a deposition in Hughes's breach of contract suit. In his testimony, Vazquez asserted that while attempting to buy UPI he talked with Nogales only ''two times, by telephone.'' He said he had no recollection of ordering Hughes to fire all the Washington editors, saying that instead he told Hughes, ''You are the chief. Do as you will in your department.''

Most of his assets stripped away by a humbling bankruptcy, Joe Russo became a well-salaried property manager. Despite losing nearly $2 million on UPI, he did not entirely regret the experience. In retrospect, however, he wished that he and Vazquez had simply turned the management of UPI over to Luis Nogales.

Ben Cason, Barry Sussman and Kim Willenson, the Washington Post team that became embroiled with Vazquez in suits over their lucrative contracts, continued to draw their salaries from a Vazquez escrow account long after leaving UPI. Cason searched for a media job; Sussman set up a private polling operation; Willenson worked on two books.

George Bason, denied a new appointment as a federal bankruptcy judge, set up a private law practice in Washington. He continued to stew over his ouster, wondering whether his handling of the UPI case had been a factor.

Despite all the hoopla over the company's emergence from bankruptcy in June, 1986, UPI's unsecured creditors did not receive their first payments for a year and a half, when the first $4 million was distributed. Three years after the end of bankruptcy, much of the remaining $6.1 million was still frozen. Lawyers argued over the many claims that had poured in, including some from Ruhe, Geissler, and their cronies, and awaited the outcome of Bill Small's suit and an age discrimination complaint filed by senior employees dismissed by Ruhe and Geissler. Jules Teitelbaum, lawyer for the creditors committee, died in 1988 after a long bout with cancer.

With the retirement of Ed Estlow, Larry Leser rose to become chairman of the E.W. Scripps Company, which after ridding itself of UPI, profited handsomely from an investment in cable television. In 1988 the E.W. Scripps trust and Scripps Howard went public for the first time, offering 8 million shares at $16 a share. In the first six months of 1989 alone, the E.W. Scripps Company reported more than $40 million in profits. Ted Scripps, UPI's most loyal ally among the family members, died on June 15, 1987 at the age of 57.

Authors' Note

This book was written in narrative form, but the authors have worked painstakingly to ensure it represents an objective, journalistically factual account of the events and circumstances surrounding the crises and controversies at UPI. *Down to the Wire* is the product of more than four years of research, including an estimated 700 interviews with at least 200 individuals, both central and peripheral to the drama.

We flew to Nashville, for example, to spend a weekend interviewing former UPI owners Doug Ruhe and Bill Geissler. We also spoke with several of their civil rights era contemporaries, including football legend Gale Sayers, who joined Ruhe in a University of Kansas student protest against racial discrimination. We tracked down longtime Unipresser Maggie Richards, retired in a mobile home outside of Las Vegas. She obligingly recounted her memories of a half-century earlier, when she worked in the United Press Kansas City bureau with Walter Cronkite, then a fledgling seeking his journalistic spurs. We spoke with Gene Autry, who gave Luis Nogales an entry into the world of American business.

We collected massive documentation, including corporate records, court papers, daily appointment calendars, and even diary entries. Many interviews were tape-recorded, and almost all were done in tandem by the authors to assure maximum accuracy and context. When those we interviewed had conflicting recollections, we researched further to assure accuracy, checking other sources, seeking documentation, assessing the quality of the recollections. When an interviewee demonstrated a reliable memory and reliable records, and tended to tell the verifiable truth more frequently, that was given more weight. If an interviewee exhibited memory lapses or tended to give vague answers or answers not supportable by our independent investigations, that, too, is reflected in our narrative. In those instances where there is an obvious and unresolvable conflict, we have spelled it out, either in the narrative or in an occasional footnote. Surprisingly, for a book of such conflicting viewpoints, few refused to be interviewed. We note, where necessary, those who did refuse; and we sought characterization of their roles and motives from people of varying viewpoints.

Dialogue has been set down, for the most part, on a nonattributed basis. It often is a distillation of accounts from two, three, or more sources. Obviously, few of the quotations are the precise words spoken at the time. We pledge, however, that so far as possible the reconstructions represent the best recollections of the most accurate sources, faithfully mirroring the spirit and essence of the conversations and the styles and personalities of the characters. The sources often included the speaker; many times they include others involved in the conversation; and in a few instances, they include people not directly involved but who were reliably informed afterwards of the substance of the dialogue.

Because at times we played significant roles in the events at UPI, we felt it was necessary that we be included in the story. Our journalistic training taught that personal involvement should be avoided whenever possible, and so we tried to minimize intrusions in the narrative relating to our own roles.

Index

417